PEACE IN IRELAND

The War of Ideas

RICHARD BOURKE

PIMLICO

Published by Pimlico 2003

2 4 6 8 10 9 7 5 3 1

Copyright © Richard Bourke 2003

Richard Bourke has asserted his right
under the Copyright, Designs and Patents Act 1988
to be identified as the author of this work

First published in Great Britain by
Pimlico 2003

Pimlico
Random House, 20 Vauxhall Bridge Road,
London SW1V 2SA

Random House Australia (Pty) Limited
20 Alfred Street, Milsons Point, Sydney,
New South Wales 2061, Australia

Random House New Zealand Limited
18 Poland Road, Glenfield,
Auckland 10, New Zealand

Random House South Africa (Pty) Limited
Endulini, 5A Jubilee Road, Parktown 2193, South Africa

Random House UK Limited Reg. No. 954009
www.randomhouse.co.uk

A CIP catalogue record for this book
is available from the British Library

ISBN 1-8441-3316-8

Papers used by Random House are natural, recyclable products made from wood
grown in sustainable forests; the manufacturing processes conform
to the environmental regulations of the country of origin

Printed and bound in Great Britain by
Mackays of Chatham, Chatham, Kent

PIMLICO

608

PEACE IN IRELAND

Richard Bourke grew up in Dublin. He studied English and Philosophy at University College, Dublin, and did his PhD at Cambridge University. He also has a BA in Classics from Birkbeck College, University of London. He has been a lecturer in English at University College, Dublin, and currently lectures in Enlightenment intellectual history and the history of political ideas at Queen Mary, University of London. He has previously published on Romanticism, the Enlightenment and the political thought of Edmund Burke, and has commented on Northern Irish affairs in *Fortnight* magazine and the *Financial Times*. This is his second book.

Contents

Acknowledgements

My greatest debt is to John Dunn who encouraged the idea of writing this book from the start, commented on the manuscript in more than one version, and challenged many of the basic positions which I wanted to advance. I have benefited from Seamus Deane's sceptical engagement with the argument presented here, but also from his general advice and criticism over many years. Ian McBride has been truly generous and incisive, both as a reader and as an interlocutor. My argument and text have been greatly aided by the rigorous and dissenting scrutiny of Ultán Gillen. I have had invaluable help and critical commentary from Paul Bew, John Burrow, David Dwan, Peter Hennessy, Matthew Kelly, Frank Millar, Emer Nolan, Peter Rose, Brendan Simms, and Jim Smyth. I have also benefited from discussions, whether informally or in formal interviews, with Alex Atwood, David Ervine, Gerry Fitt, Jim Gibney, Chris McGimpsey, Mitchel McLaughlin, George Mitchell and Danny Morrison. I am grateful to J. H. Burns, Istvan Hont, Philip Pettit, Adam Przeworski, Ian Shapiro, Michael Sonenscher and David Wootton for discussion of the broader topics in political theory which bear upon the claims set out in these pages.

It has been of inestimable help to me to have had a range of people comment on this work and take issue with many of my formulations and conclusions. My especial thanks in this regard go to Beatrice Collier. To the following I am also particularly indebted for having read chapters along the way, and for having offered me the benefit of their advice: Steven Bourke, James Coen, Cornelia Cook, Liza Cragg, Andrew Fitzmaurice, Paul Hamilton, David Lee, Daniel Pick, Rachel Potter, Chris Reid, Jacqueline Rose, Tamsin Shaw and Clair Wills. Versions of the argument in this book have been delivered to seminars at Columbia University, Cambridge University, and the Institute for Historical Research in London, and at the annual conference of the American Political Science Association in Philadelphia. I would like to thank the following in particular for their critical engagement on those occasions: Andrea Bartoli, Gregory Claeys, Ross Harrison, Melissa Lane, Michael Levin, David Runciman, Quentin Skinner and Gareth Stedman Jones. Responsibility for the errors which have doubtless survived all this scrutiny lies, unfortunately, with me.

I owe enormous thanks to my agent, Maggie Hanbury, who acted with such resolution and commitment on my behalf, and to my publisher, Will Sulkin, for his practical and intellectual support for this project. My editor, Jörg Hensgen, indulged me beyond what it was reasonable of me to expect, and offered cogent advice about the substance of my argument. The copy-editing of Beth Humphries was also more than I could have hoped for. I am grateful to Stephen Snoddy for his expert prompting, to Willie Doherty for his 'Border Incident', and to Friederike Huber for her conspicuous skill in design. I would also like to thank the staff of the Linen Hall Library in Belfast, the National Library in Dublin, the Official Publications section of the British Library at King's Cross and the Newspaper Library at Colindale, the Pamphlet Collection at the London School of Economic and Political Science, the National Film and Television Archive in London, the Film and Sound Resource Unit at the University of Ulster in Coleraine, and the Public Record Office at Kew in London, all of whom supplied me with assistance in unearthing material relevant to my research.

Preface

This is a book about war and peace in Northern Ireland, about the causes of the war and the character of the peace. Accordingly, it traces a line of development through the political events that lead from the end of the 1960s to the more immediate past. It tells of the emergence of the Civil Rights movement before the start of the 'troubles', and of the slide from political protest into open sectarian violence as the conflict advanced; it relates how Unionism fragmented under pressure from events, and how Britain sought to manage the interplay of forces as the situation deteriorated from discord into crisis. This makes for a striking, yet dispiriting story in which human arrogance and miscalculation, common fear and misunderstanding, played a large role. But the book explores the process that led away from conflict too. It examines the gradual co-ordination of British and Irish policy, the evolution of thinking inside the Republican movement, and the twists and turns within Unionism that prepared for the present settlement. It charts the passage, in other words, from apparently insurmountable civil strife to the achievement of political agreement.

The escalation of sectarian antagonism in the aftermath of 1968 in Northern Ireland took its bearings from the Home Rule crisis that had inflamed political attitudes within the United Kingdom toward the close of the nineteenth century. The establishment of Northern Ireland in 1920 was part of a political package designed to overcome the impasse, but by the end of the 1960s that settlement was in serious difficulty, and heading towards imminent collapse. But even today that collapse remains significantly misunderstood. A genuine explanation of the catastrophe that befell Northern Ireland requires a more comprehensive perspective than is usually employed for the purpose. It requires, in fact, an examination of the fundamental values and perceptions which have been involved in giving direction to political action in the modern world.

Consequently, the purpose of the argument developed here is to unravel the significance of the collision of ideas that sustained the battle of wills throughout the conflict. Having said this, the point is not to argue that the crisis under review should be understood as the product of a merely intellectual dispute which erupted inexplicably into violence. Ideas on their own did not simply make the war – but still, without a clash of ideas there would have been no war. This book sets out to take a fresh look at how the conflict in Northern Ireland was informed by opposing doctrines, and sustained by opposing arguments and ideas. It advances a new claim about what the underlying collision between political doctrines was, and concludes that this collision was not a residue of ancient history but was instead very much a product of specifically modern political values.

The claim that the war in Northern Ireland was fuelled by modern values as those values became embodied in rival factions involves insisting that the conflict was not driven by tribal loyalties, nor by mutually exclusive political identities, nor even by blind sectarian hate. This book argues that, on the contrary, the dispute in Northern Ireland was a product of modern democracy: the prime issue in contention was the core value of democracy – namely, the value of political equality. In fact, most modern political struggles have centred around the struggle for equality. Equality, in the end, is a perpetual, yet fractious and elusive aspiration which modern politics seeks to realise through the procedures of democracy. However, even under the most propitious of circumstances, the realisation of equality by means of the democratic process is fraught with difficulty. But in Northern Ireland, the democratic expectation of political equality was actually thwarted by the mechanisms of democratic government. As a result, political competition led to strife, and then to breakdown.

A democracy aspires to form a unity of equals. But actual politics within a democracy risks disunity and inequality: its procedures are competitive, and so potentially exclusive. Typically, competition takes place between the minorities and majorities which result from electoral choices and the changing fortunes of political parties. Of course, usually, over the longer term, the contest is felt to deliver an approximation of equality. But since the achievement of long-term harmony is still secured by a competitive process in which successive majorities and minorities vie for their own success, the expectation of equality is not always immediately apparent as the underlying demand of the democratic sensibility. Consequently, the identification of democracy with the decision of the majority becomes an obvious temptation for political analysis: indeed, the idea that democracy is basically equivalent to majority rule begins to look like a reasonable assumption. However, the assumption is in fact radically misconceived and, more importantly, it can lead to political disaster.

By now, this misconception deserves some serious attention, not least because it still affects the prospects for the peace settlement agreed in 1998. The claim presented here, then, is that the conflict in Northern Ireland was the product of a fundamental misunderstanding about the organising principles of modern politics. That misunderstanding derives from the stubborn assumption that the procedures of democratic government offer a sufficient guarantee for the achievement of political equality in modern states. And while this assumption has dogged the history of Northern Ireland, it continues to confuse political judgement in the Balkans, in the Middle East and in Central Asia as well.

The fact is, however, that harmony requires a further condition to be fulfilled: every democratic government operating in the world today depends, for its success, upon the simultaneous existence of a democratic state in which the *entire* population is pledged to the common good. It should be obvious, although it remains a seriously neglected reality, that since democratic states are based upon equality, they are ultimately founded on a principle of unanimity: they are not meant simply to service the exclusive preference of a majority. Majorities ought properly to be accepted as decisive in determining both the selection and tenure of democratic governments, but not as a means of prescribing the terms of democratic inclusion in the state. The history of Northern Ireland in the twentieth century presents a cautionary tale about the dangers involved in failing to abide by this injunction.

Democracies, in other words, are ordinarily formed *e pluribus unum*, as the motto on the Great Seal of the United States is at pains to emphasise. In the absence of such unity, democratic governments can all too easily operate as instruments of division in defiance of their accepted role as arbiters of peace. In this context, it is of vital importance to grasp the essential difference in political analysis between democratic governments and democratic states. The confusion between the two is responsible for our inherited, dogmatic attachment to the idea that political majorities constitute a reasonable basis on which to establish the legitimacy of democratic states. Democratic procedures of government like decision by the majority are expected to operate for the benefit of a community of citizens – for the benefit, in other words, of what we term a nation-state, not for a sectional interest in what might be called a 'majority state'.

Here the case is made that a majority state such as existed in Northern Ireland down to 1972 is liable to exacerbate a war between rival aspirants to equality, with both parties insisting on the justice of their claims to form alternative democratic governments of their own. Any attempt to manage the conflict between these characteristically antagonistic and murderous popular forces by means of nominally democratic mechanisms of government is, sooner or later, bound to fail. The failure of Northern Ireland, which proceeded from the attempt to establish a form of majority rule in the absence of an integrated democratic state, might therefore usefully be understood as an exemplary failure, prolonged by the refusal on the part of the protagonists all round to abandon their commitment to flawed democratic principles.

The effort to resolve the British–Irish problem was for precisely this reason a protracted and exacting process for the participants involved. Over the course of more than a quarter-century of conflict, there was no decisive military climax that secured political victory to one particular side. There was no final depletion of capability that affected the outcome between the belligerents: no concerted advance along enemy lines, no conclusive reversal through the infliction of casualties, and no exchange of territories. It was a long and dirty war, sustained at once by guerrilla assaults and counter-insurgency operations – by torture, assassinations and emergency powers, bombings, shootings and assorted 'spectaculars'. But after the grim cycle of terror and repression had been exhaustively rehearsed, the stark reality of a military stalemate remained conspicuously in place. Yet so too did the apparently intractable issue which had provoked the original contention. That issue comprised the very meaning of democracy, disputed among the combatants. Each party to the dispute continued to advance the legitimacy of its claims on the strength of its democratic credentials, but this apparent conformity of principles resulted in disastrously incommensurate objectives. Democracy, in fact, was the root of the problem, yet the contestants mistook it for an easy solution.

And so an uncomfortable problem begins to emerge: the appearance of such violent hostility in the face of a common commitment to democratic values points to a conflict within the framework of principles that inform our practical understanding of the world we now inhabit. In analysing that conflict through a reconstruction of developments in Northern Ireland, this book tries to uncover the clash of expectations and confusion of ideas that lurk beneath the surface of political attitudes today.

That confusion is surely evident in the Manichaean assessments which inform political judgement in our unipolar world. From the perspective of the contemporary *pax Americana*, political power in the international arena is licensed to defend democracy against the perpetrators of terror. But in the eyes of the United States' embattled opponents, the ultimate ambition of American foreign policy is the elimination of resistance to its own special brand of imperialism. However, the international strife arising from such incompatible perceptions is not completely accounted for by the disparity between competing representations of a shared reality. Conflict is actually intensified still further by the basic incoherence which orientates political decision-making *within* each opposing frame of reference: on one side the meaning of democracy is protean, on the other the significance of imperialism is diffuse.

But if confusion can be lethal, it is not permanently insurmountable. Modern political argument is burdened under a weight of misconceptions, haphazardly adopted into the present from the past. The impact of these misconceptions can obviously be brutal, indeed devastating; but their influence in the end can nonetheless be curbed by incremental advances in analysis and appraisal. It would certainly be naïve to expect any immediately decisive benefit to follow from such efforts at analysis and appraisal. But it would equally make no sense to hope for nothing from the attempt whilst still continuing to contribute to political discussion.

Grounds for hope in this capacity for reappraisal can be found in the trajectory of the 'troubles', culminating in the peace process of the 1990s. In the early 1970s, the Provisional IRA launched a campaign of terror against the political deformations allegedly foisted upon Northern Ireland at the behest of British imperialism. Imperialism, in this account, was represented as the historic enemy of the rights of an Irish democracy whose legitimacy Republicanism was labouring to restore. But if the Republican insistence upon the perfidious designs of British imperialism did scant justice to reality, neither did the objection raised confidently in response that Northern Ireland had always been a recognisable democracy, impartially protected by a responsible British power.

Yet, whatever the discouraging paralysis of the past, now the political ground has positively shifted. It would seem that the IRA has come to accept that Britain no longer has, as the British government was brought to declare in the early 1990s, any 'selfish strategic or economic interest in Northern Ireland.' It might, then, be the case that the spectre of imperialism has finally been laid to rest in Ireland. This development can surely count as at least one identifiable victory for focused political reappraisal: the settlement was clearly enabled by military exhaustion, but it still involved a process of productive reassessment.

Nonetheless, at a deeper level, confusion still persists: it is still accepted by the signatories to the 1998 Agreement that the actual status of Northern Ireland ought by right to be determined by the decision of a majority of its citizens – whether Catholic or Protestant, nationalist or unionist, whichever happens to pre-ponderate with the passage of time. But a democratic state cannot credibly be presented as the property of some part of its member-ship, however large. To suggest otherwise is no less alarming in its implications today than it was originally in 1920, and again in 1968.

Modern complacency about the potency of democracy needs urgently to be challenged. The idea that democratic institutions of government are automatically equipped to resolve the most intense disputes about who is actually to be included within the ambit of a given democracy is manifestly misconceived. Such disputes are very much in evidence today on the streets of north and east Belfast. Yet a familiar misconception still haunts the workings of the current Agreement: a bare numerical advantage amongst the Northern Ireland protagonists is still entitled to decide whether the population as a whole should ultimately form part of a British or an Irish democracy. Since there exists an expectation that the size of the nationalist electorate will continue to expand over the coming generation, and since the unionist majority is acknowledged to have undergone a steady diminution over the course of the preceding eighty years, the hope that democratic hostilities have been definitively placated by the Good Friday Agreement is not certain to be satisfied.

The losers in this demographic struggle might well, over the longer term, accept their loss. But ultimately the struggle will be perceived as a matter of political survival, and acquiescence cannot be guaranteed. It is certainly possible that either party, anticipating defeat, might decide to trust in the political process already up and running. But equally they might just as soon decide to fight for better terms. This dilemma captures the crisis of modern democracy, immediately apparent in Sri Lanka, the Lebanon, Afghanistan and Kashmir. But it would be a grave political error to assume that democratic governments, however ingeniously constructed, were miraculously ordained to make the dilemma disappear.

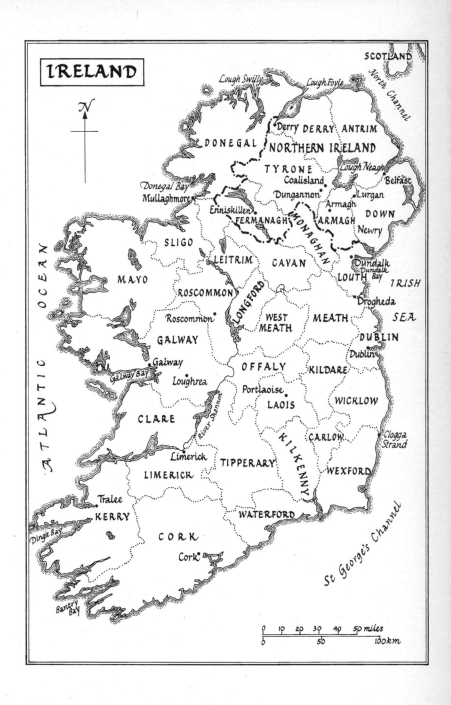

IRELAND

N

SCOTLAND

North Channel

Lough Swilly
Lough Foyle

Derry DERRY ANTRIM

DONEGAL

NORTHERN IRELAND

TYRONE
Coalisland
Lough Neagh
Belfast

Donegal Bay
Mullaghmore
Dungannon
Lurgan
Armagh
DOWN

Enniskillen
FERMANAGH
MONAGHAN
ARMAGH
Newry

SLIGO

LEITRIM
CAVAN
Dundalk
Dundalk
Bay
LOUTH
IRISH

MAYO
ROSCOMMON
LONGFORD
Drogheda
SEA

Roscommon
WEST
MEATH
MEATH

GALWAY
Galway
DUBLIN
Dublin

Galway Bay
Loughrea
OFFALY
KILDARE

CLARE
Portlaoise
LAOIS
WICKLOW

River Shannon
CARLOW
Clogga
Strand

Limerick
TIPPERARY
KILKENNY
WEXFORD

LIMERICK

Tralee
KERRY
WATERFORD

Dingle Bay
CORK
Cork

Bantry
Bay

St George's Channel

ATLANTIC OCEAN

0 10 20 30 40 50 miles
0   50   100km

Introduction

A kind of parable is told about Northern Ireland and then offered as a lesson to the world. On the local, provincial level, the story tells how thirty years of war was finally ended, and how a settlement at long last was secured. And in the broader context, regarding politics within an ampler and more cosmopolitan frame, the message reveals how democracy solves the riddle of history and brings about an end to human conflict. But the parable just doesn't fit the facts.

The substance of the peace settlement in Northern Ireland is contained in the Good Friday Agreement concluded at Stormont Castle, in Belfast, in 1998. With the arrival of this Agreement it seemed clear that the bitterest of rivals on the Northern Ireland scene had decided to try things differently. Republicans, on one side, had come to their senses, abandoning the path of war in favour of an honourable peace; and unionists, for their part, had given up on pretensions better consigned to the past. But what is the deeper meaning behind this transformation? Old enemies, we are told, had been drawn together to embrace a common *democratic* faith, leaving political commentators to observe that even here the war of ideas was finally over.[1] Yet however much this analysis might appeal, it hardly captures the complexity of the truth.

Allowing for that complexity, it would be more accurate to view the Good Friday accord as merely pointing to the possibility of a democratic settlement which could evolve in the course of operating the provisions of the Agreement. But even if this Agreement is to be more modestly understood as no more than the harbinger of a final democratic settlement, we ought still to have at least some sense of what the ultimate realisation of democracy might entail.

It would seem reasonable to insist that it should embrace, at a bare minimum, agreement about the terms of inclusion in this democracy, and then secondly about the means that will be employed to reach decisions. A democratic settlement must involve, in other words, concurrence about which people are to be equal members of the state, and a consensus on how the government is to represent the people.[2] In the light of these requirements, it must be obvious that democracy poses fundamental problems for modern societies, and so can hardly be relied on as the ready answer to political conflict. But Northern Ireland has not yet been exempted from these problems: while agreement has been reached about how the government is to function, a final settlement remains outstanding on the terms of inclusion in the state.

The Republican party in Northern Ireland today – in other words, Sinn Féin and the IRA – remains pledged to an island democracy as the final form of a solution. However, most unionists are committed to a British federal democracy which shares in the common citizenship of the United Kingdom. It is perfectly possible that either one of these scenarios might ultimately win a more general acceptance. Equally, it is plausible that both preferences might be supplanted in the end by some other alternative. But in the meantime, the occasion for friction continues to exist because the Agreement actually defers a final decision on the issue.

So, while the form of democratic government for Northern Ireland has been settled, the long term democratic make-up of the state remains undecided. Under the terms of the Agreement, this uncertainty can be resolved by a simple majority mechanism: whichever preference wins the allegiance of the greater number of people will determine whether a Republic or the Union should prevail. But the problem is that the demography of Northern

Ireland is unstable: currently, the unionist allegiance is preponderant in the North,* but the trend appears to favour the long term prevalence of nationalists.[3]

The adoption of a simple majority procedure to resolve the outstanding question of the status of Northern Ireland is therefore quite a gamble under the circumstances. In proposing to settle the dispute over democratic sovereignty by means of the principle of majority decision, the Agreement is reverting to the problematic principle which provoked the original crisis in Northern Ireland. This principle states that a democracy derives its legitimacy from the allegiance of a majority of its members.[4] Instead of being a sustainable principle, however, in reality it is a spurious criterion whose application has been resisted throughout the history of democracy.[5] The United States of America, for example, aspires to generate unanimous allegiance among the members of an integrated democracy, united in the aftermath of civil war. In the same vein, the opponents of the French *ancien régime*, throughout the course of the Revolution, contended for the establishment of various constitutions, yet each of these was intended to embody an undivided democracy. However, full Northern Ireland citizenship, for almost fifty years since its creation in 1920, was the exclusive reward of one part of its population – the Protestant majority – and not the equal privilege of a united populace.[6]

Obviously the Good Friday Agreement of 1998 is not a replica of the 1920 Northern Ireland constitution as established under the Government of Ireland Act published in that year. Yet it remains a disturbing fact that the principle of majority sovereignty which underwrote the 1920 settlement has survived intact in Northern Ireland after eighty turbulent years. This survival is not only a cause for concern given the fratricidal history to which the

---

*The terms used to denote Northern Ireland as a political entity are sometimes viewed as controversial in themselves. However, throughout this book, 'the North', 'the Province', 'the Six Counties' and 'Ulster' are used interchangeably to designate Northern Ireland. The same applies to 'Derry' and 'Londonderry': both are employed here, on the grounds that they are both used in Northern Ireland, albeit by opposing constituencies.

principle has contributed – it also stands in contradiction with the ambition of the new Agreement to create the conditions for democracy in the Northern Ireland of the future. Majority sovereignty has always been incompatible with the democratic principle of popular sovereignty. The significance of this incompatibility is made apparent by the events of Northern Ireland's past: it was the institution of majority rule at the expense of popular sovereignty which bred dissension in Northern Ireland from 1920 onwards. Membership of the majority determined membership of the state: conversely, membership of the minority meant exclusion from effective sovereignty.

In the absence of a democratic state in Northern Ireland after 1920, the existence of a democratic government in the Province produced dissension, not cohesion, among its people.[7] It may be unsurprising that dissension within the population encouraged partiality on the part of the Northern Ireland government between 1920 and 1968. Nonetheless, the partial exercise of authority is, in terms of the most usual definition, tantamount to the employment of arbitrary power. With the eruption of the 'troubles' at the end of the 1960s, it was the ultimate guarantor of this arrangement – the United Kingdom Parliament – that was to find itself indicted with the charge of abetting discrimination against the minority within the population which stood to lose from the arrangement. In the atmosphere of intense suspicion which accompanied the disturbances in Northern Ireland after 1968, it was only a short step from associating discrimination with the government at Westminster to identifying British interests with the motive of imperialism.

It is important to draw the appropriate lesson from that experience as Northern Ireland faces a future that is far from certain. However, given the actual political advances that have now been made in the North, the lesson is in danger of being set comfortably to one side, at the risk of enabling a resurgence of the original problem. Political rule in Northern Ireland today has been devolved to a Provincial executive constructed on a cross-community basis: in effect, a weighted majority in the Northern

Ireland Assembly determines the tenure of the government. Yet a simple majority of the people is still entitled, under the provisions set down in the Agreement, to decide the ultimate status of the community as a whole.

So, while what might be termed a comprehensively democratic procedure has been agreed for the delivery of executive decisions in Northern Ireland, the long term survival of the democracy which has been organised in this way remains in the hands of what can only be described as an undemocratic portion of the whole: a simple majority.[8] Given this situation, it would appear timely, if not urgent, to examine with renewed vigour what exactly we take the character of democracy to consist in because, while as a theory it is the beneficiary of universal applause, in practice it is little understood.

The current wisdom has it that the Good Friday Agreement marked the point at which the appetite for war gave way to an acceptance of this unspecified 'democracy' amongst the parties to the conflict. On this understanding, the British, the Irish and the Northern Irish protagonists stood on the threshold of a new beginning: the end of imperialism and terror, and the start of a democratic process.[9] Of course, something has clearly finished in Northern Ireland, and something entirely preferable has begun. For one thing, IRA hostilities have ceased. A new administration has also been established, and a comprehensive settlement endorsed. But there had always been some kind of democratic *process* in Northern Ireland, albeit in the absence of a democratic state. Consequently, standard accounts of the meaning of these developments continue to leave a lot to be desired. In the context of what has been said so far, it should be clear that it would be overly simple to see the new arrangements as amounting to the final establishment of democratic normality. Yet this perception has become integral to the accepted understanding of the peace process, despite the fact that there are good reasons for supposing that it rather impoverishes our grasp of the serious issues at stake.[10]

The argument of this book is that a fuller elaboration of these issues can tell us something about the basic assumptions we make regarding political arrangements today. Northern Ireland witnessed a breakdown in political life at the end of the 1960s and the Good Friday Agreement still points towards the possibility of a durable reconstruction at the start of this new millennium. An inquiry into these two extremes of war and peace, asking how we got from one to the other, offers an opportunity to take a closer look than we are ordinarily inclined to do at some of the staple ingredients of modern political understanding. It provides a chance to examine what we mean by the standard idioms of the age. So while this book has a particular purpose, while it sets out to explain the descent of Northern Ireland into disarray and its re-emergence into relative stability, it also has a more general purpose. It is an attempt to throw light upon what is really covered by the terms 'democracy' and 'imperialism', and so by implication it is an exploration of what counts for political success and what for political failure at the start of the twenty-first century.

Obviously my aim is not to undermine our attachment to democracy, nor to deride what has become an instinctive hostility to imperialism. Each of these has come to epitomise the very essence of political good and evil since the end of the Second World War, and there are good reasons for the survival of consensus surrounding their relative desirability. Imperialism conjures up the spectres of tyranny and oppression. It stirs up memories of conquest and subjection, of national bondage and human degradation. The prospect of democracy, by comparison, holds out the promise of liberty and equality. So it is not entirely surprising that it is this promise which has been invoked in support of the peace settlement in Northern Ireland.

Democracy, after all, encompasses our average, uncomplicated political expectations: the expectation, for instance, that legitimate government embodies the will of the people; or that political liberty consists of an equality of rule shared across the population at large. These expectations are counted among the standard entitlements of modern citizens, but the modern world does not grant them, in their practical expression, the attributes which are ascribed to them when they are conceived of in abstraction. The reason for this can be found in the fact that the expectation of absolute political equality in modern societies is incompatible with the means by which we transact our affairs.[11]

The lure of our habitual assumptions about politics is such that the existence of this incompatibility rarely intrudes upon our settled understandings. But the pages that follow are an attempt to throw some light upon the nature of the mismatch, and to demonstrate its implications. The case of Northern Ireland highlights the existence of a shortfall between our basic political aspirations and what in actual fact transpires in the world we have inherited. The existence of this shortfall doesn't mean that we are the dupes of political ideology, nor that our lives are spent in a state of nagging disappointment. But it does mean that the residue of expectation fostered by our dominant ideas about democracy harbours the potential for serious conflict under conditions of crisis.

This residue is made up of the assumption that the citizens in a democracy are all equally the arbiters of sovereign power. Indeed, the idea of political equality is implicit in the very motto of democracy as expressed by the colloquial phrase 'Let the people decide'.[12] But the phrase conceals a basic tension intrinsic to modern thinking about the business of ruling and being ruled: a tension between the idea that autonomy consists in individuals' enjoyment of their private rights, and the idea that autonomy can only really be expressed through citizens' control over public affairs.[13] On the one hand, it is expected that political specialisation should free the individual from the burden of continuous public engagement – the assignment of a civilian role allows each individual to pursue such private enterprises as are definitively their own. But at the same time, it is presumed that the political process remains in the possession of the people as their collective sovereign entitlement – what was forfeited in the interest of individual freedom, is then reclaimed after the surrender as a common public right.

Consequently, while freedom from public affairs is a standard benefit expected from modern constitutional democracies, so too is the freedom to participate in directing political power. But this freedom to participate in controlling the sovereign power is understood to be a freedom distributed equally among citizens. That is, it is based on the expectation of political equality. The idea of popular sovereignty, in other words, assumes that the people enjoy an equal share in the corporate political and coercive power of society.[14] However, this assumption is put under immediate strain by the most cursory observation of societies which are accepted as exemplary democracies. Modern representative democracies do in some sense embody the people's will, but the popular will in a democracy does not result from political equality. Under the sway of modern representative governments, it is obvious that the people do not rule equally, but neither are they strictly given equal representation. Equality is certainly the underlying principle which motivates the dynamics of modern politics, but it is also a fraught and precarious principle which always falls short of full achievement.[15]

Modern representative democracy is an instrument designed to cater to the demand for citizen equality. But while this demand can usually be neutralised by the procedures of modern politics, it can never be fully satisfied. Genuine political equality is thoroughly compromised by the very process which is expected to provide it with expression: the process of representation itself disables the realisation of literal equality. Representative governments represent particular interests – they do not directly channel the communication of a general will.[16] They do not give equal expression to society's individual preferences, nor even sum up these preferences into a negotiated compromise. Democratic politics is a game of winners and losers: it is, at base, a competitive process in which advantages are distributed unequally.[17] But in serving a variety of particular interests over time, successful democracies nonetheless do manage to generate at least an *acceptable* version of the general interest. Generality and equality are approximately

8

gratified: inequality is never entrenched or systematically endorsed.

As a result, in the ordinary course of affairs, the conflict between the aspiration to political equality and the reality of its proximate status under representative government need hardly give us grave cause for concern. A certain equipoise is maintained in which our democratic hopes are at least minimally addressed: our interests are sufficiently protected not to offend our sense of equality. However, this equipoise is never a dependable design of nature, but is the product of political accommodation. What the peace in Northern Ireland specifically teaches is that the achievement of accommodation does not happen spontaneously, but emerges through a process of political contestation. When the contest is conducted through representative institutions, an agreed sense of equality can be adequately sustained in the midst of the political process. While this arrangement is not tantamount to popular sovereignty among equals, the demand for equal treatment is sufficiently obliged.[18]

But the war in Northern Ireland staged this development in reverse. As rival democratic aspirations took the place of a concordant sense of equality among Protestants and Catholics in the late 1960s in Northern Ireland, both parties became divided on how their interests should be represented, and so they fought to represent them for themselves. But, of course, this outcome did not exemplify an equal decision of the people, but a division of the populace into hostile factions. Moreover, a people deciding on war amongst themselves, while arguably an example of primitive democratic self-expression, cannot be taken to fulfil the modern ambition of democracy. Modern democracy, by comparison, is expected to preserve the liberty of the individual in the midst of a basic unity of political sentiment and purpose: its vocation cannot be realised through popular convulsions in which the enjoyment of private freedom is completely sacrificed to the communal welfare.[19]

By its peaceful operation – through elections, parties and political assemblies – modern democracy aims to produce representative decisions without establishing either perfect equality or homogeneity among the citizens who contribute, however remotely, to the making of those decisions. The process of democratic representation is intended to secure the greatest good for the total number of citizens without detriment to each citizen's enduring sense of freedom. Yet despite the sense of freedom secured to each person individually, this total number of citizens has to constitute a united whole: collective decisions have to represent a plausibly *common* benefit unequally distributed among equal citizens.

The argument being advanced here, then, is that political equality under modern democracy can never be substantively realised, but it must nonetheless be plausibly sought as the chief objective of the political system. It is the representative system itself that must sustain this plausibility: since representative governments represent their populations as comprising citizens who in principle enjoy an equal political status, everyone in a democracy must somehow appear to count, even if it is impossible for each person to count equally. However, the very process of political representation makes exactly the prospect of uniform 'counting' impossible to achieve. Representation, after all, selects, assimilates and excludes: political canvassing transforms voter priorities, the results of elections weed out preferences, executive decisions reduce these still more, and only victorious preferences count.[20]

As a result, decisions arising out of the process of democratic representation always risk the appearance of partiality: specific interests might seem to count significantly more than others. But the means of political decision-making in Northern Ireland between 1920 and 1972 lent a regular and constant character to the tendency towards partiality endemic to the democratic process: a particular interest was systematically privileged over the general interest. The will of the Protestant majority in Ulster monopolised the machinery of government in the Province as a calculated consequence of the majority's preponderance over the Roman

Catholic minority. In effect, the will of the majority was permanently enfranchised at the expense of the inclusive will of the people as a whole. Under this arrangement, the minority was demoted to a degraded form of citizenship, and democratic equality was systematically affronted.

Instead of procuring the greatest good for the total number of citizens, then, the political process in Northern Ireland catered preferentially to the good of the greater number. This fact explains the attraction felt among sections of the minority community in the North for 'imperialism' as a term of art which could convict the established government of petty despotism. Imperialism could be wielded as a ready synonym for arbitrary power, for the systematic partiality of the Northern Ireland government. But with the resurgence of Republicanism in the early 1970s the slogan acquired a more insinuating significance. Now imperialism denoted less the majoritarian democracy which the Northern Ireland government represented, and was instead employed to castigate the design of British power which was understood to favour the divisive politics of the Province.

The Republican extension of the meaning of the term was intended to advance a very specific implication. For the leaders of the Provisional IRA, beginning in 1969, the obstacle to be overcome in Northern Irish politics was not simply the inequality inflicted on the minority by the system of majority rule. Instead, the main problem to be tackled was a perfidious 'British interest' which somehow thrived on the partiality of political arrangements in Northern Ireland.

However, not only was the Republican diagnosis misconceived. It also entailed a wholly desperate solution: it involved projecting a new, all-Ireland democracy as the only means of overcoming the majoritarian bias entrenched in the political system of the North. Yet the solution was in reality a perfect image of the problem which an island-wide democracy was intended to resolve: an island-wide democracy would contain a new majority that would reduce its Ulster rival to an all-Ireland minority. As Republicanism armed itself to bring about this new democratic design, the curtain was being raised on an acrimonious struggle between ideas of imperialism and expectations of democracy which embroiled their opposing advocates in a bitter civil war over a period lasting more than a generation.

2

There is no necessary connection between democracy and human virtue, and likewise there is no necessary connection between empire and human vice. Despite this, the assumption persists that democracy breeds compromise among peoples, that it fosters the virtue of mutual accommodation.[21] But the fact is, there is no constitutional guarantee for the survival of a general disposition to human agreeableness. However, the very opposite assumption has tended to form the attitudes of modern political pundits.[22] Democracy promotes tolerance, we are told, and tolerance is an index of modernity. Any falling off from the expected achievements of modernity is taken to constitute a kind of abysmal regress into primitivism and superstition.[23] This explains the virtual incomprehension with which the Northern Ireland crisis was originally treated by the press in the late 1960s and early 1970s. It also explains the eagerness with which the Agreement was seized upon as a final passage from darkness into light, from tribalism to citizenship.

And so the story began to circulate that after so much death and destruction, the Northern Ireland protagonists had finally entered upon the modern stage. They came together to embrace a laudable consensus – extolling democracy, attempting goodwill and leaving bigotry behind them. An allegedly ancient quarrel had thus been put to bed and the old combatants regrouped in acceptance of values long esteemed by the civilised portion of the watching world. Indeed, it had been forecast that they would, and the far-sighted have been almost heard to mutter that this is how the world goes round, that on the final lap belligerents always opt for the reasonable course as reason says they should.

'I want this to be a pluralist Parliament for a pluralist people,' declared David Trimble on the first day of proceedings in the Northern Ireland Assembly, late in the summer of 1998. In his capacity as First Minister, he had set down a marker: he had bid farewell to that 'Protestant Parliament' for a 'Protestant State' trumpeted by Northern Ireland's first Prime Minister, James Craig, back in 1934.[24] Putting history behind him, he was apparently catching up with the rest of us. Similar gestures and similar speeches had also been made by Trimble's most bitter opponents. And there were hopes for what everybody saw as Ian Paisley's sticklers also, the myopic remnant shy of compromise: they too might catch up with the rest of us – the lucky ones for whom pride and prejudice and superstition had been cast aside like old, ill-fitting garments.

But, from the start, things were not as they seemed in Northern Ireland, and the settlement isn't what it is made to appear. Diagnoses have long been floated on the airwaves and in print, positions have been formulated and phrases crafted in an effort to capture the precise character of the slippage, the shortfall which left Northern Ireland immobilised on the wrong side of the ordinary rules and the ordinary procedures of modern political life.[25] That effort, however, has too often been freighted with the cries of expectant moralism, baffled well-wishers loudly musing – if only tolerance, for a change, could be allowed to flourish. That plea, with time, became increasingly anxious, having too often met with disappointment. 'Britain cannot be expected to sit patiently and bleed indefinitely,' insisted James Callaghan, Home Secretary under the Wilson government in 1969.[26] But there has always been some irony attached to the habit of preaching tolerance to the intolerant in tones of weariness and exasperation, and the more desperate attempt to impose tolerance with the persuasive instruments of a military arsenal has frankly begged the question of what one might take its reasonable enforcement to comprise.

Tolerance is a perfectly amiable virtue, very difficult to fault in principle. Indeed, it should come as no surprise that it is quite often a virtue shared in equal measure within the memberships of warring factions. The problem is that, between them, they are not given to extending the courtesy to one another. This, once again, begs the question: under what conditions can such generosity of spirit be made to prosper? But it is certain that the answer will not be found to lie in the application of grossly moralising norms to the exigencies of war.[27] The virtues of a peaceful life – like free discussion, or reciprocity, or democratic dialogue – are all certainly consoling, but equally beside the point precisely at the moment of their absence. We might then make a more effective start upon the reduction of conflict in the modern world by looking to the enlargement of each protagonist's sense of what could enhance their own survival. Survival, after all, is an altogether more pressing inducement to engage with one's opponent than the promise of more intangible benefits like universal approval. Only then, when the security of one's antagonist appears as a pre-condition of one's own survival, does it become relevant to nominate the political regime under which the more expensive virtues might find occasion to express themselves.

Political reconciliation does indeed require a commitment to common values. But, so far, little advance has been made by resorting to the usual list of political abstractions – liberty, equality, democracy: all attractive, yes, and compelling also, but normally left unexplained and for that reason unable to bridge the gap in political understanding. To the extent that they continue to sit there like compliant counters in ornamental splendour, their general utility can only be doubted. Without substance or content or evident meaning, they are destined to act as fillers and stopgaps awaiting elaboration. Elaboration, however, has not been forthcoming, and in its absence attempts to specify the character and the achievement of the peace accord in Northern Ireland are surely condemned to draw blanks.

The terms of the settlement, as we have seen, have been embodied in a single document, the Good Friday *Agreement*, painstakingly negotiated and meticulously drafted. It begins with a

'Declaration of Support' commending its provisions to the people of Ireland, North and South, in good faith and in the spirit of concord. The opening sentence reads: 'We, the participants in the multi-party negotiations, believe that the agreement we have negotiated offers a truly historic opportunity for a new beginning.'[28] This 'new beginning' rests upon the expectation that Republican and unionist ideologies, at least as these had been mobilised over the preceding thirty years, will bury their differences in a common purpose.

It goes without saying that such a commitment would entail a radical process of realignment in which relations between Republicanism and Unionism would undergo comprehensive redefinition, and so also in turn would their relations to some of the canonical terms of recent political conversation: loyalty and democracy would no longer mean quite what they meant before in Northern Ireland, tyranny and imperialism would no longer be invoked in quite the same old way. For, since the Northern Ireland parties have long advanced their respective claims to justice with reference to these two elusive components of modern political discussion – democracy and imperialism – it might be expected that recent developments in the Province would oblige the various protagonists to overhaul the framework within which such appeals to justice are made.

'The tragedies of the past have left a deep and profoundly regrettable legacy of suffering,' proclaimed the signatories to the Good Friday Agreement.[29] Certainly these 'tragedies of the past' had a distinct resonance for each of the different parties. But for Republicans, tragedy had been visited upon Irish politics by Britain – the imperial interloper – and the Union, on this understanding, was synonymous with empire. However, according to the Agreement, the Union still stood, yet – as we have seen – a 'new beginning' remained in the offing. How had imperialism in that case disappeared?

The signatories equally pledged themselves to 'reconciliation and rapprochement within the framework of democratic and agreed arrangements'.[30] But were they pledging themselves to a democracy different in character from the one to which they had variously committed themselves on previous occasions since 1968 before finally subscribing to these new 'agreed arrangements' in apparent harmony in 1998? Presumably it was expected that the character of the debate about Unionism and democracy, and about Republicanism and imperialism, would be significantly recast much as it had been recast on previous occasions when the Irish problem aggravated British politics in the late nineteenth and early twentieth centuries. But what was the political content of this expected transformation?

This book is an attempt to assess the nature of this transformation by setting the Northern Irish settlement in the wider context of political doctrines and their historical descent. This, it is hoped, will mark an improvement upon the familiar practice of using what has not yet been explained as a means of explanation. It involves an effort of scrutiny in which our assumptions about established values and ideologies are subjected to a more rigorous inquiry. And there are, I think, good reasons for believing that this exercise in reconstruction has implications that extend beyond the limits of its particular subject: its conclusions might serve a more general benefit in awakening us from the complacent presumption that the gift of democracy, having delivered almost half the world from fratricidal disintegration, might readily be used to civilise the political savagery of the remainder.

3

The endeavour to remedy political collapse has a very long and discouraging history. But our efforts to go one better than the political architects of the past give little by way of dependable grounds for wide-eyed optimism in the future. President Clinton, during the course of his second visit to Ireland in support of the 1998 settlement, expressed confidence that the peace accord could be held up as an example to those parts of the world still fastened in the grip of sectarian conflict. The standard formulations tripped eloquently from his tongue: dialogue was good, compromise a virtue, democracy an asset, and peace the dividend. Now it's true that it takes little by way of intelligence or insight to expose the purely gestural nature of such linguistic diplomacy. But when pundits and analysts repeat the performance, simply replicate the language without the occasion, it's fair to assume that little progress is being made toward a more searching understanding. After all, to commend a document in a shower of superlatives is not to say very much at all. At this stage it would be better to untangle the confused strains of ambition and belief that have defined the conflict in Northern Ireland together with its passing. Inevitably, this requires of us more than the stock vocabularies employed in accounts of post-Cold War conflicts, and it asks us to draw on more than a collection of alluring formulas intended to promote their resolution.

In the United States since the end of the 1980s, conflict resolution has been a minor growth industry, and it is set to grow still further. Studies are commissioned, techniques are devised, instruments prepared, and strategies advanced for ministering to desperate persons in desperate parts of the globe. Obviously these vary from the optimistic to the utopian – from spirited exhortations to earnest resolutions in support of a number of possible responses: sanctions, armament, intervention, diplomacy. This world of political trouble-shooting has its personnel, its media and a variety of fora. Participants collaborate in international colloquia, looking for an easy fix. They have their institutes, their colleges, conferences and plenaries. They launch think-tanks, pressure groups, focus groups and NGOs. They have long had the ear of editors in specialist periodical journals, and they now want the ear of the press.

They travel into the Middle East, into the Balkans, to Rwanda, to Algeria, with a sense of mission. They speak to each other, they speak to the locals, they speak to the armies and they speak to officials. All the while, they hope for the attention of movers and shakers back home in the capital, waiting for the blessed break, returning at last to take up research posts or journalistic careers, to become advisers to Congressmen or forecasters dealing in scarce information. But either way their language has made its mark, ambitious maxims have been constructed and a political culture has been established around the expectant search for *solutions*.

President George Bush Senior's New World Order offered a glimpse of a whole new field of opportunity. Next, the peace accord at Dayton became a source of inspiration, and then Northern Ireland appeared, offering encouragement and succour. Not even the wreckage of America's '9/11' could dispel the ingrained expectation that the old political remedies would ultimately be to hand. The war against the forces of international terror – as the White House made clear – would have no precedent in the past, but the crisis that it was anticipated might ensue in Central Asia was nevertheless forecast to respond to the familiar treatments: the jealousies and dissensions that were expected in Afghanistan in the wake of a US military victory would be pacified, it was predicted, through the employment of a ready method – the settlement would be 'chosen by the Afghans themselves'.[31]

The bad news is that combatants cannot be made suddenly to agree following the use of apparently dependable instruments of brokerage and mediation. It is probably more productive to assume quite simply that they will agree when they end up agreeing. Beyond this, assistance may come from the advent of exhaustion, from nuances of persuasion or cogency of argument, from gestures of goodwill or the application of force. The choice between them is a matter of judgement and judgement has no guarantees. There are indeed tools, stratagems and methods – the more refined the better, the more versatile the better. But this versatility is obliged to move in the human world of ambition and reticence. On its way it encounters the unpredictable disposition of passion and interest, of diffidence and vanity, and it cannot consequently be rationalised into a technique.

This is not a plea for some older and more reliable method, tried and tested. Such methods have enjoyed ample scope for application in the past and they too have been found wanting. But it is to register scepticism in the face of the current intellectual wizardry that promises to broker agreements by means of a transferable calculus and with the aid of transferable skills. The most common political calculus today professes to separate the good from the bad: democracy brings peace, we are advised, and imperialism brings war. But unhappily, as this book tries to show, democracy is not a simple recipe for justice, and imperialism has come to mean whatever we don't like. These considerations put some strain upon our powers of discrimination: they unsettle our basic political assumptions, and they disturb our cherished values. In the process, they inevitably call into question the usefulness of the instruments we have devised for ending conflicts, all of which are nourished by a naïve trust in democracy.

One expects one's tools to be fitted to one's trade and the trade to be conducted in the interest of the larger enterprise. But a multitude of enterprises are pursued in the modern world, and not all of them are obedient to the same strict laws of consequence nor amenable to the same explanatory logic. The same goes for crises, wars and disturbances, before which our salvage operations have often appeared uncertain and unavailing. But individuals have always been confronted with inhospitable occurrences and unforeseen disasters and so they have always been forced to make a response.

Our various responses over time can almost be said to compose a sort of history, with the result that from the point of view of palliating crises we do not find ourselves now exactly where we first started. It is true – for instance – that we no longer inhabit martial cultures, relaying heroic feats in epic verse. The chroniclers of today instead write lyric poetry in bad prose. Equally, we no longer conduct our affairs in the shadow of courtiers, counselling princes with elegant maxims gleaned from the archive of Classical learning. On the other hand, we are surrounded by eager moralists conjuring with abstractions and contriving solutions without sufficient circumspection. Likewise, we are less under the influence now of social science in the Enlightenment style, projecting revolution and counting costs. But we do live with ideological enthusiasts offering the most speculative science of politics by the back door to the State Department and the Pentagon.

It may be the case that nothing in this historical sequence is particularly to be admired, that the response to political crisis has always been fraught or incomplete. But we need reminding that it is just as clearly the case that today there has been no great leap forward. The human species seems always to have lived with strife, and there is no reason to expect the incidence of conflict suddenly to discontinue. All that can be done in the face of this fact is to mitigate its consequences, to offer our own examples of trial and error and to set about adducing the reasons for failure or success. This is not a recipe for a final deliverance. But it is better than prayers recited in the form of an incantation – tolerance, equality, democracy – and leaving the rest to providence.

PART ONE

REPUBLICANISM AND IMPERIALISM

I

Prologue

I

'Violence in Ireland is the result of British Imperialism, of the British connection and the British presence.'[1] So argued Gerry Adams in September 1976. He was writing from Long Kesh prison, near Lisburn in Co. Antrim, as pressure was mounting on the Irish Republican Army to end its campaign of terror. The campaign was then in its seventh year. While pressure to call off the war was coming from a variety of sources, it came most immediately from the Peace Movement which had recently been established to challenge the growth of militancy in Northern Ireland, and the methods of the Provisional IRA in particular. Throughout the month of August, peace rallies had been held in Belfast, and soon there were marches in London and Dublin as well. In response, Adams set about providing a defence of the Republican position. Responsibility for the war, he insisted, lay with the British government. More specifically, it lay with the government's policy of imperialism. Imperialism, however, has meant many things over the course of modern history, and it requires some investigation to discover what significance it carried for Gerry Adams in 1976. Republicanism, we are led to believe, was endeavouring to secure the defeat of imperialism in Ireland. It had set about ending the 'British connection' and removing the 'British presence'. But what in more specific terms did Republicans like Adams imagine they were replacing, and what in the wake of victory did they think they would achieve?

The war in Northern Ireland lasted nearly thirty years. In the late summer of 1969, when British troops had just been deployed in the Province, the dominant feeling among the Catholic population was one of palpable relief. The situation had been coming to a head for over a year. Then, between 12 and 14 August, Catholics in the Bogside area of Derry became involved in a desperate battle with police for two and a half harrowing days. Fearing a final assault upon their enclave by an armed militia of the Stormont regime, the residents of the Bogside welcomed the British Army as a kind of deliverance. But gradually relations began to deteriorate as soldiers came into conflict with rioting youths in the city. 'Life was very bleak,' as James Callaghan, the British Home Secretary, confided to Richard Crossman on 11 September: 'there was no prospect of a solution.' Callaghan had apparently anticipated that 'the honeymoon wouldn't last very long and it hadn't. The British troops were tired and were no longer popular.'[2] Events had moved very rapidly indeed. In the space of less than a month, sectarianism had worsened, the military presence was interpreted as exacerbating tensions, and dissidence was spreading among the disaffected, the young, and the unemployed across the Province.

That attitude of dissent was later captured by Eamonn McCann, a radical activist in Derry at the time: 'British imperialism', he recalled, 'took a lot of stick.'[3] But the specific nature of this imperialism remained shrouded and obscure. Ireland in the 1920s was frequently invoked as a way of somehow proving the point. Aden was similarly mentioned, and the example of Cyprus was confidently cited. However, as McCann put it, 'We never got down to defining with any precision what British imperialism was . . . it was the thing the Bogside had been fighting against.'[4] Nonetheless, tales of imperial perfidy steadily proliferated. Attitudes were formed and re-formed as arguments intensified. Clarity, however, was slow to emerge. Another prominent activist in those early days, Bernadette Devlin, presented her own version of what the radical youth of Northern Ireland ought to be 'fighting against'. She was, she admitted, 'generally opposed to the system', and so it was 'the system' that would have to be replaced.[5] But months passed, the crisis deepened, and positions became more finely honed.

By 28 December 1969, it was the Republican response to developments that supplied the spectre of imperialism with more definite characteristics. On that day, the Irish Republican Army split into its Provisional and Official wings. The Officials were seeking to assimilate the conflict to the language of class struggle, the Provisionals to 'reaffirm the fundamental Republican position'.[6] In a retrospective account of the first period of the Northern Ireland troubles, Gerry Adams, once again, provided his own analysis of what that fundamental Republican position had been.[7] The Civil Rights movement, which took off in the Province in the late 1960s, had succeeded in highlighting what Adams termed the 'reactionary and colonial nature' of Northern Ireland, together with 'the responsibility of the British government for this situation'.[8] In his view, the Official IRA were endeavouring to reform the irreformable, but the Provisionals would bring the system to its knees.

That system now had a definite content. It comprised a 'colonial' government manned by 'reactionary' unionists, and it was kept in existence by the occupying forces of the British Crown. But the further reaches of the Provisionals' analysis exposed an additional lurking menace: in the background, behind the outward signs of oppression – behind the colonial prop on the one hand, and the military establishment on the other – lay the historic ambitions of the British Empire. This, then, was 'imperialism', in case anyone hadn't noticed. It had been introduced into Ireland in the sixteenth century – by some accounts in the eleventh.[9] It survived as a result of the partition of the island into North and South in 1920, and it had been maintained since then at the behest of British political and economic interests.[10] Imperialism, therefore, had both a political and an economic dimension, and it was embodied in a colonial administration. But most importantly, what imperialism denied, as Adams saw it, was 'democracy' – and democracy, in turn, could only be secured by a 'campaign for national self-determination'.[11]

It was the task of Provisional Republicanism to spearhead that campaign.

But in the face of these Republican formulations, it is worth recalling that much of what Adams set down in the name of popular insurgency had its original source within the tradition of British liberal thought.[12] The essentials of that tradition deserve examination still, not least because the difficulties which afflicted what had originally been a radical liberal case against imperialism were to return to haunt the mainstream of Provisional doctrine. At the beginning of the twentieth century, the advanced English liberal, J. A. Hobson, had openly declared that the 'antagonism with democracy drives to the very roots of Imperialism'.[13] He was writing in 1902, at the close of the Boer War, when Britain's confidence in its imperial mission was on the wane. Having been a focus of national pride for close on thirty years, imperialism was now presented by a growing band of critics as a sign of civic corruption and political decline.[14] As public morals degenerated, democracy – in Hobson's mind – would be the first to suffer.

In this account, the threat to democracy came from the pursuit of an aggressive foreign policy which aimed at territorial annexation. By the progress of expansion, the proper functioning of national government was thought to have been disabled. The British Cabinet, Hobson observed, had grown to absorb the powers of the House of Commons in direct proportion to the extension of imperial control over diverse parts of the globe. In specific terms, the burden of expansion had required increasing specialisation throughout the organs of government. As a result, the business of empire exceeded at once 'popular knowledge and popular control'. The Foreign Secretary, the Colonial Secretaries and Governors in the dependencies were no longer answerable 'directly or effectively' to the 'will of the people'.[15] Accountability declined, autocracy emerged, and the means of popular resistance were – in consequence – imperilled.

In Ireland, within two years of the appearance of Hobson's book, Michael Davitt – already a committed Irish separatist and by

26

now an advocate of Boer autonomy – was presenting what in essence had been the main Hobsonian line: 'In Great Britain, parliamentarism or imperialism must die. They cannot live together.'[16] But in Hobson's further estimation, it was the murky world of finance capital and entrepreneurial interests that had been undermining parliament by stealth.[17] He advanced his claim with the sturdy support of recent historical developments: between 1870 and 1884, 3.75 millions of square miles were added to the British Empire. After the Franco-Prussian War in 1871, Germany and France had begun to pursue an active policy of foreign annexation. Britain in due course followed suit, in defence of the balance of power in Europe. It was Benjamin Disraeli who, notoriously, supplied this project with its ideological gloss. Speaking at Crystal Palace in June 1872, he advertised the virtues of 'Imperial consolidation' with a view to making the country 'great' again.[18] The speech was intended as a challenge to liberalism and to the advocates of *laissez-faire*. It was a self-conscious departure from the world of Richard Cobden and John Stuart Mill, and, in local strategic terms, it was a political assault upon the principles of Gladstone.[19] Soon the government was committing the energies of the British nation to foreign war and political subjugation. Italy in due course joined the race, and Portugal and Belgium followed fast upon her heels. The partition of the African continent had begun.

This was the era of the Zulu War, the conquest of Egypt and the annexation of the Transvaal. It was the period of the Afghanistan adventure, and the time when Victoria became Empress of India. And it was in the context of these developments that 'imperialism' acquired a positive political resonance in British public life. The term, as is well known, had started life in the middle of the century as a synonym for despotism. The personal rule of Napoleon III at that time was the target.[20] Now it stood for national glory and righteous expedition. But, according to Hobson, behind the trappings and the pageantry, behind the militarism and the patriotic fervour, lay the problem of domestic under-consumption and the search for profitable foreign investment: 'The economic root of Imperialism,' he declared, 'is the desire of strong organised industrial and financial interests to secure and develop at the public expense and by public force private markets for their surplus goods and their surplus capital.'[21]

Imperialism now meant war and conquest, it was sustained by jingoism and popular pride, but it was driven by the acquisitive zeal of organised economic interests. The exporters of surplus financial and entrepreneurial capital appeared to have succeeded in harnessing the resources of the state to their own imperial impulse. According to Hobson, then, it was through the subordination of national politics to the 'clear-sighted calculation' of industrial and financial interests that the appropriation of new territories had been effected on a massive scale, that protectorates and Crown colonies had been established across the southern hemisphere, and that an attempt had been made to exploit all regions of the earth.[22] Responsible government was left to the old empire of colonial settlement, while autocratic rule became the norm for a new emerging empire of commercial and military aggrandisement. Imperialism in the developed world spelt the decline of parliamentary democracy, but it also entailed for less developed regions the creation of primitive forms of despotism. In this context, every pretence on the part of the metropolitan establishment to be advancing the cause of civilisation amounted, in Hobson's judgement, to 'wanton exhibitions of hypocrisy'.[23] It signalled that English perfidy had been effectively transformed: the national reputation for treacherous self-regard was no longer just imputed to Britain's European diplomacy – instead, dissimulating selfishness was now ascribed to its global policy.[24]

Hobson's analysis fast gained recognition, and its currency survived for another eighty years. First Marxists around the First World War, then Fabians between 1920 and 1945, and ultimately an array of national movements in the period of European decolonisation, seized on the equation of economics with empire as a welcome explanatory tool.[25] If that equation was vague in terms of specifying with precision a chain of cause and effect, it was nonetheless versatile. Already in 1918, campaigning during the months before the Anglo-Irish War, Éamon de Valera could pose the question to an American audience: 'Does the Trotzky phrase "most cynical imperialism" not immediately occur to us as the best and truest description of England's attitude?'[26] But the association of imperialism with cynicism, and cynicism with capitalism, still retained the power to persuade well into the 1970s. And for the IRA it had obvious attractions. For its Official wing in 1969, economic interests guided the political will of empire. Those interests, however, were understood to serve established social privilege. Social discontent in Northern Ireland would therefore have to be politically harnessed before economic progress could be made: unity across the Catholic and Protestant working classes in the Province would help to precipitate the reform of the Northern Ireland government, and 'Stormont could then be used against imperialism'.[27] Reform would have to be engineered in advance of revolution, and revolution would then terminate imperial control.

For the Provisionals, on the other hand, it was the political will of Unionism that would have to be broken first before economic justice could be adequately addressed. And since Unionism in the Six Counties was seen as little more than a malleable creature of British policy, Republicanism would have to launch itself against the designs of British power. As Ruairí Ó Brádaigh, President of Provisional Sinn Féin between 1970 and 1983, came to elaborate the position within a few years of the break with the Officials, the escape from 'economic imperialism', and so the transition to publicly administered socialism, had to begin with Irish revolutionary secession.[28] The order of precedence here was defended by resort to a time-worn *apologia*. It had, Ó Brádaigh insisted, been Britain's purpose to advance its own domestic interest by 'dividing and ruling the people' of Ireland.[29] The remote cause of that endeavour was an abstract 'Imperial system'.[30] But that system could only be practically engaged by attacking its more immediate manifestation: by a direct assault, in other words, on the commercial and military capacity at the disposal of the British government.

But if the ambition to terminate imperialism in Ireland could impose such stark political choices upon the main Republican organisation, carving up the IRA into militarists and politicians, the attempt to identify the cause of imperialism was to prove a more desperate undertaking. As late as 2003, it remained the stated objective of Provisional Sinn Féin to remove the fundamental 'cause of conflict' in Northern Ireland. But since that 'cause' had – from the beginning – been deliberately identified with the designs of British imperialism, it would seem a matter of overwhelming concern to discover the true identity of this responsible, moving agent. However, as early as 1970, the endeavour to characterise the inner workings of imperialism had, in general terms, acquired a complicated history. Immediately in the wake of Hobson's diagnosis, the confused medley of economic and political forces ostensibly shaping the world of imperialism had entered the canon of socialist thought. The Austrian Rudolf Hilferding contributed to the debate; so too did the wayward Otto Bauer.[31] Then, in 1916, came Lenin's infamous response. Imperialism, in his account, was the 'highest stage of capitalism'. That stage, the final stage of crisis, was characterised by the decline of free competition and the emergence at once of big banks and industrial monopolies: the replacement of private business and banking by high finance, cartels, syndicates and trusts.[32] These were the motors of domination compelling the European powers of the day towards rivalry and conquest.

With the translation of Lenin's *Imperialism* into French and German in 1920, the argument spawned disciples, and disseminated. At the same time, the more narrowly Hobsonian thesis was reclaimed by a string of Fabian publicists between the two world wars: 'The white man,' as Leonard Woolf put it, as early as 1920, 'must cease to seek his own economic interests in Africa.'[33] But by the end of the 1950s, influential figures within the British Labour Party were declaring that the end of imperialism was definitely in sight. John Strachey revealed their thinking in 1959: 'An end of the imperialist epoch,' he affirmed, 'is both possible and a precondition of our survival.'[34] That expectation burgeoned among the devotees of Labour, leaving debate about 'economic imperialism' to the heirs of V. I. Lenin. But while Leninism is hardly a major player on the ideological battleground of our new century, in the late 1960s, particles of the doctrine still had the power to seduce.[35] Snippets even survived into the middle of the 1970s: 'Every imperialist system lives through monopolised capital,' declared Tom Hartley, a prominent Sinn Féin publicist, in 1976.[36] But the original occasion for the recrudescence in anti-imperialist rumination was the experience of European decolonisation among former African and Asian colonies.

It was on the back of this experience that the opinion began to prosper that imperialism had in fact survived, although disguised in 'neo-colonialist' apparel.[37] In 1965, Kwame Nkrumah, President of the newly independent Ghana, offered the view that 'World capitalism has postponed its crisis but only at the cost of transforming it into an international crisis.'[38] The immediate arm of conquest had been withdrawn to base, but solely with a view to re-equipping its ambition. In the future, the direction of operations would be conducted by altogether subtler means, through more insidious machinations: 'neo-colonialism,' as Nkrumah declared, 'acts covertly, manoeuvring men and governments.'[39] Its agents were still Lenin's ailing monopolists, regrouped in multinational corporations: by their actions, pan-African underdevelopment had been effectively guaranteed, while the ascendancy of the developed world had been comfortably assured. But the original inspiration for Nkrumah's reassessment had itself derived from the developed world: it was in Europe and the United States that the theory of neo-colonialism had originally been formulated. Yet, unhappily for Nkrumah, the partisans of the theory construed the current leaderships in Africa as themselves a band of hapless stooges managed by the world-capitalist system.[40]

The developed world has changed since then: scarcely anyone would declare themselves convinced by Lenin's prognoses today. But the image of sinister monopolies and cartels channelling competition into savage conflict hasn't quite disappeared. Yet how cartels actually emerge and how, once established, they succeed in influencing the policy decisions of their respective governments, rarely receives such full and sustained attention. It was a standard Marxist assumption in the earlier part of the last century that the advance of capitalism led to large-scale production, and that large-scale production tended towards the unlimited concentration of industries into monopolistic combines and trusts. Markets, from this perspective, are ultimately swamped by monopolies, and monopolies in turn seek protection from tariffs. But an effective monopoly behind a protective tariff encourages sale above the market price. This, according to the standard Marxist view, inevitably leads to dumping on poorer countries as home consumption fails to keep pace with monopoly production. Faced with rival cartel interests in foreign markets, competition can lead to ineliminable friction, to the need for diplomacy, even for war, and the search for colonial markets.

Such was the argument Hilferding and Bauer sought to mount, and these were the conclusions Lenin sought to develop and exploit. But the argument was always open to powerful objections: for one thing, monopoly is not a necessary product of capitalist competition. Neither does its operation plunge the whole world into escalating crisis. By any historical reckoning, conflict is uneven and unpredictable, but never total. Equally, if monopolies can only be said to flourish under the supervision of a protective tariff, tariffs are hardly the inevitable outcome of capitalist development. Moreover, the political clout of cartel industries continually meets with substantial opposition from competing economic interests within each capitalist democracy. They too have votes, publicists and lobbyists, with the result that monopoly and merger scrutiny and anti-trust legislation have become a familiar feature of twentieth-century economic policy. Faced with this situation, it was the Austrian political economist Joseph Schumpeter who advanced the claim that '*it is a basic fallacy to describe imperialism as a necessary phase of capitalism, or even to speak of the development of capitalism into imperialism*.[41] Never-theless, the association of capitalism with imperialism persisted, and their mutual hostility to democracy became an enduringly popular refrain.

2

This brisk narrative of the fortunes of imperialism is presented with a particular point in view: imperialism's evolving status as everyone's political nightmare was accompanied by its progressive obfuscation as an identifiable actor in the world of mundane circumstance. As imperialism rose in the minds of its various critics to the heights of omnicompetence, it disappeared from the field of reality as a definite plan of action associated with a specific set of agents. Each time it was invoked, its campaigning zeal could only ever be construed *at the back* of discernible actions and outcomes, never actually showing its hand. 'With England's designing hand removed', de Valera could confidently predict, 'religious differ-ences would not figure in Ireland more prominently than in other countries.'[42] That prediction has been shared across the range of separatist opinion in Ireland: James Connolly made the point before the Rebellion of 1916, and P. S. O'Hegarty repeated it at intervals in the ensuing years.[43] But by the spring of 1969, the presumption had returned with a vengeance as the organising principle of Republican propaganda: 'English imperialist rule . . . has used religious sectarianism to delude generations of Protestant workers that in some way Irish democracy is the enemy.'[44] Partition, and then sectarianism, seemed to answer to the needs of modern conquest, in conformity with the method of the ancients: they bore the hallmarks of the tried and tested strategy, *divide et impera*.

But the policy of 'divide and rule' can never actually be produced: no person ever proposed it, no government ever tried to bring it about. Instead it lingers, like a perpetual insinuation, or a Republican hunch, which aims to close the distance between the fact of Northern Irish dissension and the assumption of a British imperial contrivance. So the policy of imperialism is demoted to a rumour – an intention endlessly imputed, but never actually owned. In the run-up to the peace negotiations in 1998, the northern chairperson for Sinn Féin, Mitchel McLaughlin, could refer to the British orchestration of 'religious and cultural differences' in 1920 as part of a larger purpose 'to create a form of social and political apartheid' in Ireland. Even if no such purpose had in fact been entertained, confirmation could still be found in the immediate results: 'British interference meant that a healthy democracy failed to develop and religious differences were exploited as a means of maintaining control.'[45] And then again, with reference to the end of the twentieth century, McLaughlin could allege that the control of Northern Ireland remained an abiding British project, despite the fact that final control had actually been renounced.[46] So imperialism lived on, as an implacable suspicion. Like the ghost of the old King on the battlements, having retreated from the mortal world, it was assumed it dictated the course of events remotely, from beyond the grave.

But the drama of life does not replicate the drama of the stage: departed souls do not direct affairs within the terrestrial world. They can of course be conjured in imagination, but in pursuit of such bodiless images of the brain, even the most eager of seekers is obliged to fix their attention on real forces and ascertainable persons. These real presences might well be imagined to be the bearers of some spectral significance lurking behind their manifest appearance, but they have, in truth, no genuine meaning beyond the assemblage of motives and actions which gives them their existence. For Nkrumah it was imperialism that still manoeuvred 'men and governments'. The origins of this imperialism lay in the development of capitalism, but its result could be discovered in the political fragmentation which affected the African continent as a whole: 'The greatest danger at present facing Africa', Nkrumah argued, 'is neo-colonialism and its major instrument, balkanization.'[47] Imperialism, therefore, was again equated with the strategy of 'divide and rule'. But the search for the contemporary agents of this wanton process of division was ultimately doomed to failure: the policy and the perpetrator just could not be aligned.[48]

In like manner, the first critics of imperialism found that modern war was haunted by the spirit of capitalism, but that spirit soon dissolves in the face of further investigation and leaves the fact of bellicosity in the wake of its dissolution. So also the Republican assault upon British colonial government in Northern Ireland: here it was found that British policy was possessed by the phantom of imperialism, but when the ghostly remnant is allowed to bow out, it is the fact of a million Protestant unionists which remains as a solid political reality. Curiously, the leaders of Provisional Sinn Féin seem to know this. It was Mitchel McLaughlin, after all, who conceded the point in speculating that if 'unionists were to find that they could become a minority within the North of Ireland it is difficult to believe that they would not resist . . . change violently'.[49] But the developed Republican taste for spirit-raising always distracts from the problem at hand, displacing the immediate cause of contention on to a disembodied residue that can only ever be reached by presuming its survival in the flesh of the living: in this instance, the United Kingdom system of government as a seeming relic of an imagined British imperialism.

Every such battle against intangible spirits, whose demonic purpose is misattributed to tangible persons in the world of politics, is bound to extend the moment of reckoning into a bloody struggle. But with the progress of the twentieth century, the battle-lines themselves grew steadily more faint. Since the spectre of imperialism was never supplied with any definite shape of its own, it has been easy to cast its formless features into a plurality of moulds. The results of this process are clear to see: imperialism over the longer term came to cover a multitude of sins. It meant the social relations which we do not like, or the authority we oppose. The example of Indonesia's President Sukarno exemplifies the tendency: at the Bandung Conference of Afro-Asian powers in 1955, he warned his audience that imperialism did not exclusively appear in its 'classic form' of old: 'It has also its modern dress in the form of economic control, intellectual control, and actual physical control by a small but alien community within the nation.'[50] As conflict raged around the geo-political upheavals which attended the aftermath of the Second World War, the traits of imperialism were progressively found to be subtle, disguised, or indeed invisible: as Egypt's Gamal Nasser described it, again in 1955, imperialism was 'the great force that is imposing a murderous, invisible siege upon the whole region'.[51] Likewise for Nkrumah, in 1963, imperialism had 'begun, and will continue, to assume new forms and subtler disguises'.[52]

It would be ridiculous to suggest that what is complained about in the name of imperialism disappears with every attempt at description. But the injustices that individuals do obviously encounter have a perfect reality all of their own. In addressing the experience of injustice in abstruse and general terms, it is altogether more expedient, if redress is to be secured, to launch the general criticism with the particular complaint in view. In the early part of the twentieth century, criticism of imperialism certainly had a definite purpose: it was to promote the spread of responsible government and raise the level of general prosperity. But that purpose was never going to be profitably advanced by elaborating the dynamics of global trade and politics in terms better suited to a world which had long passed. This belatedness was the basic problem with the repudiation of imperialism, beginning in 1898. However, the attempt at repudiation had itself started off as part of a deliberate move to supplant an older orthodoxy.

In the eighteenth and nineteenth centuries there emerged a commonplace presumption that belligerence would reduce in the face of an expanding network of international trade and the modern institution of representative government: extensive commerce between rival states and public opinion within them would contribute to the promotion of peace and prosperity.[53] But a century of war and carnage did little to enhance that argument's appeal. After the Boer War, and in the middle of the Great War, the thesis began to wear thin. And so Hobson and Lenin, in their different ways, shifted the frame of reference. Now it was said that commerce congeals into monopolistic control, that monopolies hijack public opinion and that opinion grows to favour war. Imperialism, on this account, governs the international order. However, observable reality – such as it is – offers little encouragement to the concomitant view that conquest is the secret goal of modern European states. Britain, in this regard, is hardly an exception: despite some flights of national fantasy, it was never another Rome.

The example of Rome inevitably haunts the history of modern European conquest, and so it pervades every charge of imperialism mounted in response to global conflict.[54] But while it might seem obvious, it is still important to emphasise that the dynamics of modern warfare are not conducted on the model of the ancients. That model received astute recapitulation in early modern Florence: in 1529, Niccolò Machiavelli made the point that states in the real world of perilous conflict are compelled to preserve their fortune. They do so, he observed, by defence or by expansion. Venice exemplified the former model, while Rome conformed to the latter. And since initiative is always preferable to indolent optimism, it was Rome that was destined to reap the benefit of proactive self-assertion. The necessity of conquest, he further argued, was most productively served by a patriotic militia. But the existence in a city of an armed citizen body required that power be placed in the people's hands, and from political and military enfranchisement arises the supreme aptitude of martial republics for empire: 'there never has been another republic so organised that she could gain as Rome did. The efficiency of her armies caused her to conquer her empire, and the order of her proceedings and method . . . caused her to keep it when conquered.'[55] Empire became a Roman *raison d'être*, the object of Republican greatness.

Now, the Republicanism of the Provisional IRA obviously falls

37

far short of these pretensions, but so too did the orientation of British imperial policy. To refer to an imperial 'policy' is already to stretch the point. War, trade and commercial advantage were certainly objects of national ambition. This is as true of the age of Pitt as it is of the age of Disraeli. But at no stage was foreign conquest sought as a principal reason of state. This, moreover, was clearly the case with Britain in the 1960s. The 'thing the Bogside was fighting against', recalling Eamonn McCann's phrase, was not an acquisitive military machine. Neither was it a British will to despotic usurpation. And nor was it a sinister cabal of imperialistic capitalists. Apart from anything else, it is a little less than credible to suggest that organised private capital controlled the entire political agenda of successive post-war governments.

3

Nevertheless, the legacy of former conquest continued to linger beneath 'the dreary steeples of Fermanagh and Tyrone' in 1969 and 1970.[56] Three waves of political extirpation in the sixteenth and seventeenth centuries, extensive settlement and resettlement in the same period, a penal code in the eighteenth century, sectarianism and famine in the nineteenth . . . they all combined to cast a long shadow over twentieth-century memory in Ireland. Moreover, a Provincial government in Northern Ireland, subordinate to the Westminster Parliament since 1920, yet armed with an arsenal of emergency legislation and a sectarian paramilitary police force, was poorly calculated to diminish bitterness and suspicion. Similarly, petty Unionist local government, electoral gerrymandering, and discrimination in housing and employment, did little over the course of fifty years to enhance the prospects of Northern Ireland's political success.

At the start of the 'troubles', in 1968 and 1969, when the Stormont regime was confronted with resistance, Unionism responded with minimalist concessions, and then with partiality and violence.[57] Britain was encouraged to intervene, but it did so with reluctance: 'Jim Callaghan and I considered whether we should propose . . . intervention,' recalled the British premier, Harold Wilson. But, in the end, they both agreed that the measure 'would be unwise'.[58] And when the request for military assistance was finally made by the Stormont government, Wilson acceded, but with grim anticipation: 'I remembered that in that remarkable maiden speech of Bernadette Devlin's earlier in the year, she had said that one answer to Northern Ireland's problems must be ruled out; a decision to introduce British troops, which would unite both sides against them . . . I was disposed to think that she might be right.'[59]

As it turned out, she was wrong. Yet still the problems multiplied: 'British troops and the British Government were bearing responsibility for an intolerable situation,' Wilson was soon complaining: 'we were exercising responsibility without power.'[60] But into the vacuum, connecting British responsibility with the exercise of power, the spectre of imperialism would ultimately be installed at the behest of Irish Republican propaganda. In the meantime, before Republicanism had become a decisive player in the conflict, the British Cabinet was already in serious trouble. The 'Irish problem, after nearly 50 years of relative stagnation, was on the move again', commented the Home Secretary to Cabinet colleagues at the start of September 1969. The only consolation was that the Army on the ground was not 'emotionally involved' in the situation, and the Tories were 'no longer totally committed to the Protestant North'.[61]

But despite freedom of manoeuvre on the domestic front, the Labour government was apprehensive in the face of calls for concerted action. This reluctance to commit its energy to any radical plan of action was disguised by the appearance of being in command when tackled in discussion. However, difficulties stemming from half-hearted intervention were compounded by genuine ignorance of the actual Ulster situation.[62] As a result, a policy which sought adjustment to the balance of forces in Northern Ireland was never closely considered or assessed. The reality was, Britain wanted neither responsibility nor power. Having inherited responsibility, she would not act upon her power, the extent of which was significant, although not decisive.

Then the Southern Irish government, in the midst of the unfolding crisis, began to challenge the wisdom of partition. Expectations were raised among the Catholic minority without the slightest chance of being satisfied. Soon, ministers in the Irish government were conspiring to supply weaponry to vigilante defence committees which appeared throughout Northern Ireland in the closing months of 1969. The committees were heavily populated by Northern members of the IRA, but it was the Provisional contingent within this Catholic vigilantism which was most likely to benefit from any Southern arms procurement: the government in Dublin already favoured straightforward militants over the socialist subversives who, by and large, ultimately affiliated with the Official IRA.[63]

The South had become involved in the upheavals of the North: the Northern minority were encouraged to look with optimism to the Southern majority as a significant resource against the majority in the North. By the middle of 1970, the Provisionals were brandishing one of the founding political tenets of the Southern establishment, but with revolutionary intent: 'the Six County boundary was drawn by careful design to form an artificial pro-British majority'.[64] Soon the example of the Anglo-Irish War was being preached to the inhabitants of the Belfast ghettos: as had occurred in 1922, so now in 1972, the British could be 'swept' from Ireland 'by a people who are the MAJORITY'.[65] Such expectations contributed to an explosive mix which had already fanned the flames of sectarian hatred and now opened the way to civil war. Militant Republicanism was reborn, so British imperialism had to be reinvented.

But the truth is that behind the rhetoric of Republicanism and empire lay a recognisably modern dispute about the nature of democracy. Hostilities in Northern Ireland after 1968 derived from the most basic and elusive problem to have afflicted politics in the twentieth century. That problem once troubled the Ottoman Empire, and it came to trouble the USSR. It has destabilised Quebec, disturbed Sri Lanka, and harassed the Lebanon and Kashmir. But in Northern Ireland the problem of democracy has been more easily misapprehended since here its features have all along been subtly distorted by the political assumption which associates democracy with the procedure of majority decision.

Democracy is the name for a modern system of values, dominant across the globe; yet democracy itself has been endlessly subjected to misunderstandings so severe as to provoke fundamental crises. On the one hand, democracy refers to an established form of government, but on the other it refers to a form of state: it covers both the way in which self-determination is exercised, and the unit of population by which that self-determination is authorised. In Northern Ireland the distinction proved significant: while the Province was administered by a democratic government after 1920, that government was obliged to function without a democratic state. In fact, the government operated as an instrument of division, exacerbating conflict between rival democracies: a Catholic minority, excluded by the majority, which ultimately aspired to form a democracy of its own; and a Protestant majority which tried to count as the whole democracy, while only forming in reality a major portion of the state.

The first part of this book traces the collision between Republicanism and imperialism from the emergence of political protest in the late 1960s to the resurgence of Republican militancy through the early 1970s, and it charts the development of the politics of Provisional Sinn Féin from its adoption of an electoral strategy after the hunger strikes of the early 1980s, to the party's pursuit of a peace strategy in the 1990s. Along the way, I present the earlier struggle between Republican resistance and British policy from the 1890s through to the Irish Civil War. This involves recovering previous debate about the conflict between democratic self-determination and the imperial strategy of 'divide and conquer'. Self-determination as a political formula has always been as problematic as it is ideologically attractive. In Northern Ireland over this past generation, its problems have been dramatised in the theatre of war. What follows is an attempt to draw some conclusions about the peace, and the means by which democracy became a cause of war.

II

Protest: 1968

I

A crowd of demonstrators fled in disarray along Duke Street as two cordons of police advanced simultaneously toward their front and at their rear with batons drawn. Suddenly, from every angle, the Royal Ulster Constabulary set upon confused bands of protesters groping each way for escape. Next, a water cannon stationed on Craigavon Bridge hosed marchers in retreat. Everywhere men and women scattered in dismay, or huddled together in fear.

Soon the immediate panic lifted. Sections of the crowd began to cross over the River Foyle and head toward Derry's city centre. Shocked and wearied, some went home. Others gathered in discussion and alarm in the lounge of the City Hotel. But outside on the streets, around the Diamond area of the city, clusters of young men gradually emerged and by sunset fighting had broken out again. As daylight failed, police were driving Catholic youths back along Butcher Street and down into the Bogside. Barricades went up in Fahan Street, petrol bombs were thrown and shop fronts were smashed. Rioting continued through the night and then into the morning.

It was the first Saturday in October, 1968. The Derry Housing Action Committee had organised a protest march to be held that day in the city. The planned route was to lead across the centre of the town, from the Waterside, over the River Foyle, through the city walls to the Diamond. This would take the marchers, mostly Catholics, through traditionally Protestant areas. Unionist organisations had already objected, confrontation had been anticipated, and so the march was banned the previous Thursday by William Craig, Minister for Home Affairs in the Stormont government. Despite the ban, the organisers decided to proceed. They were animated by a spirit of defiance, gripped by a sense of the justice of their cause, and so on the afternoon of 5 October a small contingent of protesters assembled to begin a public demonstration.[1]

In the summer of 1968, tension was rising throughout Northern Ireland. Indeed, it had been rising over the two preceding years. Across the world at large, a decade of unrest seemed to be heading towards crisis: disturbances were manifest from Algeria to South Africa, Cuba had plunged itself into socialist revolution, and civil disobedience had shaken the United States. Then came 1968. The Tet Offensive was launched in Vietnam in February, the Prague Spring challenged Soviet power in Czechoslovakia, Martin Luther King was assassinated in Memphis, Tennessee. In March students did battle with police in Rome, they revolted in Paris in May, in August they rioted outside the Democratic Party Convention in Chicago. And so it seemed that Northern Ireland also was on the verge of some kind of reckoning.[2]

The pervasiveness of social and political inequality had steadily contributed to resentment among the Catholic population of the North. Since 1921, the Unionist Party had held the reins of power in the Northern Ireland Parliament located, after 1932, at Stormont outside Belfast. The Stormont regime was created in the face of bitter opposition from the Catholic third of the Province's population, yet it continued to preside over a total number of one and a half million citizens for more than fifty years.[3] From the start, the government of the Province was armed with a formidable array of emergency powers under the Civil Authorities (Special Powers) Act of 1922. Annually renewed up to 1928, the Act was then passed for another five years until 1933 when it was finally made permanent.[4] By 1963, it had attracted both the envy and the admiration of South Africa's Minister for Justice, Mr B. Johannes

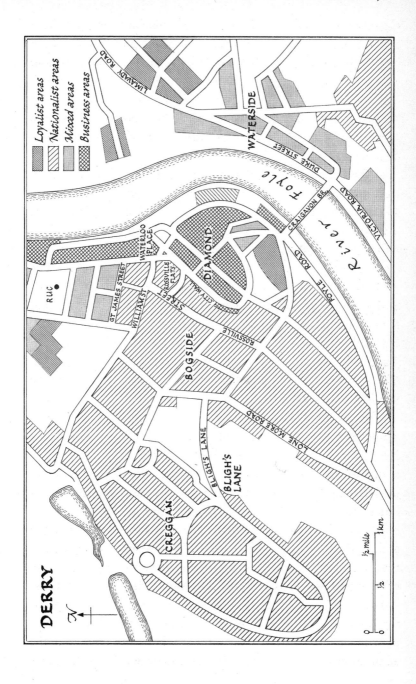

DERRY

Loyalist areas
Nationalist areas
Mixed areas
Business areas

WATERSIDE

River Foyle

LIMAVADY ROAD

DUKE STREET

VICTORIA ROAD

CRAIGAVON

POYLE ROAD

DIAMOND

WATERLOO PLACE

ROSSVILLE FLATS

CITY WALL

ROSSVILLE STREET

WILLIAM ST

GT. JAMES STREET

RUC

BOGSIDE

LONE MORE ROAD

BLIGH'S LANE

BLIGH'S LANE

CREGGAN

½ mile
½
¼ km

45

Vorster: he would, as he confessed, trade all the coercive powers at his disposal 'for one clause of the Northern Ireland Special Powers Act'.[5] The extremity of these powers had been a source of nervous pride for loyal Protestants during the early period of Northern Ireland's existence, but later their excessiveness was to be privately acknowledged by members of the Stormont government itself.[6]

The Civil Authorities Act had originally gained approval in the Northern Ireland Parliament during the spring of 1922 in an atmosphere of resounding urgency and crisis.[7] The creation of a devolved administration in the six north-eastern counties of the island of Ireland after 1920 was assailed by bloody violence from the very beginning. Over the next two years, with sectarian tensions rising in the North and civil war in progress in the South, the government of Northern Ireland moved to secure its faltering position by the implementation of emergency provisions.

The general purpose of these provisions was to avoid the necessity of recourse on the part of the Northern Irish government to the Restoration of Order in Ireland Act which had been passed by the Westminster Parliament in 1919 as part of the British effort to combat Irish Republican guerrilla tactics during the Anglo-Irish War. But, more immediately, the new Act was intended as a way of conferring legality upon the radically coercive measures then required for the defence of a newly established regime struggling at the time for its survival. To the unionist and Protestant majority in the Province, the Act had seemed a matter of survival. But close on half a century later, with the Act of 1922 still manifestly there, the pretext of necessity began to lose conviction.

At its inception, then, the Northern Ireland Parliament had recourse to draconian emergency legislation which effectively put an end to any functional separation of powers in the Province, and by 1968 the expedient had long survived the critical circumstances which had prompted its original employment. In practical terms, that meant that the arm of government in Northern Ireland was placed in a position to interfere directly with the personal and political liberties of the civilian population in the absence of any due process of law throughout the entire period of the government's existence.

It was of course the personal and political liberties of subversive elements within society which were likely to be undermined by any invasive government action. However, subversion was all too easily linked to any show of dissatisfaction on the part of the Catholic community at large. It was a term for branding disaffection and so a ready means of denominating the nationalist population, virtually all of whom were at least nominally Catholic by persuasion. Sectarian antagonism in the form of emergency legislation was therefore embodied in the permanent political machinery of the state. The unavoidable result of this arrangement was that the sense of security enjoyed by the Catholic population was systematically threatened and impaired. But where the security of a people is threatened, its allegiance is correspondingly dissolved.

Under the Special Powers Act, a significant range of prerogatives ordinarily exercised by the judiciary were conferred upon the Northern Ireland executive, and drastic means of legal enforcement were concentrated in the hands of the Minister responsible for home affairs in particular. This meant that in 1968 a large retinue of judicial powers fell to the notorious William Craig, the unrelenting Minister for Home Affairs in the O'Neill government. It was he who was empowered, as the opening clause of the 1922 Act stated, to take 'all such steps and issue all such orders as may be necessary for preserving the peace and maintaining order' in the Province as a whole.[8]

The power to search and detain without warrant lay with police under the control of the Minister for Home Affairs. He could outlaw organisations and ban publications, impose exclusion orders and declare curfews. He could secure an arrest on the mere suspicion of seditious intent. The provisions of the Act were therefore nothing if not truly comprehensive in character. But on the afternoon of 5 October 1968, as disgruntled Roman Catholics were taking to the streets, no less than three generations had passed since the first desperate period of trouble in Northern Ireland had prompted the introduction of obviously desperate measures. The Second World War had intervened, great empires had been overturned, the map of Europe and the globe had been redrawn. Habits of thought, the grouping of parties, and the outlook of affairs had all been subject to violent change in the deluge of the world. But as the deluge gradually receded, and the determined optimism of the 1960s emerged, the Northern Ireland Special Powers Act remained, its provisions more or less unaltered in the cataclysm which had swept the world.

If anything, their scope had been augmented. A Public Order Act of 1951 had reinforced them, and the Flags and Emblems Act of 1954 had extended political control over opposition to the regime.[9] Once again the public welfare was defined in terms of a Protestant majority, and so at the expense of a large Catholic minority, both bound together under a common constitution, although scarcely as equal citizens. This Protestant welfare was maintained by a Protestant security establishment cast in the form of a paramilitary police force and a part-time auxiliary militia. These were the Royal Ulster Constabulary and the Ulster Special Constabulary, both of which had been founded in the early 1920s, and each of them surviving to the end of the 1960s as a source of mounting tension within community relations.[10]

The Ulster Special Constabulary had grown out of the remnants of the Ulster Volunteer Force. Formed as a private army back in 1912, and revived in 1920 as an instrument of loyalist defence, the UVF was co-opted into the Special Constabulary as a localised force comprising three divisions – A, B, and C – which encompassed both full and part-time members and an additional body of reservists. Each division had originally been charged with assisting the regular Crown forces in their fight against Republican insurgency during the Anglo-Irish War. After the war, the Specials were adopted by the government of Northern Ireland and, by 1926, although they had been cut back and reorganised, the second division of the Constabulary – the B Specials – remained as a part-time militia available to support the Royal Ulster Constabulary in maintaining peace and security.

The RUC had itself been commissioned during the combustible month of April 1922 but, like the B Specials, it was to remain well beyond that first period of excited expectation in Northern Ireland. For nearly fifty years they both stood vigilant in the apprehension of armed rebellion. In reality, however, significant rebellion was neither planned nor possible in 1968. The Irish Republican Army had barely a few hundred members and less than half that number was stationed in the North.[11] Their armaments were paltry and dilapidated, their activities increasingly political in character.

Yet whatever the unlikelihood of militant insurrection, the majority of Northern Ireland's half-million Catholics still saw themselves as existing in a kind of internal exile. Their representatives at Stormont had no chance of influencing policy; their MP at Westminster was a solitary voice. The Civil Service was dominated at every level by members drawn from the Protestant community, and in local government it was again Protestants who held sway throughout the upper echelons out of all proportion to their numbers. Bias had been alleged in judicial appointments as well: by 1969, only six senior posts were held by Catholics out of a total number of sixty-eight. The same pattern was reproduced in the security services. The 3,000-strong membership of the Royal Ulster Constabulary was 90 per cent Protestant, and the 8,000 part-time volunteers in the divisions of the Special Constabulary were almost completely so.[12] Between them, they commandeered a sizeable arsenal of military hardware which included revolvers for individual members, Sterling sub-machine-guns, water cannon, armoured cars and gas projectors.

The Northern Ireland government had never sought nor secured the allegiance of its Catholic population and the Protestant majority regarded the minority with suspicion and alarm. With the advent of the 1960s, ongoing discrimination in employment and unfair treatment in housing allocation provided a focus for the established sense of grievance. The expectation of equality was rising among the disaffected members of the population, the historic settlement of 1920 was coming under strain, and the spirit of protest was rekindled among the Catholics of the North.

The first significant sign of disquiet came in 1964 with the establishment of the Campaign for Social Justice in Northern Ireland. The Campaign was the product of disgruntlement over local government housing policy in parts of east Tyrone which had first been highlighted through research conducted by the Homeless Citizens League. The Campaign made its appearance, however, at a moment of general political change in the United Kingdom as a whole. With new personnel at the helm in Ulster and Westminster, the climate for discussion was expected to improve, encouraging the assumption that murmurings of patient protest might at least begin to prosper. In October 1964, Harold Wilson took the British Labour Party into government and, just eighteen months earlier, Captain Terence O'Neill had succeeded to the premiership of Northern Ireland with the promise of introducing some forward momentum into the stagnant fold of Ulster politics.[13] This hardly amounted to a startling shift in direction, but small gestures could have a large impact upon the cramped world of Provincial affairs. The nationalist population hoped for credible progress: the Unionist regime looked ready to make some concessions.

Within months of taking office O'Neill released a public message of condolence upon the death of Pope John XXIII. A couple of years later he invited the Taoiseach, Sean Lemass, to lunch at Stormont House, and within another month he had himself braved a visit to the government of the republican South. Soon he was visiting Catholic schools and allowing himself to be photographed with an array of nuns and priests. But these gestures amounted to diplomacy and not reform, and as diplomacy O'Neill's efforts appeared uncomfortably close to a kind of strained *noblesse oblige* extending its favours out of season: 'If you treat Roman Catholics with due consideration and kindness,' he remarked as late as 1969, 'they will live like Protestants in spite of the authoritative nature of their Church.'[14] At best, he was picking his way through the limited options which a divisive history had imposed upon conduct in the present – though he thought he was blazing a trail.[15]

O'Neill had served as Finance Minister for seven years in the Northern Ireland government under the feckless leadership of Viscount Brookeborough before becoming Prime Minister himself in 1963. The immediate result of his succession was a drive for numerous policy initiatives and the public display of a benignly conciliatory tone. Policy was directed toward economic planning, good deeds toward the amelioration of chronic communal strife. Straight away, his government evolved a strategy for advancing regional development and enticing outside investment into the eastern counties of Ulster. New industries were pioneered, multinationals arrived, and ambitious public works abounded. The old manufacturing sector declined – the linen mills languished and the shipyards contracted – but then Grundig, Du Pont, ICI and British Enkalon appeared to stem the tide of overall stagnation. Four motorways were built, a new city was created, and a second university was sited at Coleraine.

The impact on community relations was intended to be swift. 'In twenty years as Prime Minister,' O'Neill was later to comment on the laxity of Lord Brookeborough, 'he never crossed the border, never visited a Catholic school and never received or sought a civic reception from a Catholic town.'[16] These were to be exactly the emollient actions by which the incumbent would try to signal his own progressive stand. O'Neill's hope was that an outward show of magnanimity coupled with the benefits of marginal growth would jointly operate as catalysts for an eleventh-hour *détente*: with the simultaneous advance of material prosperity and symbolic displays of good-neighbourly behaviour, the dark impulses of atavistic hankering would be safely conducted towards benevolent compromise.

The venture, however, ultimately failed: 'As the Party would never stand for change', O'Neill ruefully conceded in 1972, 'I was really reduced to trying to improve relations between North and South; and in the North itself between two sections of the community.'[17] But already by the end of 1966 the dream of sudden harmony looked more remote than ever. In December of that year, in the aftermath of a resurgence of sectarian strife, O'Neill was openly bewailing his predicament as an honest broker trapped between the implacable energies of opposing ideological extremes: on one side stood republicans 'who sought to flaunt before our people the emblems of a cause which a majority of us abhor' and on the other 'those self-appointed and self-styled "loyalists" who see moderation as treason, and decency as weakness'.[18]

But all the while, as Protestant loyalism was progressively inflamed, Catholic frustration was ratcheted toward despair. Despite all the tokens of liberality brandished as pledges of substantive improvement, not a single concrete measure of reform had been embraced by the Northern Ireland Prime Minister.[19] In the end came the disturbances of 5 October 1968 with the pressing demand for immediate change. Ten days after that event, reflecting upon its consequences in Northern Ireland's House of Commons, O'Neill delivered his considered response: 'In the last resort, change has to be acceptable change.'[20]

But by then the judgement of acceptability had itself become an overwhelming problem: acceptable change was a common goal pursued by the two communities, yet the shape which that goal might actually assume was being lost in the clash of rival perceptions. O'Neill had inched forward in circumstances of rising expectations on the part of the Catholic population which he tantalised but did not satisfy.[21] The resulting blend of hope and disappointment propelled Catholic disillusionment toward further protest. At the same time, fretful elements within the unionist family bristled at the imagined spectacle of betrayal: as O'Neill sought to mollify the minority's sense of disadvantage, loyalism branded him an apostate and a traitor. For the government, all this meant steering a course through opposing pressures imposed by mutually antagonised communities. In the end, antagonism bore fruit in dramatic form with the disorders of 1968. And by then the Catholic pressure for reform was half a decade old.[22]

2

Pressure built up from a modest start. In the spring of 1963, the very year in which O'Neill came to power, a group of sixty women from Dungannon in east Tyrone established the Homeless Citizens League. The League was a product of local circumstances, and its aim was to challenge the procedures for housing allocation operated by Dungannon Urban District Council as they affected the needs of Catholics in the vicinity of the town. Dungannon had a majority Catholic population of slightly more than 50 per cent, yet the Council was still subject to Unionist control. Public housing was awarded by a voting system as a result of which young married Catholics had been disproportionate losers in the distribution of council homes. Allegations of unabashed discrimination mounted, and the Homeless Citizens League became a filter for complaint. 'They talk about Alabama,' declared a column in the *Dungannon Observer* in September 1963. 'Why don't they talk about Dungannon?'[23] Certainly the Unionist establishment stayed quiet. The League picketed, petitioned and broadcast its complaints, but MPs at Stormont still refused to talk. Lack of prompt and evident progress called for a more concerted approach and so, in January 1964, the Campaign for Social Justice was formed to build on the activities of the Homeless Citizens League and to make itself a more dynamic engine of focused public criticism.

Housing was the issue around which criticism was to rally. It also provided the link which would connect the activities of the Campaign for Social Justice with the escalating crisis of 1968.[24] A major effort had been required throughout Northern Ireland from the late 1940s through to the early 1960s to replace the stock of public housing destroyed in the Second World War but, since the disbursement of funds for building programmes had been linked to economic expansion, the growth areas in the eastern regions of the

Province had benefited in comparison with those western regions where Catholics tended to challenge and surpass the numerical preponderance of the Protestant population in Northern Ireland as a whole.[25] The scarcity of housing was more marked where deprivation was most entrenched, but also where Catholic numbers posed a threat to the political security of their Protestant neighbours. Consequently, west of the river Bann – in parts of Fermanagh and Tyrone, and notoriously in Londonderry – local political competition was fierce, with disputes about housing supplying the controversy around which a bitter conflict raged.

The situation was certainly immediately antagonising, but it was also potentially explosive. Five years later, in June 1968, in the village of Caledon just outside Dungannon, the preferential allocation of a new council house to a single Protestant woman in spite of the burgeoning demand for homes on the part of growing numbers of large Catholic families in the area provoked direct action from the Nationalist MP for East Tyrone, Austin Currie. Having raised the issue in the Stormont Parliament on 19 June to no avail, Currie proceeded to squat in the building and focus attention on a tangible bias.[26] The event became an immediate spur to action: within a couple of months, the first extensive public demonstrations were staged in Northern Ireland.

Mass demonstrations were to provide the scene for sectarian conflict on the streets. But the path to conflict had been opened in 1964 when complaints against Unionist local government practices were quietly invigorated under the auspices of the Campaign for Social Justice. Founded by a group of Catholic middle-class professionals, the Campaign was launched with the purpose of collecting what the original organisers' press release described as 'comprehensive and accurate data on all injustices done against all creeds and political opinions' in Northern Ireland.[27] The targets for complaint were to be palpable and local, but the consequences of criticism were intended to spread and ramify.

Attention was to be directed towards the existence of prejudicial practices in housing, employment, elections and public appointments in an effort to expose 'the Government of Northern Ireland's policies of apartheid and discrimination'.[28] The tired old Irish quarrel between nationalists and unionists about the wisdom of partition was finally to be removed from the political agenda. Instead, influenced by the principles of the civil rights movement in the United States, the aim of the group was to secure equality of treatment for Northern Ireland citizens within the existing framework of the British constitution. By 1965 the Campaign was affiliated with the National Council for Civil Liberties in London and seeking to establish stronger links within the British political establishment more generally.

As it happened, debate about the anomalies besetting Northern Irish politics was already being generated in the British corridors of power. Harold Wilson, for one, had a sizeable emigrant Irish population in his own Liverpool constituency of Huyton, and in the months before the general election of 1964 he had conducted a correspondence with a leading committee member from the Campaign for Social Justice in which he highlighted his commitment to a programme of reform: 'I agree with you as to the importance of the issues with which your campaign is concerned,' he declared in a September letter, 'and can assure you that a Labour Government would do everything in its power to see that the infringements of justice to which you are so rightly drawing attention are effectively dealt with.'[29]

But it soon became clear that 'everything in its power' would amount to precious little. The Campaign for Social Justice had already been in contact with sections of the Tory administration under Sir Alec Douglas-Home, writing to the Prime Minister and his Home Secretary alike, only to have it established that the government considered itself incapable of action: the areas of complaint, they were informed, lay outside the remit of British government action, falling squarely within the jurisdiction of the Northern Ireland administration.[30] And despite the apparent promise contained in Wilson's pronouncements in opposition, victory in the October general election saw his government likewise avoiding legislative intervention in Northern Ireland. Wilson was happy to threaten the Stormont government with drastic action, but he never moved to intercede.

The reason for this isn't difficult to discover. Perceptions about Northern Ireland were frankly confused in the British Cabinet. In ministerial conversations, opposition to the status quo was paraded as a point of principle. But despite this, discussion never got to the point where specific principles were produced. Orangeism was frowned upon, and discrimination was despised. But what perpetuated the existence of injustices in Northern Ireland eluded the firm grasp of British ministerial intelligence. The symptoms of disorder were acknowledged to be in evidence, but explanations never delved into the organisation of Ulster politics. O'Neill contributed to this failure by treating the British to diversions. Typically, he would inform the British Prime Minister that 'we are convinced that the real issues underlying the current agitation are predominantly social'. Political arrangements in Northern Ireland were perennially 'defendable', and so the litany of complaints was pinned on social deprivation.[31] The government in London was loath to refuse this explanation and risk absorption into the perplexities of Irish politics. Wilson, accordingly, deferred engagement, shunned intervention, and submitted to the convention whereby the affairs of Northern Ireland were not addressed inside the chamber of the House of Commons.

The convention by which successive British parliaments had exempted themselves from discussion of the affairs of Northern Ireland was as old as the Stormont regime itself. It was established in 1923 when a question in the British House of Commons from the Nationalist MP Joseph Devlin about sectarian attacks in Belfast was ruled out of order by the Speaker. Under Section 75 of the 1920 Government of Ireland Act it had been declared that, notwithstanding the establishment of the Northern Ireland Parliament, 'the supreme authority of the Parliament of the United Kingdom shall remain unaffected and undiminished over all persons, matters and things' in the Province.[32] But as the Speaker's ruling of 1923 was to clarify, that supreme authority referred to legislative competence, and not to regular executive control.[33]

In practice this meant that, with reference to all business devolved to the competence of the Northern Ireland government, Westminster had no right of intervention short of implementing appropriate legislation. However, such a course of action Douglas-Home was not prepared to take. And neither, as it transpired, was a cautious Harold Wilson.[34] Consequently, the situation in Northern Ireland could not normally be discussed in the House of Commons. Nonetheless, in the context of this apparent impasse, in alliance with the Campaign for Social Justice, the Campaign for Democracy in Ulster was formed in London in 1965, seeking to draw some modicum of benefit from the plenitude of power reserved to the United Kingdom Parliament.

Plans for the Campaign for Democracy were originally hatched in a public house in Streatham in advance of the organisation's public launch at Westminster with the support of sixty Labour backbenchers eager to expose the realities of discrimination in Britain's Northern Irish Province. Paul Rose, MP for Blackley in Manchester, became the driving force behind the activities pursued by the Campaign, but Stanley Orme, Lord Fenner Brockway and Kevin McNamara became tireless spokesmen for the cause. When Gerry Fitt entered Westminster as the Republican Labour MP for West Belfast in 1966, he lent his eloquence and influence to the ambitions of the group. Soon the Campaign enjoyed the support of more than a hundred Labour MPs, but advances under the Westminster Convention proved tedious and abortive.

The group pressed for an impartial inquiry into the administration of government in Northern Ireland, they sought to bring electoral law in Ulster into line with the rest of the United Kingdom, and they agitated for the application of the Race Relations Bill to be extended to the Province. Furthermore, the Bill was to be amended to include religious discrimination and incitement so as to provide it with some purchase in the circumstances of the Six Counties. But at each stage, and with every scheme, the government fell dumb behind the established parliamentary convention. The efforts of the Campaign for Social Justice in Northern Ireland were stymied, recourse to the courts in the Province had failed, and now the Campaign for Democracy in Ulster was hamstrung by the Labour government's resistance to an active policy in Northern Ireland. But as criticism progressed without results, confrontation came closer too and, within a short span of time, lobbying would succumb to more rigorous agitation.

Inside that span, the fateful year of 1966 would intervene. Easter marked the fiftieth anniversary of the 1916 Rising, July the anniversary of the Battle of the Somme. Both occasions brought hostile political traditions on to the streets of Northern Ireland. The Republican tricolour adorned the terraced rows of west Belfast for weeks on end around April. Through the spring, and then into summer, the loyalist ultra Ian Paisley thundered against ecumenism and appeasement in response. In May the Ulster Volunteer Force was re-formed. They first mistakenly targeted an elderly Protestant widow in an arson attack on the 7th, and by the end of June a twenty-eight-year-old Catholic had been shot. Within a month, another Catholic had been injured when shots rang out in Malvern Street off the Shankill Road in Belfast. At the start of July, Gerry Fitt was bracing himself before the 'long hot summer' that almost everybody expected to follow. The marching season had arrived. Reports appeared of families forced at gunpoint from their homes. Rumour slowly circulated, relations promptly worsened and the interest of the media had finally been awakened.[35]

Years later, O'Neill himself surmised it had been 1966 that marked the point at which everything had started to 'go wrong'.[36] For all the advances which he considered himself to have made in recent years, the two communities of Northern Ireland remained tacitly divided and potentially even hostile.[37] The Ulster Unionist Party was stalling anxiously behind a leader who was himself trailing in arrears of the Catholic expectation of advancement. Paisley goaded Protestant resentments while the loyalist suspicion of developments festered. Meanwhile, Catholic confidence in the government declined. Certainly by the time the year had drawn to a close, complaint against the political iniquities of the Province had grown noticeably more resolute. As an immediate sign of that resolution, in January 1967 the Northern Ireland Civil Rights Association was founded. Soon options were being canvassed, strategies were selected and plans were under way. The watershed of 1968 was in construction and the shift from pressure-group activity to protest politics had begun.

The Northern Ireland Civil Rights Association was launched on 27 January at the International Hotel in Belfast with over a hundred delegates from a range of organisations in attendance. Amongst those present were members of the established political parties together with activists from a variety of affiliations: the Wolfe Tone Society, Republican Clubs, the Campaign for Social Justice. From the outset, the Association attracted a spectrum of opinion spanning the compass from radicals to moderates. Membership ranged from socialists, trade unionists and veteran republicans to civil libertarians, a Liberal and a Unionist. Although the first inklings of a civil rights organisation had emerged earlier at a conference staged by republican activists in Maghera, Co. Derry over an August weekend in 1966, by January 1967 these had fused with a variety of progressive factions drawn from all ranks of dissident and liberal opinion in Northern Ireland. This same sweep of critical opinion was to find itself represented on the Association's committee which proceeded to agree a date of 9 April for the presentation of the outlines of a draft constitution. This document was to stand as a blueprint for principles urging the defence of basic human freedoms.

It was the aim of the Civil Rights Association to succeed, under the banner of civil liberties, where conventional political organisation had failed. In time, that would involve a reappraisal of the customary methods of political opposition, the abandonment of conventional parliamentary avenues, and the seizure of opportunities for peaceful protest: it would involve petitioning, publicity drives and demonstrations, sit-downs, lobbying and symbolic marches. Political engagement amongst the nationalist population became prized as a index of civic duty. The intention of activists was to agitate in a manner that would be measured and responsible, yet unrepentant. In the process, it was hoped that the movement would acquire a moral force derived from its evident reasonableness and restraint: frustration would be managed by a programme of action which would challenge the authorities without recourse to violence. Confrontation, for the moment, would stop short of serious provocation yet maintain a momentum for political dissent.

That momentum was all the more necessary because, by the time that the Civil Rights movement was placing its credentials before the public, political opposition in Northern Ireland had acquired a pretty sorry history. Since the end of the Second World War, the rural Catholic vote in the Six Counties had been monopolised by the Nationalist Party which toiled at the margins of political relevance in the absence of professional organisation. Dominated by the clergy and the middle classes of the towns, its employment of transient registration committees was as close as it came to wielding the instruments of a modern party machine.[38] At the start of the 1960s, then, it was a low-key and somewhat slipshod affair, although its roots stretched back to the original Irish Parliamentary Party of the later nineteenth century. In Northern Ireland after 1921, reeling from the triumph of a more militant Sinn Féin, and cut off from the nationalist vote in the South, the party confronted a defeated and disconsolate electorate which it never roused or mustered. It was left with a single political platform – dogged opposition to the fact of partition – around which it sought ineffectually to mobilise: episodes of parliamentary participation were succeeded by bouts of determined abstention without either option delivering results.[39]

The Nationalist Party's only constitutional competitor for political favour among Catholics in the North centred on Belfast and a smattering of larger towns. That was the Northern Ireland Labour Party, which rallied around issues of urban deprivation and the standard slogans of workers' rights. It was this party's good fortune that from 1924 to 1949 it was in a position to take a neutral stand between nationalism and Unionism on disputes about the Irish border. But when the Irish Free State left the Commonwealth in 1948 and established an independent Republic for the South in the face of rising British anxieties over Cold War preparations, the Northern Ireland Labour Party was shunted by Clement Attlee's resolve to meet these developments with the Ireland Act of 1949 into declaring for partition: 'in no event', the Act of 1949 made clear, would the constitutional status of Northern Ireland be subject to alteration without its own Parliament's free agreement.[40] Inadvertently catapulted into support for the established border, the Northern Ireland Labour Party was overtaken by events. Protestant support for the cause of Labour rose, but the party's urban Catholic vote was splintered into a range of go-it-alone outfits such as Irish Labour and Republican Labour which offered some room for political manoeuvre to emerging aspirants like Gerry Fitt, but none of these micro-political groupings could ever wage a concerted assault.

The same applied to the Republican tradition of physical force in Ireland. By the early 1960s, the Irish Republican Army was languishing in the aftermath of the border campaign which it had launched in 1956. That campaign was effectively over before it had even begun: the blowing up of a series of targets along the Irish border in December 1956 was met by the introduction of internment, North and South, in 1957. Starved of ready personnel and distressed by the lack of public support, the organisation was on the brink of being militarily crippled. But still only on the brink: there followed a burst of IRA activity in 1958, a few fatalities in 1959, and then barely so much as a bravado escapade by the close of 1960.

In February 1962 the campaign came to an official halt, Cathal Goulding replaced Ruairí Ó Brádaigh as IRA Chief of Staff, and Republican morale sank into total depression. Over 400 activists had been imprisoned in the course of the campaign. Upon release, they emerged into a world at best indifferent to their exploits. Soon the erstwhile verities of age-old Republican dogmas were being laced with elements of neo-Marxist doctrine under the influence of a new leadership.[41] Bruised and resentful, stalwart members of the old guard departed to the margins of the movement, and the military option steadily fell to the bottom of the agenda. Interviewed in the early 1970s by the *Sunday Times*, Goulding was to reveal that in August 1967 'we called a meeting of local leadership throughout the country to assess the strength of the movement. We discovered that we had no movement.'[42]

Nonetheless, attempts at making headway among the ossified structures of Ulster politics continued outside the ambit of Republican activity. In the middle of the IRA campaign of 1956–62, National Unity was inaugurated as a pressure group within the Nationalist Party to push for more efficient organisation, and the modernisation of the party platform. The Republic's Prime Minister, Seán Lemass, had addressed the Oxford Union in 1959, and in the course of his delivery he managed to accord *de facto* recognition to the position of Northern Ireland within the United Kingdom. It was a quiet, tentative and understated move. But in response, National Unity urged the adoption of the principle of Irish unity by consent upon a reluctant party leadership. Criticism of the historic absence of any unified action on the part of nationalist political forces in Northern Ireland soon followed. Then, at a convention in 1964, a series of broadsides were delivered against the party's Stormont representatives in which a lack of professionalism and accountability was alleged.[43] Next came the birth of the National Democratic Party from the loins of National Unity, but it enjoyed precious little electoral success, and soon disappeared from the political scene.[44]

Meanwhile, Eddie McAteer became leader of the Nationalist Party at Stormont in 1964, accepting the title of Official Opposition in the Northern Irish House of Commons the following year. But the party never rose effectively to the challenge. Responding to Unionist proposals for the reform of local government in early 1968, after reams of adverse publicity had been dispatched by a myriad pressure groups, and after five long years of repeated demands for reform had been issued on the part of a plethora of organisations, McAteer rose to give his assessment: 'I want to say quite frankly that our party's view has not yet fully crystallised on this subject.'[45]

At the start of 1968, then, political opposition on the part of the constitutional parties in Northern Ireland could promise little and deliver nothing. Armed Republicanism was in the doldrums, reassessing its options and redefining its purpose. The Homeless Citizens League and then the Campaign for Social Justice had agitated furiously over a number of years, but their core objectives had not been advanced. The Campaign for Democracy in Ulster had set about tackling what it saw as irregularities in the political conduct of the Province from the benches of the Westminster House of Commons, but it encountered a seemingly insur-mountable blockade. Then the Northern Ireland Civil Rights Association was formed. Immersed in debate and preparatory discussions, it dithered for a period of eighteen months until the moment to act ultimately arrived in the summer of 1968.

The occasion for action was supplied by a case of discriminatory housing allocation in the village of Caledon which had attracted the attention and provoked intervention by the MP for the area, Austin Currie: fresh from his experience of occupying the council home awarded on the basis of what looked like favour to a single Protestant woman, Currie telephoned a meeting of the Civil Rights Association in July and proposed a march from Coalisland to Dungannon. A date was fixed for 24 August, and before long the first mass demonstration in Northern Ireland was under way.

3

Two and a half thousand people came together under the evening light of the 24th to begin the five-mile trek out of Coalisland. In good spirits, with a carnival atmosphere rife among a sea of civil rights rosettes, the protesters made their way along the stretch of country road until they reached the outskirts of Dungannon. Across the width of the highway, a cordon of police with dogs confronted the oncoming flow of marchers, and the procession came to a halt: the officer in charge approached the crowd assembled at the head of the march to announce that in the interest of peace and public order the demonstration was to be re-routed away from the Market Square in the centre of the town and towards the Catholic neighbourhood of Dungannon. 'I do believe that then for the first time it dawned on people that Northern Ireland was a series of Catholic and Protestant ghettos,' Bernadette Devlin was later to report.[46] The children were immediately led to safety, a makeshift platform was hastily constructed, and a sit-down protest was conducted on the spot. But on the far side of the police line, over a thousand loyalist agitators had congregated to register their objection. They chanted old-time choruses and hurled sectarian slogans, brandishing their clubs and staves. But behind the outward signs of aggression, the essence of the loyalist complaint had crystallised into anger at the sheer effrontery of what purported to be a non-sectarian protest being conducted in the name of equality for Catholics.

Betty Sinclair, the chair of the Civil Rights Association, mounted the podium and called the demonstration to order. Leading participants were invited to address the crowd. Austin Currie and then Gerry Fitt appealed to the massed rows beneath them in exasperated tones: 'My blood is boiling,' Fitt shouted, gesturing toward the 400 officers of the RUC stationed along the police barricade. 'We are the white Negroes of Northern Ireland,' declared another speaker to a raft of loud applause.[47] Sinclair appealed for calm, emphasising the peaceful nature of the protest. She then struck up the civil rights tune, 'We Shall Overcome', while pockets of individuals responded uncomprehendingly with the strains of the nationalist anthem, 'A Nation Once Again'. By nightfall, the organisers had departed for their homes. The remaining group of protesters banded in large circles about the road, singing until midnight, before the demonstration finally came to a close. The event passed off without serious incident.

On that first civil rights outing in the North, the two sides in an escalating conflict were discernible on either side of the police line. Two weeks later, on 5 October, the RUC joined battle on the Protestant side of that divide. In Derry the situation was more fraught than in Dungannon: there was alarm among sections of the police force that agitation in the Maiden City of the Province might give encouragement to subversive tendencies, which they considered to be on the increase within the Catholic community; there was a palpable fear among Protestants that their political ascendancy in the city was under threat; and there was a high degree of outrage among their Catholic adversaries about the subordinate position to which they thought the Unionist establishment had condemned them. The ingredients for confrontation were present in abundance. In addition, among the more radical advocates of change, there was a preparedness to invite a collision with the authorities as the most efficient way of securing the root and branch transformation of an intolerable situation.

The likelihood of such a collision intensified on Thursday, 3 October. The Northern Ireland Civil Rights Association had given notice on behalf of the Derry Housing Action Committee for a march which was to proceed on 5 October from the railway station in the Waterside to inside the walls of Derry City. But it was banned on the Thursday – two days before it was scheduled to depart – on the orders of the Minister for Home Affairs, and the expectation of trouble heightened accordingly. A day later, on the evening of the 4th, members of the Civil Rights Association met with leading figures from the Housing Action Committee to try and prevent them defying the ban.

It was Eamonn McCann and Eamonn Melaugh – one a radical activist in the local Labour Party, the other a freelance dissident with no specific affiliation – who had taken the lead in preparations for 5 October. They were both in the vanguard of complaint and agitation in Derry at the time. Each had enjoyed a prominent role in the Derry Housing Action Committee: they had obstructed the work of the Corporation by invading the public gallery of the council chamber; they had endlessly petitioned the local Housing Trust over the plight of the poorly housed in the area; and they had famously blockaded the Lecky road with a caravan which had become the sole residence of a Catholic family of four.

Having gained support and drawn attention to their cause, they were anxious not to squander their gathering momentum. In their own minds, they already had the Nationalist Party on the run and they believed that the intensity of deprivation in Londonderry had primed the populace for a more radical conversion. Under the circumstances, they thought that the ideals of civil rights could be made to yield to a socialist agenda which alone had a chance of bridging the sectarian divide. When on that Friday evening, the day before the march was set to start, McCann and Melaugh threatened to stage the event whatever the attitude of the civil rights representatives, they all agreed to the original plan within the space of just two hours.

There was no Civil Rights Association branch in Derry in October 1968 and, compared with the local activists, the Association's delegates had a less than perfect grasp of circumstances in the area. Never before had a Catholic march presumed to enter the central walled area of the town. The imposing stone edifice of the Londonderry Walls had acquired in the minds of the Ulster Protestant population the character of an unyielding citadel: behind them, for months on end in middle of 1689, 7,000 military supporters of William of Orange, together with 30,000 Protestant refugees, held out against an onslaught by the Catholic forces of James II. The achievement had entered unionist annals as a moment of seismic recovery: the defiant refusal to surrender had saved at once the beleaguered city and the Protestant settlement in Ireland, as well as the Williamite Crown in Britain and the Protestant cause in Europe.[48]

Every year on 12 August the Apprentice Boys of Derry, a local division of the Orange Order, commemorated that deliverance which had transformed the city into an icon of Protestant resistance under siege. But, three centuries later, an embattled Protestant resolve still reigned: Londonderry was now a frontier county whose western hinterland faced on to the border with the South and the unionist population maintained its position by exercising an exclusive monopoly over the local institutions of power. Among Catholics, however, Derry had grown to represent the very 'Capital of Injustice' in Northern Ireland, and the city was seething with resentment.[49]

Unemployment throughout Northern Ireland was high – over two and a half times higher among Catholics than Protestants – but in Derry it stood at over 20 per cent. There had been many complaints about housing discrimination in the western parts of the Province – in Dungannon, Lisnaskea, Portadown, Enniskillen, Caledon and Cookstown – but in Londonderry, where the need for homes had reached epidemic proportions, discrimination was bound to provoke a more aggravated response. Over a thousand properties in the city's environs were occupied by more than one family, yet only a handful of new corporation homes was built in 1968. Existing houses in the Bogside frequently lay in a dilapidated state and overcrowding had become a serious menace. However, the local Unionist authorities had refused to extend the city boundary for fear of upsetting the electoral balance and losing control of the Corporation.[50]

In addition to all this, the location of Northern Ireland's second University at Coleraine was seen as a deliberate move on the part of the government to bypass the opportunities for expansion offered by Magee University College in Derry. The Great Northern Railway line had been closed, the factories of the British Sound Reproducers had shut down, and despite the desperate situation regarding unemployment and general economic depression, the O'Neill government had created the new town of Craigavon in the middle of the Province at the expense – as local residents saw it – of development for Derry. Various self-help schemes had been organised – a Credit Union was established, a housing co-operative was founded – but the gains were insufficient to sustain community morale. Relief from unabated hardship was not even in the offing: repeated appeals to the public authorities were repeatedly rebuffed. By the autumn of 1968, as a journalist with the *Belfast Telegraph* was to comment, 'the city was ready to explode'.[51]

Politics in Londonderry was controlled by the local Unionist establishment. This was of course a familiar occurrence in many parts of Northern Ireland. A quarter of the parliamentary electorate in Ulster was deprived of the vote in local government elections due to the limited nature of the franchise: the vote was confined to rate-payers and their spouses, while some large property owners – company directors in particular – qualified for a number of votes. Given the relative poverty of Catholics and the commonness of the situation where a large number of Catholic adults were obliged to cohabit under a single roof, the electoral system at local government level adversely affected the nationalist vote in disproportionate measure.

But the manipulation of electoral boundaries had been used to altogether greater effect. Gerrymandering had been alleged against a slew of borough and county councils with evident justice in the cases of Omagh, Armagh and Co. Fermanagh. However in Derry, once more, the evidence for corruption was at its most compelling. Within the city boundaries, there was a large Catholic majority, about twice the size of the Protestant population. This state of affairs was managed, however, by dividing the City into wards – the North, South and Waterside wards – with the vast majority of Catholic voters penned into the Bogside and the Creggan Estate in the South ward of the city. While the South ward returned eight councillors to the Corporation, the other two wards returned twelve, and so by the careful fixing of voting arrangements Unionist control of the Council was assured.[52]

These, then, were the circumstances in which the Derry Housing Action Committee had been pursuing a campaign of disruption in the city, and this was the context in which the Civil

Rights Association had agreed to participate in a public demonstration. In September 1969, the Cameron Commission of Inquiry which Terence O'Neill was obliged to set up to report on the disturbances of October 1968 was to comment that 'in Northern Ireland the public procession has historically expressed the territorial domination of one or another group, but especially that of the Protestant majority'.[53] However on this occasion, it was a small embassy from Derry's Catholic majority which was taking to the streets in defence of the principle of equality for all citizens.

Of course, the ambassadorial pretensions of the demonstrators were swiftly discounted in many quarters. Indeed, there were those on the march who openly disputed the political credentials of its vanguard participants. But while doubt surrounding the representative status of the marchers on 5 October supplied their opponents with grounds for criticism, this was not the overriding difficulty which the protest was about to encounter. The fundamental weakness of the Catholic position did not result from the attitude of the established authorities to the popularity of protest as such, but from the reaction of significant sections within Unionism to the agenda of civil rights itself. The difficulty in which they found themselves, then, was a product of the delicacy of their case, given the conjunction of circumstances at the time: from the point of view of their adversaries, the passionate impulse to strike for equality automatically registered as an attempt to outmanoeuvre and cajole, and so implicitly to seek for a comparative advantage.

In the ordinary course of affairs, any fresh bid for equality is an encroachment upon the existing arrangement of things. But in the apprehensive atmosphere of Northern Ireland, encroachment risked the very closest proximity to an attempt at usurpation. Within the settled political environment of the modern world, equality is the common currency of social and political life. In this setting, the principle of equality is really used to monitor an established equality of equals, and can hardly be regarded as a laborious commitment: it poses no great challenge to reciprocal generosity. But as a practical pursuit rather than an accomplished fact, it involves striking a supremely anxious balance between assertion and concession on either side. Northern Ireland was to prove the point: as the weeks and months and years which followed made clear, the achievement of an agreed sense of equality all round proved nothing if not gruesome in the attempt – and elusive, barely tangible, in the attainment.

But for the moment, at about three o'clock on 5 October, there were various knots of individuals milling around the front yard of the Waterside station in Derry: politicians at the microphone conducting interviews, associations unfurling an assortment of banners, students hoisting ready-made placards, and stewards calling for organisation. Suddenly, some 400 participants set off up Duke Street in pursuit of equal rights for the citizens of Northern Ireland. Among the column of marchers, there were members of the Young Socialist Alliance and the Derry Housing Action Committee, activists from the Liberal and Northern Ireland Labour parties, and individuals from the Connolly Association and the Wolfe Tone Society; there were marshals present from the Republican movement, representatives from the Civil Rights Association, and then the familiar faces: Eddie McAteer and Austin Currie, both Nationalist MPs at Stormont, appeared; John Hume took up position under the blue colours of the Civil Rights flag; and Gerry Fitt arrived from the Labour Party conference in Blackpool with a trio of Westminster MPs in tow.

When the demonstrators advanced upon the line of police tenders stationed 300 yards from the starting-point of the march, the front rank of RUC men stepped forward to stem the tide of their approach. Gerry Fitt was immediately clubbed across the forehead with a baton, and then dragged away from the scene. A participant pleading with the police for restraint was smacked with a truncheon in the solar plexus. Eddie McAteer was injured in the groin. Having shown that they meant business, the police regrouped across the barricade to arrest any further incursion. But now tempers began to flare among the crowd. There were intermittent blasts of singing and shouting, and placards were hurled at the police in fury. For thirty minutes, evident confusion was shared by the protesters. A voluble hum of voices rose clear into the air while Betty Sinclair struggled to yell instructions at the demonstrators from a small chair positioned in their midst. Speakers addressed the crowd in rapid succession, urging restraint and uttering defiance by turns.

At this point, the more moderate stewards called upon those present to disperse and peacefully to make their way back to their homes. Stray bars of 'We Shall Overcome' were faintly heard, and then the muffled voice of a Belfast inspector from the RUC broke in upon the proceedings with barely comprehensible directives issued through a loudhailer. In the end, a sudden surge from the crowd was met by a methodical onslaught by the police. But by now a further barricade had been erected at the marchers' backs, down at the other end of Duke Street, barring every avenue of escape. Trapped in the middle of two simultaneous charges, men and women were assailed by a flurry of clubs, running the gauntlet of blows in the hope of relief. Mayhem ensued: batons were wielded with indiscriminate vigour as arms flailed in the scramble of ducking and diving.

Protesters gradually seeped out to the far side of the RUC tenders, but then water cannons sent them fleeing in every direction. The assault had been disorganised and vicious, more a rout than an effort at containment, and television cameras caught the moment. Within hours, footage was relayed around the globe. Later in the Bogside, the mood darkened as news of police brutality travelled with electrifying speed through the Catholic ghettos of the city. Days were to pass before the first wave of utter dismay subsided. In the words of Eamonn McCann, a 'howl of elemental rage was unleashed across Northern Ireland'.[54] For young and old alike, among moderates and radicals, there was a definite sense that things were never going to be the same again.

The leadership of the Derry Housing Action Committee was frank in its summary verdict: they had indeed set out to make the authorities over-react, but they had not expected such inordinate hostility from the police.[55] On a single afternoon, the seeds of a movement had germinated from a protest – or rather from the reaction to it. The authorities, as it seemed, had vented their abhorrence upon a Catholic demonstration. Moderates were now propelled into a position of leadership within the gathering storm of protest in Derry City, but moderation did not distract them from their singleness of focus: the earliest possible achievement of their reasonable demands.

In response to the events of 5 October, a meeting was arranged to take place in the City Hotel on the following Wednesday with a view to assessing the implications of what had already transpired and to plan for the immediate future. At that point, the Derry Citizens' Action Committee was born, eclipsing the Housing Action Committee, and constituting a more restrained and cautious body. Ivan Cooper was elected into the chair while John Hume became vice-chairman. In an attempt to ventilate the searing anger now rampant among the Catholic residents of the city, a sit-down protest was planned for 19 October when 5,000 men, women and children packed into Guildhall Square to show unity of purpose in opposing the Unionist establishment. Speeches were delivered in the drizzling rain, and a British television *World in Action* team arrived to document the occasion: 'If the people's demands are not met, leadership will pass to individuals less committed to non-violent action than ourselves,' Hume predicted to a reporter: 'that's not a threat, but an assessment of the facts.'[56]

Another march was called for 16 November with the intention of covering the original route of the 5 October parade. By now all marches had been banned from within the City Walls, but again the organisers flouted Craig's decree, this time with a mass of 15,000 people appearing in support. The occasion was anticipated with heightened suspense, and there was ample room for hazard: bloodshed, in fact, was generally expected. The night beforehand, prayers were muttered and vigils staged in the Protestant and Catholic Cathedrals in the city. But in the end, when the event got under way, order and discipline were maintained, and a conflagration was averted: a stand-off with the police was deftly managed, marchers filed past the RUC barriers in a trickle at Carlisle Square, and finally reassembled at the Diamond. The Walls had at last been symbolically breached. 'By the time the demonstrators dispersed peacefully,' as the deputy editor of the *Belfast Telegraph* put it, 'they had destroyed the Protestant ascendancy in the city.' It only remained, he concluded, for the government to recognise the fact.[57]

But the disturbances in Derry had ignited a wave of protest in Northern Ireland generally. In Belfast, three days after the results of 5 October had begun to impact upon Catholic opinion across the Province, students were returning for the start of term at Queen's University. A meeting of the Students Union immediately called for a demonstration to be held on Wednesday the 9th. On that day, about 2,000 young men and women set off for Belfast City Hall to protest against the police brutality in Londonderry. Both Protestants and Catholics took part in the affair. For the most part, the gathering comprised an embarrassed yet indignant group of demonstrators, somewhat reluctantly brought to the point of protest.[58] The plan was to proceed into the city centre by way of Shaftesbury Square. But a counter-demonstration had been organised by Ian Paisley, and so the RUC decided to redirect the procession.

Having accepted the diversion, the students ultimately arrived at Linenhall Street, close by the City Hall, but police called the march up short again. There they waited for about three hours while the RUC set about clearing the group of Paisleyite supporters who had arrived in advance of the student parade by a route that led more directly to the centre. In the end, the students broke up their demonstration and trouble was avoided. But on returning to the university campus, the participants reassembled for a lengthy debate, going into session until one o'clock in the morning, and drawing up proposals for a further plan of action.

In the aftermath of those hours of intense and heated discussion, a group of earnest young protesters launched the People's

Democracy in Ulster. In its early days, the organisation was a broad coalition of interests composed for the most part of student activists, but embracing a segment of more advanced ideological operators, some of whom were a few years out of college: Michael Farrell, for instance – a lecturer and socialist republican at the time – and Eamonn McCann – expelled from Queen's back in 1965. In its infancy, the People's Democracy adopted a platform with broad appeal, advancing six objectives which ultimately became the official demands of the civil rights movement as a whole. They were simple, crisp and pretty inoffensive by the standard of liberal taste current at the time: one man, one vote; fair elections; freedom of speech; jobs on merit; fair housing; and the repeal of the Special Powers Act.

Armed with a programme designed to be media friendly, the People's Democracy scheduled another rally for the middle of October. On that occasion conflict – once more – was avoided, and the group advanced its reputation for moderation and restraint. Soon, ardent apostles of the six-point plan were descending upon Omagh, Newry and Dungannon to further the cause and muster support. Marching continued without respite well into November, with scores of enthusiasts for reform rallying to the Civil Rights agenda: the Province entered upon a period of ferment. But with each fresh sign of a Catholic advance, loyalist dissidents grew openly more desperate, and pressed for immediate action to oppose the new developments.

On Saturday, 30 November, a newly formed branch of the Civil Rights Association organised another protest march, this time to be held in Armagh City, the ancient ecclesiastical capital of Ireland. Paisley gave notice to the RUC that 'appropriate action' would be taken should the demonstration be allowed to proceed. Large notices appeared on walls around the town during the week before the march: 'For God and Ulster', the posters read, 'Don't let the Republicans . . . make Armagh another Londonderry'.[59] During the small hours of the night preceding the day's expected activity, a virtual cavalcade of thirty cars filled with Paisley supporters flooded into Armagh. When the convoy was inspected by the RUC, a couple of revolvers were seized together with a stash of crude but lethal weaponry. The next day, a mood of acrid bitterness surrounded the events. There were some acrimonious and turbulent clashes, but full-scale sectarian violence was kept in abeyance: there were no deaths in 1968. But through repeated bouts of confrontation, ever greater numbers of discontented civilians were being recruited into the rival factions agitating for opposing causes in Northern Ireland. The more irreconcilable elements within Unionism were attracting converts to their standard and so, at every level of society, mutual suspicion and recrimination were reaching fever pitch.

Polarisation had extended toward the most precipitous of limits. Indeed, the point had arrived at which sections of the Unionist Party itself were at polar extremes. With the situation rapidly deteriorating in the Province, O'Neill was invited to meet with Harold Wilson at Downing Street on 4 November. He was accompanied on the trip by William Craig and Brian Faulkner. Faulkner, at the time, was Minister for Commerce in the Northern Ireland government, but he had long had his eye on the top job in the administration. So too had William Craig. Behind the scenes, they had both conspired to limit their Prime Minister's room for action, and so O'Neill took the precaution of bringing them along: whatever was agreed at the Wilson meeting would have to gain at least their outward approval. After their discussions, Wilson reaffirmed the United Kingdom's pledge on the constitutional status of Northern Ireland: four days earlier Jack Lynch, the Prime Minister of the Irish Republic, had rattled Unionist nerves by challenging the justice of partition, and so the situation called for a measure of reassurance.[60] But in the privacy of a closed conference with the sombre representatives from Ulster, Wilson hammered home the necessity for change.

On the following day, in the British House of Commons, Wilson called for an impartial inquiry into the events of 1968. Craig and Faulkner were strenuously opposed to any such inquiry, but for the moment their government bought time. However, the real results of the Downing Street talks unfolded over the weeks that followed. By 22 November, O'Neill had presented his package of reforms to his own parliamentary party: a new method for the allocation of council homes was to be introduced, using an impartial points system; an ombudsman was to be appointed to investigate allegations and complaints; a development commission was to be assigned to take over the functions of the Londonderry Corporation; the company vote in local government elections would be abolished, and consideration would be given to a more general review of the franchise; and finally, those sections of the Special Powers Act which were in conflict with the United Kingdom's existing international commitments on human rights would be subject to scrutiny when the threat of civil commotion had subsided.

Harold Wilson, however, remained unimpressed. He had written to O'Neill, on 19 November, to press for immediate action on the local government franchise: 'It seems to us that the local government franchise, which is symptomatic of many present anxieties, represents a way forward to reform, and we cannot regard the absence of firm proposals for action on this topic as satisfactory.'[61] But if the franchise represented a 'way forward to reform', it then needs to be asked what actual reform might have comprised. The truth is that the British government lacked a policy for reforming political arrangements in the Six Counties. The Cabinet was keen to improve the minority's position, but its members could not conceptualise what such improvement might entail. If the Westminster government made the decision to exercise direct control over the Province, what species of reform would it even then start to introduce to lead the problems of Northern Ireland towards a positive solution? Whitehall and the Cabinet simply didn't know.

When O'Neill responded to British pressure on 6 December, two weeks after the Stormont package had already been announced, he made his excuses by way of appeal to an understanding which

Britain shared: 'The franchise is primarily an issue appealing to political activists; but it is jobs and houses which most concern the mass of the people.'[62] This, of course, was exactly the presumption of the British Home Office as well. It was disseminated inside the Cabinet by means of the advocacy of James Callaghan. What was at issue in Northern Ireland, Callaghan insisted to his colleagues, was 'the growing contrast . . . between the relative prosperity of a section of the people and the continuing poverty of the majority'.[63] The incredible fact is that this analysis came in April 1969, more than four months after Wilson had intervened to lean on a reluctant Terence O'Neill.

In July of the same year, officials at the Home Office were still endorsing the old view, and further concluding that the situation was 'encouraging' to the extent that 'the issues are not seen as the legitimate political grievances of a minority against a repressive government'.[64] But of course this is quite precisely how the relevant 'issues' *were* in fact seen. Notwithstanding this reality, as late as September 1969, three weeks after British troops had intervened in the spiralling conflict, Callaghan still saw fit to explain to the members of the Cabinet that 'while civil rights and non-discrimination were of cardinal importance, the problem of Northern Ireland was also to a very large extent an economic one'.[65] Certainly, poverty in Northern Ireland posed a gravely serious problem. But the overriding difficulty was the absence of any procedure for absorbing minority opinion into the established political process.

Back in November 1968, the British Prime Minister was alarmed by what had begun to look like intransigence on the part of the government in Northern Ireland. He was committed to making an impact but still uncertain about how to move. It was becoming necessary for the Cabinet to 'contemplate legislative action', he had insisted in a memorandum to his colleagues at this time.[66] But what ameliorative policy would they be legislating for? Neither Wilson, nor Callaghan, nor Denis Healey had a plan for integrating the minority into the politics of Northern Ireland.

Roman Catholics in the Province stood outside the political process. They were not meaningful participants in the machinery of state. They were designated by Unionism as a sectional interest in the polity, yet their interest found no expression in the apparatus of government. They lived under the authority of the Northern Ireland constitution, but without the opportunity of wielding power through that constitution. In practical terms, this meant that they had no representation in the Province: the public interest was constituted through the preferences of the majority.

As a result of the political impasse created under the auspices of majority rule, the Wilson government resorted to an alternative expedient: in the name of reform, the Northern Ireland government would be made to grant concessions to the minority under pressure from Westminster. But a reform which has this character is indistinguishable from a favour. The Wilson government was indeed anxious to award these favours to the minority as nothing less than its democratic entitlement. But there was no plan to institute a democratic process so that the Catholics could negotiate their own objectives for themselves. At the same time, O'Neill was unable to go forward with party unity intact if he capitulated to implementing the civil rights demands at the insistence of 10 Downing Street. As O'Neill was to confide on 6 December, to press for changes to the franchise was tantamount to urging 'a course of action which is not possible in political terms'.[67]

In effect, this was a confession of political defeat on O'Neill's part. Yet the British Cabinet did not push the point for fear of losing the Northern Ireland government to more vigorously implacable forces. Wilson himself, however, was sorely tempted. Before the Stormont government announced its proposals for reform on 22 November, Wilson had been steeling himself for a major confrontation. Anticipating the failure of O'Neill's government to comply with the full implementation of the measures which had been suggested on 4 November, Wilson had informed his own colleagues at a Cabinet meeting in Downing Street that 'a grave constitutional crisis' might shortly be provoked, culminating in 'the fall of Captain O'Neill's Government'. Since any other administration imaginable in Northern Ireland would most likely prove less amenable than Terence O'Neill's had been, it seemed that 'the consequences must be faced of a suspension of the Northern Ireland constitution and direct rule from Westminster'.[68]

But Wilson pulled back from the brink. His government's preference was for the maintenance of law and order in the Province in the hope of improving community relations. More concerted intervention in the form of direct rule from Westminster would require a scheme for reconstructing Northern Irish politics. The prospect of such an awesome and elaborate undertaking struck fear into the mind of the London government. It seemed preferable to temporise, and to assess the reaction on the ground in Northern Ireland to the package of measures which the Unionist government had been made to support.

After all, in the space of just two months, the Catholic population of Northern Ireland had made more tangible political progress than it had even idly fancied over the course of the preceding fifty years. However, it was also true that the most potent instrument of civil rights agitation remained in the hands of the Unionists' critics. With the government's proposals on the table, and 'one man, one vote' yet to be conceded, everybody paused to take stock and make assessments. Developments through the year had raised a hurricane, and its effects upon popular sentiment would need some time to recede.[69]

So the mood of rancorous agitation had yet to settle down. With tensions at a nervous extreme, O'Neill appeared on television on 9 December to make a public appeal over the heads of his opponents in the Unionist Party: 'Ulster stands at the crossroads,' he began, '. . . our conduct over the coming days and weeks will decide our future'. In a pinched accent which he weighted with a flow of measured cadences, he continued: 'What kind of Ulster do you want? A happy and respected Province, in good standing with the rest of the United Kingdom? Or a place continually torn apart by riots and demonstrations, and regarded by the rest of Britain as a political outcast? As always in a democracy, the choice is yours.'[70]

The following day, William Craig openly challenged O'Neill's authority, and was sacked. But on the Wednesday, two days after the Prime Minister had made his plea, the Civil Rights Association called a halt to demonstrations, and the Orange Order duly made a statement in support of the government: two antagonised communities had stood back from the abyss. But as the month and the year were drawing to a close, and as the population reflected upon the fallout from events, elements within the Catholic community still pondered the fate of the local government franchise, and the People's Democracy declared its intention to stage a Long March from Belfast to Londonderry. Ulster drew breath, and waited anxiously for the new year.

III

Perfidy: 1969–1972

I

When Belfast was burning during the August days of 1969, Gerry Adams was sent by his Officer Commanding to monitor the situation on the ground. It was Friday the 15th, and the city had awoken to scenes of utter devastation. Barricades were piled high across street entrances, and flames still blazed from gutted buildings. In west Belfast, a mass of debris littered the area around Divis Street: telegraph poles and burnt-out cars were strewn about the place; fragments of glass and masonry carpeted the ground. Under the morning light – along Conway Street, Percy Street and Dover Street – Catholic homes stood charred and abandoned. A pall of smoke hung over the Falls Road.

That evening, Adams toured the Ardoyne area of north Belfast, collecting what information he could before moving south again to Clonard, which lay to the west of the city. The whole area, at this time, was in a state of wild confusion. Protestant crowds were on the rampage through the maze of frightened streets, and gunshots spluttered at irregular intervals. By this point, Adams was aware that British soldiers had taken up position further south, along the Lower Falls, and he headed for a safe house on the Kashmir Road. Dusk by this stage had turned to dark and, as Adams was being bundled through the front door into safety, the terraces on neighbouring Bombay Street were ablaze from end to end.

Once inside the building, Adams joined the company of exhausted Republican activists in the midst of an historic conflagration. There had been rioting and gunfire over the course of the past two nights. Seven civilians lay dead in Belfast, and over a thousand Catholic families had been forced to leave their homes. The pervasiveness of terror recalled the pogroms of the 1920s – except that, this time, it seemed as though a holocaust was at hand.[1] 'We definitely thought we were going to get help from the South,' a veteran Irish Republican was later to recall.[2] But intervention came from another quarter. On the Thursday the British Army had arrived in Derry, and by the afternoon on Friday troops were stationed in Belfast. In the eyes of Gerry Adams and his comrades, British perfidy had been unmasked.[3]

Having grasped how the Stormont government appeared as an 'Orange faction in power', the Cabinet in London had then resolved to send its military to shore up the position of precisely that regime whose credit at this stage lay in tatters.[4] Accordingly, segments of militant nationalist opinion in Northern Ireland came to the conclusion that British policy, which had long concealed its purpose behind a show of magnanimity, had finally been forced to declare its hand.

Stepping into the breach in mid-August 1969, the British armed forces risked the appearance of a final line of defence for a marauding Protestant ascendancy. That appearance was soon transformed into a determinate construction. The claims of advanced Republicans had seemingly been vindicated as circumstances conspired to reveal an apparent truth: 'In our view,' as Adams was later to put it, recalling the events of 15 August 1969, 'the British government had been using the RUC and the unionists to uphold and disguise the nature of their rule in this part of our country.' But when Unionism faltered, the veil was lifted: 'Although the unionists were still in charge, it was now the British soldiers who were holding the line for the British government.'[5]

That perception soon won out as an abiding political nostrum. It was to become, in effect, the central tenet of Republican doctrine that would sustain an insurrection for close on thirty years. In the aftermath of the mayhem in Belfast and Londonderry in the late summer of 1969, as real fear pervaded each mounting

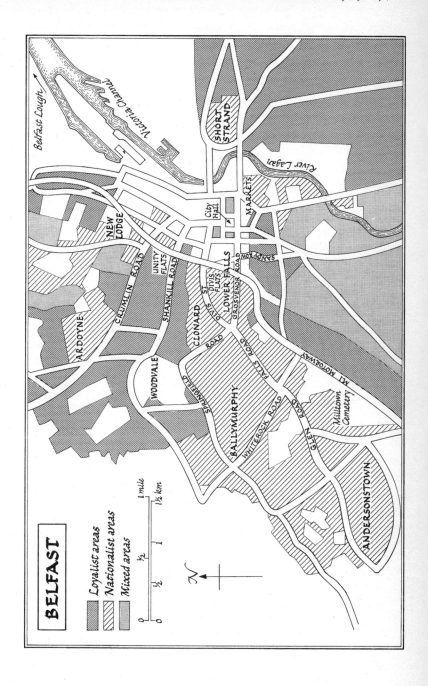

BELFAST

Loyalist areas
Nationalist areas
Mixed areas

1 mile
1½ km

½   1

½

0   0

N

Belfast Lough

Victoria Channel

SHORT STRAND

River Lagan

MARKETS

City Hall

SANDY ROW

NEW LODGE

CRUMLIN ROAD

UNITY FLATS

SHANKILL ROAD

ARDOYNE

ST DIVIS FLATS

CLONARD

LOWER FALLS

GROSVENOR ROAD

OATS ROAD

WOODVALE

SPRINGFIELD ROAD

BALLYMURPHY

WHITEROCK ROAD

FALLS ROAD

GLEN ROAD

M1 MOTORWAY

Milltown Cemetery

ANDERSONSTOWN

confrontation in the North, attitudes among elements within the Catholic population had begun to crystallise into the certainty of political conviction. A powerfully compelling assumption had taken root, and it would ultimately disseminate throughout the Catholic ghettos dotted haphazardly across the Province: despite every assurance to the contrary – despite the outward manifestations of decency and justice – it was argued that 'British imperialism' was discernible in the current operations being directed from Westminster.[6]

The military presence on the streets of Northern Ireland was a distressingly conspicuous symptom of collapse, and physical-force Republicans were ready with a diagnosis. The explanation for the current disorder in Northern Ireland, it was claimed, was to be found in the dynamics of British statecraft: the aim of British policy was the control of Ireland's destiny, a project furthered by the method of divide and rule. On this understanding, partition was the legacy of an abiding imperial strategy, and sectarianism in Ulster was a modern consequence of that endeavour.[7] As rival accounts of recent developments vied for a more general acceptance within the nationalist community late in 1969, this particular conception already had a history stretching back into the early twentieth century. Now, as tensions in the Province rose, it refused to disappear. By the middle of the 1980s, it was confidently being publicised as the fundamental article of the Sinn Féin credo. Britain capitalised, it was maintained, upon Irish divisions, and on the back of this divisiveness it maintained its 'dreadful scheme'.[8]

As Adams was to insist, this benefit to Britain should cause no great surprise, since it was an object of British policy to manufacture these divisions. Ireland had been subjected to this treatment not once, he argued, but twice: first with the creation of a northern 'statelet', carved out of the island democracy in 1920, and then with the establishment of a Unionist monopoly whose sectarian foundations 'divided us once more'.[9] But while Adams' appraisal of the situation could draw support from a long line of nationalist analyses stretching back – at the very least – to 1912, its purchase derived from the more pressing context of British intervention in 1969. As Adams commented, with that specific set of circumstances acutely before his mind: 'while there were initially mixed feelings about the British army, once it became apparent what their role was, then all ambiguity went out of the window'.[10] What seemed to have become 'apparent' was the fundamental purpose taken to be guiding Britain's forces on the ground.

That purpose, Adams contended, could be traced back through several stages of remove to the animating principles of the British Empire. These principles gave direction to the ambition of British power to secure hegemony among rival nations. But Irish freedom, Adams believed, placed an obstacle along the path towards that objective, with the result that Ireland's liberty had to be curtailed. Its curtailment, however, was a complicated business, effected through a matrix of political surrogacy and dependence. Circumstance dictated that Britain's ultimate design would have to radiate into the Province from 'the colonial power in London'.[11] Thus British interests, Adams insisted, were efficiently disseminated through a hierarchy of operatives, positioned along an elaborate chain of command. Behind the Protestant population stood the Protestant police, while Provincial security was duly managed by the Stormont government. Yet, at a further distance, behind the Stormont government, there appeared the British Army consolidating Unionism's monopoly on power. And then finally, behind the Army, lurked the establishment at Westminster, managing the enterprise with seamless craft.

Adams' argument arose from a combustible combination: elements selected from traditional Republican doctrine were grafted on to an impression of developments as they unfolded through the summer of 1969. But while the position which Adams came to espouse throughout the 1980s would have represented, at the start of the 'troubles', a rather specialised interpretation of the situation he had originally encountered, after August 1969 it was elevated into a guiding assumption which would orientate the propaganda wing of the Provisional IRA.[12] It was to become, in short, militant Republicanism's organising precept, whatever the movement's avowed contempt for political ideas.[13]

While ideas might usually, in the ordinary course of things, furnish a synopsis of reality, they also often operate as a crude distorting medium through which the intentions of others and the events of the time are summarily obliged to pass. After August 1969, a febrile mix of militancy and dismay facilitated precisely such a distortion, while ideology was on hand to give direction to blind panic and lend authority to the adoption of a militant posture. It was a powerful alliance since, in the late 1960s in Northern Ireland, ideas could spread like rumours in the atmosphere of alarm and anticipation.

Gerry Adams, once again, caught the mood of expectation which had taken hold of radicals since the turning-point of 1968: as the fallout from the events of 5 October rearranged opinion within the Catholic population, the view that 'everything was about to change' could appear a sober reckoning.[14] Moral indignation and intellectual exhilaration alike fired an attitude of political enthusiasm. Nationalist insurgents, like Connolly and Nkrumah, stole upon the imaginations of self-styled revolutionaries as exemplars of legitimate resistance. The struggles of yesterday, it seemed, could give succour to the struggle of today, and also credit the ideas required to orientate the task. The 'battle for ideas', Adams recalled, 'was being fought out on TV screens', but a propaganda victory would secure a handsome dividend because 'people were moved by ideas then'.[15]

But after 15 August 1969 events began to move at once in contrary directions. The IRA itself soon bifurcated, dividing ever more deliberately into antagonistic factions as the months progressed.[16] Towards the end of August, while the Belfast IRA adjutant – Jim Sullivan – was establishing the Central Citizens' Defence Committee for the protection of Catholic enclaves in the city, dissidents who at that time were under his nominal control were preparing to challenge the prevailing thrust of Republican strategy.

Sullivan was loyal to the Dublin leadership under Cathal Goulding, and in command of the Belfast area since the arrest of Billy McMillen on 15 August. But already on 24 August, a group of militants connected with the movement – Joe Cahill, Seamus Twomey, Jimmy Steele, Leo Martin, Jimmy Drumm, Billy McKee, David O'Connell, Seán MacStiofáin, Billy Kelly and John Kelly – were gathering in north Belfast to concert their opposition to Sullivan's defensive posture of citizen protection. The militant opponents of Jim Sullivan had either recently left the movement, or had been struggling on the inside against the policies being pushed by Goulding. And by 22 September, after the release of McMillen, they were ready to force the issue by confronting the Belfast leadership.[17] In the event, an open split was avoided: a temporary compromise was concocted. But the die had been cast, and a total rupture in the movement would occur within three months.

In addition to the ructions within the ranks of the IRA, the Catholic population itself was in general ferment. All shades of opinion within the nationalist communities – both North and South – shuddered in disgust at the ferocity of the aggression unleashed by a desperate loyalism without censure from its own regime. But in Northern Ireland itself, while some Catholics were still banking on incursions from the South, or – at least – on intervention headed by the United Nations, others were now looking to the influence of the British government to mollify the aggravations in the Province. Yet others still, facing the open onslaught from Ulster loyalism, put their hope in a push for discipline, enforced in their own favour by the preponderant strength of British arms. The IRA itself, however, inspired little trust: its capacity to mount defence at the point of greatest need had been altogether wanting.[18] It was now riven by internal discord, and its coveted supporters pondered virtually every option except dependence on the initiative of a Republican militia.

So nationalist solidarity, united in dismay, was divided in its preferences for the future. But already, long before the final pinch in August 1969, the Civil Rights movement had itself divided as the aftermath of October 1968 unsettled established patterns of political affiliation. The radical supporters of the Civil Rights Association had refused to countenance the pleas for moderation, sent out in late December by both the Northern Ireland Prime Minister and the Association's executive in an effort to quell the growth of sectarian hatred. Anticipating that the momentum built up through agitation would be stymied by the truce which brought 1968 to a close, and doubting the earnest remonstrations from O'Neill, broadcast to the Province on 9 December, the People's Democracy resolved to continue with its protest, and forced a division in the ranks of Northern Catholics at the outset of 1969.[19]

The Civil Rights movement had divided, in other words, at the 'Ulster crossroads' which trailed off in the opposing directions that O'Neill had been at pains to signpost in his bid to bring relief to a bewildered populace: 'What kind of Ulster do you want?' he frankly pleaded – a Province constantly sundered by dissensions, or a place which earns respect in the wider world: 'As always in a democracy, the choice is yours.'[20] On 20 December, the People's Democracy came forward with their choice, announcing a march from Belfast to Londonderry that was to set out on 1 January from the City Hall. But the resolve of the PD put cautious Catholic opinion under strain: coming in the immediate aftermath of the turmoil to which Northern Ireland had been subjected during the closing months of 1968, and with a halt to demonstrations now generally agreed, tensions within both the Northern Ireland Civil Rights Association and the Derry Citizens' Action Committee (DCAC) began to rise to the surface.[21]

The marathon procession westward across the Province was modelled on the Selma Montgomery march staged by Martin Luther King in 1965. But here the aim in conducting a seventy-five-mile trek across Northern Ireland – crossing through stretches of Protestant Ulster along the route – was to protest against what vocal activists within the People's Democracy saw as the derisory and 'half-hearted reforms' on offer from the O'Neill government, and to demand the introduction of 'one man, one vote' as a matter of urgency.[22] The demonstration was to extend from Wednesday into Saturday, but already as the marchers assembled at 9 a.m. on New Year's Day they were confronted by a group of Paisleyite supporters, headed by Major Ronald Bunting, threatening to 'harry and harass' participants from start to finish.[23] The protesters had received a bitter foretaste of things to come.

Bunting and his supporters surfaced at intervals along the march, drumming up disturbances and offering abuse. But on each occasion that Bunting appeared on the horizon, the marchers were re-routed – at Antrim, Randalstown, and Maghera – until they reached the open road which leads from Claudy into Derry: there, as they approached Burntollet Bridge, about two hundred loyalist opponents of the protest lay in ambush in the fields adjacent to the highway. The night before, missiles had been assembled into piles and now, as the marchers gained upon Scribetree Lane which abuts on the Derry road at an oblique angle, a shower of quarried masonry cascaded down upon the People's Democracy supporters. A hail of bricks and bottles immediately followed, pelting a group of demonstrators lagging to the rear of the procession.

But as the marchers struggled forward to escape the first bombardment, they were met by a second round of assaults: on the corner of Scribetree Lane itself, Bunting stood in wait with a band of attackers wielding crowbars, cudgels and lead piping. The protesters were shown no mercy as they advanced. In the distance, stationed along Burntollet Bridge, contingents from the RUC remained tucked away in their tenders with a blind eye turned to the violence around them: the victims were not offered any protection, the assailants were spared the severities of the law. Indeed, in the fields on either side of the main roadway, policemen were happily consorting with Bunting's gang. And as for the gang itself – about half of them had seen service in the Ulster Special Constabulary.[24]

Originally, the plan to stage a Long March across Northern Ireland to Derry had been opposed by majority vote in an assembly of the People's Democracy. But that decision was later reversed at a Christmas meeting – attended by a fraction of the participants responsible for the initial opposition – and the march was allowed to proceed. With this turn of events, the differences in approach inside the PD became explicit. The radicals – Bernadette Devlin, Cyril Toman, Eamonn McCann and Michael Farrell – were coasting ahead of the movement's mainstream members. Eamonn McCann gave his own view of the respective differences in position: while he and his associates were in the business of transforming a deluded Northern Ireland 'consciousness', his more circumspect opponents seemed haplessly confined inside a blinkered mental outlook with limited expectations.[25]

But the architect of the December volte-face was Michael Farrell, another man of ideas in Northern Ireland at the time.[26] A lecturer at the Belfast College of Technology, he had long struggled to compose any apparent clash of opinion into a common view – essentially, his own. Arriving on that Saturday at Derry's Guildhall Square, having suffered by ordeal along the road from Burntollet Bridge, his hour at last had come. He had been wounded in the shower of stones targeting the marchers as they entered upon the last leg of their journey, and now – bloodied and bedraggled – he appeared upon a platform erected in the square at the behest of the DCAC: although the committee had been critical of the apparent provocation which parading through Protestant districts might seem to offer, they had by this stage agreed to greet the marchers in a manner that befitted their commitment and resilience.

Eighty individuals had begun the march, but hundreds were appearing at the finish, and by their evident travail they had managed to attract the spontaneous support of angry thousands. The stresses that had weighed down upon the DCAC were now relieved as the Catholics of Derry resolved their differences: in the face of hostile treatment by the security establishment, subtle variations in position disappeared. On that Saturday afternoon, after the speeches and commotion in the Guildhall had stirred the crowd, anger deteriorated into rioting in the city. Emotions were fraught, and the outbreak of disturbances was not contained until late evening.

But that night, after the battle between protesters and police had long subsided, a band of RUC reservists erupted into the Bogside around 2 a.m., breaking residents' windows, inflicting assault and battery on individuals in their homes, and hurling sectarian abuse at startled onlookers. On Sunday morning, the residents responded. Barricades went up around the entrances to the Bogside, vigilante patrols were organised to repulse the security forces and, painted on a gable end in St. Columb's Street, the words appeared: YOU ARE NOW ENTERING FREE DERRY.

The events of 4 and 5 January had shattered the confidence of Derry Catholics, and apprehension spread across Northern Ireland. Seán Keenan, a Republican ally of MacStiofáin's in the Bogside, became prominent in the co-ordination of vigilantism in the city. Everybody's blood was up in response to the RUC, and the outlook for future compromise looked grim. From now on, the DCAC would have to struggle to direct the sense of outrage, implacable among its wavering supporters. And beyond Derry, an undercurrent of vengeance began insidiously to attach itself to the cry of 'civil rights' among Catholic demonstrators. As early as 11 January a Civil Rights rally in Newry descended into clashes between moderates and radicals contending for the control of sentiment on the Catholic side. The outcome portended ominously for the future – even the semblance of restraint was now abandoned: violence and anarchy prevailed for several hours as protesters turned their anger against the police.

During the months that followed, a hardening of attitudes seemed almost certain: through the spring, and then into early summer, relations further deteriorated between the denominations. There was trouble, once again, in Londonderry on 19 April when, after a battle between Catholics and Protestants around the Diamond, it was the Catholics who were batoned by police back into the Bogside. Over the course of the night of rioting which flared up in response, large sections of the RUC rampaged through the Catholic district, convincing a team of British reporters that the police had themselves degenerated into 'a sectarian mob'.[27] In William Street a family was assaulted in its home: Samuel Devenny, the father, was hospitalised, and later died.[28] The next day, as the RUC milled around the access points to the Bogside, thousands were evacuated to the Creggan by John Hume, and the residents returned only on the condition that the police would stay out of the area for the foreseeable future. An incursion by the RUC had for the moment been forestalled, but everyone was now impressed with the need for preparation, anxiously anticipating the next time: 'No one doubted that there would be a next time.'[29]

That same weekend there were disturbances elsewhere in the Province, too. Earlier, on 30 March, there had been an explosion at the electricity supply station at Castlereagh in east Belfast; on 4 and 25 April there had been attacks on water installations in Co. Antrim and Co. Down; and now, on 20 April, an electricity pylon at Kilmore in Co. Armagh was blown up; finally, on the next night, there was an explosion at the Silent Valley reservoir in the Mourne mountains. IRA PLAN BEHIND THE BLASTS SAYS RUC, ran the headline in the *Belfast Telegraph* on the following morning. It was later discovered that the bombs had been the work of Protestant extremists affiliated with the Ulster Volunteer Force.[30]

The garrison of British troops in the Province was then strengthened as a precaution, with soldiers posted to defend the public utilities from attack. Here was evidence of a British desire to consolidate its 'tyranny', the Dublin leadership of the IRA was later to declare.[31] But the fact is that by then the British government was considering a withdrawal, partly rejecting that course of action on account of the vulnerability of the minority – or at least in view of how the abandonment of Roman Catholics could be made to appear.[32] Naturally, at this time, pronouncements from the IRA inspired minimal conviction within the minority community. Nonetheless, Republicans had exploded eleven petrol bombs in

Belfast on 20 April, there were scuffles with the police in the Ardoyne in mid-May, and anxiety continued to rise. Before long, the Protestant marching season would arrive with the high summer, and frustrations would be vented on the streets.

2

Caution and moderate calculation were thus gradually over-whelmed by communal strife as Ulster politics was propelled towards the precipice. Whatever residual credibility the Royal Ulster Constabulary had enjoyed was now annihilated in Catholic areas, while trust in the Special Constabulary had never been established. Moreover, the Stormont government could not be dissociated from the actions of the police on account of the wide discretionary powers at the disposal of the Minister for Home Affairs. The results here were disastrous: in the opinion of Harold Wolseley, the Commissioner for Police in Belfast in 1969, responsibility for law and order had been conferred upon a 'State force'.[33] Consequently, as the security situation worsened, the partiality of the government was steadily confirmed and the sense of civil obligation within the minority community correspond-ingly eroded even further.

The Catholic section of the Northern Ireland populace became a virtual people unto itself: a community living under the state without being fully a part of the state – a disaffected element set against the communal good. Since the majority alone was taken to constitute the public interest at large, the minority was converted into an aspirant democracy embedded within the polity as a whole.[34]

This predicament points to the basic problem in Northern Ireland which erupted into violence in 1969. Where a majority and a minority compose distinct communities of interest, democracy degenerates into factions. Strictly speaking, democracy quite simply disappears as a common venture and is bisected into opposing democratic interests. Since 1920, it was this situation which had prevailed in Northern Ireland and which obtruded into its politics with varying degrees of aggravation until, with the emergence of the Civil Rights movement in the late 1960s, reform held out the promise of a regime of equality.

But as the agenda for reform incrementally expanded, the prospect of its achievement receded. Under the fraught conditions of communal antagonism which accompanied this process, the absence of an integrated democracy in the Province exploded into conflict by the middle of 1969. The majority regarded themselves as custodians of the whole democracy, while in fact they only comprised the larger portion of that whole. But as the minority failed to secure an inclusive democratic equality, they imagined their detachment from the existing constitution, and aspired to the creation of a sovereignty of their own.[35]

Between January and August 1969, the conditions fostering that aspiration came ever closer. In increasing numbers, Protestants doubted the wisdom of conciliation, and Catholics began to wonder about the utility of peaceful protest. 'The monster of sectarian violence is well out of its cage,' declared the *Sunday Times* in April.[36] The gulf between the communities had seriously widened, and what had started as protest had rapidly descended into bigotry and aggression. Confronted at once by the slackness in the pace of progress and the lack of generosity evinced by the Stormont government, the Civil Rights Association began to flounder. At the same time, the government of the Province was struggling to keep pace with the rate at which society was imploding. Indeed, it struggled – in a basic sense – simply to govern: each progressive lunge towards pervasive conflict saw the Unionist authorities straining to align themselves with the shifting priorities of their own grassroots supporters, but at the price of further alienating the minority population.

'Enough is enough,' declared O'Neill in response to the disturbances of early January. However, the focus of his criticism was the continuance of protest, not the lawless depredations of the Specials and the police. He soon snapped: 'We have heard sufficient for now about civil rights.'[37] But if anything had been clarified at Burntollet Bridge on 4 January, or in the Bogside in the early hours of the 5th, it was the vulnerability of Civil Rights in Northern Ireland as a system of entitlement enjoyed evenly across the community. Under pressure from events, the historical reality of Ulster politics began to surface: the government of the Province displayed a primary obligation to a particular constituency within the society it governed – namely, the constituency comprising the Ulster Protestant majority.

But attitudes within the majority community were changing, and the authority of O'Neill was badly shaken by the change. Back on 15 January 1969, the Prime Minister had announced the establishment of a commission of inquiry under Lord Cameron to look into the causes behind the upsurge of disorder since October. Nine days later, his Minister of Commerce, Brian Faulkner, resigned from the government: reliance on a statutory commission to make decisions represented an 'abdication of government responsibility', he contended – it was an 'initiative to avoid initiatives', and a betrayal of the parliamentary party and the country.[38] The next weekend, the Minister of Health and Social Services followed Faulkner, and then finally, on 30 January, a junior whip abandoned ship. By the time that anti-O'Neill Unionist MPs were meeting in Portadown in early February to call for the election of a new leader, it was clear that the Ulster premier was losing grip on his own party, so he scheduled a general election for 24 February, hoping at last to bolster his position.

However, Whitehall and Westminster were growing ever more concerned. A draft bill 'to make temporary provision for suspending the Parliament of Northern Ireland' was prepared by Home Office officials around this time.[39] In the event of Her Majesty's government reclaiming the reins of power from Stormont, it was anticipated that the Civil Service in Northern Ireland would co-operate – 'to the extent at least of 70%' – and that the RUC would also lend its support to an emergency government.[40] It was expected that the legislative functions of the Northern Ireland

Parliament would be carried on by means of Orders in Council at Westminster, and that the British Governor in the Province would act as the principal instrument of administration in the emergency. However, there was no plan for reforming the constitution of Northern Ireland. A statement for the Governor had already been prepared: 'There is no intention to use the emergency powers themselves to implement particular policies in the transferred field favoured by the Government in London but not by the erstwhile Government in Belfast.'[41]

In any event, a British resort to emergency intervention was avoided, despite the fact that O'Neill's venture failed. Although technically the Captain emerged victorious from the polls, it was a narrow scrape, and the margins were insufficient to grant him the standing he required to patch up disagreements in his party. Ian Paisley had fallen short of ousting the Prime Minister in his own constituency of Bannside by a mere 1,114 votes. O'Neill's opponents – William Craig, Desmond Boal, John Taylor, Harry West and Brian Faulkner – were all returned to Stormont. It seemed as though the pressure on the Prime Minister would not abate. Then, on 23 April, O'Neill urged the adoption of 'one man, one vote' on the Unionist parliamentary party. But on the morning that the vote was carried, Major James Chichester-Clark resigned from the Cabinet. There were rumours of further defections likely to follow, so O'Neill finally opted to quit.

In Belfast, bonfires were lit on the Shankill Road to celebrate his departure. O'Neill himself was beginning to countenance direct rule from Westminster.[42] But for its part, the British government, while disappointed by these developments, remained uncertain about the best course for the future. The expulsion of Northern Ireland from the United Kingdom was considered, but ultimately rejected: 'A threat to expel Northern Ireland could be made only to serve the purpose of protecting the minority,' commented a top secret report prepared by the British Home Office in the wake of O'Neill's departure.[43] However, it seemed obvious that 'expulsion would in any event worsen their condition'. Regarding that option,

Whitehall officials were consequently to conclude: 'In the worst case, we would be accused of precipitating another Congo.'[44]

Independence for Northern Ireland was also considered by the Home Secretary himself, and then rejected on similar grounds, which his own departmental officials had already adumbrated: 'even if we could unilaterally change the national status of Northern Ireland, we would be abandoning the minority we are desiring to protect'.[45] Therefore, the possibility of intervention loomed ever larger, but this would probably be accompanied by the full-scale involvement of Westminster – 'Partial intervention ... might well lead to total intervention.' It was not a course which Callaghan believed should be adopted 'out of choice'.[46] At the same time, the possibility of convening a 'Round Table Conference', representing the different political opinions in Northern Ireland as a whole, was considered without a conclusion being reached.[47] The preference of the Home Secretary, whose department exercised the greatest influence within the British government on the design of Northern Ireland policy, consequently came down to this: 'I believe that the cardinal point of our policy must be to make Northern Ireland solve its own problems.'[48]

This sentiment was entirely noble, but practically redundant, and under the circumstances politically irresponsible. It was being suggested that 'participation by Roman Catholics in the institution of Government' should be encouraged at 'every level'.[49] However, it was participation of this kind which the constitution of Northern Ireland had effectively made impossible. But if the British government remained concerned about the welfare of the Province whilst being nervous about a commitment to any definite course of action, the government in Dublin was altogether less engaged, and at the same time less circumspect in its attitude and pronouncements. Dublin feared the drift towards a breakdown in the Province, but did nothing to avert the general trend in that direction.[50]

As mutually incompatible postures were being struck by an assortment of ministers inside the Irish government, and while policies were being endlessly devised but never actually adopted by the government at Westminster, the conflict in Northern Ireland just rumbled on without a decision. Moreover, O'Neill's successor to the premiership brought further drift: it was Chichester-Clark himself who was elected into the leadership on 1 May, defeating Brian Faulkner by a single vote. The Major was a party man and a committee man, punctilious about procedure; blundering if straightforward, he lacked purpose and real drive. By common consent, he preferred farming to the cut-and-thrust of politics: hardly the best person for a crisis in the state. And yet it was a crisis which appeared to be in the offing. Then, on 12 July, it seemed it had arrived.

Up until that date, there was a period of respite. Restlessness continued, but there was no tragedy on the streets, and the security establishment had in any case been strengthened. Anticipating the worst, the Minister for Home Affairs, Robert Porter, had been authorised to mobilise the B Specials for police duties the previous January. A new Public Order Act had been in place since March to meet any unexpected challenges. Now, under Chichester-Clark, police officers below the age of sixty who had retired from the RUC were invited to apply for service with a new supplementary reserve. But more positively, the Cameron Commission, established under O'Neill, had begun to take evidence in Derry. A programme for jobs and housing was announced by the Londonderry Development Commission responsible, since the demise of the Council, for the administration of the city.

A plan for the reform of local government was widely publicised, and an amnesty for all offences connected with the disturbances since October 1968 was granted. Ian Paisley and Ronald Bunting were reprieved. So too were the B Specials and the RUC. In light of the events in the Bogside and at Burntollet, this posed a problem.[51] In fact, the problem in Northern Ireland altogether remained the police. This included, by implication, the power to which the police were themselves responsible: the Stormont government.

During the course of the summer marching season, this problem came to the fore. Each year in Northern Ireland, a series of public festivals in July and August advertises the Protestantism of Ulster. The principal event throughout the run of celebrations – the annual commemoration of the Battle of the Boyne – falls on 12 July. But this year, with tensions heightened in the Province, trouble was expected between Catholics and Protestants; and, more critically, between Catholics and the police as well. Chichester-Clark, however, remained curiously complacent during the run-up to this flashpoint in the Northern Ireland calendar: just forty-eight hours before the event was set to proceed, both he and the Inspector-General of the RUC were assuring the General Officer Commanding in the Province – Sir Ian Freeland – that Orange marches had never been a source of communal strife.[52]

The Cabinet in London was similarly complacent – nothing new since the raft of May proposals was brought before the government in London at this time, and nothing old was implemented. And in any case, in the event of the July procession descending into violence, neither the Home Office nor the Ministry of Defence was alert to the likely consequences: 'Why don't they realise,' Freeland wondered to a member of his staff, 'we are on the brink of civil war?'[53] But, as it happened, a full catastrophe was avoided for the present: there was fierce rioting in Derry and in Lurgan throughout the day; in Dungiven, the B Specials fired a fusillade of shots, contravening orders from Ulster's Minister for Home Affairs; there were disturbances around Unity Flats near the Shankill Road in Belfast, and battles between Catholics and police in the Ardoyne; but a truly calamitous outbreak was avoided.

On 12 August it wasn't. On that day, the Derry Apprentice Boys were due to stage the second major Protestant celebration of the year in commemoration of their deliverance from the Catholic siege of the city prosecuted three hundred years before. Nearly every dispassionate observer expressed the view that the march should not proceed – Harold Wilson inclined toward a ban on the procession, as did his Chancellor, Roy Jenkins. But Chichester-Clark was eager that the event should go ahead, and James Callaghan, as Home Secretary, agreed to the parade.[54] On Sunday, 10 August – just a couple of days after Chichester-Clark had given his assessment of the prospects for a peaceful celebration to the Home Office in London – Eddie McAteer was giving his own apocalyptic forecast for the future: events on the following Tuesday, he wagered, might 'raise the curtain on the last terrible act of the age-old Irish drama'.[55] Until recently, McAteer had been the Nationalist MP for the Londonderry constituency of Foyle. As he was making this prediction before an audience of 2,000, bottles were being stockpiled for petrol bombs in the Bogside.

By one o'clock on 12 August, 15,000 marchers had swarmed in bowler hats towards the city to begin their ritual circuit around the Londonderry Walls: columns of determined men congregated in dark suits striped with the blazing colours of collarettes and Orange sashes. As the drum bands, flute bands and pipe bands assembled, members of the Apprentice Boys tossed penny coins into the Bogside as a 'gesture of contempt' towards the Catholics below.[56] An hour and a half later, the first missiles had been thrown – over the crush barriers and beyond the police lines – towards the marchers from the direction of the ghetto. Battle was soon joined by the RUC, still firmly in position between the Catholics and the procession. Violence then escalated throughout the afternoon.

The police barriers across William Street were overwhelmed by the insurgents in the early evening; in response, around 5 p.m., the RUC breached a barricade situated on Little James Street. Within an hour, a further barricade was erected by the residents of the Bogside, hiving off the area from attack along Rossville Street. An RUC armoured vehicle stormed the Catholic defences on Little James Street to gain access to the district in revolt: an invasion of the Bogside was now conducted by the police, with about a hundred Protestant civilians following at their rear. The incursion only lasted twenty minutes – but from then onwards, there was total unanimity in opposition to the police.[57]

The first barrage of petrol bombs was launched from the top of Rossville Flats to repulse the RUC: the battle-lines had now been drawn. For the best part of three days, and for two exhausting nights, the RUC were kept at bay while the Catholics held their ground. In the middle of it all – on the Wednesday – the Taoiseach intervened: 'the Stormont Government is no longer in control of the situation . . . the Irish Government can no longer stand by,' Jack Lynch contended.[58] The statement was a bluff, but still a threat – the Catholics were galvanised, the Protestants appalled: 'This clumsy and intolerable intrusion . . . will be . . . resented,' the Ulster premier retorted.[59] Meanwhile, Harold Wilson was on holiday in the Scilly Isles; the Leader of the Opposition was sailing in the Atlantic; and James Callaghan was just rousing himself from his summer retreat in Sussex. But still the battle raged.

By Thursday, the Bogside was blanketed in a smog of CS gas, the whole neighbourhood was deluged with bottle shards and paving stones, and a climax to the collision was at hand. The police were now at breaking point, but the insurgents would not relent – utterly convinced, by this stage, that surrender could only bring disaster. However, on the afternoon of the 14th, as the B Specials were massing on the outskirts of the Bogside – armed with their own rifles, revolvers and sub-machine-guns – British troops arrived at five o'clock, taking up position on William Street. Subsequently, a verdict on the whole affair was delivered by an *Evening Standard* reporter on the ground: 'The Bogsiders had won.'[60] But had they? The Catholics had been victorious in the battle, but the Province stood on the brink of civil war, and the politics of Ulster was still to play for.

Anarchy reigned in Belfast. On 13 August, Catholics had taken to the streets in Newry, Dungannon and Dungiven – by now resentment seethed across the Province – but in Belfast the mood was frantic: there were clashes between civilians and police in the Falls Road area, and rioting erupted in Ardoyne. First there was a stand-off, then the antagonists came to blows: around 10 p.m. shots were fired at a police vehicle on Leeson Street, and a hand grenade was thrown. But the RUC responded – with energy and zeal – until, by early morning, Sterling sub-machine-gun fire was streaming from the rooftop of the police station on Springfield Road. On the next day, the situation deteriorated further still. At 3 p.m. the B Specials were mobilised throughout the Province. That evening, in Armagh, they opened fire into a crowd: a Catholic, John Gallagher, was shot dead. In Belfast, by comparison, there was bedlam: street battles, arson attacks and shootings became general as the Thursday night wore on.

Barricades went up and petrol bombs were prepared. In the warren of streets connecting the Shankill Road to the Falls – at the interface between the Protestant and Catholic neighbourhoods – fighting became pervasive. Shots rang out – fired south towards Divis Street, close by the Lower Falls – and angry loyalists surged into the frontier streets bordering their own territory. By midnight, Catholic homes on Dover Street and Percy Street had been torched. But still the crowd pushed forward. Suddenly, a swathe of automatic fire was unleashed upon the Protestant advance: a handful of Republicans had commandeered a Catholic school. At this point, the assumption that the city had risen in rebellion began to dominate the actions of the RUC.[61] Shorland armoured vehicles roared through the Catholic districts, scattering bursts of heavy-calibre fire to devastating effect. Soon loyalists were mustering behind the Specials and police, petrol-bombing houses further west, in Conway Street. Belfast had now been overwhelmed by a wave of consternation. The Protestants were alarmed at the appearance of insurrection, the Catholics electrified by the fear of annihilation.

The night of 14 August saw a frenzy of suspicion rampage through Northern Ireland, polarising the communities distributed into ghettos and consummating in violence the very democratic divisions which political arrangements over the previous fifty years had buttressed and rigidified rather than surmounted. Months before this, on the evening of 29 April, during the course of his resignation speech broadcast to the Province, Terence

O'Neill had pointed to the fundamental principle which Northern Irish politics had betrayed: 'Democratic government,' he observed, 'must rest upon the consent not just of those who elect the governing party, but of the people as a whole.'[62] The statement contained a truth which O'Neill now happily commended, although it was not a point on which he had delivered: true democracy comprised 'the people as a whole', he had proposed. But significantly, in the wake of the Irish premier's intervention over the Bogside on 13 August, Chichester-Clark thought himself at liberty to controvert the proposition: during an emergency session of the Stormont Parliament held on 14 August, the Prime Minister defended Northern Ireland's current 'status' as an arrangement which was supported by 'a majority of our electorate'.[63] So the Province, on this analysis – enjoying majority 'status' – ought really to be understood as constituting a majority state: it was a partial, an incomplete, a majoritarian polity – falling some way short, in other words, of constitutional democracy.

On the same day, an editorial in *The Times* reflected on developments in the Province over recent months. It took the line that politics had moved beyond the stage of civilian protest and 'was engulfed in something much more primitive and volcanic, tribal fears and hatreds'.[64] The take here was shambolic, although somehow it still managed to set the terms of discussion for years to come. There was nothing 'tribal' about the fear of being overwhelmed by a new democracy – precisely the situation which the majority now expected; and there was nothing 'primitive' about the desire to be full participants in the state – the aspiration which the minority now embraced.[65] The situation, in a certain sense, was indeed volcanic: it was explosive. But the trouble had not risen from obscure historic depths. It was the product of a set of recent circumstances where the burgeoning of modern democratic expectations had collided with the absence of democracy in Northern Ireland.[66]

The *Sunday Times*, four months in advance of the diagnosis offered by *The Times*, came closer to the mark: 'The issue now is no longer civil rights or even houses and jobs,' the paper observed. Instead, as early as April, the question was 'whether the state should exist and who should have the power, and how it should be defended'.[67] The question, in other words, hinged upon Stormont: upon the tenure of the government, its obligations to the governed, and the manner in which the peace should be secured. The main players at Westminster, in principle, knew this – but without really wanting to grasp the implications.[68] The British Prime Minister was later to spell these out, pointing to the basic anomaly in Northern Ireland: the ruling party had gone 'unchallenged' for fifty years. He was also able to offer an explanation: it was 'unchallengeable'.[69] For half a century in the Province, without a moment's interruption, the executive was bolstered by a majority in Parliament since Parliament was perpetually controlled by the major party – the Ulster Unionists. And because the Unionists were guaranteed a permanent majority, Unionism gave priority to the majority constituency.

Consequently, it was not just the government, but the *system* of government, that catered to the Protestant component of the community. The obligation to modify this aberration now fell to the United Kingdom government. The government of Northern Ireland was no longer in a position to guarantee security to the Province. For that reason, it had effectively been forced to abdicate responsibility, falling back upon the resources of the British military.[70] But since Ulster had been edging towards a state of war between Stormont and the Catholic population, Britain's obligation was not just to dam the breaches, but to address the situation which had brought about the crisis.

'It was unthinkable in these circumstances,' James Callaghan was later to insist, 'that either the British Government or Parliament would have supported a proposal to hand over British troops to prop up a régime which had lost so much authority, unless reforms were made.'[71] However, it was not at all clear to the British what kind of reforms were required. They had not at this stage formulated a comprehensive policy to address the balance of forces in Northern Ireland: 'our mind was made up by events,' Richard Crossman would later disclose.[72] The reason for this is obvious: serious political involvement was the last thing Westminster wanted. This reticence carried with it a reckless degree of risk. Callaghan, once again, had reckoned with this risk: 'if the British Army were to appear to be an arm of the Ulster Unionist Government, the Catholics in their turn were likely to regard the troops with the same distaste as they regarded their Government'.[73] Nonetheless, the Home Secretary – indeed the Cabinet – took the gamble.

3

The size of Britain's gamble was almost immediately apparent. In Belfast, as parts of the city plunged into murderous hostility after the upsurge of violence in Derry, the first inkling of suspicion about British intervention was spawning on the margins of the Catholic community. Suspicion centred on the military operation conducted by the Army on 15 August. On that day, at around 4.30 p.m., in the Clonard area of the city, Bombay Street was black with smoke. Five hours later, a contingent from B Company of the First Battalion, the Royal Regiment of Wales, arrived at the junction of Cupar Street and Kashmir Road, to discover that the houses on either side of Bombay Street were consumed in a blaze of fire: 'they did not intervene when loyalists burned down the whole of Catholic Bombay Street', Gerry Adams was later to pronounce.[74]

But the Army was too late to intervene. And earlier, around eight o'clock, when the 2nd Lieutenant of B Company had embarked upon a surveillance of the area, he was still engaged in ascertaining the points of interface dividing the communities: the sectarian geography of Belfast was not yet clear to the British Army.[75] In any case, the military presence was too small to take control. The total effective strength available for deployment lay somewhere in the region of four companies of soldiers – amounting, in effect, to a mere 300 men.

The fact is that, up until the last, Healey, Callaghan and Wilson were determined to stay out of Belfast. As a result, the concentration of British forces was woefully inadequate. 'I don't care a fish's tit what Freeland wants,' a senior admiral with the Navy was heard to growl upon hearing of the requests for reinforcements coming from the General Officer Commanding in Northern Ireland.[76] Denis Healey himself was similarly dismayed by the influx of statistics from the Ministry of Defence: estimates for troops required to meet the worst predictions were soaring into the region of 30,000 men. However, the policy of the government was to minimise engagement as the best way of avoiding long-term intervention: hopefully hostilities would diminish in a short time. But if they didn't, imposing order on the situation might prove impossible: in addition to the tiny number of troops available, military intelligence was extremely poor.[77] If partiality, or even confusion, was exhibited by the Army, expectations of British perfidy were bound to prosper. And slowly, but surely, they did. 'The Troops and the RUC and the Specials are all one force,' came the message from the radicals behind the barricades: 'They must be resisted.'[78]

But this, in August 1969, was a sparsely credited position, promoted by youthful radicals and also disaffected militants on the fringes of the Irish Republican Army. Among the youthful radicals, Michael Farrell set the tone: 'the root cause' of Ireland's present discontents, he proclaimed at a PD meeting on 7 October, 'went back to British imperialism' which had 'created' the Irish border.[79] Teenage Republican activists, eager to prove their credentials, found encouragement from Belfast stalwarts who had been prominent in the movement, but who by this point were disillusioned with IRA GHQ.[80] The potential for competitive belligerence spurring Republican militants was therefore blossoming into existence on the outskirts of pacific life. But this was the very period in which Belfast was pervaded by sectarian alarm. If anxiety intensified, fears over security might increase demands for defence. More disturbingly, it was equally possible that the organisation of defence might cover clandestine preparations for war.[81] However, war requires an enemy, and the allegiance of supporters. Yet for the moment, inside the mainstream of Catholic opinion, allegations of collusion between the Army and Ulster Unionism appeared utterly implausible. So a fragile truce was temporarily secured and, for a period in September, even the barricades came down.

So whatever the outrage among the minority over the actions of the domestic security forces in Londonderry and Belfast through the summer, the response to the British presence was one of evident relief. Even members of the People's Democracy were happy to concede that they 'were pleased to see the troops. They behaved well.'[82] Republican assumptions about British cunning and betrayal were not yet popular, nor even meaningful; and an immediate plan to mount an offensive against the Army's intervention was simply out of the question. For that matter, the wherewithal to organise the most basic means of defence was wholly lacking: 'We were without guns or direction,' explained a young Republican volunteer, recalling the desperate straits in which the IRA had found itself during the rioting of 14 August: a couple of Thompsons, a Sten gun, one Lee-Enfield rifle and half a dozen handguns accounted for most of the weaponry available to Republicans in the city at the time.[83]

Cathal Goulding, in Dublin, had withheld a supply of armaments from activists in Belfast urgently seeking guns; Seán Keenan, in the Bogside, had refused a consignment of rifles offered by a Republican splinter group on 13 August.[84] 'Today, the stock of the IRA has never been lower,' declared one organ of radical socialist opinion in the early autumn: the nominal 'defenders' of the Catholic community 'sat on their fat arses' when defensive action had been most desperately required.[85] The rhetoric of the IRA had certainly resounded with strains of anti-imperialist effusion, but the main strategists in the movement were opposed to committing their resources to a military campaign.[86] 'The North is imperialism's strongest bastion in Ireland,' declared the *United*

Irishman back in 1968.[87] But the assertion had carried with it a particular significance under the circumstances in which it was composed. Later, in January 1969, the same Republican paper came to elaborate the point: the 'root cause' of communal unrest in Northern Ireland was – yet again – 'imperialism', but imperialism was revealed to comprise a range of social evils, spanning 'capitalism and the rule of big business and international monopoly'.[88]

This equation of imperialism with the world of monopoly capitalism had become a pivotal principle for the Official IRA: it was being peddled in the main organ of Official Sinn Féin propaganda, the *United Irishman*, just after the final schism that split the IRA in December 1969. As it related to Northern Ireland, the equation was significant. It identified British policy with a substratum of interests – 'big business and international monopoly' – which an alliance between agitation and conventional parliamentarism could eventually aspire to overthrow: when the organs of Ulster governance had been sufficiently overhauled, they would lend institutional assistance to the long term Republican project of revolutionary social change. For this reason, it was assumed that a combination of politics and protest could productively impact upon the situation in Northern Ireland.[89] It was no longer military activity that would prepare the ground for politics, as IRA tacticians had classically supposed. Instead, political activity would create favourable conditions in which a military strategy could be successfully pursued. But this casting of priorities was anathema to the traditional Republican policy of abstention: it depended on participation in the parliamentary process as an intermediate stage along the road to revolution.[90] Any involvement in parliamentarism – even as an interim, strategic option – would commit the IRA to the Northern Ireland constitution, albeit with the object of securing its reform.

In the eyes of dissident members of the Army Council, and doctrinaire supporters of established Sinn Féin policy, any move that ascribed validity to a Northern Ireland government conceded the legitimacy of the British Act of Parliament that legalised the political partition of the island back in 1920. As MacStiofáin put it, there was a choice to be made – 'between accepting the institutions of partition or upholding the basic Republican principle of Ireland's right to national unity'.[91] But the political point of principle bore on a military point of strategy. Acquiescence in the existence of a Northern Ireland government entailed deferring confrontation between the advocates of Republicanism and the sovereign political agency which secured the British Union. It was that agency – the Westminster Parliament – which held final sway over the balance of forces in play in Northern Ireland; and it was the arm of Westminster – the British government – which authorised the personnel who would embody that sway: the British Army. So elements within the IRA began openly to push the point that Stormont was a screen between the British Army and the Irish people. Remove the screen, they implored, and the underlying conflict could be brought to a conclusion by mobilising resistance against the resources of British power.[92]

Ironically, it was Chichester-Clark himself who lent credibility to this construction. In response to the upheavals which rocked the Province in mid-August, he released a statement from Stormont Castle that made his own perspective clear: 'in the last resort,' he let it be known, 'our enemies face not only the determination of Ulster but the might of Britain.'[93] The general import of the statement was immediately apparent. The resilience of the Ulster Parliament drew its strength from the Protestant people, but it was the resolution of Britain that allowed the majority to prevail. The dissidents within the IRA accepted this analysis. Yet they also felt encouraged to take the argument one stage further. The very choice of the majority, they surmised, depended for its survival on the support of British arms. A corollary seemed to follow from their reasoning: if Britain's fidelity to the Union was progressively worn down, the 'might' at her disposal would no longer be decisive. Moreover, once Westminster's determination had finally been buckled, the position of the Protestants would be immediately transformed. Unionism would be forced to come to terms. As MacStiofáin saw it – and Cahill, O'Connell and Ó Brádaigh now agreed – the majority in Ulster would re-examine its position and join forces with the majority on the island as a whole. The goal of the Republic would, at that point, be to hand.[94]

The advocates of the traditional Sinn Féin policy of abstention calculated that engaging the British enemy directly promised to deliver the Republican objective without insult to the integrity of the movement's established principles. It also promised to deliver this with consummate efficiency. Armed struggle, it was assumed, could achieve by the most immediate route what political activity could only hope to attain on the back of an incalculable interlude of reform. On the strength of this assumption, the Provisional IRA was formed in the middle of December. Straight away, Seán MacStiofáin was elevated to Chief of Staff. David O'Connell, Ruairí Ó Brádaigh, Leo Martin and Joe Cahill were elected on to the ruling Army Council. At the beginning of 1970, by the time the Sinn Féin annual conference had convened in the centre of Dublin, the split in the IRA had been formally recognised.

The Provisionals immediately endorsed an absolute policy reversal: 'we made the abolition of Stormont one of our primary objectives,' as MacStiofáin recapitulated the new drive. Volunteers were expected to be 'ready for the summer'.[95] The abolition of Stormont would disclose a basic reality – Westminster's responsibility for the Ulster situation – and hasten the arrival of the final showdown: the Provisionals' encounter with 'the forces of British imperialism'.[96] It was anticipated that conflict between Catholics and Protestants would accelerate the progress towards that encounter. An outbreak of disturbances was expected to resume with the advent of the summer marching. Army restraint would be at a premium in the ensuing climate of recrimination, but sensitivity on the part of the military could hardly be guaranteed. 'I'm not having my men stoned like that,' protested a British officer during the Ballymurphy riots which spiralled into serious violence on Easter Tuesday in 1970.[97] Still, the government at Westminster had already assumed that the worst was over.[98] Its energies were now absorbed by the British general election, scheduled for mid-June. But the Provisionals were digging in for a long haul: 'Should British troops ill-treat or kill civilians, counter-operations would be undertaken when the Republican units had the capability.'[99]

Capability on all sides was fast expanding. Nervy loyalist defence committees had been importing armaments from Scotland. The Officials were trawling the countryside for hidden, or even discarded, dumps: competition with a rival guerrilla faction gave impetus to the hunt. By this stage, Sullivan and McMillen had reputations to salvage and, besides, defence was still a burning concern in beleaguered Catholic communities. But the Provisionals went at it with a consuming focus, gearing up for the contest that they hoped would decide the crisis. Defence would be followed first by acts of retaliation, but then – in the long term – an offensive would be staged against the British occupation. Funds poured in, arms poured in and, as time went on, recruits poured in, joining up with the Provisionals in the housing estates around Belfast. By the summer of 1970, both wings of the IRA were engaged in bitter feuding. The Officials were still dominant across most of the Province, and throughout the South; in Belfast, they also held on to the Turf Lodge area, the Lower Falls and the Markets. But preference was given to the opposition in Ballymurphy, Andersonstown, Ardoyne and the Upper Falls. Belfast had already proved the capital of militancy, and from that point of concentration the Provisionals would swell and dominate Republicanism for the coming generation.

Circumstances in Belfast gave a certain pace to this expansion. It was there that sectarian rivalry was at its most intense. Catholics in the city were in an especially precarious minority, while loyalists, for all their strength, were an *aggravated* majority. The size of their advantage did not relieve the strain of conflict: instead, the disparity in numbers only exaggerated the acrimony evident throughout the Province as a whole. Outrage among Protestants was more likely to occasion open confrontation with their Catholic antagonists precisely because victory was assured to the greater number if both sides were to meet in a straight fight. So the Protestant advantage was a recipe for panic among Catholics in the absence of effective means to offset the imbalance. The British Army was their most immediate resource should the IRA prove feeble. With Republicanism in abeyance, if the Army enforced a peace between the antagonised communities in the context of a programme of political reform, the belligerent disposition welling among the minority might gradually be composed.

The practical viability of successfully pursuing this particular course of action in the face of hostile resistance from the Protestant majority is now a matter for speculation.[100] But the fact remains that, when Britain intervened in Northern Ireland in 1969, her armed forces were charged with lending their support to the maintenance of a majoritarian constitution: the Army had arrived 'to aid the civil power' without an accompanying political plan to redress the majority status which characterised the political organisation of the Province.[101] Belfast was the nerve centre of the struggle that ensued: within the minority community, popular alarm gave currency to the adoption of desperate measures. Without a scheme for the overhaul of the balance of forces in Northern Ireland, the aspiration to realise a competing majority arrangement was perfectly amenable to encouragement. Against the majority in Ulster the Catholic minority could counterpose the hinterland majority in the South: the sum of each would constitute a victory for the Republic. Back in 1968, a leading Sinn Féin activist had dwelt upon the Republican provenance of this calculus while addressing a group of supporters at the annual Wolfe Tone commemoration: the doctrine of Tone, Sean Garland advised his audience, was contained in the idea of 'the Greatest Happiness of the Greatest Number'.[102]

With a bitter political stalemate now entrenched by the British Army in the midst of deepening sectarian animosity, it only remained for the suspicion to be confirmed that the United Kingdom government had appeared upon the scene as a broker for the discredited regime. The coarse brutality of the Army in policing civilian districts soon lent an air of credibility to Britain's partisan appearance, and the Provisionals grew expert in fomenting disaffection and sowing the fertile seeds of Catholic suspicion. Republican militancy was reborn amid a hunger for security in an atmosphere which continually bred mistrust. 'The British could not be trusted,' MacStiofáin insisted; the 'mentality' of her Army was 'imperial'.[103] As the perfidy of the British was steadily revealed, imperialism was bound to stand apparent.

In reality, imperialism was difficult to pin down. Two years after the rupture in the Republican movement, *An Phoblacht*, a southern organ of Provisional Sinn Féin, still felt it relevant to advance the observation that 'Ireland north and south is controlled by monopoly capitalism'.[104] Imperialism, it seemed, remained what it had been before, in advance of the divisions within the IRA: it was still somehow related to the subtle machinations of what the Officials were also presenting as the work of 'monopoly capitalism'. The political landscape of Northern Ireland had been utterly transformed by April 1972, but one isolated element of IRA propaganda had survived the realignments cemented in the aftermath of 1969. Everything in Ulster had been either shaken or uprooted, except the association among Republicans of British statecraft with imperialism, and the identification of imperialism with capitalist control.

The government of the United Kingdom had now changed: the Conservatives, under Edward Heath, had come to power in 1970, with Reginald Maudling taking responsibility for Northern Ireland. The Prime Minister of the Province had also changed – Chichester-Clark was replaced by Faulkner at the start of 1971. The Inspector-General of the RUC was long gone: Sir Arthur Young had taken charge to restore confidence in the police at the point when sectarian hatreds were at their most intense – but then Young himself was relieved within a year. Sir Ian Freeland, as GOC, had by now likewise departed, replaced by Harry Tuzo after the Conservatives had come to power. And Northern Irish politics had altogether changed. The Alliance Party had been established in April 1970 with the aim of distinguishing the cause of the Union from the bullishness of hardliners. The following August, the Social and Democratic Labour Party was also founded under the auspices of Paddy Devlin, Gerry Fitt and John Hume. Then, by the end of September 1971, the Democratic Unionist Party had formed under Ian Paisley and, in the same month, a new Protestant militia – the Ulster Defence Association – was established under the leadership of Harding Smith. But across the whole landscape of reorientation and upheaval, the suspicion of imperialism had remained a solid fixture.

However, now, there was a difference: the suspicion was profound. The daily Catholic experience of politics was transacted through encounters with the British Army – it was now the public face of the Stormont government and Westminster – but the Army gave every appearance of being an instrument of oppression.[105] The blunt force of the military had been turned against the Protestants during rioting around the Shankill in October 1969. But gradually, after 1970, the sheer invasiveness of the Army worked increasingly to incense the Catholic population. Meanwhile, the Provisionals had garnered additional support since their success in defending Catholics around the Short Strand in east Belfast in June 1970. In July of the same year, Sir Ian Freeland ordered a curfew to be imposed on the Lower Falls with a view to seizing armaments held by the Officials. Four civilians died during the course of a reckless operation. Suddenly, the militants seemed justified in their recourse to armed struggle: the defence of 'law and order' had again brought dividends to the Provisionals.

And then there was internment: thousands of soldiers had been dispatched across Northern Ireland to begin the swoop on 9 August 1971. Hundreds of Catholics were piled on to the *Maidstone*, moored at Belfast docks, or corralled into Magilligan and Long Kesh prison camps. The fallout was, by any reckoning, appalling: the arrests were ineffectual from the point of view of security while the measure wildly exacerbated existing Catholic estrangement. Protestants were effectively exempted from the sweep: no attempt was made to imprison members of Protestant paramilitary organisations. The use of torture against the internees was bitterly resented – and publicised extensively – within the Catholic community. The violence of the IRA and the loyalists duly escalated: by Tuesday, 10 August, the day following internment, there were already eleven fatalities on the streets of Belfast.

Naked sectarian retribution also took its toll: well over 2,000 families were forced out of their homes. Throughout the month as a whole, there were thirty-five deaths and over a hundred explosions. And it was now, directly after internment, that the Provisionals really went for it, hoping to collapse the Province: there were gun battles almost nightly for weeks on end, and the frequency of bomb attacks accelerated catastrophically – 131 explosions occurred in August, 196 in September, and in October there were a further 117. Loyalists placed a bomb at McGurk's Bar on 4 December, leaving fifteen dead; Republicans exploded a furniture shop on the Shankill Road in the same month, killing two young children together with two adults. Next, on 30 January 1972, came Bloody Sunday: thirteen Catholic civilians were shot dead by members of the First Battalion, the Parachute Regiment, after a Civil Rights march held in Derry to demonstrate against internment. At this point 'alienation' was 'pretty total', in the words of the SDLP MP, John Hume.[106] The consequences of imperialism, it could credibly be claimed, were clear to see.

Social and political dysfunction were not difficult to discover in Northern Ireland. The challenge was that of deciding on the culprit, and then sorting out the damage. But the Provisionals were precocious in meeting both these challenges: Britain, they were sure, was responsible for the distress in Northern Ireland – and so withdrawal would bring about relief. The pressures of political collapse across the Province, together with the military presence on the streets, united Catholic sentiment against brutality and despotism. But it was the Provisionals who were quickest to apportion blame for this adversity: responsibility for the situation lay with imperialism.

It only remained to identify what made imperialism tick – what had ignited this secret impulse to tyranny and domination in the age of democratic politics? The answer was to be found in monopoly capitalism, the seemly underbelly of British policy – the hidden motive, impelling the institutions of the state headlong into conquest.[107] The world of monopoly capitalism was cast as a world of organised greed: its endless appetite for expansion could be made convincingly to dovetail with the hankering for empire. This underlying motive obviously required an identifiable strategy to succeed, but here again Provo publicity would not be found short of compelling proposals.

The means of assuring conquest was identified by the IRA with the method of 'divide and rule': the British possessed 'an empire', *An Phoblacht* came to observe at the close of 1972, 'whose underlying policy would always appear to be one of "divide and conquer"'.[108] Divisiveness had been introduced by the hands of conspiring men to disrupt the natural unit of democratic decision in Ireland: division was therefore to be understood as an instrument of imperial control. Such doctrinaire pronouncements could readily find endorsement in the programmatic writings of Republican icons like Patrick Pearse: 'The nation is of God; the empire is of man,' Pearse once observed.[109] But still there was a problem. Republicans had long championed the 'rightful' unit of democracy on the island of Ireland.[110] But the 'unit' of democratic decision up for grabs displayed no tangible sign of actual unity. Not only had the island already been partitioned, but sectarianism in the North was brutal evidence of further rupture.

Ruairí Ó Brádaigh was not shy of stepping forward with a solution: 'Stormont must go and the British get out *before* Irishmen can be brought together.'[111] If only Britain would stand aside, he was suggesting, the inevitable democratic unit of decision would come together and be as one. This particular piece of optimism already had a long history at the time when Ó Brádaigh spoke. It constitutes the true foundation of the Irish Republican analysis of the character of Ulster Unionism, stretching back into the 1890s: its very antiquity bestows an outward semblance of truth upon the reality of obstinate and impoverished understanding.

IV

Perfidy: 1891–1923

I

During the fifth plenary session of the Anglo-Irish Treaty negotiations conducted in the autumn of 1921, with the participants edging towards what was generally hoped would be a final solution to the Irish Question, Arthur Griffith approached the British Prime Minister, David Lloyd George, with suggestions for a settlement of the Ulster problem. It was mid-afternoon on Monday, 17 October, and Griffith was armed with the Provisional Irish government's clause for resolving outstanding differences concerning the six counties of the north-east of Ireland.

Under the Government of Ireland Act, which had already passed into law in December 1920, a federated Home Rule Parliament had been established with devolved authority over the counties of Antrim, Fermanagh, Tyrone, Armagh, Down and Londonderry. Now the Provisional Irish Cabinet, headed by Éamon de Valera, were poised to argue that the six-county area should consider surrendering its position under the 1920 arrangement and submit itself instead to the authority of a Dublin parliament. In the event of Ulster refusing this offer, the Northern Parliament would be permitted to retain possession of its subordinate jurisdiction, but the overriding powers then vested in the British Imperial Parliament, together with the federal representation of the Six Counties at Westminster, would be transferred to a Southern parliament, and so the 'essential unity' of Ireland would be maintained.[1]

It was of course expected on all sides that the North would prove recalcitrant in the face of such an offer. Substantial proportions of Protestant opinion in Ireland had by this stage been agitating energetically against a Home Rule settlement for over a quarter of a century, and Ulster had formed the mainstay of the opposition at each stage. Unionist sentiment throughout the island was alarmed at the advance of Irish nationalism, so for the Protestants of Ulster the partition of the country was intrinsic to political survival: it was a promise of security against submersion in the South. Therefore, whatever fresh schemes bearing on the plight of Ulster might emanate from either the British or the Irish delegations, the North was set to stand militant against further compromise. But for the moment, Griffith did not lay the Southern Irish offer on the table. Rather than declare his hand at the outset, he urged that the British government should 'stand aside' from the proceedings, and thus oblige the elected leader of the Unionists in the North to deal directly with representatives from the South.[2]

The British side demurred, recrimination followed, and so a final confrontation on the subject was postponed. But Griffith's strategy at this point in the discussions, however tactical the position he was advocating, nonetheless betrays a fundamental assumption integral to the Irish nationalist perception of the effects of British imperial policy. That assumption pervades the entire history of Republican ideology and insurrection. It was fundamental to separatist thinking after the fall of Ireland's 'Chief', Charles Stewart Parnell, in 1891. It sustained irredentist attitudes towards the politics of partition well beyond the duration of the Irish Civil War. And more than this, as we have seen, it was to form the very cornerstone of IRA demands throughout the latest phase of Republican militancy in the North. If only the British would 'stand aside', Griffith was suggesting, negotiations would naturally proceed towards agreement: the British presence, in other words, was the major obstacle to Irish unity.

As Griffith was declaring his understanding that Britain was the source of Irish divisions, the negotiations were entering their second week and the process would continue into the middle of

December. Both sides had set themselves a formidable undertaking: it was the task of the British government, together with its Irish Republican opponents, to scout out how 'the association of Ireland with the Community of Nations known as the British Empire may best be reconciled with Irish national aspirations'.[3] For the British, that meant securing the allegiance of Ireland within the Empire. In intermittent conferences over a three-month period at 10 Downing Street, the merits of Britain's case would be commended to the attention of the Irish negotiators by a British delegation including Lloyd George himself, Austen Chamberlain, Lord Birkenhead and Winston Churchill. On the other side, the substance of 'Irish national aspirations' was staked out by a group of Republican plenipotentiaries selected from the Cabinet in Dublin: first Arthur Griffith, who led the team, and then Michael Collins, Éamon Duggan, Gavan Duffy and Robert Barton, with Erskine Childers attending in the capacity of secretary.

Back in Dublin, the head of the Irish Cabinet, de Valera, anxiously awaited a result. When it came, in the form of the Anglo-Irish Treaty, and after its provisions were debated in the frenzied atmosphere of the second Dáil in December 1921, he rejected it.[4] So also did a pair of pivotal members in the Dublin government who had remained behind in Ireland throughout the course of the negotiations – the Minister for Defence, Cathal Brugha, and the Minister for Home Affairs, Austin Stack. W. T. Cosgrave, who had also stayed in Dublin as Minister for Local Government, joined with Griffith and Collins in recommending the settlement to the Dáil, and then to the Irish people. After both of these had died – Griffith following a cerebral haemorrhage, and Collins as a result of Republican assassination – it was Cosgrave who was left to take charge of the Irish Free State government. But in the meantime, as the rival British and Irish delegations faced each other across the negotiating table throughout October and November in 1921, a grim despondency unsettled every anticipation of a breakthrough: Irish autonomy could not be made to square with the sovereignty of the Empire, while the exclusion of Ulster could not be harmonised with the island unity of a national state.

Indeed, pessimism was surely to be expected. Each side had just emerged from a lacerating war, and embarked upon a nervous – and uncertain – truce. From early on in 1919 until the middle of 1921, the bloody toll of guerrilla outrages, police brutality and military reprisals had ensured that an air of profound suspicion would settle on the peace proceedings. During the Anglo-Irish War, the British press had teemed with reports of unconscionable extremities – of brutal assaults, degrading tortures and an endless train of assassinations perpetrated by the Republican forces. Hostility had frequently reached a state of high-pitched intensity. At the end of two and a half years of bloodshed in Ireland, the total strength of the British military forces in the country lay somewhere in the region of 80,000 men. Up until then, the Royal Irish Constabulary had been acting in open defiance of their civilian duties, while Britain's Auxiliary forces had terrorised the population. But all this was only the most recent phase in a long and dispiriting succession of misalliances and confrontations.

Since 1891, unity of purpose had eluded the protagonists in the struggle over Ireland. The whole period in Irish politics after the fall of Parnell was marked by the experience of drift and disappointment. Ever since Herbert Henry Asquith had assumed power in 1910, the British political establishment had indeed been bracing itself for a showdown on the Irish Question – the Conservatives mustering with their Ulster allies in defence of a fully incorporated Union, the Liberals consulting with the Irish Party in the expectation of agreement on a Home Rule Bill. The Liberals, for their part, had in fact sought to introduce some form of legislative devolution on two previous occasions – in 1886 and 1893 – only to have met each time with a damaging defeat, the first time in the House of Commons and the second in the Lords. Ten years of Conservative government had followed, and under its auspices the hope was that constitutional innovation could be stifled by concessions to outstanding grievances about

Irish land tenures. But still nationalism hankered and would not abate.

However, even with the advent of a Liberal victory in 1906, at a time when Irish constitutionalism was harassed and demotivated, and when Arthur Griffith's Sinn Féin organisation had barely stumbled into existence, a commitment to Home Rule scarcely figured on the agenda at Westminster. Within four years the situation was to be utterly transformed. After two general elections in the United Kingdom, brought forward as a result of the budget crisis of 1909, by December 1910 the Irish Party under John Redmond held the balance between Liberalism and Unionism in the House of Commons. Political stalemate gave way to a period of high drama in Irish affairs. The 1911 Parliament Act immediately reduced the power of the Lords in Britain, a Home Rule Bill passed through the House of Commons in April 1912 and, after delay in the Upper House for a period of two years, was placed upon the statute book in an atmosphere of international crisis in September 1914. However, the measure brought scant relief to national turmoil and vexation.

The Act, of course, was suspended in its operation for the duration of the First World War. But despite this frustration, the settlement seemed to its architects to proclaim the comfortable ascendancy of constitutionalism in Irish politics. Yet waiting in the wings, behind this apparent herald for the triumph of parliamentarism, lay the resurgence of a determined paramilitarism preparing to direct the course of events. By January 1913 the Ulster Volunteer Force was already drilling in the North, inflamed by Edward Carson to take a stand against Home Rule. By November, in the same year, the defiance of the UVF was being matched with the creation of the Irish Volunteers.[5] The Volunteers in the South were represented by MacNeill, a figure who had given every impression of a commitment to moderate constitutionalism. But within the ranks of the militia, indeed within the inner councils of the organisation, Irish Fenianism had installed itself and connived at the management of its military affairs.[6]

The insurgent wing of separatism at that time was embodied in the Irish Republican Brotherhood. Four members of the IRB sat on the original Provisional committee of ten which controlled the activities of the Volunteers, and when the committee expanded its representation to thirty, eight of the new accessions came from the Brotherhood's own ranks. But when the First World War came, the Volunteer movement split, the vast majority following Redmond's call to advance to 'wherever the firing-line extends',[7] while the membership of the IRB maintained allegiance to the rump. By this stage, the Supreme Council of the Brotherhood had been overhauled under the influence of Thomas J. Clarke, a veteran revolutionary who helped to oust the older leadership and revive the movement's flagging fortunes by the addition of young blood. At this point – in addition to Clarke – Bulmer Hobson, Sean MacDermott and Denis McCullough sat on the Supreme Council. So too did Patrick McCartan, Sean MacBride and P. S. O'Hegarty. But by May 1915, unknown to the majority of senior figures within the IRB, the executive of the Supreme Council was establishing a Military Council to prepare for a resort to arms.[8]

The Military Council was key: the seven signatories of the 1916 'Proclamation of the Republic' were all members – Patrick Pearse, Joseph Plunkett and Éamonn Ceannt from the beginning, with Sean MacDermott and Tom Clarke joining in September, and James Connolly and Thomas MacDonagh being co-opted in due course. The Rising itself, beginning on Easter Monday, ended as a military fiasco for the rebels. But after the protracted execution of its leaders; after the imposition of martial law throughout the island as a whole; after the mass arrests, the deportations and the infliction of civilian casualties involved in crushing the insurgents; after all this, disaffection began to permeate and intensify throughout the country: the tide had begun to turn against good faith in British promises.[9]

When Griffith stalled in the Treaty negotiations in the autumn of 1921, floating the idea of direct talks between the representatives of North and South and imploring his British counterparts to 'stand aside' to relieve the impasse, he was invoking a long tradition of analysis and description which cast Britain in the role of the divisive interloper. British divisiveness, on his understanding, was the product of imperial rapaciousness which could just as readily disguise itself as stand out proud. Under cover, imperial policy declared itself in the language of civility, only open to exposure when it slipped its specious guard. Imperialism, indeed, was an affair of craft, a dissimulating business, and a traitor to the high ideals it claimed as its true motive. Back in 1916, as the weeks after Easter stretched into a period of draconian surveillance and reprisal, that treachery began to move more steadily into public view as nationalist opinion grew increasingly dismayed at the severity of British measures.

In the eyes of nationalist Ireland after 1914, Britain had elected to fight a war for the freedom of small nations and summoned the neighbouring island to her standard for that purpose. Now, as the war dragged on, and as the response to 1916 pitted Irish nationalism against her, Britain was perceived to have turned her liberating zeal into an instrument of calculated repression: in what seemed a sudden revelation of her inherent disposition, the Mother of Parliaments, the guardian of liberty and democracy, had authorised the suppression of an earnest bid for freedom on the part of an ally in the fight against military expansionism. Griffith, for his part, had already expressed his scepticism about Britain's intentions early in 1916: 'England having destroyed our consti-tution, suppressed our Parliament, loaded her debt on to our shoulders, ruined our trade and commerce, turned our tillage fields into cattle-ranches, trebled our taxation and halved our population – all within a century – wants what is left of us to fight for her supremacy over the world.'[10] Griffith, of course, considered himself quite expert in the art of uncovering British hypocrisy, but a more general and more widespread mistrust of England's high vocation began to burgeon throughout Ireland as the year progressed.

Later in 1916, with popular opinion all but universally affronted at the continuance of the British clamp-down, disaffection mounted in support of Roger Casement, hanged for acts of treason at Pentonville in August. Just over a year later Thomas Ashe, a leader in the Rising and now on hunger strike in Mountjoy jail, died after the authorities subjected him to force-feeding, and again the temperature in Ireland rose. 'Ireland does not demand any kind of liberty which she does not wish to see England, France, Belgium, Poland, and all the other nations enjoying in equal measure,' wrote Robert Lynd, a prolific Sinn Féin advocate at the time. He went on: 'Ireland, in her struggle against English Imperialism, is the close counterpart of England and (closer still) Belgium in their struggle against German Imperialism.'[11]

In the months and years following the Easter Rising, the rebellion of Pearse, Clarke, MacBride and the rest – the phalanx of conspirators within both the IRB and Connolly's Irish Citizen Army – was identified with the gospel of self-reliance, autonomy and an 'Irish Ireland' long preached by the propaganda organs of Arthur Griffith's Sinn Féin movement.[12] And now, as events unfolded, that party inherited the advantage: in January 1917, in a by-election in North Roscommon, Count Plunkett, father of the executed Joseph Plunkett, took the seat with the backing of Sinn Féin. Later in that year, in a by-election in East Clare, de Valera, standing on a platform of Sinn Féin abstentionism, precipitated a landslide in his own favour. Then, in a singular example of impeccable bad timing, came the long-awaited threat of compulsory conscription as Britain made a final push to end the First World War. Nationalism in Ireland was driven towards resistance, and Sinn Féin was swept to victory in the general election of December 1918. England, as William O'Brien – a renegade from the Irish Parliamentary Party – was to put it, had been saddled with a 'meet reward for her politicians' perfidy'.[13]

O'Brien, who had long campaigned for land reform and responsible government in Ireland, came in retrospect to see the humiliation of Parnell as the harbinger of a catalogue of political disasters for his country. In his judgement, since the early 1890s,

Irish parliamentarism had been passionless and ineffective. It had steadfastly refused to conciliate the North, and had eschewed the path of compromise under the influence of John Dillon. Moreover, the Irish Parliamentary Party itself had been converted into an engine of sectarian division through the offices of the Ancient Order of Hibernians spreading like a cancer from its centre in Belfast.[14] But while MPs bungled their own project of Irish unity, they were simultaneously vulnerable to the charge of capitulation.

To an emerging generation of self-assertive nationalists, constitutional politics became increasingly identified with fractiousness, incompetence and, not least, corruption.[15] As O'Brien was to observe, party members in the Commons had discredited themselves in the eyes of advanced extra-parliamentary opinion by having agreed to receive their salaries from the imperial coffers of the British treasury. In contrast to the personal pride and self-respect inculcated by the teachings of Sinn Féin and the Gaelic League, the huckstering posture of the Irish Party in its dealings across the water began to savour of a fawning and degraded slavishness.[16] But the cowed machinations of constitutional politics did not merely affect the reputation of the party in the disillusioned quarters of the population, it also undermined the provision of deliberate policy in the lobbies and on the benches at Westminster. The argument steadily began to gain momentum that the utility of parliamentarism had perished with Parnell, that now Irish MPs deferred obsequiously to the whims of the British parties, that they played the role of courtiers in the palace of world power and so betrayed the Irish interest they were obliged to represent.

Holding, in their very own hands, the balance of power at Westminster after the general election of December 1910, Redmond and his followers had fumbled on the margins, squandering the chance of wielding decisive influence, as Edward Carson and Bonar Law were adopted into the wartime coalition Cabinet. O'Brien stood aghast, and later commented: 'The Irish Republic arose to take up the power which the Irish Parliamentary Party had shamefully misused. The young men of Ireland, long chafing under the spectacle of incapacity in Parliament and venality at home, heard their hour of deliverance from the Hibernian nightmare strike when the World-War proclaimed new and giddy possibilities of Self-Determination for "small nationalities".[17] Acquiescence in the settled rhythms of public life, a partiality for political *rapprochement* and – in particular – the commitment to Home Rule itself, were all discarded as super-annuated relics in the maelstrom of dissent directed against British perfidy. The stage was set for the resurrection of what was increasingly presented as an historic Irish democracy proclaiming its legitimacy in the teeth of British imperialism.

2

As Michael Collins advanced preparations for the Irish Republican Brotherhood – now styled the IRA – to resist the inevitable British onslaught against the progress of secession, the first Sinn Féin assembly in Ireland, Dáil Eireann, was gathering at the Mansion House in Dublin to ratify 'the establishment of the Irish Republic' that had been proclaimed on Easter Monday 1916. It was 21 January 1919, and the theory of political abstention had at last been animated into virtual life. With the majority of deputies in prison, on the run, or otherwise unavailable, twenty-seven parliamentary representatives elected themselves out of the Union and estab-lished a government of the Republic in defiance of British sentiment and authority. Of course, the policy of abstention had been fielded on numerous occasions in the nineteenth century.[18] But more importantly, by this stage, it had been broadcast with singular tenacity and conviction over the course of the preceding fifteen years by the progenitor and chief architect of Sinn Féin.

Between 2 January and 2 July 1904, in the columns of his own weekly newspaper, the *United Irishman*, Arthur Griffith had set about narrating the history of Hungary's struggle to restore its 'rightful Constitution of 1848' in opposition to the conniving and usurpatory designs of the Austro-Hungarian emperor, Franz

Josef. Later in the same year, Griffith's account was republished in book form, with the travails of Hungarian resistance explicitly presented as an exemplary, almost allegorical, 'parallel for Ireland': 'Sixty years ago,' as he declared in the Preface, 'Hungary realised that the political centre of the nation must be within the nation. When Ireland realises this obvious truth and turns her back on London the parallel may be completed.'[19] It is obvious that, in elaborating the details of the Hungarian 'resurrection', Griffith's purpose was less to focus attention on the course of events in Hungary – the tract was conceived as a witty, journalistic *tour de force* – than to defend two specific measures with a view to making progress on the Irish Question: first, he proposed that the objective of independence could best be secured under a dual monarchy on the Austro-Hungarian model; and second, that Ireland could most readily achieve her goal by the method of passive resistance pioneered by Ferenc Deák.

At this point in his career, Griffith was still a member of the Irish Republican Brotherhood, although since 1867, and more particularly since the early 1890s, the physical-force tradition of Republican separatism had been in a dilapidated, almost moribund state. The year 1898, the centenary of the United Irishmen's rebellion and the French invasion under Wolfe Tone, saw a revival of enthusiasm for displays of rhetorical and ceremonial militancy, but little by way of concerted plans to translate these into deeds. Maud Gonne, William Butler Yeats, John O'Leary, and an assortment of less prominent members of the Brotherhood, eagerly endeavoured to capitalise on the legacy of 1798 with a series of processions, demonstrations and monster rallies held throughout the year. But Fenianism was bound by its own amendment to the IRB constitution of 1873 proscribing any armed initiative in the absence of a democratic mandate, and so the movement was given more to bluster than revolt.[20]

After the death of O'Leary, and faced with the eviscerated condition of the organisation, Bulmer Hobson, Denis McCullough and Sean MacDermott set about revitalising the IRB some time between 1904, the year in which Hobson was inducted into the movement, and 1907, the year in which Tom Clarke returned from the United States. But despite the foundation of such hives of paramilitarism as the Dungannon Clubs and the Fianna Éireann, and notwithstanding the infiltration of the Gaelic League and a variety of other literary and sporting societies designed to stimulate the regeneration of national consciousness, the membership of the IRB, together with its prospects, remained negligible until the period after 1916. Griffith therefore dedicated all his resources after 1904 to filling a vacuum in Irish political life – channelling militancy into a constructive programme of engagement and seducing the Irish Party away from parliamentary wheedling.[21]

The 'mass of Irish people were not separatist', Griffith is reported to have confided to Bulmer Hobson: they 'would not support a rigidly separatist party'.[22] Therein lay the logic of his attraction to dual monarchy, an arrangement which was deliverable in the absence of armed struggle. In *The Resurrection of Hungary*, Griffith spelled this out: 'a policy of Passive Resistance and a policy of Parliamentarianism are very different things, although the people of Ireland have been drugged into believing that the only alternative to armed resistance is speech-making in the British Parliament.'[23] Griffith concentrated his fire on the scheme devised by Anton von Schmerling, Habsburg minister from 1860, to inaugurate a federal structure for the Empire by inducing Transylvania to send deputies to the Austrian Reichsrat. In Griffith's judgement, the British proposals for a system of federal Home Rule in 1893 were an exact replica of the Schmerling blueprint of 1861. Indeed, Joseph Chamberlain's desire to rescue the British Empire from implosion by the device of 'Home-Rule-All-Round' was likewise construed as the child of Schmerling's brain.[24]

But for Griffith, the problem with Home Rule as it was envisaged for Ireland in the late nineteenth century derived precisely from both its federal complexion – Irish members at Westminster would be detached from the Irish interest – and from the derisory extent of power to be devolved to an Irish legislature. These were exactly the objections which Griffith was later to raise against both the Home Rule Bill of 1912 and the Government of Ireland Act of 1920 although, at the time of the earlier Bill, he held back in the interest of nationalist unity from giving voice to outright rejection.[25] But his later position still drew on his original 1904 analysis of the inadequacies contained in Austria's proposals for compromise with Hungary's 'historic claim' to national independence.

Griffith dwells at some length in his text on the series of addresses made by the Hungarian Diet to 'His Imperial Majesty, Francis Joseph', in response to various of the emperor's *douceurs* designed to bend their resistance. '"All matters relating to money, credit, the military establishments, customs and commerce of Hungary",' as Griffith declares, in the voice of Ferenc Deák, '"– these essential questions of a political national existence – are placed under the control of an Imperial Parliament".'[26] Now, all of these matters, in respect of Ireland, were in due course to detain the participants in the Treaty negotiations of 1921 in heated discussion. But what is clear is that for Griffith, as early as 1904, the reservation of such powers of control and regulation as coinage, credit, customs, commerce and defence to Westminster would fall short of an acceptable settlement. But so too, as we have noted, would any federal plans for the retention of Irish members at Westminster: Irish participation in the House of Commons, like Hungarian participation in the Imperial Parliament, would constitute a concession to the political power of the centre at the expense of Ireland's representation in the corridors of power.

In Griffith's reconstruction of the situation, between 1861 and 1867, under the leadership of Deák, Hungary stood at once on the Pragmatic Sanction and the Constitution of 1848 to wrest control of its political destiny from the conspiring hands of Austrian court ministers. The achievement of historical concision in Griffith's account is brought about by the most remarkable sleight of hand: the fact that Magyar nationalism comprised barely a third of the

Hungarian population – that Serbs, Slovaks and Romanians constituted a dissenting majority with which the subsequent history of Europe was to grow familiar – is resolved by construing every rival secessionist claim within the Empire as the product of a false consciousness afflicting the 'Slav hordes'.[27] But, in the spirit of propagandising wilfulness, no extraneous complication is permitted to detract from Griffith's central ambition of upholding the merits of the 1867 *Ausgleich*, and the method of passive resistance which was responsible for its success.

Deák's methods of abstention and obstruction may have staked their claim to legitimacy upon a pacifism of principle. But for Griffith, forgoing violence and embracing the Hungarian example was a matter of opportunity and expedience. The 'fight for Ireland's independence' was being waged in 1904 – as he made clear – at a time when 'circumstances do not permit it to be waged with the sword and the gun'.[28] But if the question of ways and means was not hemmed in by the requirement of strict principle, the overriding objective of Griffith's argument was to show that flexibility on the question of Irish autonomy certainly was subject to this demand.

The *Ausgleich* was secured by a 'bloodless war' prosecuted with the sole resource of sustained Hungarian obduracy at a time when Prussian forces threatened to overawe the Habsburg lands. In the face of impending disaster, Franz Josef disposed of the services of the man whom Griffith cast in the role of the pugilistic first minister – Richard Belcredi – and dispatched Count Beust instead to cut a deal with the Hungarians. Now the time had come for the restoration of the Austro-Hungarian compact, and so for a reconciliation – in Griffith's words – between 'two independent nations, agreeing for their better security and territorial integrity to have a common sovereign and to act in concert in regard to foreign affairs'.[29]

The ostensible illegality of Hungary's subjection to Austrian might between 1849 and 1867 is matched in Griffith's account by what he took to have been the unconstitutional passage of the

British Act of Union under the supervision of Pitt and Castlereagh in 1801. On the reading of Irish history put forward to justify this thesis, the patriotism of Molyneux, Swift and Charles Lucas is seen as having finally borne fruit in the period of Henry Flood and the Irish Volunteers with the lifting of Irish commercial restrictions, the establishment of Grattan's Parliament, and – more particularly – with the Renunciation Act of 1783 by which Britain agreed to cede the authority, already granted to the Irish legislature in 1782, in perpetuity. Griffith concluded: 'Six hundred years after the English invasion of this country, the English Parliament renounced all claim or title to govern this country. Its Renunciation is still inscribed on the British Statute-Book.'[30]

The sweeping narrative of eighteenth-century Irish history fabricated in the pages of *The Resurrection of Hungary* is perhaps no more extraordinary than Griffith's travesty of the *Ausgleich*.[31] However, precision was not its point: political purchase was. But the fact is that here too the enterprise was found wanting. Griffith's allies continually met with such a barrage of criticism and incredulity in their attempts to sell the message that the Sinn Féin platform was steadily eclipsed after its brief flourish in 1908 until the radical reversal of 1916.[32] But Griffith's rehearsal of past history did serve a definite and consequential purpose. To start with, it supplied the claims of modern Irish nationalism with a compelling foundation in narrative history which, whatever its shortcomings from the perspective of factual rigour, could nonetheless easily trump the appeal of arid philosophical pleading. But – more than this – it perpetuated, and lent a measure of sophistication to, a range of political motifs whose very durability stands as a mark of their success.

Griffith's aim was to construct a broad political platform on which Republicans and Home Rulers could overcome their differences and unite in a common front against the enemy. In the absence of such unity, being faced with a situation in which each individual protagonist in the struggle was armed with their own 'scheme for the final settlement', the ensuing factionalism would beget weakness and division, and so also the strangulation of the endeavour as a whole.[33] Accordingly, the Sinn Féin position represented a bid for realignment and inclusiveness in the interest of national renewal. For that purpose, the platform was to be enlivened – and thus to make its impact – with the aid of ideologically compelling maxims which built upon inherited perceptions from the past, refining the general import of familiar slogans, and then adapting them for the future.

With this end in view, the story of Britain's treacherous betrayal of the spirit of 1782 with the destruction of the Irish Parliament in 1801, and the enforced incorporation of the Irish Kingdom into the Union, enabled Griffith to extend a new lease of life to received suspicions about perfidious Albion, and so to underwrite his case, in the terms of a recognisable idiom, against a secret imperialist conspiracy to conquer by the tactic of divide and rule. It was, Griffith insists, Britain's 'divide-et-impera policy' which succeeded in bringing to fruition Pitt's policy for uniting the two kingdoms, thereby yoking Ireland's fortunes to a controlling British interest.[34] However, the price of imperial Union was the continuance of sectarian hostility in Ireland, itself originally fostered by the ruling power. The reality of that hostility in twentieth-century Ireland was apparent in the unionist intransigence of Ulster. If only Britain would stand aside, Griffith was beginning to insinuate, intransigence would be eased and hostility assuaged.[35]

3

Already in 1892 William O'Brien was contributing to the outlines of this argument, which was to achieve its most elaborate expression in Arthur Griffith's *Resurrection*. In a lecture delivered in Belfast in that year, O'Brien remarked that 'Irish quarrelsomeness is English policy. It is not a provision of nature. It is the invention of cunning conquerors.'[36] That perception, as we shall see, was soon to become *de rigueur*. At the first Annual Convention of the National Council, held on Tuesday, 28 November 1905, Griffith mounted the podium in Dublin's Rotunda to outline the agenda of Sinn Féin. At the close of his speech, he turned to relate party policy on 'the Orangeman of the North': Sinn Féin ought, Griffith declared, to extend to its northern antagonists the same 'greeting of Brotherhood' as was currently being offered to its potential southern allies. Such an overture, he was suggesting, would begin the process of coaxing Orangeism away from its accidental unionist affiliation. The Orangeman was to be seen, as Griffith put it, as the 'blind instrument' of imperialist ingenuity.[37] And while this understanding of the insidious artifice of sectarianism stands at no great distance from O'Brien's account of Britain's 'cunning' contrivance, Griffith was to extenuate the thesis, and to provide during the course of his career a more ambitious and robust analysis of the historical operation of imperialism's ruse.

It was Griffith's view that British imperialism had sprung from an anxious absolutism which, with the aid of England's sovereignty of the seas, had sought with unremitting diligence to maximise the benefits of its foreign trade. Absolutism in this context meant English avarice which, it was alleged, sought to eliminate from the world of commercial competition the first hint of any challenge to an exclusively domestic advantage. With regard to Ireland, that meant the reduction of her economy to primitivism and penury: her meagre role was now to be 'the fruitful mother of flocks and herds'.[38] Ruthless egoism was England's secret; national attrition became Ireland's lot.

In August 1906, in the pages of the newspaper which he began to edit in the same year – the aptly named *Sinn Féin* – Griffith felt compelled to warn his readers that the British Empire was 'more a trading concern than a philanthropic institution'.[39] But more alarming still from the perspective of Irish separatists, imperialism was specifically construed as raw self-interest under wraps. As Griffith outlined the case in his Sinn Féin manifesto, the reality of zero-sum commercial self-aggrandisement was occluded by the pretence of a generous philanthropy.[40] Behind the smoke and mirrors, behind the numerous professions of liberality and consensus, conquest by stealth plotted and intrigued as the true *arcanum imperii* of the 'mistress of the seas'.

At this stage in his career, Griffith's pronouncements were already registering the influence of Friedrich List's polemical crusade, *The National System of Political Economy*, translated into English in 1885. Here one could discover, Griffith felt sure, the real reasons behind England's exclusion of Ireland from both the Chinese and the Indian trade, and an explanation for Ireland's failure 'to form colonies of her own'.[41] On Griffith's reckoning, it was in 1785 that the Dean of Gloucester, Josiah Tucker, betrayed the depth of England's hunger for world mastery. Tucker had campaigned long and hard during the American crisis against Edmund Burke's proposals for conciliation with the Colonies, before turning after the war to fix his attention upon Ireland: after the Dublin legislature had rejected Pitt's design for the regulation of Irish trade in the late summer of 1785, Tucker – as Griffith recounts – advised the 'English shipowners to fit out vessels under the Irish national flag' since by this time 'the Irish marine was ousting' its British rival.[42] But if Tucker in a fit of pique gave the game away, it was List who had been able to discern the inner motive.

'In all ages,' List had argued, 'nations and powers have striven to attain to the dominion of the world': but none had quite succeeded with such dexterity as the British.[43] In Griffith's adaptation of List's assessment, it was an independent Ireland which, after 1782, occupied a prime position from which it could harass the supremacy of English trade. In 1911, in a series of articles which appeared in the columns of *Sinn Féin*, Griffith identified William Pitt as the mastermind who had lighted upon the seriousness of this threat: 'He saw clearly enough,' Griffith announced, 'that if the Parliament of Ireland retained the independence it won in 1782, the government of the empire must within 30 years be equally shared by the two countries. Mr. Pitt was determined that the empire should remain England's private property. His Imperialism spelled England absolute.'[44] But that end required an effective means, together with the wherewithal to seize the opportunity.

The opportunity came – according to Griffith – in 1789, as a response to Ireland's refractory self-confidence at the height of the Regency crisis. With the intention of bringing to an end any possible occasion for future conflict with England, John Fitzgibbon – the Lord Chancellor of Ireland, and a vital link in Pitt's scheme for effecting a United Kingdom – was set the task of rekindling the fires of sectarian bigotry in Ireland: the advent of religious disturbances was to act as the pretext for English intervention. And when they came, culminating in the Battle of the Diamond in Armagh in 1795, with the Orange Order founded in the aftermath of the collision, and Catholicism in reaction spawning a Hibernian movement, Fitzgibbon's undertaking seemed complete: mutually hostile religious institutions would now fulfil their allotted role as the sorry 'puppets of English statecraft'.[45] Except, as Griffith observed, the project did not quite deliver: in the place of sustained sectarian acrimony came the ambition of the United Irishmen for a cordial union among '*all the people of Ireland*',[46] the republican ministrations of Theobald Wolfe Tone, and ultimately the Rebellion of 1798.

The Rebellion, outside Wexford, was suppressed within ten days, and then Wexford fell in June. Griffith's account of its proceedings is of a piece with his other didactic histories: events are made to correspond to an ulterior design, but the lesson, at least, remains apparent. Accordingly, Griffith's message declared that from this period dates – all at once – the desire for an Ireland united in independence; the reality of a country riven by religious antagonisms; the division of Ireland into political factions for the benefit of English rule; and the decline of Irish prosperity as a result of imperial manipulation.[47] But the grim trajectory of Ireland's humiliation still conduces, in Griffith's telling, toward a positive result whose lineaments, once again, had been drawn by Friedrich List.

List's account of the emergence of English hegemony begins with the discovery of the secret of modern power. By the seventeenth, and especially by the eighteenth, century, the folly of emulating the Roman ambition to achieve universal dominion by means of conquest, annexation and pacification was exposed by England's prescience and skill as she converted 'her entire territory' into a world emporium. Without any need for military virtue or the expense of endless war, England instead erected itself into an 'immense manufacturing, commercial, and maritime city'.[48] Having been elevated to a position from which it was possible to control world trade to its own advantage, England soon occupied the pinnacle of international supremacy by capitalising on the policy first proposed by Adam Smith.[49]

Under Pitt, the doctrine of free trade was disseminated throughout Europe until gradually Smith's teaching was accepted by every government on the continent as securing an optimum arrangement for its own national prosperity. But, List counselled, while a free trade might be equally favourable to equal competitors under market conditions, it was detrimental to the weaker partner forced to bargain in an unequal trade. However, as List went on to reveal, it was precisely this fact which was concealed behind the alluring array of 'cosmopolitical expressions' coined by the ingenious Adam Smith and peddled by the craft of William Pitt.[50] Hoodwinked by the bluff, with the British free to import their raw materials and export their manufactures without restriction, agricultural producers like the German states were forced to labour at a discount. And so we are brought to see that the *pax Britannica* had been built upon the handicap of its rivals, although it was marketed as the means to their deliverance.

Griffith follows List in pointing to the unexpected climax to this subterfuge. It was ultimately Castlereagh who upset the grand design, resigning commercial policy to the protectionism of grandees who thus 'killed the hen which had laid the golden eggs'.[51] Aristocratic resistance to free trade was duly vented in the passing of the Corn Laws in consequence of which the Germans were thrown back upon their own resources. Since Germany was now obliged to cultivate its manufacturing base, the country's fortunes were at last permitted to rise to the challenge posed by Britain's ascendancy. It almost seemed to List that 'Providence' had organised this redress and, marvelling at the outcome, he was encouraged to offer this prediction: as a result of the growth of the United States, he expected that 'in a not very distant future' the external pressures which imposed on the French and Germans 'the necessity of establishing a Continental alliance against British supremacy, will impose on the British the necessity of establishing a European coalition against the supremacy of America'.[52] Griffith, however, does not pursue List's line into the future, but focuses again upon the legacy of the past.

After defeat in the American War in 1783, Griffith recollected, the fortunes of the Empire hung in the balance. England was presented with the option of constructing 'an invincible naval and military Anglo-Hibernian Empire' on the ruins of its former greatness.[53] However, Pitt instead chose an incorporative Union, the subjection of Ireland to foreign interference, and also – but unexpectedly – the ultimate demise of English power. The Union was to be ushered in as an emergency solution to the outbreak of violence ignited in Ireland by the policy of divide and rule. But the project was to backfire: under a dual monarchy, the ascendancy of an Anglo-Hibernian emporium would certainly have been unassailable in Griffith's estimate. But, under the regime of an exclusive imperialism, with Ireland weakened and degraded, England confronted an anarchic world of competitive power politics harried by the disaffection of her closest ally. The world, Griffith anticipated, 'will surely rock with a war waged to secure the hegemony of Europe'. With England standing at the head of a European coalition, a powerful Germany 'must face a world in arms'.[54] And in this prospective fight, the chink in England's armour will be lying on her flank: 'England's enemy will have no Irish enemy to face.'[55]

If, however, England should survive this latest conflagration, her ambition was ultimately bound to fail. And so Griffith comes to his point, and makes an appeal to 'the Irish Unionists': the Act of Union was 'not only the destroyer of Ireland's organised nationhood', but more vitally it would also prove 'the destroyer of England's Empire'.[56] Artificially hitched to a doomed enterprise, Irish unionists would best serve their own future by renouncing their inheritance: the most elementary maxim of self-preservation enjoined Unionism to liberate itself from the legacy of England's 'divide-et-impera policy', to refuse the Machiavellian inducements of the neighbouring conqueror, and exchange English perfidy for the tangible benefit of an integrated, national cause.

War, in Griffith's presentation of his case, is an inevitable concomitant of capitalist rivalry. But a year before Griffith had embarked upon his project to seduce Irish unionists away from the allure of English imperialism by alerting them to the pitfalls of Pitt's chauvinism, Norman Angell had set about challenging the assumption of trade's dependence upon militarism, and more particularly the idea that colonies could yield profit. Angell, in the first place, was arguing against the inevitability of war. His criticism, set out in *The Great Illusion*, was directed at the pervasive tolerance of English jingoism, at Roosevelt's association of martial exploits with civic virtue, and in particular at the survival of the Hobsonian equation of imperialism with commercial expansion. Colonies might be a matter of honour, but not of material profit, he insisted. Equally, war might result from the promptings of national glory, but not from the pursuit of purely economic interests.[57] And since Angell's argument was fated to achieve wide diffusion, its tenets were soon being scrutinised within the ranks of Irish Republicanism.

Shortly after the publication of *The Great Illusion*, Terence MacSwiney saw fit to take exception to the unabashed utilitarianism contained within the covers of Angell's book. MacSwiney had been a leading Volunteer in Cork in 1916 and, although he saw no action in Easter week, he was imprisoned in the aftermath of the Rising. Elected to the first Dáil in 1919, he was subsequently selected as Lord Mayor for Cork in March 1920. But he was arrested again within five months, went on hunger strike immediately, and died in prison after fasting for seventy-four days.[58] He had also been a budding literary and political commentator in the period before Home Rule passed into law, and in that capacity he found himself rejecting Angell's thesis. What rankled with MacSwiney was the suggestion which he detected in the *Great Illusion* to the effect that when reason and argument had finally exploded the customary association of military might with national power, and after a durable and enlightened peace had been settled on the community of Great Powers, it would fall to this victorious coalition to police the 'backward races' of the globe.

Angell's argument is thus convicted of complicity with the fundamental tenets of what MacSwiney dubs the 'imperial creed', committed – as he understood the phenomenon – to a hierarchy of nation-states instead of a common fellowship of free and equal republics. And since, in MacSwiney's estimate, a Home Rule settlement, retaining (as it would) the remnants of the imperial edifice, was a virtual certainty in the near future, it fell to advanced Republicans to evoke the 'tyranny, cruelty, [and] hypocrisy' which constituted ineradicable components of this creed in operation.[59] The imperialist project arrogated to itself the righteous undertaking to 'civilise the barbarians', but the hoax had won few friends among the disenfranchised nations whose votaries were now united in their pledge to both a cosmopolitan fraternity and the defence of 'the weaker ones of the earth'.[60]

Portions of MacSwiney's argument include residues of thinking which survived from the long history of polemic directed against the indignity of 'dependence', a history which stretches back through the reforming and revolutionary sectaries of the English Civil War to the heyday, and then the last gasp, of Roman republican nostalgia.[61] The impact on MacSwiney of this traditional harangue against the evil of political servitude is conspicuous: 'while there is any restraint on us by a neighbouring power, acknowledged superior, there is dependence to that extent,' he declared. And he went on: 'To avert the moral plaque of slavery men fly to arms.'[62] But with each display of republican zeal, MacSwiney is advertising the distance between his own ideal of liberty and the virtues of dual monarchism advanced by Arthur Griffith: 'let not the hands of the men in the vanguard be tied by alien King, Constitution or Parliament,' MacSwiney demanded, as if his own political objectives might otherwise have remained obscure.[63]

Conflict over the competing political agendas of Griffith and MacSwiney was to reverberate through the years of Republican struggle down to 1923, and beyond. Both parties to the debate were anxious to avoid any damaging confrontation, but each was to charge the other with responsibility for the provocation: Griffith's insistent endorsement of the Constitution of 1782, MacSwiney warned, would precipitate a 'mighty collapse' of the whole edifice of independence in the event of a serious nationalist advance. Griffith, as we know, entertained a corresponding fear, focusing his anxiety on the implacability of separatists. As it transpired, these fears were not disappointed. With the Treaty signed in December 1921 and ratified the following January by the Dáil, the Irish Free State was now established as a member of the British Commonwealth of Nations. But intense political dissent accompanied these developments, and a plague of recrimination was in the offing.

Fifty-seven votes were cast against the Treaty on 7 January 1922, with the majority – sixty-four – accepting its provisions. The elections to the third Dáil the following June increased this proportion in favour of the settlement on offer – with fifty-eight members returned supporting the Treaty, and thirty-five members against. But by now the Irish Republican Army was profoundly divided. At a Convention held two months after the ratification of the Treaty in the Dáil, the Army reaffirmed its allegiance to the Republic, vesting authority in an executive of its own choosing in defiance of the tenure of the provisional Free State government. The military supporters of the Treaty did not attend the Convention, placing themselves instead under the command of the

Free State authorities, while their opponents combined to form an army of Irregulars pledged to make a stand for the Republic. The stage was now set for a contest in arms which would end in civil war.

That catastrophe arrived in earnest in the summer of 1922, ending in the spring of the following year with the defeat of the Irregular forces. But in tandem with this finale came the survival through succeeding generations of the bitter enmities occasioned by the collision. The contemporary Provisional IRA, it will be remembered, was formed in December 1969 out of a split within the residual Irish Republican Army which was itself bequeathed to posterity by the descendants of the irreconcilable elements from the 1922 Irregulars. But if the Provos saw fit to trace their lineage back to the recusant stalwarts of the Irish Civil War, the central plank of their complaint had an altogether different source. The ferocious energy of modern Republican insurrection was sparked into action less by an unwavering adherence to the principle of republican sovereignty in the South – although this too played its part – and more by enduring acrimony over the legitimacy of partition.

The failure of Irish unity, the Provisionals were to insist, was an elaborate Machiavellian ruse contrived by the imperial power: in the event of a British withdrawal political hostility would cease. This argument, as we have seen, has a definite pedigree extending back to the period of nationalist commotion which greeted the first promise of Home Rule. In fact, with a view to genealogical exhaustiveness, it can be traced back to the writings of Wolfe Tone.[64] But the point here is that the claims advanced in the early twentieth century about England's secret ambition to enforce Ireland's submission by means of concocted sectarian divisions did not so much provide material for conflict across the range of advanced nationalist and republican opinion as supply a common perspective on the character of northern Irish unionism. With respect to this core component of Republican doctrine, the Provisionals were to stand united, just as Griffith and MacSwiney before them had, on this score at least, presented a common front.[65]

Composing the Preface to his posthumously published *Principles of Freedom* in Brixton prison in September 1920, MacSwiney delivered the outlines of the thesis: 'our enemies,' he wrote, 'sowed discord in the North, with the aim of destroying Irish unity.' But the appearance of division was to his mind an entirely 'unnatural' occurrence which was destined to dissolve under the conditions of 'political Freedom'.[66] This optimism was to survive the most brutal manifestations of sectarian hatred in the early 1970s in Northern Ireland, but more immediately it guided the Republican plenipotentiaries in the Treaty negotiations of 1921. At the close of the proceedings, the Irish delegates did of course accept compromise, although still in the hope of eventual success. It was agreed under Article XII of the Treaty that, in the event of Northern Ireland continuing to repudiate the jurisdiction of the Free State, a Boundary Commission would be established to re-examine the area to be included in the territories of North and South. Griffith and Collins expected the process to lead to the revision of the existing boundaries in favour of the South, thus hopefully bringing about the demise of Northern Ireland. But the expectation, as it turned out, was radically thwarted.

The work of the Commission was brought to a halt with the resignation of its Free State representative in 1924, and the original partitioned area of 1920 was accepted as matter of established fact, if not of established principle, by the Irish government under W. T. Cosgrave in 1925. But the principle continued to assert itself without respite, and the logic of its defence in 1970 exhibited no great difference from the terms in which it had been recommended in 1910 – except that, in the earlier phase of Republican polemic, the imperialist tactic of British governments had been associated with concrete historical agents, and with an original creative intelligence who fashioned its design. For MacSwiney, that intelligence belonged to none other than Niccolò Machiavelli who, it is claimed, formulated a scheme for conquest which could be seen to fit 'exactly' the 'English occupation of Ireland'.[67]

In the third chapter of *The Prince*, Machiavelli lays down the best method available to a ruler for securing the conquest of a province 'different in language, customs and institutions' from his own. First, he advises, colonies should be settled in the region as a means of avoiding the expense and insecurity occasioned by military garrisons. Next, resistance should be ruthlessly crushed, and its perpetrators destroyed, since a more indulgent policy would leave to the injured party the option of revenge. And finally, a foreign prince wishing to exploit new territory should befriend the 'lesser potentates' envious or fearful of those who are more powerful in their vicinity. By this method the more vulnerable party, seduced by the new ruler, will at once 'unite with the state he has conquered to form a single body'.[68] Observing in all this what appears to be a strategy for manipulating the allegiance of one section of the population in order to secure the conquest of the other, MacSwiney draws his own conclusion: 'Here,' he writes, 'is the old maxim, "Divide and conquer"' in operation, its applicability to the case of Ireland obvious to anyone who cared to notice.[69]

By this stage in the argument, MacSwiney had long prepared his readership for the neatness of this correspondence. At the very outset he had maintained that 'there is no religious dissension' in Ireland – or none at least that was of a purely native origin: on the contrary, it was clear that 'English politicians, to serve the end of dividing Ireland, have worked on the religious feelings of the North'.[70] In order to lend historical weight to this claim, MacSwiney rests his case on what to him was the most significant moment of sectarian unity in Irish history: namely, the moment when the Republican standard was first raised against foreign tyranny, 'in the Rising of 1798' when 'Catholics and Protestants were united in its cause'.[71]

But while few would want to rush to the defence of this particular rendition of 1798 and its aftermath, MacSwiney could at least have found some endorsement for the broad implications of his argument in the writings of that figure most commonly associated with the 'spirit of '98', if not with the event itself –

Theobald Wolfe Tone.[72] Writing to Arthur O'Connor from Philadelphia in October 1795, Tone set out his own 'theory of Irish politics' by tracing all the miseries suffered by his country to the 'blasting influence of England'. That destructive influence was maintained, he continued, by 'perpetuating the spirit of internal dissension, grounded on religious distinctions'.[73] But while such remarks might well be taken to coincide with the general thrust of MacSwiney's diagnosis of sectarian divisions in Ireland, Tone's subsequent attempt to anatomise the various factions in the country for the edification of the French government in 1796 points in an altogether different direction.

In his *Memorials on the Present State of Ireland*, addressed to the French Directory with a view to encouraging it to embark upon a military expedition to Ireland, Tone describes the established Protestant religion in the country as comprising a 'colony of strangers' who have 'always looked to England for protection'. But, he went on, 'it is very different with regard to the Dissenters, who occupy the province of Ulster'.[74] Quite unlike the 'Protestant aristocracy' of the island, the dissenters of the north-east – far from requiring England's protection as 'necessary for their existence' – were in fact explicitly opposed to the 'usurpations of the English'. Moreover, until the recent *détente* between the two religions, there had been in existence since 1620 – since, that is, the first settlement of Protestantism in the province – 'a continual animosity' between settler and native 'grounded on the natural dislike between the old inhabitants and strangers, and fortified still more by the irreconcilable difference between the genius of the religions of Calvinism and Popery'. In Tone's view, these dislikes and differences had indeed been capitalised upon by the adherents of the established religion in Ireland, and fomented in turn by the 'English party'.[75] But since the division did not originate in the clandestine recesses of imperial policy, it had certainly not been fabricated as an instrument of conquest.

Naturally, Tone's analysis proves nothing in itself, although clearly it can offer little comfort to the conventional pieties of

Republican doctrine as these were advocated around 1910, and again since 1969. But the larger effort in which Tone involved himself – to effect a 'cordial union' among the sectaries of his own country, independent of any foreign interest – still raises questions of considerable delicacy which bear upon the specific political upheaval with which this book is concerned. The cordial union espoused by Tone was to be established upon the solid foundation of a common interest. The social and political divisiveness of a partial ruling interest would, as the Revolution in France had apparently shown, be overcome by constructing a representative interest through the effective means of a representative government.[76] But the individual most closely associated with this argument was not so much Tone himself as Thomas Paine, whom Tone had been reading since 1791.

In the second part of *The Rights of Man*, published in 1792, Paine pointed to the sole method available to modern political wisdom for constructing a 'government established and conducted for the interest of the public', putting an end in the process to the perfidious and arcane practices of European *raison d'état*.[77] It was under a republican regime alone that nations could have 'no secrets', while also answering to the fundamental purpose for which 'government ought to be instituted' – that is, the '*res-publica*, the public affairs, or the public good'.[78] But while every republic was founded on the principle of democracy – it had democracy, as Paine put it, 'as the ground' of its proceedings – modern republicanism was most naturally associated with representative institutions. In other words, of all the modern expedients available, it was representation which best served a common, united 'public good'. However, the struggle to evolve an agreed public good in Northern Ireland, and the competing claims to representation which the participants in that struggle sought to advance, oblige us to explore the precise import of these inherited components of political perception, and so to examine with a degree of care and attention the precise nature of the collision between democracy and imperialism as it unfolded after 1972.

V

Politics: 1972–1998

I

The hunger strikes of 1981 marked a complicated turning-point for the Republican movement: they signalled the climax of the war, and they laid the foundations for the peace. On 5 May, the former Officer Commanding of the Provisional IRA in the H-Blocks of the Maze prison, Bobby Sands, passed into Republican martyr-dom. It was just after one in the morning, on the sixty-sixth day of his fast, when Sands died. Within hours, protests and rioting convulsed the Catholic ghettos across Northern Ireland. By the time day broke, gasps of anxious disbelief were whispering through the South.

Throughout the island, the mood amongst republicans was desolate, yet expectant. 'I am standing on the threshold of another trembling world,' Sands had confided to his diary at the start of his protest.[1] But by now it seemed that a tangible deliverance might be to hand: everything that Republicans had struggled to achieve suddenly appeared to be about to happen.[2] However, by the end of May, with another three strikers dead, Margaret Thatcher remained confident that the venture would miscarry: the whole desperate effort might prove to be the Provisionals' 'last card'.[3] Over the months that followed, both predictions sought approval as rival propaganda. Did these events announce the consummation of twelve successive years of struggle, or were they tokens of enraged defiance just before defeat? It remained to be seen what the hunger strikes would ultimately produce.

On Thursday, 7 May, two days after Sands had finally expired,

100,000 mourners lined the route from St Luke's Church as his coffin passed toward the republican plot at Milltown Cemetery in Belfast. There was a profound and enduring silence throughout the crowd in the drizzling rain. A lone piper led the procession down the stretch of the Stewartstown Road. Then came the military ceremony, and the oration: 'Bobby Sands, your sacrifice will not be in vain,' proclaimed Owen Carron.[4] It was certain that the war of liberation would continue with renewed vehemence. But armed action would now be bolstered by a new political endeavour.

On 1 November 1981, at the annual Sinn Féin party conference at the Mansion House in Dublin, the new departure was already being publicised as the pursuit of a dual strategy: electoralism was to accompany ongoing military operations. It fell to Danny Morrison, the party's director of publicity, to unveil the change in direction by posing a question to the conference floor: 'will anyone here object if, with a ballot paper in this hand and an Armalite in this hand, we take power in Ireland?'[5]

Years later, Jim Gibney, a member of the Executive Committee of Provisional Sinn Féin, and an associate of Adams since his internment at Long Kesh, would elucidate the message which had been planted in the question. Supporters of the Republican movement were being primed to think strategically 'beyond the IRA': 'it was shorthand for Republicans being convinced of new forms of political struggle'.[6] Nine years earlier, things had been very different: 'You've got to have military victory first and then politicise the people,' argued MacStiofáin.[7] But the attitudes of the 1970s were to be purged and overhauled. Now, in the early 1980s, popular participation was a key component of the struggle: agitation was a vital part of the struggle, and mobilisation was a part of the struggle. And, since the massive displays of defiance on the part of the strikers in the Maze, funerals were now a part of the struggle too.

The day after Sands' funeral, Joe McDonnell joined the strike. He then died on 8 July after sixty-one days on hunger fast. At his funeral, there were serious confrontations between the mourners and the security forces as the British Army moved to arrest an IRA firing party. By this stage, a spirit of bitter resistance held the republican heartlands in its grip. But the mood was spreading – the whole of nationalist Ireland was growing steadily more incensed by the endless chain of sacrificial deaths.

The legendary IRA commando, Francis Hughes, had already died. So too had Raymond McCreesh, another member of the IRA, and Patsy O'Hara, of the Irish National Liberation Army, both on 21 May. In mid-July another Provisional, Martin Hurson, died; and then followed Kevin Lynch, of the INLA, on 1 August. Next Kieran Doherty, of the IRA, died after seventy-three days on strike. Another IRA member, Tom McElwee, died on 8 August, and finally Michael Divine, of the INLA, on 20 August. By the time that the strike was ended, on 3 October, there had been ten republican funerals in Northern Ireland. The media coverage had been extensive, each funeral turnout had been substantial, and the publicity for the Republican cause beyond historical comparison.

But while there were funerals, there were also elections. It was the election of Bobby Sands to the House of Commons in early April which laid the groundwork for the Republican movement's conversion to electoral politics.[8] On 5 March, four days after Sands had first refused his prison food, Frank Maguire, an independent Member of the Commons at Westminster for the constituency of Fermanagh–South Tyrone, suddenly died. At a meeting of the Sinn Féin Executive Committee on the Saturday following, the idea was floated that Bobby Sands might be persuaded to contest the seat. Within days, Gerry Adams, Jim Gibney, David O'Connell and Ruairí Ó Brádaigh came out in support of the proposal. By the 26th, the decision was official. Owen Carron would act as Sands' election agent. On 9 April, the day of the by-election arrived. Carron was at the count: Harry West, a former leader of the Ulster Unionist Party, had been defeated. Sands had won by 30,492 votes to 29,046 in a poll which brought out 87 per cent of the electorate.

The prisoners in the Maze were inwardly exultant – open displays of jubilation were scarcely viable under the circumstances.

But on the outside, among republicans at large, the response to events was more volubly ecstatic. 'To say that I was elated would be an understatement,' recalled the veteran Republican Seamus Kerr, looking back on that climactic day from the vantage of the 1990s.[9] The result of the Fermanagh–South Tyrone by-election represented a monumental victory for Sinn Féin and the IRA. But more elections were now to follow.

In Northern Ireland itself, the local government elections fell on 22 May. On this occasion, Sinn Féin declined to participate in the proceedings.[10] Nonetheless, in general terms, Republican participation was beginning to be feared in case advances through the ballot box might seem to vindicate armed struggle. Accordingly, the House of Commons had amended the Representation of the People Act immediately following the success of Bobby Sands: starting at the end of June, prisoners would be excluded from contesting parliamentary seats. But already, in the South of Ireland, a new opportunity had arisen.

The Taoiseach, Charles Haughey, called for a general election to be held on 11 June. Nine republican prisoners, standing under the aegis of the National H-Block/Armagh Committee, and supported by Provisional Sinn Féin, ran in the contest. The committee had been established in October 1979 to spearhead the campaign led by a clutch of Relatives' Action Committees which had themselves formed back in April 1976 to publicise conditions in the Northern Ireland prisons as these affected protesting republican inmates in the Maze and Armagh jails.[11] In 1979, as Gerry Adams was subsequently happy to concede, both himself and Jim Gibney were 'looking positively at electoralism', and generally trying to realise some political 'advances'. In fact, as early as 1975, Adams had been prepared to consider the merits of electoral politics, although at that point his flexibility was not being openly advertised. But now – four years later – an alliance had presented itself in the form of the H-Block/Armagh Committee, and Sinn Féin could avail of a platform from which to promote 'the political character of our struggle'.[12]

Co-operation within the alliance was agreed on a strategic basis. Endorsement of the prison protest would not be equated with commitment to the legitimacy of the Provo war.[13] It was intended instead that the committee would work, in a purposefully exclusive way, to promote the prisoners' five demands – the right to wear civilian clothing, exemption from penal labour, free association, the right to recreation and education, and the restoration of remission.

From the start, the committee had included the Trade Union Campaign Against Repression, Women Against Imperialism, People's Democracy, the Irish Republican Socialist Party – as the political wing of the INLA – and naturally Sinn Féin itself.[14] Its first major political triumph had come with the victory of Bobby Sands and now, just under two months later, the chance of additional forward movement had arrived with the elections for the Dáil. The result was encouraging. Altogether, the prisoners secured some 40,000 first preference votes in the Republic. Kieran Doherty and Paddy Agnew won seats in the Irish Parliament, while Joe McDonnell was defeated by a mere 300 votes.

The OC in the H-Blocks wrote approvingly to Adams, 'we have effected the political change you spoke of'.[15] The Provisionals had made an impression on the politics of the South. The Fianna Fáil government led by Haughey had been narrowly swept from power. Garret Fitzgerald was now forced to lead a minority government in the Dáil, with abstaining TDs in the Maze cast into the parliamentary balance. But still the hunger strikes continued, with no conclusion yet in sight. Early on, an appeal had been made to the European Commission on Human Rights to intervene in the dispute. Subsequently, the Irish Commission for Justice and Peace had tried to intervene. In late July, the International Committee of the Red Cross had likewise attempted to broker a deal. And, of course, the Catholic Church had interceded on numerous occasions. But every effort at mediation had failed to produce a result.

However, the family of Patrick McKeown, on the forty-second day of his strike, then agreed to medical intervention to save the ailing striker's life. This was the second intervention made at a family's behest. The momentum of the death fast was beginning to unwind. It was 20 August. On that same day, Owen Carron was elected to fill the seat that Sands vacated. Buoyed up by this development, the Northern leadership of Sinn Féin could enthuse its rank and file about the advantages which accompanied electoral campaigning. But such enthusiasm would be difficult to sustain in the long term: soon the unprecedented scale of the publicity stirred by the protest in the Maze would be brought to an abrupt conclusion, and the priorities of the Republican movement would be subject to dispute.

But, for the moment, at least this much was clear: the propaganda skills of Sinn Féin had flourished during the hunger strikes. The perspective of the Republican movement gained media attention as never before, and the party's more prominent Northern Ireland members had to engage politically as never before. Indeed, the balance of power within Republicanism shifted decisively to the Belfast leadership as a consequence of the hunger strikes. Ó Brádaigh, for instance, was confined at this time to operating out of the South since an exclusion order banned him from entering the North. Senior Provos in the Irish Republic had been gradually ceding initiative since the middle of the 1970s, but now they were surely losing even the remnants of control.

Public exposure was the most obvious gain secured by Adams and his associates as a result of the dramatic protest staged by Sands and his prison colleagues. At the same time, invaluable experience in public relations and political negotiation was acquired by the Northern cohort, again at the expense of the Southern veterans. Even the expansion of the party base would ultimately be mobilised to benefit the Adams faction: with the decision to embrace electoral politics after 1981, branches of the National H-Block/Armagh Committee were seamlessly absorbed into the Sinn Féin organisation, supplying Adams and his allies with a fund of young and loyal support which would ultimately facilitate the shifts in Republican policy through the middle of the 1980s.

Martin McGuinness, Tom Hartley, Jim Gibney and Danny Morrison operated in support of Gerry Adams. Gradually, 'they got into positions of power and influence' within the wider movement, as Ó Brádaigh was later to describe the situation.[16] Coveted positions in both the party and the Army were marked and finally taken over; there was a move to control publicity within the organisation through the amalgamation of Belfast's *Republican News* with the Southern weekly, *An Phoblacht*.[17] Strategic alliances were fostered right across the movement. Ideologues and politicians were employed to refine the Republican platform: Mitchel McLaughlin, Ted Howell and Richard McAuley were variously committed to political planning and development. But notorious militants would advertise the Provisionals' purity of purpose: senior operators associated with the military campaign were dispatched to assure hardliners that the political wing of the movement was still on message and on board.

Well-placed opponents were patiently won over to endorse controversial new departures, although more usually they were overwhelmed by the dexterity of younger strategists. Alternatively, they were sidelined, and ultimately dropped. Billy McKee, at one time a leading Belfast figure, had already been unceremoniously ousted in 1977, while Seamus Twomey and Jimmy Drumm were gradually co-opted in support of a deliberate policy of political engagement. Since 1975, an effort had been under way among ardent Provisional activists to mobilise durable popular support behind a professionalisation of the guerrilla war. By the end of the decade, that effort was meeting with considerable success. McGuinness, Adams and Ivor Bell were set to politicise the terror. The plan was to combine political progress with a streamlined military operation. But, for that combination to succeed, the fiction of the 'people's army' would have to be reinvigorated: popular disaffection inside the Catholic ghettos would have to be converted into mass political support.[18]

The bid to harness civilian support behind the military campaign had begun in the early autumn of 1975 when the fortunes of the Republican movement were at their lowest ebb. But the purpose behind this strategic shift was not to politicise the leadership of the Republican Army – it was to radicalise the Republican base in its commitment to guerrilla struggle. The idea was that the constituency of passive support behind Provisional militancy could be fired by the same passions which sustained armed insurrection, while the members of active service units inside the IRA could operate in isolation from this community of support: the Army would be protected against British infiltration, while the war could be pursued without Republican demoralisation. On the back of this effective reorganisation of the movement, the Provisionals would be able to sustain a long campaign.[19]

By the end of 1978, the new plan was in full swing: IRA GEARED TO LONG WAR, read the headline of *Republican News* in the second week of December.[20] Provisional operators had been organised into cells instead of battalions; mass allegiance to the Provo cause was being established from the grass roots up; and both military strategy and political planning were increasingly subjected to a tightly managed, centralised control.[21] The idea of a permanent leadership was put into operation to secure the organisation against the loss of purpose and direction which came with fitful changes of the personnel who staffed the upper reaches of Republican command. As a result, the most senior activists inside the movement would be obliged to place themselves above suspicion by shunning direct involvement in operations on the ground. A Revolutionary Council had also been created as a vehicle for Northern radicals to increase their hold on the organisation as they outmanoeuvred both the Southern leadership and the old guard in the North.[22] In this way, both initiative and authority in political planning and military strategy were falling to the ambitious pragmatism of the Adams generation.

The restructuring of the movement had been planned inside the prisons in which key members of this emerging generation of leaders had been interned since the early years of the 1970s. Martin McGuinness had actually been imprisoned in the South on a judicial charge of membership of the Provisional IRA, but Gerry Adams, Brendan Hughes and Ivor Bell had been detained in the prison 'cages' of Long Kesh before the H-Blocks had been built. Various schemes and proposals made their way out of the cages where they had at once fraternised and plotted. Amongst the numerous schemes devised was the plan to establish a Northern Command over the eleven Irish counties which either comprised or directly abutted the primary conflict area of the North. A separate Southern Command would service the Northern war zone with the requisite training, explosives and military equipment to keep the struggle up and running without compromise or interruption.[23]

With the coming of Northern Command and the Revolutionary Council, and with the centralisation of control over military operations; with the tightening up of security and the increase in efficiency generated by the creation of specialist active service units; and with the establishment of a programme of popular politicisation spearheaded by Sinn Féin but still directed by the Army – with this recasting of the structures of the Republican organisation completed by the end of the 1970s, a young cohort of Northern militants were poised to take control and prolong the movement's capacity to endure a protracted war. By 1979, Adams was Vice-President of Provisional Sinn Féin, while McGuinness is alleged to have climbed to the position of Chief of Staff.[24] Both of them had yet to reach their mid-thirties. By the time they did, in the autumn of 1983, their ascendancy over the movement looked virtually unassailable: McGuinness was by this point Vice-President of Sinn Féin and Adams had been elected into the presidency itself.

But over the course of the next three years under the Adams leadership of Sinn Féin, tensions grew apparent in the Republican organisation over the extent to which party politics were in conflict with armed struggle. Between 1983 and 1985, that conflict came to a head within the exclusive inner recess of Republican decision-making: Sinn Féin's ongoing involvement in electoral campaigning had polarised opinion on the IRA's Army Council, and among members of the Army's Executive as well.[25] That battle ended quietly with the fall of Ivor Bell, who is reputed to have succeeded Martin McGuinness as Chief of Staff, and to have held on to his tenure from 1982 until a period of imprisonment in 1983 obliged him to relinquish the top military command. The denouement came in 1985. Thereafter, Adams and McGuinness reclaimed their hold on the organisation. A potentially disastrous battle inside the Republican inner council had been decisively surmounted without a public show of struggle.

But then in 1986, an open collision seemed inevitable: a resolution to abandon the Sinn Féin policy of abstention had been placed on the agenda of the annual Ard Fheis, scheduled for the beginning of November. The resolution was designed to boost the fortunes of Sinn Féin in its struggle to win over the electorate of the South without prejudice to the principle of abstaining from Westminster and refusing to participate in any parliament in Northern Ireland. If the motion succeeded, Republicanism in the South of Ireland would remain a revolutionary movement, but the revolution would be represented by a constitutional party.[26]

An IRA convention, assembled around September, had already given the go-ahead for a major change in direction.[27] At the same time, news of the importation of over 100 tons of weaponry, supplied to the IRA by Libya's Muammar Qaddafi, was spread among party waverers during the run-up to the conference to allay incipient fears of an impending sell-out of the movement: swayed by a raft of rumours about this sudden new capacity to wage a massive offensive against the British occupation, potential doubters were won over to the swelling band of supporters prepared to countenance an historic shift in the politics of the Republican movement.

Such a major change in policy required a clear two-thirds majority in favour of the motion: a serious division within the ranks of the Republican movement, or a humiliating defeat for the leadership of Sinn Féin, were both definite, if diminishing, possibilities. But, in the end, the motion was carried. It was McGuinness who rallied the delegates to the necessity for a change: 'We are not at war with the government of the twenty-six counties – the reality of this fact must be recognised by us all,' he simply stated. He then insisted: 'By ignoring this reality, we remain alone and isolated on the high altar of abstentionism, divorced from the people and easily dealt with by those who wish to defeat us.'[28]

The partnership between 'the Armalite and ballot box' had emerged victorious. However, back in the summer of 1981, after the election of Bobby Sands to the Westminster House of Commons, Republicans had been confronted with the necessity of choosing between significantly divergent options. They could revert to their original policy of developing the alliance between popular radicalism and guerrilla warfare which had been nurtured in the aftermath of 1975. In that case, electoralism could still be drawn upon as a strategic form of intervention without subjecting the Republican movement to constant pressure from constituency opinion. Alternatively, they could embrace electoral politics as the settled policy of the party and permanently expose themselves to the mixed blessings of publicity. As it turned out, they chose publicity. But now, in 1986, they chose to mix insurgency with constitutionalism as well.

Gerry Adams would later comment on the dynamics of the Provisional onslaught prior to 1981: 'Our struggle, faced with the armed forces of the imperial power, had limited itself for long periods to an almost exclusively military perspective and failed to build a political alternative.'[29] After 1981, that 'alternative' had brought Republicans to submit themselves to elections as an adjunct to the terror tactics of the military campaign. But by 1986, in the South of Ireland, the new commitment to electoral politics had transformed Sinn Féin into a virtually constitutional organisation. How would this transformation affect the expectation of a military victory which still guided strategic planning inside the Provisional IRA? In the Republican and journalistic parlance of the time, the Provisionals had begun to go 'political'. But how would Sinn Féin's progress in the ambit of constitutionalism affect the military conduct of the war?

2

Fourteen years earlier, the reverse question was being posed, as speculation focused on how the militancy of the Provisionals might be restrained by subjecting their organisation to the pressure of public opinion exercised from inside the Catholic community. At a private meeting with the United Kingdom representative in Northern Ireland on 11 April 1972, members of the Social and Democratic Labour Party were endeavouring to impress upon an anxious British official the extent to which they were engaged 'in a struggle with the IRA', and insisting that the Westminster government 'should help [them] in this struggle'.[30] That would involve the British government assisting them in the competition for Catholic support by depriving Republican insurgents of their ultimate resource – namely, passive endorsement within the nationalist community of the IRA's self-presentation as the final line of defence against the threat from hostile elements in this corner of the United Kingdom.

Two months later, in discussions with William Whitelaw, the new Secretary of State for Northern Ireland, John Hume and Paddy Devlin were setting out their stall in a more purposeful and forthright fashion: 'the Provisionals would not respond to pleas or argument,' they both contended; instead, 'they needed to be exposed to political pressures'. A first step in that direction would be the ending of internment: then the pressure to end the violence 'would be irresistible'.[31] Within a month, the British government was already considering this proposal, weighing up the merits of judicially based detention as an alternative to arbitrary internment without trial.[32] It took another three gruesome years before this proposal became actual policy, and by then a Labour government had succeeded the Conservatives. But in the meantime, a more significant constitutional initiative was being drafted in an effort to placate political passions in Northern Ireland.

A major drive towards constitutional reform in Northern Ireland was being actively debated inside the British Cabinet in the early months of 1972. 'The Roman Catholic minority had now become totally alienated,' reported the Home Secretary, Reginald Maudling, on 2 March: the need for a comprehensive political reassessment seemed by this stage to be perfectly obvious.[33] A month earlier, only a matter of days after Bloody Sunday, Edward Heath had already indicated what such a reassessment might entail: 'it might be possible,' he informed his colleagues, 'to reach an acceptable solution on the basis of ensuring the minority community an active, permanent and guaranteed role in government.'[34] In fact, this idea had first been mooted in the autumn of 1971 when the full consequences of internment still looked uncertain to 10 Downing Street.[35] But, for the moment, it was some distance from being adopted as an immediate objective. However, as violence in Northern Ireland spiralled to abysmal depths as 1972 progressed, the establishment of cross-community, representative institutions came into focus as the British government's preferred policy for the Province.

'It had been found possible elsewhere, for example in the Lebanon, to devise an acceptable method of allocating government responsibilities between representatives of different religious groupings,' Heath was suggestively reflecting before his Cabinet colleagues early in 1972.[36] But, in just over a year, there were more definite plans which enjoyed a full measure of government support and a degree of forward momentum: by March 1973 the attempt to move the constitutional parties in Northern Ireland towards a resolution of the Ulster crisis was being vigorously pursued under the stewardship of William Whitelaw who by this stage had been acting as Secretary of State for almost a year. In preparation for the negotiations which aimed at reaching an accommodation between what were generally presumed to be the mainstream representatives of Northern nationalism and Unionism, a border poll was held on 8 March to determine the actual status of the political unit up for discussion.

The result was decisive. With the nationalist population abstaining from the vote, 57 per cent of the electorate in Northern Ireland opted to remain within the United Kingdom. On the day of the poll, the Provisionals responded with a series of car bombs in the British capital, miraculously claiming only one civilian life but still injuring a further 180 individuals when the devices which had been deposited at Great Scotland Yard and the Old Bailey detonated in the afternoon. Whitelaw, and the British Cabinet, remained undeterred. However, the Provisionals were gradually discomfited by developments as the movement towards an agreement from which they would be excluded began to gain momentum.

On 20 March, a White Paper on the future government of Northern Ireland was published as an indication of the remit for negotiations. Over the course of the months that followed, as more progress was being made in coaxing nationalists and unionists to take their place around the negotiating table, the Provisionals became increasingly disoriented and alarmed. At one point, they considered contesting elections in Northern Ireland, but rapidly rejected that course.[37] Instead, they mounted bomb attacks and planted incendiaries on the mainland of Great Britain, and launched devastating offensives throughout the North. But still they could not credibly feel that they were directing the course of events: discussions were proceeding towards a constitutional settlement for Northern Ireland while Republicans battled furiously on the margins of the debate.

A year earlier, things had looked very different. With the collapse of the Stormont government in March 1972, the Provisional IRA thought it was in the vanguard of developments.[38] In fact, the signs had seemed propitious throughout this period more generally: outrage after Bloody Sunday induced a flood of volunteers to join up with the Provisional IRA; a ceasefire by the Officials left the control of the Catholic ghettos more firmly in the hands of the

Provisionals; and a hunger strike in Belfast prison, led by Billy McKee, ended with 'Political Status' being granted to the internees.[39] In the same year, a Libyan connection for arms procurement had been established by Brian Keenan, and the car bomb had been invented on the initiative of Seamus Twomey. On 20 March, a vehicle exploded on Lower Donegall Street in Belfast, killing six civilians. On 14 April, a further twenty-six explosions created mayhem across the Province. Then, at the end of June, the Provisionals announced a ceasefire, which was to last for just two weeks. But even with this briefest of interludes in hostilities, the IRA had come close to negotiations with the British government: by the end of the first week in July, an IRA delegation had arrived in London for discussions with the Secretary of State for Northern Ireland.

But the talks were a 'non-event', as Whitelaw was later to summarise his reaction. The Provisionals, by all accounts, agreed.[40] However, the preliminary negotiations between the British government and the Northern Ireland constitutional parties which were getting under way in March 1973 held out an altogether more promising possibility of success. Without the prospect of inheriting more political leverage on the horizon, while the Provisionals could increase both their ferocity and brutality, they could not actually increase their overall advantage. As a result, beneath the ruthless determination of the military campaign there was political hesitation among the leadership of the movement.

The attitude of the Southern government was a further setback. Over the course of the past three years, the position of the government in the Republic of Ireland had progressively hardened. In August 1970, Jack Lynch had written to the British Prime Minister about the need for 'Right-wing Unionists' to find 'their proper place in the Irish nation'.[41] In September of the following year, the Taoiseach still had no compunction about informing Edward Heath of his opinion that both 'the settlement of 1920 and the Border were invalid'. He could not even 'recognise' Brian Faulkner as possessing any 'authority' over 'the people of Northern

Ireland'.[42] Up until January 1972, he had also been optimistic about the prospects for some kind of agreement which might emerge when the Provisionals had been significantly weakened in Belfast while the Protestant community was still awed by the threat of Republican violence.[43] But by 31 July 1972 Lynch's patience had run out: by this stage, 'he could not care less' about 'Irish reunification', as he informed the British Ambassador in Dublin.[44]

And so, by 1973, with the Irish government's tacit indulgence of the basic tenets of Republican thinking effectively at an end, and with the likelihood of an agreement between the SDLP and the Ulster Unionists beginning to look more certain, the Provisionals began to grow nervous about the long term prospects for their struggle. But despite this underlying anxiety, Republicans continued to utter their defiance. Between the border poll of 8 March 1973 and the British government White Paper which was to appear in a couple of weeks, an article in *Republican News* could still presume to emphasise the unassailable strength of the IRA position: 'it will be recalled that there is one sort of fight which the British Army has never won – when it is ordered into a war of attrition against a hostile population'.[45]

At a Cabinet meeting back in March 1972, the British Home Secretary, Reginald Maudling, had displayed his appreciation of precisely this political reality: while it was reasonable to hope for British Army successes in disrupting the activities of the Provisional IRA, it 'would never be possible by military means alone . . . completely to root out urban guerrilla warfare so long as a substantial element of the population remained alienated from the forces of law and order'.[46] But with the movement towards some kind of political agreement in Northern Ireland advancing through 1973, there was the definite possibility that nationalist alienation might ultimately be redeemed. At that stage, the IRA's dependence upon 'a hostile population' whose antipathy to the status quo could be bought off with an offer of political concessions from the British government would expose the Republican movement to the possibility of defeat.

By the end of 1975, that possibility had come to look more like a probability.[47] Although the plan to establish a power-sharing government in Northern Ireland lay in tatters since the collapse of the Sunningdale Agreement in 1974, the Provisionals still gave the impression of being politically irreconcilable. A ceasefire called at the end of 1974 had developed into a bilateral truce between the British and the IRA early in 1975. But the truce had petered out by September of that year, although its official end was not declared until the start of 1976. The aim of the truce from a British perspective had been to 'educate' the Provisionals into appreciating that a programme of political 'disengagement' would be a long-drawn-out and sensitive affair: there was never any desire to effect an immediate withdrawal.[48] However, members of the Provisional leadership had been rather more expectant, although by the middle of 1976 their expectancy looked rash: their hopes for a united Ireland were undiminished, yet their chances of achieving this seemed more remote than ever.

Billy McKee was ruined by his handling of the truce, while David O'Connell and Ruairí Ó Brádaigh were severely compromised. Not only had Republicans secured no meaningful advance, but the setbacks the movement had evidently endured exposed the leadership's insistence that some degree of progress had in fact been made. Throughout 1975, elements in the Provisionals continued to engage in violence, much of it explicitly sectarian in nature. Late in 1974, the Official IRA had itself divided, leading to the creation of the Irish Republican Socialist Party, with the Irish National Liberation Army as its military complement. A feud between the Provisionals and the INLA ensued. In due course, both factions were being pressed by the pacific demands of a new Peace Movement: on account of its continuing militancy, and its apparent political bankruptcy, republicanism was being radically and effectively demonised.[49]

After the bloody carnage wrought by the Provisionals in 1974, including bomb attacks against civilian targets in London, Manchester and Birmingham, the reputation of Republicanism was not going to be hard to shatter outside the pockets of IRA support in Belfast, South Armagh, Tyrone and Derry. But the vilification of the Provos received an additional boost from British policy. In July 1974, the first Secretary of State for Northern Ireland under the second Wilson government, Merlyn Rees, announced to the House of Commons his intention to embark upon the phasing out of internment. At the same time, he was keen to bring an end to the 'special category' status which had been introduced by Whitelaw as a concession to republican prisoners. With the publication of the Gardiner Report on prisons policy in Northern Ireland on 30 January 1975, Rees got independent backing for his plans. Accordingly, from 1 March 1976, 'political status' was to be terminated: henceforth, republicans convicted of terrorist offences would be categorised demeaningly as 'common criminals'.[50]

During Rees' term of office, security policy was also reconstructed. The presence of the British Army was to be reduced in Northern Ireland as their duties were assumed by the local forces of the Royal Ulster Constabulary and the Ulster Defence Regiment. Counter-insurgency was to be handled by the SAS and the intelligence services. British efforts would thus concentrate on the prosecution of a 'dirty war' while the security services of Ulster would bear the brunt of the front-line conflict: the open engagement of the IRA had been effectively 'Ulsterised'.[51] But while 'Ulsterisation' and 'Criminalisation' were an affront to both the tactics and the esteem of the IRA, Republicans were not slow to mount their own response. The Provisional counter-offensive likewise had two elements: the 'professionalisation' of the military struggle and the 'politicisation' of the Catholic ghettos.

Three months after the concession of 'political status' had been withdrawn, Richard McAuley gave his assessment of the British government's design: 'it is imperative for the British that the political nature of this struggle be played down'.[52] McAuley was later to operate as press secretary to Gerry Adams, but at this point he was writing from the compounds of Long Kesh. Nonetheless, even then his message was neatly crafted: since the British were now anxious to criminalise Republicans, Republicans should learn to emphasise 'the political nature of this struggle'. But whilst reclaiming the mantle of politics was essential for the purposes of Provisional propaganda, it was also the case, in McAuley's eyes, that popular politicisation was the only effective means of combating the purpose behind the policy of 'Ulsterisation'.

'What does Ulsterisation mean?' McAuley asked in *Republican News* the following December. He then answered his own question: 'It is a term borrowed from the American involvement in Vietnam.' But the aim of Ulsterisation was equally based on American precedent: 'Vietnamisation ... entailed the bolstering up of the Saigon administration through using locally recruited forces.'[53] So also in Northern Ireland: the British were keen to isolate Republicans as criminals whilst stabilising the security and politics of Northern Ireland. This was a standard colonial 'method' of defusing militant struggle, claimed an article in *Republican News* in 1977: it was 'used by the Brits in places like Kenya, Aden, Palestine, Cyprus, Malaya, and [in] other colonial wars'.[54] But it was the insurgents' response to the counter-insurgency strategy of the British that would be decisive: by reconstituting the IRA as a professionalised guerrilla outfit comparatively secure against infiltration, and by politicising the constituencies which had spawned Provisional militancy between 1969 and 1972, the radical opponents of the 1975 truce aimed to rejuvenate Republicanism as a revolutionary movement which would ultimately prevail against the pacification and containment that 'Ulsterisation' and 'Criminalisation' had originally been intended to effect.[55]

The main impetus behind a programme of political rejuvenation came from inside the prison communities, with Gerry Adams prominent among the principal exponents of change. Already in November of 1975, Adams was loudly advocating 'a complete fusing of military and political strategy'.[56] But this fusion would be a subtle and incremental business. Provisional activists would be separated from their old battalion areas, hived off in their capacity as guerrilla operatives from the communities from which they had originally emerged, while the localities themselves would be deliberately transformed into pockets of political resistance: the resistance would be co-ordinated by Provisional Sinn Féin, while Sinn Féin would be directed by former guerrilla activists who were to be elevated to the leadership of the Provisional IRA.

In this way, the Provos' active service units would aim to steal a march on the information networks established by British intelligence, while Republican areas would be radicalised through orchestrated encounters between the local population and the forces of law and order. Adams put his finger on the inevitable result: when the security forces had occasion to move into an area, they would not be able to identify specific perpetrators of violence but would instead be forced to deal with 'an aggressive Republican or People's resistance structure'. Once drawn into such a conflict, 'the Brit must remove everyone connected, from school children to customers in the co-ops, from paper-sellers to street committees'.[57]

Soon the editor of *Republican News*, Danny Morrison, was elaborating on the position: 'IRA Battalion areas are the ideal structures upon which street political units could be organised. They are existing identities which people associate with, and roping together the many street committees, tenants associations, action groups, bands, cumainn [party branches] etc., they could take over effective governmental control.'[58] The idea here was to promote a programme of 'active abstentionism' within each Catholic area with a decent measure of Republican support – to carve out districts of opposition with their own executive controls, and so effectively to establish autonomous popular enclaves with alternative government structures inside the Northern war zone. The original Sinn Féin policy, pioneered by Arthur Griffith, of practically seceding from an 'illegitimate' sovereignty was to be adapted to the political circumstances of the North.

But this was Griffith with a difference, as Adams in particular understood. Not only would the precincts of Provisional resistance make up a discontinuous patchwork of liberated quarters – Griffith had set his sights on a singular unit of secession – but each discontinuous district would be dragooned into supporting the militant forces of armed struggle: 'I'm not advocating a diversion from the war effort,' as Adams had already clarified in October 1975. 'Far from it! I'm advocating an extension of it plus an implementation policy.'[59] The Adams 'implementation policy' as it was conceptualised in the mid-1970s would ultimately fail: it was diverted, and then overtaken, by the politics of Sinn Féin as the party sought expansion through the middle of the 1980s. Nonetheless, the original conception had been vitally important, if only because it galvanised the political energies of the younger militants. The success of Gerry Adams, Ivor Bell and Brendan Hughes, and the consequent longevity of the Provisional IRA, resulted from the perception that some kind of durable 'policy' had become absolutely necessary if Republicanism was to survive.

A new initiative had become urgent on account of British Army advances. The initiative was to comprise an alternative administration which would be built up from inside the Catholic ghettos, replete with 'People's Councils' and 'People's Courts'. 'The people must have a rallying point,' Adams had declared in the autumn of 1975: the ghost of the Irish Republic of January 1919 was not sufficient to harness popular support behind the modern struggle. Consequently, the appeal of the IRA would have to be based upon the 'understandings and needs . . . of the ordinary Irish people, the people of no property'.[60] Some time later, Adams expanded on the idea: 'We must undermine support for the enemy and we must counter him by emerging ourselves with the people.'[61] But the fact is that this emergence would in effect be a re-emergence since it was British Army incursions into the Northern nationalist ghettos in the summer of 1972 which forced the IRA to retreat from its strongholds in the cities.

With the British now established in the former 'no go areas' of Belfast and Derry, the Provisionals were forced on to the defensive, with successful operations after July 1972 usually being launched from the rural IRA fastnesses in Tyrone and South Armagh.[62] The bombing campaign in London distracted attention from the new reality: by 1973 there was drift in the Republican movement. Then came a conspicuous decline: first a spate of loyalist assassinations which terrorised the Catholic community, next the truce of 1975 which polarised IRA strategists, and finally the internecine struggle among an array of republican factions, sapped the morale of nationalists in the ghettoes. The Provisionals desperately needed a substantial political presence if they were to rally the flagging fortunes of the IRA.

Ironically, the Provisionals' first significant political presence in Northern Ireland arrived with the establishment of truce incident centres to monitor the progress of the 1975 ceasefire. Soon, in the words of Tom Hartley, these had 'developed as we had foreseen into complaint centres and political advice centres'.[63] Other tokens of Republican power, as Adams himself had again realised, already included 'people's taxis . . . Social Clubs . . . welfare committees . . . refugee groups . . . and local policing'. The incident centres consolidated this nascent political presence. Next, the expansion of the Republican base to include more ambitious projects like People's Councils and People's Courts would enable the IRA to fashion a 'mini-Republic' in the midst of British Ulster – 'in effect the Republican alternative to the Brit war machine'.[64]

However, the reality of the situation in 1976 was that the existing Republican war machine was in a pretty parlous condition. Up until the summer of 1972, it was British policy that nourished the growth of the Provisional campaign. More specifically, it was nourished by the absence of any concerted political programme which could guide the British military intervention. Way back in August 1969, the British Foreign Secretary, Michael Stewart, had noted at a Cabinet meeting that the Prime Minister of Northern Ireland 'had spoken of a more broadly-based administration'. Indeed he had – just after the August riots, on Sunday the 17th. Two days later, Stewart had counselled his colleagues: Chichester-Clark 'should be asked what he meant by this'.[65] He certainly should have been. But the matter slipped, short term priorities intervened, and it was another three years before the establishment of a 'broadly-based administration' became an overriding priority for the British government.

In the meantime, it was not so much the existence of an alternative approach as the difficulty of discerning any overarching approach that was noted by British forces on the ground in Northern Ireland. As late as December 1971, the man at the forefront of British counter-insurgency operations, Brigadier Frank Kitson, could plead in a secret memorandum composed for the British government that 'it is necessary for us to receive some direction beyond the immediate mission of destroying the IRA'. The problems in the Belfast area were most acute, on Kitson's reckoning: 'we are handicapped by lack of government policy relating to the way in which the community in Belfast should develop'.[66] But it was not until the middle of 1972 that temporising measures on the part of the British government were replaced by a programme of deliberate political action.

After the new Tory administration had come to power in the summer of 1970, advice from the Cabinet Secretary, Burke Trend, to the British Chiefs of Staff had pointed to the difficulties involved in deciding to 'wash our hands of the whole business'. Short of recourse to such drastic action, perhaps it was necessary to 'accept that we are now in effect back in 1920; that the settlement enshrined in the Act of that year has broken down; and that we must start again . . . something like a Round Table Conference would be unavoidable'. But a Conference including the constitutional parties in Northern Ireland, together with the government of the Republic, remained in abeyance until 1973. Trend was left remarking: 'nobody has yet succeeded in devising a convincing new political approach to the basic problem'.[67]

The three-year hiatus in developing a policy of constitutional reform in Northern Ireland saw the desperate counsels of the Provisionals prosper amongst those sections of the nationalist opposition with least to lose from the deepening crisis: militancy filled the vacuum left by political inaction. But then came Bloody Friday, 21 July 1972. Twenty-six bombs were exploded by the

Provisional IRA around Belfast in the afternoon. The warnings had been inadequate, and the death toll was correspondingly high. One device ripped through the Oxford Street bus station, another was detonated in north Belfast, while the bulk of the explosions devastated the heart of the city centre. The operation slaughtered a total of seven civilians and two soldiers, while it mutilated scores.[68] Ten days later, the British Army launched Operation Motorman to impose its own control on the 'no go areas' of Belfast and Derry.[69] The Provisionals were from then on seriously curtailed in their urban strongholds: watch-towers and army forts were constructed in the city enclaves out of which Republicans had previously operated.

Operation Motorman and its aftermath amounted to a major setback for the Provisional IRA. Ivor Bell, Brendan Hughes and Gerry Adams naturally knew this. Adams would in the end concede as much: 'And what of '69? What hurt the Brits most? Not the first few nights of violence but the danger [to] their interests when huge sections of people withdrew from the system into their own system . . . Didn't government exist behind the barricades?' But the barricade days of 1969–72 were now over, as Adams knew. Both the spirit and the infrastructure of orchestrated resistance would have to be rebuilt if militant Republicanism was to stay in business. 'What of '71 and '72, when the people withdrew even further?' Adams continued: 'The only practical Governments were those in the liberated areas . . . "People's Government".'[70] But by 1976, after Operation Motorman and the bilateral truce had shaken the Provisionals' resources, and after both Republican feuding and the loyalist campaign of terror had weakened the IRA's support, 'People's Government' was rather an aspiration than an established fact in the Catholic ghettos. Disorganised and dispirited after a series of decisive blows, the Provisional Republican movement would have to be rescued from defeat.

3

But if popular politicisation was to be a significant component of the rescue plan designed by the Northern cohort around Adams, how would a 'People's Government' which could embody these popular forces be made tangibly to operate in the face of a British occupation? On 26 June 1972, a leaflet issued by the Second Battalion of the Provisional IRA appeared in Ballymurphy: 'We claim the traditional allegiance of the Irish people,' it announced. The flyer concluded: 'We are the Provisionals, Provisional until, subject to revision, the Irish people can decide who is to become their final representative.'[71] Was Adams' new 'People's Government', proposed in 1975, to be distinct in its essentials from the military representation on offer to Ballymurphy civilians in 1972?

He certainly said it was. The representation proposed by Adams was described in endless detail as a move beyond the militarism which had so far dominated Republican thinking. 'England is at war with the I.R.A. and thus with the Irish people,' Adams declared in January 1976.[72] But in what sense could the IRA be made to represent these people? How could the Provisionals make good their claim to constitute the embodiment of the Irish population? The answer was simple: the gap between the Republican army and the civilian population was to be narrowed using the mechanisms of politicisation and control. In 1986, Adams coined a term for the Provisional plan of action: 'republicanisation'.[73] First the Catholics in the North, and then increasing numbers in the South, would be subject to this process of republicanisation.

But that process had begun less with the politics of the street – less with a local democracy ascending through tenants' associations and local councils, reaching an apex of representation in the people's assemblies of the North, as Adams and his associates had expected – than with the escalating impact of the protests in the prisons. The blanket protest beginning in 1976, then the dirty protest continuing into 1980, and the original hunger strike of October 1980 conspired to broaden the mood of sympathy with both the plight and the motivation of Republican insurgents. It was in this context that the Relatives' Action Committees, and thereafter the National H-Block/Armagh Committee, began to liaise with activists in Provisional Sinn Féin. But it was the hunger strikes in the Maze in 1981 which represented the first significant step towards substantial 'republicanisation'. Adams was keenly focused in his assessment of the implications: 'Identification with the IRA increased very significantly.'[74]

This sentence captures the train of Republican thinking down to 1986, and indeed beyond that date. Neither popular protest nor electoral politics was developed as an alternative to Republican goals or methods. The progress of politicisation as such did not defuse the movement's fundamentalism.[75] Neither the IRA cease-fire of August 1994 nor the acceptance of the Good Friday Agreement in 1998 bore witness to an inevitable development intrinsic to Republican politics. On the contrary: republicanisation aimed to create a nationalist consensus in its own image. The point is that this venture failed. The campaign of the Provisionals was inadvertently trumped by the encounter between its principles and the requirements of its survival.

The requirements of survival brought the movement into an alliance with the forces of constitutional nationalism on the island of Ireland. The plan had been to build on the momentum of 1981: to infuse Irish constitutionalism with republicanising zeal. The hunger strikes were a climax, not because they signalled a con-version, but because they embroiled Republican politics in a larger political process which neither Sinn Féin nor the IRA could effectively control.[76] In the same way, the ending of abstentionism in 1986 was part of a long term strategy to infiltrate the South, not the outcome of steady progress towards the Grail of compromise. Brutalised and radicalised by fifteen years of struggle, the Provisionals were desperate to ensure that they could win, but winning entailed expanding, and the cultivation of a broader front. That ambition was perfectly evident in 1976. But a decade later, immersion in the processes of broad front politics and electoralism had started to produce the very opposite result from the one which had been intended by the decision to go 'political'.[77]

Of course, the objectives of the Provisionals had always been 'political'. Their politics, moreover, had from the start been ideological: they were committed to a doctrine of democratic fundamentalism.[78] The chief antagonist of this commitment was a rival democratic populism, identified with the Ulster majority and the Protestant preference for the British Union.[79] But the motivation behind the ambition of Sinn Féin and the IRA to destroy the existing Protestant democracy in Northern Ireland did not derive from a simple attitude of unadulterated prejudice, nor from sheer sectarian hate. Republican determination was not fuelled only by blind hostility, nor inspired by the welling up of religious fervour. Equally, the Provisionals were not spurred on by disguised religiosity, exemplified by the martyrdom of Bobby Sands or Patrick Pearse.[80] Instead, the war was driven, on the Republican side, by politically focused hatred which targeted the Ulster majority through Britain's defence of their regime.

The existence of this focus was obvious from the start: the Provisionals did not seek redress for injustices within Northern Ireland; instead they sought to undermine the foundations of the regime. In other words, it was not the *character* of the regime as such that provoked the IRA to take the actions which it took, but the democratic make-up of the polity itself.[81] Joe Cahill's response to the emergence of the Civil Rights movement in the late 1960s exemplifies the train of Provisional speculation. He had a 'theory', as he would later put it, that 'you cannot have civil rights without national rights'.[82] This meant that Republicans would have to concentrate their efforts on challenging the foundations of the Northern Ireland state, and not merely on reforming a majoritarian regime.

Indeed, this was exactly the position that the Provisional leadership had publicised after the prorogation of Stormont back in 1972: 'We hold,' declared *Republican News* in the autumn of that year, 'it is impossible to create democracy within a basically undemocratic state.'[83] But even earlier, just as the 1960s were coming to a close, this was already the basic principle that guided the strategic thinking shared by those Republicans who would soon inaugurate the Provisionals: democracy in Northern Ireland required a union with the South, while the disestablishment of the existing Union between Great Britain and Northern Ireland would depend on the resurgence of a military campaign.[84]

As far back as the spring of 1969, military preparations were effectively under way to provoke a confrontation between the Catholic population and the forces of law and order which secured the existence of Northern Ireland. At this time, auxiliary guerrilla units were being established throughout Belfast by dissident Republicans like Joe Cahill and Jimmy Steele without the knowledge of the Southern leadership of the Irish Republican Army.[85] Events were soon to favour the militant posture of the Belfast dissidents: beginning in the late summer of 1969, deteriorating relations between Roman Catholics and their Protestant neighbours, succeeded by the severity of British military operations conducted in the absence of a long term government plan of action, devastated the nationalist impetus to aim for a *rapprochement*: the August violence, the Ballymurphy riots, the Falls curfew, internment without trial, and Bloody Sunday, together served to bolster the credibility of the Provisionals.[86]

But, as we have seen, by 1972 the luck of militant Republicanism had started to run out, and by 1976 the movement was in the doldrums. The skill of Gerry Adams and Martin McGuinness in resuscitating the Provisionals in the aftermath of the mid-1970s lay in their refusal simply to trust in the basic righteousness of their cause: the cause would have to be serviced by a Republican campaign. But this shift did not hail the advent of Provisional politics. Rather, it signalled the intention to sustain a war machine with the assistance of political co-ordination: it marked the comprehensive fusion of military and political strategy. That fusion included harnessing the vicissitudes of popular passions. It embraced popular protests, prison protests, proselytism and electoralism, although the People's Councils perished at the moment of their inception: with the British Army 'sitting on the doorsteps of the people', it soon became pretty obvious, as Jim Gibney later reflected, that '1977 was not 1919'.[87] But the new programme also included a further essential component: it embraced the ambition to intervene in the politics of the South.

In reporting the contributions to a prison 'conference' staged in cage 11 in September 1976, Adams presented Brendan Hughes as advocating the inauguration of a new campaign in the Republic: he 'proposed that Sinn Féin organise a massive agitation campaign in the Free State and that they affiliate themselves with all anti-state groups'.[88] Adams himself had already advertised his own optimism about the prospect of a steady Sinn Féin advance. The previous May, he had offered the view that Liam Cosgrave, then head of a Southern coalition government, was 'creating a vacuum which only we can fill. He has surrendered the Republican platform to the Republican Movement.' That surrender was the occasion for Sinn Féin infiltration: it created the opportunity to instil Republican values, starting from the 'grassroots' up: 'If the people of the North are not to be let down, Republicans living in the Free State must involve themselves in arousing the national consciousness of our people in that part of our country.'[89]

Within two years, by the time that Gerry Adams and Danny Morrison were preparing the annual Bodenstown Oration to be delivered by Jimmy Drumm in the spring of 1977, the Sinn Féin commitment to the development of broad front politics beyond the pale of Ulster had been elevated to the top of the Republican agenda. The war could not be won in the North alone, Drumm was to insist: 'Hatred and resentment of this [British] army cannot sustain this war.' Republicans had no choice but to turn their attention to the South: 'we need a positive tie in with the mass of the Irish people'.[90] But by 1978, Morrison was aware that any progress in the South would be an arduous and protracted business. The population of the Twenty-Six Counties was less prone to 'republicanisation' than the nationalist population of the North.[91]

The 'low level of political agitation in the 26-counties must be breached', declared the Provisional Army Council at the start of 1978.[92] But Danny Morrison's apprehension was soon to be confirmed: the high-point of Republican electoral success, coming on the back of the 1981 hunger strikes, was rapidly followed by a slump in Sinn Féin's fortunes in the Southern general election of 1982. In that year, Morrison, Hartley, McGuinness, McAuley, Joe Austin and Gerry Adams decided that the policy of abstention would have to go: it was a clog on the attempt to build 'across the island as a whole'.[93] But by the time it went, in November 1986, a new breakthrough in the relations between the Irish Republic and the United Kingdom had already begun to unsettle the calculations of Sinn Féin. While the Provisionals were desperate to make headway in the South, the government of the Republic was negotiating with its British counterpart to broker an agreement that would foil Sinn Féin's ambition to 'republicanise' the electorate in the South.

These negotiations triumphed in 1985: in November of that year, the British and Irish governments signed up to the Anglo-Irish Agreement. It was a watershed for Sinn Féin and the IRA. Despite the continuing stream of Republican violence in Northern Ireland, despite the bombing of Harrods in December 1983, and despite the attempt to annihilate the British Cabinet in Brighton in October 1984, the representatives of the British and Irish administrations had established a common position from which to approach the Ulster crisis. The impact of this diplomacy would prove decisive for Sinn Féin: during the aftermath of the Agreement there was major political debate among senior members of the Republican movement in an attempt to gauge the options remaining open to the Provisionals.[94]

The accord of 1985 had conceded a new role to the Irish government: Dublin was to be consulted for its opinion on political matters affecting the situation in Northern Ireland. The concession was a clear advance on the part of constitutional nationalism, secured through a major effort at conventional negotiation. But, at

the same time, the Southern establishment had officially surrendered the Republican principle that the North was by right a
component of an island-wide jurisdiction. From the perspective of
the Provisionals, while the British had moved forward in truckling
to nationalist sentiment, the Irish government had retreated in
accommodating unionist principle: they had accepted the right of
the majority of the citizens of Northern Ireland to determine the
jurisdictional status of the six-county political unit. Sinn Féin had
sought to radicalise republican sentiment in the South, but the
government of the Republic had effectively scuppered its advance.

After the Anglo-Irish Agreement, the Provisionals sought to
combine ongoing military operations with the attempt to forge
alliances with nationalist opinion throughout Ireland: it was a far
cry from the proposal which had been advanced by Brendan
Hughes that Republicans should team up with 'anti-state groups'
across the island. However, in treating with the forces of
constitutional nationalism in Ireland, Sinn Féin would not be
dealing from a dominant position.

Between 1985 and 1990, the Provisionals were holding discussions with the nationalist leaderships, North and South: openly
with the Social and Democratic Labour Party, secretly with the
Irish government. The party was also in secret talks with the
British government under Margaret Thatcher. In the midst of these
first gestures towards a diplomatic encounter came the Enniskillen
bombing of 1987, attracting a deluge of adverse publicity for Sinn
Féin and the IRA. But soon the long term thrust behind IRA
strategy would become clear. Sinn Féin would aim to bring the
twenty-year-old conflict to a close with the greatest benefit to
Republicans short of fulfilling their final objective: by the end of
the 1980s, it was being acknowledged among leading figures inside
the Provisional movement that the war was beginning to enter into
its final phase.[95]

In abandoning its commitment to an indefinite resort to war, the
Provisional leadership was aware that it would not achieve a
Republican peace. Nonetheless, they would press for the most

advantageous terms available. In an interview with Mary Holland recorded for *Weekend World* back in 1974, David O'Connell had called on the British 'to simply state that they have no interest'.[96] He received no definite reply. However, sixteen years later, on 9 November 1990, the Secretary of State for Northern Ireland, Peter Brooke, declared publicly that his government had 'no selfish strategic or economic interest' in Northern Ireland.[97] This did not amount to the announcement of an intention to withdraw, as Republicans had demanded since the beginning of the 1970s, but it did show a preparedness to negotiate with Sinn Féin. Within two years, the Provisionals were subtly acknowledging a basic willingness to comply.[98]

Accordingly, between 1992 and 1998, the focus of the Republican leadership was to ensure its participation in negotiations for a settlement of Northern Ireland, to maximise its advantage when the talks got under way, and to avoid any major divisions when the size of the compromise became obvious. Each of these three purposes was secured through military action: a series of major explosions in London — at the Baltic Exchange in April 1992, at Bishopsgate in 1993, at Canary Wharf in February 1996 — applied the appropriate pressure at the appropriate time. But that pressure did not deliver the final Republican goal of terminating the partition of the island of Ireland.

Mounting the podium to address a Sinn Féin conference specially convened to debate the Good Friday Agreement in 1998, Adams had to concede that the Republican objective had not been secured: the Agreement, in his opinion, ought properly to be seen as a kind of 'interim' arrangement — as part of 'a rolling process' which, projected into the future, would ultimately facilitate the achievement of Irish unity on the basis of concerted action through political struggle alone. That struggle would have to call upon the assistance of nationalist Ireland, and also draw on the support of Irish America. But, in any case, it could happily proceed without the accompaniment of armed struggle since, as the recent seismic advances of the party had already shown, Sinn Féin in alliance with others had the definitive capacity 'to transform the political landscape in Ireland'.[99]

But in actual fact the transformation had worked the other way. Back in cage 11 in 1976, Adams had denounced the 'Quisling' activities of 'our partitionist assembly south of the border'.[100] At that point the Irish government was presented as a stooge and a parasite. It certainly could not claim to be genuinely representative: 'The main establishment parties in the Free State have always represented Irish Gombeen interests.'[101] The figure of the 'Gombeen' connotes usurious intent; the Provisionals, by comparison, were a true embodiment of the people. 'Like after all we are the local people,' as Adams protested: 'We don't become elitists just because we maybe do the operating.'[102] This was not the disconnected, theoretical representation on offer from the Provisionals down to 1975. Now, in 1976, the Republican activist should be understood as occupying the position of both a political and a military 'servant of the people'. That required an effort to 'coordinate, direct and push all Republican activity' – to personify the popular interest by redefining the popular interest.[103]

But while the Provisionals had the wherewithal to sustain their representative status within the ghettos of the war zone in Northern Ireland, in the South they had to contend with an array of private, pacific interests untouched by the exigencies of war: they encountered an electorate which was evidently less amenable to 'republicanisation' than had originally been anticipated. At the start of 1977, Adams had cited the authority of the nineteenth-century radical, James Fintan Lalor, as part of a New Year's message which aimed to remind his audience that the 'mass of a people' is liable to exhibit passivity in the face of the forbidding burdens of political struggle: they do not, he cautioned with Lalor, spontaneously 'move' themselves so as to constitute a force in politics – rather, 'it is the man by whom that mass is moved and managed' who forms the 'real and efficient might' of popular insurrection.[104]

But exposure to the cut and thrust of political life in the South of

Ireland did not in the end enable the Provisionals to move and manage people. On the contrary, they were moved by an electorate that had shown itself to be happy to condone the Irish government's abandonment of Republican principle through the signing of the Anglo-Irish Agreement in 1985. In due course, in the wake of the negotiations for the Good Friday Agreement in 1998, Adams was anxious to insist that 'Sinn Féin and republicanism' had become a 'pivotal and growing force in Irish politics'. As that force gained in power, the implication went, the ability to drive Republicanism towards its proper goal would surely prosper: having closed one phase of the struggle, Republicans could proceed to open another.[105] But the first phase of the struggle had been closed by political forces beyond the control of the Provisional movement, and the outcome of the second still lay in the future.

PART TWO
UNIONISM AND DEMOCRACY

VI

Prologue

I

On 27 June 1998, the results of the elections to a devolved shadow Assembly for Northern Ireland signalled the arrival of a new political dispensation for the Province. The supporters of the Good Friday Agreement had been vindicated at the polls. They just held the balance of power in the Assembly, and so the Agreement looked set to succeed. The situation promised nothing less than a new era of politics capable of purging an older reign of crisis and of terror, of hostility and division. But what, in broader terms, did this actually mean? In Britain and the United States, in the Republic of Ireland and in Northern Ireland, the outcome was heralded as a final victory for democracy: a victory, indeed, for peace and democracy, as if the coupling were inevitable. But in fact, the new situation has to be seen as some kind of end for democracy: more properly, as the end of two conflicting democratic ideologies – one Republican, the other Unionist – both now ready for a new beginning.

This assertion stands in need of a more comprehensive explanation, and a fuller explanation is precisely what the remainder of this book will seek to provide. That task, however, is made all the more difficult by a particular irony deriving from the fact that Northern Ireland had been canvassed as a democracy all along. Margaret Thatcher led the way: from 1979 to 1990 her efforts had apparently been directed towards 'upholding democracy and the law'.[1] And so democracy, we are asked to believe, reigned before Good Friday, yet democracy, we are also told, now rules in its wake. What, then, are we to make of the Agreement – the replacement of democracy by democracy? If developments in Northern Ireland have been momentous – at least within their own frame of reference – this formulation can scarcely be said to exhibit their fundamental characteristics.

Discovering the reassuring features of democracy in Northern Ireland through the 1980s, as was standard practice in British high political circles at the time, may well – to coin a phrase – have just been so much spin.[2] But during the same period, it was its absence that was lamented to such devastating effect by all other interested parties. All the major players in the Northern Ireland conflict agreed that it was democracy's institution that was urgently needed to facilitate the transition to an equitable settlement. But since this measure of agreement could produce nothing more edifying than the bitterest animosity, it would seem self-evidently to follow that conflict centred on the character of the democracy so earnestly esteemed on all sides.[3] The deal embodied in the Good Friday Agreement, concluded some two months prior to the Assembly elections, made plain that the core representatives of Unionism and Republicanism had retreated from their respective optimal positions as these had been publicised over the previous decades. Abandoning in this way quite fundamental political objectives, surely it was the mutually exclusive commitment to a set of democratic ideologies displayed by two competing political factions that had been left behind by the prevailing political opinion in June 1998.

Of course, in the middle of 1998, Ian Paisley's Democratic Unionist Party (DUP), together with Robert McCartney's United Kingdom Unionist Party (UKUP), still stood outside the Agreement. Indeed, up to the very last, it looked as if they might seriously hamper its realisation. Being certain of their dissent, and anticipating stirrings of unrest within his own ranks, David Trimble, the leader of the Ulster Unionist Party (UUP), had been obliged to arm himself with a promissory note from the British Prime Minister, Tony Blair, as a sort of coda to the Agreement of

10 April – apparently, though not really, securing the inclusion of what had been excluded from the deal. In the Prime Minister's opinion, yet not in the Agreement, the decommissioning of paramilitary weapons 'should begin straight away', and the conditions of tenure for executive office in the Assembly could, if this proved necessary, be subject to review.[4]

It was enough for David Trimble, but too little for the aspiring Jeffrey Donaldson, MP for Lagan Valley, and a prominent negotiator for the UUP during the course of the talks. Too little also for Willie Ross, UUP member for East Londonderry, for William Thompson, UUP member for West Tyrone, and for the Reverend Martin Smyth, UUP member for South Belfast – though it is true that they were never going to be on board. Too little, in other words, for a significant portion of the Ulster Unionist Party's parliamentary membership.[5]

The signs were therefore a little ominous as Trimble faced into a future in which there could clearly be discerned, first the necessity of receiving endorsement from the Ulster Unionist Council, then the requirement of a positive mandate in a referendum on the Agreement to be held in both the North and the South on 22 May, and finally the need for a good showing in the elections to the shadow Assembly itself. Endorsement from the Council came on a Saturday, eight days after the Good Friday deal had been struck, and then the Agreement was duly ratified by an equally large margin – 71 per cent – in the May referendum.[6] But between that time and the day of the Assembly elections on 25 June, the pro-Agreement unionist lobby was continuously harassed by allegations of betrayal as the cries – ever more shrill – of 'traitor', 'Lundy' and 'Judas Iscariot' whipped up opposition among unionists to the accord.[7] And on the day that the results of the elections were finally calculated, it seemed that the charge of treachery might finally have borne fruit.

Though not quite. The Ulster Unionist Party's performance had been its worst in living memory. Its share of the vote was down to a shocking 21 per cent, with John Hume's SDLP down from its

Westminster performance, losing ground to Sinn Féin but, at 22 per cent, still higher than the UUP. Nonetheless, Trimble retained more than the requisite proportion of unionist votes to carry the Agreement, and he could look forward to being further buoyed up by support from the Progressive Unionist Party, the political wing of the paramilitary Ulster Volunteer Force, headed by David Ervine. Progress, as viewed from the serried ranks of pro-Agreement forces, would continue towards the full implementation of the accord, with the possibility of significant defections to the anti-Agreement lobby standing as the sole remaining obstacle identifiable on the horizon. A sentence, a phrase or, at the least, an abstract noun was required to welcome these advances, and an *Irish Times* editorial from the end of June – 'A Functioning Democracy' – was typical in its choice: 'Now should be the time to rejoice and celebrate the new birth of democracy.'[8]

However, it is noticeable that those who had held back from the process of negotiation since the entry of Sinn Féin into the talks process in 1997 – in other words, the DUP and the UKUP, both now worsted though not quite neutered – stuck to an old mantra. Both parties felt impelled to castigate the accord as a sop to terrorism – as a deal struck with the forces of darkness. But more than this, and perhaps not unpredictably, they also chose to couch their rejection of the Agreement in terms of an overriding commitment to democracy, and thus to represent the new arrangements proposed for Northern Ireland as a departure from accepted democratic principles.

In defence of unionist democracy, Paisley had supported a policy of fuller political integration between Northern Ireland and Great Britain back in 1972. However, by the middle of the 1970s, he had come to lend his support to the provision of some kind of devolved assembly as a preferable arrangement for the Province. By 1989, he was setting out his commitment to devolutionary government in the following terms: 'I believe in the British democratic system . . . those that can have a majority in the House are entitled to form a government.'[9] The implications of the statement are clear to see. The executive functioning of any Northern Ireland assembly required the support of a simple majority of its delegates to authorise its actions. Any retreat from this majoritarian principle – and the Good Friday Agreement manifestly was in due course to represent such a retreat – appeared to contradict the tenets of normal democratic practice.[10]

But while Paisley's position amounted to a recommendation to reinstate the *status quo ante bellum* of 1968, McCartney found himself opposing the settlement on the same grounds, but from a diametrically opposed perspective. 'I am not an Ulster nationalist,' he declared back in 1986, signalling his disdain not only for the prospect of an independent Ulster, but for any imaginable model of legislative devolution as well. Northern Ireland's had been 'a mean and uninspiring conflict, out of which nothing can develop'. More complete integration with Britain, 'one of the great liberal democracies of the world', remained the only compelling option. But by June of 1998, that option had been firmly displaced from the realm of political possibility by the appearance of a settlement which had been shown to command popular support, obliging McCartney to predict that this apparent 'victory for democracy' would in time be revealed to be precisely its antithesis – a sorry kind of 'sectarian huckstering' within an institutional frame.[11]

2

All this piety about democracy, the common currency of new-found allies and political enemies alike, is perhaps unsurprising in an age in which democracy itself has effectively become, in the words of one commentator, 'the public cant of the modern world'.[12] But unanimity on this scale, taking the idea of democracy as a universal panacea, might reasonably nourish a degree of scepticism, or at least provoke us into a more searching inquiry into the significance of the peace settlement concluded at Easter 1998 in Belfast.

The word *significance* might seem somewhat portentous here, or even inappropriate, to the extent that it implies that lessons could be learned. How could an exception such as Northern Ireland seems to represent offer guidance as a rule – how could an example drawn from what could be said in a European context to count as the meanest and most unprepossessing of scenarios provide instruction for the ordinary predicament of settled political communities? Is the effort not dogged by provincialism from the start?

In the context of raising questions such as these, we might remind ourselves that historical inquiry at its inception had proceeded from the opposite perspective – disregarding the mean and the insignificant, and seizing upon the grand. 'Though men always judge the present war wherein they live to be the greatest, and when it is past, admire more those that went before it,' remarked Thucydides in his history of *The Peloponnesian War*, 'yet if they consider of this war by the acts done in the same, it will manifest itself to be greater than any of those before mentioned.' He went on: 'as for this war, it both lasted long and the harm it did to Greece was such as the like in the like space had never been seen before'.[13] But while the war in Northern Ireland likewise lasted a long time, it was hardly the most catastrophic event to appear in the modern world.

Two hundred and fifty years later another Greek, Polybius, saw fit to trump Thucydides' claims as he marvelled at the mixture of finesse and fortune which enabled the Romans in the space of less than fifty-three years to bring under their rule 'almost the whole of the inhabited world'.[14] If Thucydides supplies us with the grandest of military spectacles, Polybius draws attention to the most universal of political dramas. But while it seemed fitting to Polybius to marvel at a story of unrelenting Roman success, the 'troubles' of Northern Ireland offer precious little to admire.

Polybius begins his narrative around 216 BC for the purpose of choreographing events of world-historical significance – the Social War of Philip of Macedon, the war between Antiochus and

Ptolemy Philopator in Asia and the Hannibalic war in Italy and Africa: 'Now up to this time the world's history had been, so to speak, a series of disconnected transactions, as widely separated in their origin and results as in their localities. But from this time forth history becomes a connected whole: the affairs of Italy and Libya are involved with those of Asia and of Greece, and the tendency of all is to unity.'[15] Real history, we are being told, proceeds expansively and comprehensively, but not episodically – towards grander vistas and more extensive durations: from provincialism to universalism, in short. What design could be more elevated and more capacious than this, what more desultory and diminutive than our own?

Northern Ireland is not the point at which all episodes are superseded, in Polybius' sense, by real history – not the point at which all action and reaction converge. The response of David Ervine on Thursday night, 9 April, to the deal within his sights – 'it is the emotional equivalent of the collapse of the Berlin Wall'[16] – betrays a sense of personal odyssey, but it does not pretend to be an adequate tabulation of consequences. Just as well, really: Mr Reagan, Mr Clinton, Colonel Qaddafi, and occasional bouts of attention from a handful of European powers, had played their part in the events of Northern Ireland – some parts evidently more vital than others. But so much did not depend upon this place for them: Northern Ireland was never a matter of major international strategic concern.[17]

Equally, the conflict in Northern Ireland inflicted less 'harm', recalling Thucydides' word, than a host of comparable conflicts played out in comparable magnitudes of space. Incomparable conflicts of incomparable magnitude – Angola, Algeria – are in the nature of the case even less hospitable to comparison. Even the preferred analogies of Northern Ireland's ideologues – Israel, the West Bank, Apartheid South Africa – even these prove so unrelentingly inappropriate as to discourage the remotest intimation that such a grim and quizzical conflict might exemplify anything at all.[18]

Not the grandest then, not the direst, not the most exemplary: now that the war seems over, might not the episode be allowed to slip from memory? Such a resolution would have much to recommend it, except for the fact that the situation in Northern Ireland, as it unfolded over the course of thirty years – claiming, in the process, some 3,200 lives, and proving resistant to a host of attempts by the wise and the not so wise alike to presage a solution – could be taken to have exemplified at least a vital kind of failure. To hope to learn by example is not a conspicuously empty ambition, though it is worth the effort to discriminate amongst the examples one might pick. What can be said of Northern Ireland is that it provides a powerful example of how the problem of democracy reveals a fault-line in modern politics.

In founding new states and maintaining established governments, nobody now – Machiavelli complained –. 'resorts to the examples of the ancients'.[19] This was a plea, humanistic in character, for the utility of 'studies': an enthusiasm for the literary culture – for the history, the philosophy, and the eloquence – of the ancients, facilitated the recovery of discrete 'exempla', and the exemplary affairs of the past, so the argument went, offer guidance to contemporary conduct. However, in recounting the vicissitudes of Northern Ireland's politics one is forced to deal with exemplary failure – failures of action and failures of perception.

It is obvious, but still worth emphasising, that these failures by now have an extended history, and that this history coincides with the ideological careers of both Republicanism and Unionism since 1886. But even by that date, the year of Gladstone's first Home Rule Bill, both doctrines had discernible roots in the intellectual and political culture of humanistic and Enlightenment Europe.[20] The transmission of that culture to the contemporary world has been an involved and intricate affair, but by 1912 the partisans of the Union defended their cause in terms of its democratic legitimacy, much as Republicanism in 1918 asked only to be judged in terms of its own democratic credentials. This coincidence should really serve to underline the fact that a political history of

Northern Ireland must be written with a close eye on the ideological descent of either doctrine. To plot a course through Northern Irish affairs since 1968 is therefore to examine an exemplary episode – in our sense of these words – in conjunction with something of the legacy of European intellectual history.

The French historian Alexis de Tocqueville once complained that the world of letters – of 'studies', in Machiavelli's sense – had degenerated into the most quixotic of pursuits at the hands of Enlightenment and Revolutionary ideologues in France. Elaborate speculative systems and theories of government had come to overwhelm the ambitions of philosophers and moralists. Men of letters had begun to live in isolation from 'the world' – as Tocqueville put it – with the result that abstract 'literary views on political subjects are scattered throughout the works of the day'.[21] But the world returns with a vengeance when the abstract principles of Unionism and Republicanism, each in its own way a child of eighteenth-century intellectual experiment, are judged by the example of action and consequence in Northern Ireland's politics.

3

The abstract political principles of Republicanism and Unionism have a common source in democratic theory: for all their obvious mutual hostility, both Republicans and unionists came to share a fundamental commitment to the democratic principle of self-determination around the start of the twentieth century. That principle has its roots in the American and French Revolutions, but it acquired a new force and significance during the course of the First World War.[22] In January 1917, Woodrow Wilson declared that 'every people should be left free to determine its own polity'.[23] For Wilson this simple, impeccable maxim promised to secure an age of peace. That hope, however, was soon disappointed. Then, between 1945 and 1962, the principle of self-determination was on the move again, throughout all Africa and Asia. Peace, once again, was scarcely the result.[24] But the point, for the purposes of this argument, is that it was never quite clear what self-determination meant. How was one to isolate this self – the people, the democracy – that was to be given the power to determine its future? Who was to embody this power on the people's behalf?

Commentaries on Northern Ireland have endlessly presented the political turmoil of the Province as mysteriously arising out of ethnic conflict.[25] But it has never been explained with precision what an 'ethnic' conflict means, or why this particular form of strife has come to be rife in the modern world. If the conflict in question is conceptualised as resulting from whatever hostility might be displayed between generic 'bands' of individuals, then conflicts between ethnicities have been around since the time of the Pharaohs and can hardly hope to illuminate a characteristically modern problem.[26] But if, on the other hand, the antagonism demands to be seen as founded upon rival aspirations to popular sovereignty, then the conflict has to be understood as specific to democracy. 'The plain, the undeniable truth,' exclaimed the Belfast editor William MacKnight in 1896, 'is, that there are two antagonistic populations, two different nations on Irish soil.'[27] The argument proved prophetic: between 1905 and 1911, as self-government for Ireland loomed steadily larger on the horizon, Ulster Protestants came to see themselves as constituting a democracy in order to gain protection under institutions of their own.[28]

The motive here was fear: the prospect of incorporation under a singular Irish democracy entailed subjection to the sovereignty of the majority on the island. Ulster Protestants resorted to self-determination as a means of self-defence to be secured by a government of their own. This pathology was already obvious in the early twentieth century to the unionist polemicist and historian, Ronald McNeill: 'To the Nationalist claim that Ireland was a nation,' he remarked, Ulster responded 'that it was either two nations or none, and that if one of the two had a right to "self-determination", the other had it equally'.[29] It was Ulster's claim to equality of treatment with the South that ultimately prevailed: Northern unionists refused inclusion within a unitary Irish democracy, claiming the liberty to determine themselves as a people in their own right.

However, having been vindicated in their bid to count as a distinct and separate people, Ulster Protestants then proceeded to wield precisely that political weapon which had provoked them to resist the advance of an all-Ireland democracy: majority rule was instituted as the basic mechanism of decision-making for the institutions of government in Northern Ireland. In this way, a form of democratic government was established as an instrument for maintaining Northern Ireland as an undemocratic state. Here lay the fuel for the Republican fire: over the longer term, the ruling majority in the North inadvertently succeeded in converting the local minority into a populace whose security could plausibly be seen to depend on their entitlement to self-determination in a new union with the South.

However one looks at it, the democratic principle of self-determination is fraught with difficulty, and difficulty often leads to failure. That failure, I want to argue, is exemplified by the course of Northern Irish politics since 1968. Developments in the Province over the last thirty years expose the vulnerability of the assumptions which underpin the practice of democracy. Modern democracy is founded on the institution of representative government, and political representation was conceived as a happy marriage between authority and popularity. It was intended to provide a mechanism for identifying the decisions of governments with the interests of the governed.[30] But that benign intention has no guarantee of success. The aim of identifying a people with its rulers is not necessarily maimed from the start, but it has always been open to frustration. More than this, it has often failed. It fails when the principles of identification, which are always a subject of debate in democracies, become a matter of overwhelming dispute. The institutions of majoritarian democracy in Northern Ireland made dispute, and ultimately crisis, extremely difficult to avoid.

In the chapters that follow, I shall be exploring the crisis of Unionism, the political reversals to which that crisis gave rise, and the condition of siege which both of these experiences ultimately managed to promote. That exploration will take us from the prorogation of Stormont in 1972, to the Sunningdale Agreement of 1973 and the Ulster Workers' Council strike of 1974, through the Anglo-Irish Agreement of 1985, and finally to the Good Friday Agreement. But it will also take us back to the first political reversal to which Unionism was subjected in the wake of the Home Rule crisis of 1886. The events of 1886 to 1920 help to explain the nature and significance of developments since 1972. In the process of uncovering that explanation, it will become clear that Unionism has always pledged allegiance to democracy but that democracy has throughout been a perilous commodity. It has always been subject to the possibility of crisis, and crises in democracies are harbingers of war.

VII

Crisis: 1972–1976

I

The crisis of Unionism arrived in 1972. In March of that year, the government at Stormont was finally prorogued, although that outcome had been predicted throughout the previous nine months. Since January, events had begun to spiral out of control. Internment, which had been introduced into the Province in August the year before, was still in operation. Bloody Sunday, with thirteen unarmed civilians shot dead and a further seventeen wounded by the Parachute Regiment in Derry, had brought about the recall of the Irish Ambassador from London, the burning of the British Embassy in Dublin, and, most significantly, the searing radicalisation of Northern Ireland's Catholics. As a result, a major reappraisal of Westminster's political options was in prospect: the regime in Northern Ireland would be subject to renewed scrutiny, and Unionism would be forced to re-examine its position.[1]

The burden of expectation among the Protestant population imposed a strain upon the leaders of Ulster Unionism in the Province, and their reactions to developments became precipitous, and even frantic. By 9 February, the former Northern Ireland Home Affairs Minister, William Craig, had launched the Ulster Vanguard Movement as a pressure group within the Ulster Unionist Party, and by 18 March the tone of his pronouncements had become ominous in the extreme: 'it may be our job to liquidate the enemy,' he now openly declared.[2] On 22 February, the Official IRA had bombed Aldershot military barracks; on 4 March, and again on 20 March, the Provisional IRA bombed Belfast civilians.

Within four days, the British Prime Minister, Edward Heath, announced the suspension of the Northern Ireland parliament for one year, and the introduction of direct rule from Westminster. The suspension of the Stormont parliament was followed by its dissolution in July of 1973. Both were catastrophic defeats for Ulster Unionism.[3]

However, Protestant demoralisation had been growing now for years. British troops had arrived in the autumn of 1969, and a programme of reform had been imposed upon the Province. Soon loyalists were to come into conflict with British forces on the ground as the Ulster Special Constabulary was disbanded and the Royal Ulster Constabulary disarmed. By 1972, two prime ministers had resigned in Northern Ireland – first Terence O'Neill, then James Chichester-Clark – and, in November 1971, Harold Wilson had announced his 'Fifteen Point Plan' for a solution to the Irish problem which included the consideration of a means of achieving 'the aspirations envisaged half a century ago, of progress towards a united Ireland'.[4]

The Provisional IRA itself had been seeking to provoke a resort to direct rule, and presenting its eventuality as a first step in the direction of an all-Ireland settlement.[5] Now direct rule had arrived, and unionist ranks were in disarray: 'Northern Ireland is not a coconut colony,' declared Brian Faulkner, on the verge of surrendering his premiership.[6] But, in the place of indignant protestations, substantive arguments would have to be marshalled, action would have to be taken, and decisions would shortly have to be made.

A process of consultation began almost immediately. William Whitelaw, leader of the House of Commons, had been designated first Secretary of State to Northern Ireland by the time that Stormont sat for the last time at the end of March 1972, and he began the move towards negotiations almost straight away. In June he met with the Social Democratic and Labour Party, which had formed back in August 1970 under the leadership of Gerry Fitt. In July he met with the Provisional IRA at Cheyne Walk in

London: the Officials had called a halt to their campaign in May. And, in September, he convened the Darlington Conference to discuss political options with the Ulster Unionist Party, the Alliance Party and the Northern Ireland Labour Party.

The conference produced little agreement among the participants, even with the SDLP boycotting the proceedings. But in its wake, the Northern Ireland Office, now under the control of the British Secretary of State, produced a document – *The Future of Northern Ireland* – indicating the direction which government policy might take. William Whitelaw set out the overall position in his foreword to the document: it was the British government's purpose, he made clear, to help the people of Northern Ireland to 'draw together' and 'find a system of government which will enjoy the support and the respect of the overwhelming majority'.[7]

The new departure was signalled by just two words – 'overwhelming majority': the qualification – 'overwhelming' – discreetly carried the implication that the political institutions established under the 1920 Government of Ireland Act, which were based on the principle that executive decisions in the Province required the support of a simple majority in the Stormont parliament, had been misconceived. The document itself, in a historical preamble, spelt this out: 'The most striking feature of the executive government of Northern Ireland throughout this period of more than half a century was its virtually complete concentration in the hands of a single political party, the Ulster Unionist Party. At every General Election from 1921 to 1969 this Party secured an absolute majority of the seats in the Northern Ireland Parliament.'[8]

This meant that the alternation of governing parties – 'which has for so long been a characteristic of the British political system, and which has undoubtedly contributed in a marked degree to the stability of Parliamentary Government in Great Britain' – did not exist in Northern Ireland.[9] With the population divided in its political allegiance, and with the consequent absence of a floating vote inside the Province, the government of Ulster was entrusted

– effectively in perpetuity – to a party which had made little secret of its suspicion of, and sometimes of its fear and contempt for, a third of the population.[10]

The argument of *The Future of Northern Ireland* represented a watershed in British policy, although it hardly marked a revolution in the political thinking of the time.[11] Indeed, its central point had been set out a year earlier in a pamphlet published under the auspices of the New Ulster Movement, an organisation which had been founded in 1969 to urge moderation in the face of impending disaster. In *The Reform of Stormont*, the Movement had declared that the Westminster model 'works well only in rather special circumstances. It is a system which can easily lead to tyranny, because it produces a remarkable concentration of power in the government of the day'.[12]

The Northern Ireland Office had by now come to accept the basic import of this verdict, and it was on that basis that the British government was seeking to broker an agreement between Northern Ireland's constitutional parties. But it was not absolutely clear what kind of reform was intended to follow. Obviously the suggestion was that the Northern Ireland constitution would have to be reconstructed since majoritarian government had combined with single-party rule. As a result of this combination, both legislative and executive competence in Northern Ireland had become the exclusive monopoly of the majority community at the expense of minority participation in the public life of the Province. In the first place, then, it was hoped that the system of majority rule would be replaced by a properly representative system – that the idea of mustering general consent behind the institutions of government would be reflected in the practice of Northern Irish politics. But with this reconfiguration of the apparatus of government, what would be the fate of Ulster's United Kingdom status? Would the position of Northern Ireland in relation to the British Union change?

This question had a particular urgency in 1972 because the security of the Union and the character of the Ulster government had long been inextricably linked through the constitution of Northern Ireland. Both the status of the Province and its powers of political control had been determined from the beginning by a simple principle of decision-making: they both depended upon the preference of a numerical majority voting in the Northern Ireland parliament. Under the 1920 Government of Ireland Act, the right of the Six Counties to resist incorporation into the South hinged on the decision of a majority of members sitting in the Stormont House of Commons.[13] But, equally, control of the executive in the Northern Ireland parliament had been put into the hands of the same majority. The monolithic structures of majority ascendancy were about to be deconstructed under the stewardship of William Whitelaw – yet the consequences for British sovereignty over Northern Ireland remained uncertain.

While it was clearly the case that sovereignty over Northern Ireland after 1920 had continued to reside at Westminster, the political will of Ulster, wherever it actually applied, had nonetheless been embodied in the Protestant community. In practice, this meant that both the regular administration of the affairs of the Province and the actual survival of the Six Counties as a political unit were indissolubly intertwined: as we have seen, they both depended on support from a loyal majority in the Ulster parliament. But it was precisely this constitutional interdependence between routine political decision-making and long term political survival which had ensured the conversion of the Protestant majority into a permanent political faction: unionist loss of control over the Stormont administration would entail the dissolution of the Ulster polity as a whole.

This arrangement was hardly likely to foster the spread of liberal sentiment through society at large. Quite the contrary, in fact – it was a spur to rampant politicisation among the community in charge: the minority became a threat through its potential alliance with the South, and so coalitions across the communities were disabled in the North. Consequently, unionist toleration could not be easily afforded if the Protestant democracy in Ulster was to endure. The inclusion of Roman Catholics as meaningful players in the constitution appeared to threaten Northern Ireland with subversion. As a result, democratic government in the form of decision by the majority became a bulwark against the development of a democratic state: any movement toward an equal political union of all the citizens consenting to the institutional representation of their interests was hampered and curtailed.

With Catholics condemned to merely a shadow participation in the established democratic process, and tempted as a consequence by the idea of an Irish union, Protestant society continued to be pervaded by an awareness of the basic schism. As a result, social relations became burdened with political significance – private life was amalgamated to the concerns of public life, civil society subordinated to community affairs. Public spiritedness and civic virtue, Protestant vigilance and determination, were at a premium. But such vigilant determination would not be easily relaxed since the goal of Ulster Protestantism was never sure to coincide with the long term orientation of its political master: after all, the stated preference of the Westminster government in 1920 had been for an Irish union.

The Government of Ireland Act of that year had made provision for precisely this eventuality: 'With a view to the eventual establishment of a Parliament for the whole of Ireland, and to bringing about harmonious action between the parliaments and governments of Southern Ireland and Northern Ireland, and to the promotion of mutual intercourse and uniformity in relation to matters affecting the whole of Ireland . . . there shall be constituted . . . a Council to be called the Council of Ireland.'[14] A Council of Ireland was to be a precursor to an actual parliament for the whole of Ireland: Ulster Protestants would then be incorporated within an Irish union.

It so happens that the Council of Ireland made no headway after 1920 since it depended for its progress on co-operation between North and South. Nonetheless, the fact remained that Britain's expectation had been that legislative competence would ultimately be devolved to a united Irish parliament under the authority of the British legislature. Of course, the South had left the Union in 1921, and then departed from the Commonwealth in 1948. A year later, the Attlee government responded with a guarantee for Ulster: it was declared under the Ireland Act of 1949 that Northern Ireland would not cease to remain an integral part of the United Kingdom 'without the consent of the Parliament of Northern Ireland'.[15] But, despite this assurance, Ulster Protestant anxieties over the prospect of an Irish union were not alleviated for long.

The Ireland Act was the pillar of post-war unionist politics. 'We appreciate very much your specific assurance about the declaratory provision of the Ireland Act, 1949,' Terence O'Neill wrote to Harold Wilson during a period of high political drama at the end of 1968.[16] However, in reality, the declaratory provision of 1949 offered nothing that was not already contained in the Act of 1920: 'the consent of the Parliament of Northern Ireland' still meant the consent of a majority of its members. At the same time, on the British side, the declaration was only as durable as the commitment of Westminster: it could be retracted just as easily as it had originally been made.

Indeed, preparations to revoke the commitment given in 1949 were already being undertaken by 1969. While a meeting of the Northern Ireland committee of the British Cabinet under the new Conservative administration could arrive at the view in the summer of 1970 that the 'Protestants could not doubt the strength of the United Kingdom's commitment to the integrity of Northern Ireland,' within a month it was precisely such doubt that was being voiced by Northern Ireland's Prime Minister: 'Are the Army, or are they not, here to support in an evident way the lawfully constituted Government of Northern Ireland?' demanded Chichester-Clark of Reginald Maudling.[17] But the Ulster premier's alarm was hardly totally misplaced: at the start of December 1969, the Home Office had made plans for a redrafting of the Ireland Act, determined to dilute Britain's obligation to the Province.

The wording of the relevant clause of the new Act would be

designed to enable the British parliament to take unilateral action regarding the fate of Northern Ireland. As a Whitehall official noted in his assessment of the options, a change to existing arrangements could be made to read in one of two ways: either the clause could lay down that Northern Ireland would not cease to form a part of the United Kingdom 'without the consent of both the Parliament at Stormont and that at Westminster', or it could stipulate that the integrity of the Province would not be altered 'without the consent *either* of the Stormont *or* the Westminster Parliament'. If this second formulation was adopted, the point would be clear – as the British official noted in his comments on the redrafting, Stormont could be 'overridden' by Westminster: Britain would be asserting its own freedom of manoeuvre.[18] In the end, of course, nothing became of the plan to scotch the Ireland Act in the open: instead it was made to disappear with more subtlety – on the quiet.

Eight months after the instructions had been given to find a form of words which would release the British parliament from the bonds of the Ireland Act, Harold Wilson had made the prudent decision to commit his government to the terms of the existing 1949 clause. However, now the phraseology was different. Emerging after urgent talks with Northern Ireland Ministers on 19 December 1969, Wilson had reaffirmed that no change would be made to the status of Northern Ireland 'without the consent of the people of Northern Ireland'.[19] At that point, the 'people of Northern Ireland' really meant the 'parliament of Northern Ireland' – no plans had yet been made for a referendum on the border.[20] More accurately still, Wilson's 'people of Northern Ireland' denoted 'a majority in the Stormont parliament'. But soon, the right of decision would be definitively transferred to a majority of the population in the Province.

The shift was made in 1972. It was noted by the Home Office in December 1969 that Lord Monson, in the Upper House, had proposed a referendum on the fate of Northern Ireland.[21] Three years later, the proposal was accepted by the Conservative administration: the position of Northern Ireland could 'be made the subject of a plebiscite', Edward Heath informed his Cabinet in February 1972. The poll need not be held immediately, but rather 'in a number of years' – 'this might remove the emotive subject of the Border from the centre of Northern Ireland politics'.[22] A month later, Reginald Maudling proposed instead that a referendum should be held forthwith: 'a plebiscite should be held on the question of the Border at an early date but should not thereafter be repeated for some 15 or 20 years'.[23]

It was at this same meeting of the Cabinet in early March that Maudling informed his colleagues of his having reached the conclusion that the 'least dangerous course' open to the British government in relation to the general situation in Northern Ireland would be to proceed to 'direct United Kingdom rule'.[24] But such a development could have consequences for the right of the Stormont parliament, under the Ireland Act of 1949, to determine the status of Northern Ireland: if Stormont were to be dissolved, that right would disappear. This, in fact, was one of the reasons why it was prorogued and not dissolved: 'The Unionist Party attached great importance to the Northern Ireland Parliament as a guarantee of the integrity of the Border under the Ireland Act, 1949,' Maudling correctly observed. 'He therefore proposed that during the interregnum of direct rule it should not be dissolved but should be temporarily suspended by prorogation.'[25]

As the situation stood at the end of March 1972, with Stormont in suspension and a plebiscite in the offing, any decision in a referendum to change the status of Northern Ireland would require that the Ulster parliament be reconvened to give its assent – or indeed to withhold its assent – in regard to the popular verdict. Suspension, as Maudling made clear, would necessitate the recall of Stormont 'should the result of the plebiscite make it necessary to seek its consent to the detachment of Northern Ireland from the United Kingdom'.[26] However, the Northern Ireland parliament was ultimately dissolved – in July 1973: 'The Parliament of Northern Ireland shall cease to exist,' declared the Act which ended Stormont in that year.[27] But, with the dissolution of

Stormont, the Ireland Act of 1949 was effectively repealed: the future of Northern Ireland within the United Kingdom would depend on the exclusive decision of a majority of the Province's population.[28]

This change was hardly momentous in the context of 1972: Ulster Protestants were a clear majority of the Northern Ireland population. But it was the view of the British establishment that this would not always be the position. At a meeting between Heath and Faulkner on 22 March, the British Prime Minister made it clear that a plebiscite on the border should be repeated 'at intervals of 15 years'.[29] But, three years earlier, the Home Office had calculated that there could be a Catholic majority in approximately '20 years' – in 1989, in other words.[30] For the moment, then, the Union had been secured. But, ultimately, its future could be at the disposal of a Catholic majority. As it turned out, that point had not arrived by the time that 1989 came around: indeed, as late as December 2001, Catholics made up 44 per cent of the population, with Protestants comprising 53.[31]

Nonetheless, the trend left ample room for future Protestant anxiety. In 1998, the Northern Ireland Assembly established in the wake of the Good Friday Agreement did not inherit the right which had been conferred on Stormont in 1949: the Assembly, unlike the old parliament, was not entitled to decide the position of Ulster regarding the British Union.[32] Should the apparent drift toward a preponderance of Catholics become established as a *fait accompli*, with a Catholic majority at the same time opting to vote along nationalist lines, Ulster's membership of the Union would be at an end.

2

However, in 1972, Ulster Unionism was not defined by its position on the Union alone – it was also characterised by its commitment to the existing provisions for majority rule. With the decision to hold a poll on the border in March 1973, the Union was expected to be safe for at least a further twenty years – yet the principle of government by the Protestant majority was about to be repudiated by British policy.

This prospect was itself of major significance. As we have seen, the integrity of Northern Ireland since 1920 had depended on the ability of an entrenched majority to control the Ulster parliament. This meant that as long as unionist control could be maintained, the parliament would be an instrument of Protestant opinion. But, at the same time, the control of the Stormont parliament entailed the control of the Northern Ireland government, and so the government itself became a tool of the majority. Under this arrangement, every means of effecting a separation between legislative and executive power had been abolished. But, more importantly, the powers of government were united in the service of a particular interest – they were united in the service of the larger section of the population: this was a Protestant parliament intended for a Protestant state.

As late as August 1969, the long established association between majority ascendancy in the Stormont parliament and Protestant ascendancy over the Northern Ireland state was still being celebrated in the loyalist refrain – 'We are the People'.[33] However, in the spring of 1972, as Protestants confronted an imminent Ulster crisis, the precepts of Unionism were struggling for survival. This struggle brought those precepts out into the open. As consternation spread throughout the unionist population in anticipation of a new initiative from Westminster, a notice issued by Ulster Vanguard was doing the rounds in Belfast. Its message appeared to carry an unambiguous significance: 'We reject any departure from the principle of majority rule.'[34]

But 'majority rule', in fact, connoted two things here, not one. First, it referred to the mode of endorsement which licensed the Ulster government's decisions. Accordingly, Vanguard rejected 'the adoption of electoral procedures or principles of parliamentary government which do not now apply in the remainder of the UK'.[35] Yet it also implied that it was through majority consent that political power over Northern Ireland was conferred on its institutions of government: the consent of the governed in Northern Ireland was understood to be based on adequate popular acclamation – but this acclamation comprised only 'the wishes of the majority'.[36]

The slippage here is importantly revealing, since it points to a basic confusion about the nature of democracy. Majority consent, it was being comfortably assumed, was sufficient to commend Northern Ireland's democratic credentials.[37] However, the customary reliance in democracies on the method of decision by the majority is not intended as an instrument of majority consent, but as a method of sustaining general popular support: the majority voting procedures familiarly adopted by democratic states are expected to inspire a common, democratic consent – not merely the consent of the majority. The employment of such procedures within the framework of a constitutional separation of powers, competition between rival political parties, and the formation of new coalitions of voters developing over time, are supposed to answer to the expectation of political equality – not systematic inequality in the form of majority rule.

What is consented to in a democracy is the distribution of powers and opportunities in the community, not the precise decisions of particular governments at specific points in time. However, where there is only majority consent to the basic arrangement of political power, on the grounds that the constitution serves merely the greater number of people, certain democratic procedures may well be in operation, but these procedures hardly add up to a democratic state.[38] Constitutional democracy employs majority decision procedures as one expedient among others for ensuring equal representation. But the constitution of Northern Ireland down to 1972 had been constructed with a view to entirely partial representation: politics had become a vehicle for representing the majority. What was being signalled with the publication of the *Future of Northern Ireland* was the determination of the British government to create political institutions whose endorsement by an 'overwhelming majority' of the population would enable them to become representative of the community as a whole.

Accordingly, the options under consideration by the Northern Ireland Office from October 1972 included full political integration into the United Kingdom, with the consequent abolition of the Stormont parliament; the establishment of a purely executive authority in Northern Ireland, with legislative power over the newly established executive continuing to reside at Westminster; the formation of a convention which would be charged with executive functions, and which could deliberate over legislation, but which would neither initiate bills nor pass laws; and a more powerful assembly capable of both enacting laws and administering such public services as would fall within the competence of any devolved institutions.[39]

The SDLP preference for 'joint sovereignty' between the Republic of Ireland and the United Kingdom, presented in a 1972 position paper *Towards a New Ireland*, was given little serious consideration. And neither, perhaps, should it have been: a condominium arrangement whereby Dublin and London would share responsibility for the government of Northern Ireland is in the nature of things liable to precipitate either entrenched confrontation or a union of states. Sovereignty which is 'joint' is more than a juridical paradox – it is, in truth, a radical misnomer despite the currency given to it by the New Ireland Forum in 1984 and by an assortment of academic pundits since.[40]

If truly 'joint', it is simply a sovereignty – the sovereign united states of Great Britain and the Republic of Ireland, accountable for the good government of its Northern Irish Province through any number of imaginable federal or imperial arrangements. But if the scheme was intended as an alliance – jointly co-operating bodies politic – authority is by definition divided, begging the question as to which sovereignty is more authoritative under conditions of dispute: a hydra-headed constitutional monster with all the potential for ineliminable conflict which that implies. The

Kingdoms of Ireland and Great Britain had some experience of this arrangement in the 1650s, and few with an historical sense were now keen to revisit its disasters.[41]

The Northern Ireland Office Green Paper of 1972 made clear its preference for the introduction of some form of devolved Assembly with a law-making capacity rather than either the maintenance of direct rule as it then stood, or the establishment of a full incorporative Union on a putatively more equitable basis. Equally, it indicated a bias in favour of a single-chamber legislature comprising between seventy-two and a hundred members, as against the reintroduction of a bicameral parliament, and it noted the support of the Northern Ireland parties for elections to be conducted under the single transferable vote system of proportional representation. The difficult or contentious issues, therefore, were likely to be related to the precise form that any new government should take, and to the nature of the relationship between a Northern Ireland administration and the government of the Irish Republic.

The Ulster Unionist Party had proposed a system whereby an executive commanding a majority of assembly votes would be formed in the manner customary under the British system, except now it would come under the scrutiny of 'powerful' committees which would draw their memberships from across the range of parliamentary parties. Membership of committees would be determined in accordance with party strength in the assembly.[42] The Alliance Party, by comparison, wished to depart more radically from precedent, proposing the introduction of a committee system capable of replacing Cabinet-style government altogether, with the chairmanship of committees determined by an assembly vote on a proportional representation basis.[43]

The Northern Ireland Labour Party also opted for government by committee, but in this instance with the committee elected through proportional representation and in due course electing the committee chair itself. Finally, the Social Democratic and Labour Party proposed the formation of an 'interim' administration, pending reunification with the Irish Republic, elected by the assembly on a proportional representation basis, with this body in turn electing a chief executive.[44]

The Northern Ireland Office, for its part, noted the further possibility of 'entrenched' government, whereby minority elements would, by constitutional requirement, be included in the government; 'bloc' government – or an enforced coalition – whereby the majority party would be obliged to coalesce with the majority of the remaining minority; and, finally, it considered the possibility of a 'weighted majority' government in accordance with which an incoming government would be obliged to seek endorsement from a weighted majority within the legislature. But whichever option prevailed, any agreement arrived at was expected to respect the 'strong arguments' in favour of 'giving minority interests a share in the exercise of executive power'. The importance of an 'Irish Dimension' to any new settlement was also given a degree of prominence, the precise character of this 'Dimension' remaining somewhat indeterminate: 'Whatever arrangements are made for the future administration of Northern Ireland must take account of the Province's relationship with the Republic of Ireland.'[45]

All these resolutions and recommendations are just so many historical relics now but, for all that, they are not without their interest. They formed the basis of the government White Paper – *Northern Ireland Constitutional Proposals* – of 20 March 1973, which reiterated the need 'to create a representative forum of Northern Ireland opinion', and committed Her Majesty's government to considering 'how devolution on a basis of government by consent may take place'.[46] It was, more or less, on the basis of these proposals, which were subsequently modified and incorporated into the Northern Ireland Assembly and the Northern Ireland Constitution Bills in the spring, that the Ulster Unionist Party, the Alliance Party and the Social and Democratic Labour Party stood for election to a new Northern Ireland Assembly on 28 June 1973.

It was from this Assembly that the parties would select delegates to negotiations which, in due course, would set about establishing a new executive for Northern Ireland. For its part, Provisional Sinn Féin called on its supporters to spoil their votes in the Assembly elections, but the Republican Clubs – the political wing of the Official IRA – actually stood in the contest.[47] They stood, however, in opposition to the government's constitutional proposals. But so too did Ian Paisley's Democratic Unionist Party, together with Vanguard, which by now had formed itself into the Vanguard Unionist Progressive Party under the leadership of William Craig, who was eager to challenge both the Ulster Unionist Party and the credibility of the White Paper.

Accordingly, Paisley and Craig set about forming a 'Loyalist Coalition', whose purpose was to thwart the achievement of any compromise settlement. Their chance of success, moreover, was far from remote since the Ulster Unionist Party itself was divided between those who were prepared to accept a manifesto pledge to enter into a coalition government should a deal with the SDLP be on offer, and those 'unpledged' party candidates who wished to keep their options open.

In the end, the SDLP secured nineteen seats in the new seventy-eight-seat Assembly, while the supporters of Paisley and Craig got eighteen. The Alliance Party won eight seats, but the Northern Ireland Labour Party was left with only one. The Ulster Unionist Party, on the other hand, ended up with thirty-two representatives – but ten of these had refused to put their signature to the Unionist election pledge, and now they proceeded to organise themselves under Harry West into a third flank in the loyalist opposition to Faulkner's party.

Nonetheless, despite the large proportion of dissent confronting the British government initiative, the pro-White Paper parties still held a majority of seats in the Assembly. Consequently, at eleven o'clock in the morning on Friday, 5 October, in the old Cabinet Room at Stormont Castle, formal talks between the Alliance Party, the UUP, and the SDLP, were ready to begin under the chairmanship of William Whitelaw. An Assembly had just been established, an executive was now to be formed, and so the questions to be decided concerned, first, the conditions to be placed on the formation of any new government and, then, the general issue of Provincial security. But the formation of an executive depended in turn on agreement over the legitimacy of the Assembly, and therefore on the SDLP accepting the integrity of Northern Ireland as a part of the United Kingdom.[48]

However, it also depended on reaching agreement on both the proportion of nationalists to unionists in any prospective government, and on the scope and remit of the proposed 'Irish Dimension' which was to be embodied in a new Council of Ireland. The issue of security, on the other hand, hinged on the fate of the RUC and the future of internment. Neither of these were inconsiderable issues. On the contrary, even the latter went to the heart of the conflict since, while responsibility for security would ultimately rest with Westminster, it was necessary for any potential government in Northern Ireland to agree a common approach to law and order if it was to maintain its credibility under conditions of continuing violence.

From a unionist perspective, the first obstacles to agreement were overcome on the opening day of the talks when the SDLP made it clear that it would accept an oath of allegiance to the new constitution – including, by implication, acknowledgement of the legitimacy of Northern Ireland as a politically subordinate part of the United Kingdom. Furthermore, the question of the nature and extent of the powers to be devolved to Stormont had been effectively decided in advance of negotiations with the publication of the Northern Ireland Assembly and Constitution Acts in the previous summer.[49]

It had already, therefore, been established that certain powers were to be excepted from the competence of the new Assembly – namely foreign relations, defence, electoral arrangements, the judiciary and emergency legislation. On the other hand, the powers to be devolved included social services, industry, education, planning and agriculture. But there would also be further 'reserved' matters, like the organisation of the police, criminal law, the courts and the prisons, all of which could be transferred back to Stormont from Westminster should the Northern Ireland government prove stable and dependable. And so it remained to be seen whether it was possible to reach agreement on the fate of internment, the status and organisation of the RUC, the composition of an executive, and the nature of the proposed Council of Ireland.

On Wednesday, 21 November 1973, Whitelaw convened the final long session of talks at ten o'clock in the morning. In due course, it was agreed between the participants that internment should be brought to an end as soon as the security situation permitted and that, as an indication of his positive intentions, the Secretary of State would release about one hundred internees by Christmas. The composition of the executive, which had stymied progress for weeks, was also agreed by seven in the evening, with six posts going to Brian Faulkner's party, four to the SDLP, and one to the Alliance. An additional non-voting member of the government was secured by the Unionists, two more such members by Gerry Fitt's party, and one by Oliver Napier's Alliance Party. The precise constitution of the Council of Ireland, and the finer details of policing, were both left over to be considered at a tripartite conference between both the British and Irish governments and the Northern Ireland representatives to be held at the Sunningdale Civil Service College in Berkshire from 6 to 9 December 1973.

By the time that the conference got under way, William Whitelaw had been replaced by Francis Pym as Secretary of State, and the discussion was led from the British side by Prime Minister Edward Heath, accompanied by – amongst others – Alec Douglas-Home as Foreign Secretary, Peter Rawlinson as Attorney-General, and obviously by Pym himself. The Irish delegation included Liam Cosgrave, then heading a coalition government, with Garret Fitzgerald as Minister of Foreign Affairs and Conor Cruise O'Brien as Minister for Posts and Telegraphs. The Northern Ireland parties, in turn, were represented by Gerry Fitt,

John Hume, Paddy Devlin, Austin Currie, Eddie McGrady and Ivan Cooper for the SDLP; Oliver Napier, John Glass and Bob Cooper for the Alliance; and Brian Faulkner, Roy Bradford, Leslie Morrell, Basil McIvor, Herbie Kirk and John Baxter for the Unionists. These last were indeed party delegates, however they could not be said to represent the prevailing opinion within unionist ranks – not even within their own party. Events were soon to make this clear.

But in the meantime, an understanding was reached and then compromise conceded among the various participants at the Sunningdale Conference. The Dublin government, for its part, agreed to declare that the constitutional status of Northern Ireland could not be changed without the consent of a majority of its citizens. An undertaking to put the amendment of Articles II and III of the 1937 Constitution of Ireland to a referendum could not, as circumstances in the Republic then stood, be given. These articles in effect claimed authority by right over the six counties of Northern Ireland, and although Southern Irish politics made their amendment a virtual impossibility in the short term, recognition of the North by the government of the South nonetheless meant significant progress.

The Unionists, in turn, agreed to the establishment of an all-Ireland body – a new look version of the old Council of Ireland – consisting of a Council of Ministers with executive functions, together with an all-Ireland Assembly and a Permanent Secretariat. Heath, on the British side, agreed to devolve police powers to the Assembly as security improved. The SDLP conceded that the all-Irish Assembly would have no more than a consultative and advisory role, that the members of the Council of Ministers would be mandated from within their own respective jurisdictions, and that decisions would have to be arrived at on the basis of unanimity. A Law Commission was established to consider the best means of dealing with terrorist offences North and South, and finally the details of both the 'executive and harmonising' functions of the Irish Council of Ministers would be thrashed out

213

at a later date. Official ratification would be left until the spring, but a deal, it seemed, had been done.

Nonetheless, as the power-sharing executive took office on Tuesday, 1 January 1974, loyalist and unionist opposition in the Province was already rising. Then the opportunity for action came in the second month of the new year when Heath called a general election in response to growing industrial unrest under the slogan 'Who governs Britain?'[50] Who should govern Northern Ireland with 'Dublin only a Sunningdale away?' came the response from the DUP, Vanguard and dissident Unionists, grouped together for a concerted effort under the auspices of the United Ulster Unionist Council.[51] The implication that the election would be used to display popular rejection of the Agreement was clear to see, and the demand for fresh elections to the Northern Ireland Assembly, the results of which – it was assumed – would facilitate the destruction of the new arrangements *tout court*, rose like a clarion call.

In the general election of 1974, the Labour Party came to power under the leadership of Harold Wilson, and Merlyn Rees assumed office as Secretary of State for Northern Ireland. Opponents of the Sunningdale Agreement had won 51 per cent of the vote in Northern Ireland, and eleven of the twelve Ulster seats in the Westminster parliament. The Agreement was now in serious difficulty. A renegotiation of aspects of Sunningdale, in particular the provision for a Council of Ireland, began to be sought by Faulkner to shore up Unionist support. On the other hand, the SDLP were liaising with the Dublin government with a view to pushing implementation forward. At the same time, the IRA continued its military campaign, while loyalist opposition to Sunningdale steadily expanded its basis of support. But it was in May, on Tuesday the 14th, that politics in Northern Ireland shifted towards breakdown. On that day, at eight minutes past six in the evening, a strike was called by the Ulster Workers' Council, seeking the abandonment of Sunningdale and new elections to the Assembly. At first the announcement was barely noticed. Soon it was to paralyse the Province.

The Ulster Workers' Council strike was among the most remarkable events of British post-war history. Ulster loyalism rose in a massive show of strength, threatening the British in an effort to stay British. The atmosphere of crisis was pervasive: road blocks went up across the Province; barricades lined the city streets; crowds massed in the urban ghettos. Within the space of only a fortnight there were power cuts and blackouts, there was flooding and pollution, and a state of emergency was declared.

The spectacle was immediately astounding: Protestant para-militaries gathered in broad daylight, hijacking and intimidation became a virtual norm, and services slowly ground to a halt. Shopkeepers were forced to close. Food shortages steeply escalated. Telecommunications began to collapse. The police refused to intervene, the Army didn't try. And in the midst of the confusion, a caucus of unconstitutional strikers managed to establish itself as the *de facto* provisional government of the Province. Its members occupied provisional 'ministries' and liaised with essential services. They negotiated with industry and they negotiated with private companies. Within a week they were issuing passes to the public, and soon after they organised a system of rationing.[52] This was civil disobedience on a cataclysmic scale.

The strike was a sinister, successful coup. It was a major insurrection within a civil war, and an awesome challenge to established political authority. But in the sudden explosion of activity and emotion, the true dimensions of loyalist outrage steadily became clear. Outrage, in fact, was being channelled into anger, and that anger was as bitter as it was obviously resourceful. In the early days of the stoppage, after a series of car bombs had been detonated in the Irish Republic by Protestant extremists, leaving twenty-eight civilians dead in the space of just three hours, one leading Workers' Council member uttered the remark, 'Slap it into you fellahs – you've deserved every bit of it.'[53]

But hatred and venom fuelled determination, and that deter-mination mobilised the strike. As it progressed, the Army declared its impotence while government ministers vacillated. The civil power grew suspicious of the military, the military doubted the competence of the civil power. Relations became fraught, accusations mounted, and the chain of command was put under strain. That, of course, was potentially disastrous: if the government doesn't own the Army, the Army owns the government. Confrontation, however, was averted in the face of mutual incapacity – the government was unable to issue orders, the Army unable to act. And so the Ulster Workers' Council stepped in to fill the void.

The Ulster Workers' Council had emerged suddenly from the political obscurity of back room conspiracy into the limelight on an otherwise unremarkable day in Belfast. It consisted of a twenty-one-man executive chaired by Glen Barr, a dashing Ulster Defence Association officer who represented Vanguard in the Assembly. The executive in turn came under the direction of a Co-ordinating Committee which comprised a cross-section of loyalist opponents of Sunningdale in general, and of power-sharing and the Council of Ireland in particular. Some of its members had a history of political involvement, some came from the ranks of the para-militaries, and some were representatives of the Protestant trade unions.

Paisley sat on the committee, as did William Craig and Harry West, the disaffected leader of dissidents from the Unionist Party, and in that sense the chief of the 'unpledged' Unionists. Ken Gibson stood in for the Ulster Volunteer Force on the Committee, while Andy Tyrie was brought on to represent the Ulster Defence Association. Also, and crucially, Harry Murray – a small, self-conscious, gutsy character – was spokesperson for the Co-ordinating Committee. A shop steward at the Harland and Wolff shipyard in Belfast, he was supported by Billy Kelly, a power-station operator and union convenor from Belfast, and Tom Beattie, an operator in the station at Ballylumford near Larne in Co. Antrim.

It was Harry Murray who announced on Tuesday, 14 May that the production of electricity in the Province would be reduced from the usual 725 megawatts to 400. Within days his message would be understood more clearly. It was through the supply of electricity that the strikers intended to exercise their leverage over the political fate of Northern Ireland. They could rely on the generating stations, whose workforce was about 75 per cent Protestant, to fail to deliver power to the Province. They could rely on the British Army, with its lack of technical expertise, to be unable to step into the breach. And they could rely on popular disaffection, together with Protestant paramilitary intimidation, to bring about a general stoppage.

And that is what they achieved. The various paramilitary factions spoke as one voice in the name of the Ulster Army Council which declared, again in the middle of May, that 'If Westminster is not prepared to restore democracy . . . then the only other way it can be restored is by a *coup d'état*.'[54] Power had passed, almost without notice and, as it seemed, effortlessly, out of the hands of the Westminster parliament and had come to reside, not in a newly established Assembly at Stormont, but in the hands of organised and determined men operating outside the bounds of any formal system of accountability.

The strike, which lasted for a further fourteen days, was to test relations between the British civil and military powers, it would try relations between the police and the Army, and it would push the power-sharing executive to breaking point. By the time that Faulkner finally resigned on 28 May, Ulster had come face to face with the disestablishment of constitutional government, near anarchy in the streets, and the end of a hopeful political experiment. Years later, Garret Fitzgerald, an Irish government representative at Sunningdale and subsequently Taoiseach, remarked on how the amendment of Articles II and III of the Irish constitution might have diminished Protestant suspicions.[55] However, for Conor Cruise O'Brien it was the Council of Ireland proposals that had made the collapse of the deal inevitable.[56] But Brian Faulkner, curiously, disagreed.

Faulkner pointed to power-sharing itself as just too much of a concession to bear at the time for the mass of Protestant opinion in Northern Ireland.[57] But the fact is that the difference between the components of the Agreement had become blurred. A press statement issued by the UWC in the middle of May lumped the disparate elements together: 'The Ulster Workers Council are determined that the Government shall not ignore the will of the majority of the people as to the form of government or the Sunningdale Agreement': both the power-sharing executive and the all-Ireland Council of Ministers had together come to symbolise resurgent Catholic power.[58]

But how are we to characterise the opposition to this resurgence? For the SDLP, the course of action taken by the Ulster Workers' Council had been a perfect exemplification of neo-Fascist intimidation, but for the strikers it was a popular and democratic insurrection. However, the problem for posterity amounts to setting out the principles in terms of which one could plausibly draw a distinction between the two.

On Monday, 27 May, the day before the stoppage was to come to a conclusion, with the electricity stations about to shut down power completely, with sewage flooding the streets of Belfast, food rationing in the control of the UWC itself, and voices warning of the 'point of no return', Merlyn Rees made a statement on the radio.[59] It was then that he explained how 'No parliamentary democracy, accepting as it must the rule of law and order, can accept that a group of men self-appointed and answerable to no one should decide when and where and to whom the essentials of life shall be distributed within a part of that democracy.'[60] But to whom was Merlyn Rees himself accountable? Who did he represent? And how, by comparison, did the representatives of the Ulster Workers' Council constitute a threat to democratic representation?

As Rees spoke, the Sunningdale Agreement had been effectively brought down, another failure of effort and intelligence to add to the list of false starts and disappointed hopes which observers and participants in the Northern Ireland scene have since become accustomed to expect. His remarks, however, oblige us even at this distance to ask what exactly had challenged and subverted democracy in the Province. It remains, in other words, to be asked of this catastrophe – and a catastrophe for the advent of peace and good government in Northern Ireland it certainly was – whether the breakdown had been caused by the actual democratic process which, while it bungled the situation in 1974, somehow came to the rescue in 1998, or whether the situation was not yet ripe for the blessing of democracy.

In 1998, guidance was certainly sought from the results of 1974, with 'Sunningdale for slow learners' popularly advanced as an adequate summation of the achievements of Good Friday.[61] But who or what was to bear the brunt of the joke now – was it history almost repeating itself in 1998, this time around bringing good news, the first time around bad luck? Was it nationalism out of synch with Unionism, or Unionism out of synch with itself? Was it democracy failing a people, or a people failing democracy? The Ulster Workers' Council strike launched itself with the assistance of paramilitary intimidation. It succeeded through extreme reluctance on the part of the Army to engage the forces of rebellion, and through the British government's reluctance to act with speed and resolution. But it succeeded also as a popular insurrection, one which had the support, and often the active support, of a faction – the Protestant people of Ulster.

This was the will of a faction pitched in armed opposition to the will of the British government. But both the British government and the pro-agreement parties were themselves no more than a composite faction, unable to control the actions or ambitions of a newly formed conspiracy whose membership happened to operate under their nominal authority. The strike of 1974 gave expression to the will of a people, represented by the Ulster Workers' Council, spoiling for a fight against another people, the advocates of Sunningdale represented by the established government and its supporters in the Northern Ireland Assembly. And, of course, both of these were in turn confronted by a militant Irish Republican

Army posing as the legitimate embodiment of the historic Irish nation.

It therefore becomes clear that the situation in Northern Ireland in 1974 was a contest between three hostile contenders for competing versions of democracy, between three embodied popular wills – but with each presuming to represent its rivals. One such will – the British government's – held supreme authority over the new Assembly, which it commended as properly representative. However, the supporters of the British plan for a new representative system of government in Northern Ireland – the advocates of the Sunningdale initiative, in other words – failed to win endorsement for this 'representative' regime.

Another protagonist – the Ulster Workers' Council – happily conceded its revolutionary status while nonetheless laying stress on its own democratic credentials. But its democratic legitimacy was presumed to derive from its proximity to the intensity of Protestant disaffection. The UWC thus claimed to represent the majority community on the basis of plebiscitary entitlement: the strikers believed that they 'knew the mind' of their people – they advertised the extremity of popular passion in their own persons.[62] So while the government sought to broker a representative settlement in the absence of inclusive popular representation, they were opposed by the Workers' Council offering popular representation on the basis of its rejection of that very settlement.

At the same time, as we have seen, the Provisional IRA appeared as the military wing of a prospective state, but for all that as the arm of the Irish people. Soon they would follow the example of the UWC, coming forward as the plebiscitary advocates of popular outrage. But the danger here was again the same – the eager representatives of communal uproar are obliged over the longer term, in order to secure themselves as permanent political players, to maintain their own constituency in its original state of excitement, thereby thwarting the possibility of evolving a more inclusively representative system.

So there were three political forces in play, three 'democratic' factions, with none commanding the complete allegiance of all the parties involved in the conflict. It is in terms of this contest that the Northern Ireland situation between 1974 and 1998 has to be understood. It was a war between two democratic principles grouped into three opposing factions: two of the three were avowedly populist in nature – a Unionist and a Republican populism – and a third aspired to advance the cause of representative constitutionalism. To grasp this struggle more completely, it is necessary to trace the historical sequence leading from one point to the other – from the strike of 1974 to the emergence of peace in 1998.

3

That sequence takes us through a set of political landmarks, from the Constitutional Convention of 1975 through the Prior initiative of the early 1980s to the Anglo-Irish Agreement of 1985. As it turned out, it was this last feat of diplomacy which ultimately bore upon the events of 1998. The initiative for the Good Friday Agreement was supplied jointly, by London and Dublin – a community of purpose made possible by the Anglo-Irish Agreement: although the Agreement of 1985 was not immediately decisive for the conflict at the time, it nonetheless transpired that the long term impact of its provisions proved indispensable for the developments of the 1990s. While certainly a piece of unconscionable stealth to unionists, the Anglo-Irish Agreement still offered little by way of deliverance to Republicans. It showed loyalism the limits of its own resistance, and it demonstrated to the Provisionals the vulnerability of their position when faced with the abandonment of republicanism in the South.

However, the 1985 Agreement only emerged after another series of failures had arrived in the aftermath of the Sunningdale fiasco. With the disappointments of the past having been stoically endured, Merlyn Rees brought forward new proposals on 3 July 1974, committing his government to introduce legislation for the election of a Constitutional Convention 'to consider what provisions for the government of Northern Ireland would be likely to command the most widespread acceptance throughout the community there'.[63] After so many disasters over the course of the previous year, almost every interested party was now keen to play for time. Rees had secured approval for the Convention with barely a moment's pause after the collapse of the Assembly, but he held back from actually bringing the new Convention into being until April 1975. But by that time, another general election had intervened, Enoch Powell had introduced himself into the thick of Ulster politics, and Unionism had undergone a degree of realignment.

By this point Harry West, having headed the UUP since January 1974, had lost his seat while still retaining overall leadership of his party. James Molyneaux had come to the fore as party leader at Westminster, and Faulkner had established the Unionist Party of Northern Ireland as a splinter from UUP. The 'Unionist parties now wanted delay, as did the SDLP', Rees later commented.[64] But while uncertainty and recrimination permeated the atmosphere, Rees was engaging the IRA to discover if it could be brought to a negotiable position.[65] Rumours of a British withdrawal filled the corridors, the media and the streets.[66] The Provisionals had called a ceasefire in December – their second in six years – which lasted until August, petering out but not officially ended until the start of the following year. But in the meantime, while the significance of the truce remained uncertain, Unionism waited anxiously, at once deflated and appalled.

A British withdrawal in the broadest sense was certainly contemplated at the time. The true problem was availing of the requisite ways and means: the Provisionals' bottom line – a declaration of intent to quit within a specified number of years – was judged likely to blow the lid off the most fragile of situations. Northern Ireland was not Aden, as the British recognised. But in default of discovering a way of sneaking out of the Province, a nine month truce offered ample room for the infiltration of Republicanism by the United Kingdom intelligence services, and its defeat at the hands of the Ulster courts and the Crown forces in the field.[67]

As the truce continued, tension was mounting in the loyalist heartlands, driving the Reverend Robert Bradford, then Industry spokesman for the Unionist Parliamentary Party, somewhat laconically to remark that 'We may well have to become "Queen's rebels" in order to remain subjects of any kind'.[68] But no rebellion was to follow. Instead, the constitutional parties regrouped, barely limping forward, suspended in a state of near paralysis, until the elections to the Convention were finally called for May 1975.

There were no major surprises in the elections to the Convention – except that Faulkner had been conspicuously trounced at the polls, just holding on to his seat, but losing a raft of allies. Few were optimistic about the prospect of an advance: at one extreme, the United Ulster Unionist Council (UUUC) – comprising Vanguard, Independents and the DUP – faced a beleaguered SDLP, with the Alliance Party and a solitary NILP member somewhere in the middle. Rees exempted himself from the proceedings and left Sir Robert Lowry in the chair. Progress was duly stymied from May until November – the terminal date for the deliberations – but, with even less hope of success, the Convention was reconvened in February 1976, and set to last until March. Then the final deadline arrived, but a result was not forthcoming. Through almost a year of heated discussion, no new alliances were formed, no productive understandings reached, and no settlement was brokered.

The rules of procedure had been changed for the Constitutional Convention, drawing on the experiences of the ill-starred Assembly. Back then, tactics were uncertain, but the strategy was clear: Unionism was to be shaken and nationalism cajoled. Efforts had been focused on middle-range opinion with pressure applied where the extremes of the middle would not meet. Now Westminster sat back, the Secretary of State withdrew to the wings, and a majority of unionists hostile to the earlier experiment confronted a bruised and disconsolate residue of survivors from the days of Sunningdale. There was no prior commitment on the part of Westminster to implementing the recommendations supported by the dominant forces in the Convention, and there were bounds set within which agreement would have to be reached – except that power-sharing now stood as a minimum requirement for political endorsement by Westminster.

The Convention was thus intended to secure the political education of an unreconstructed Unionism – a Unionism cut in the original mould, dismayed by recent developments in the Province, yet still dreaming of the glory days of Carson, of Brookeborough and of 'No Surrender'. It had not been out-smarted nor out-manoeuvred by conference deals and back-room pacts – so this time it was to be converted, induced by raw experience, into an appreciation of the limits set by existing political reality: to be gently pushed, but not dragged screaming, towards what hostile onlookers considered to be the requirements of the modern world.

Theirs was a quarrel 'having no relation to this century but only to the seventeenth century', mused Harold Wilson in the House of Commons in May 1974.[69] But now it was reckoned by the Labour government that loyalism could be coaxed since it could not be shunted: coaxed indeed – not by the shady machinations of charade and subterfuge, but by the stark political necessity of drawing back from the brink, of bridging the difference and averting further crises. Enlightenment through necessity, through a direct encounter with the exigencies of a deteriorating situation, usually has much to recommend it. But here it produced little except an inkling of compromise, which was in any case presently swept to one side. For when agreement did finally flicker on the horizon with the Vanguard leader, William Craig, at that time supported by David Trimble, tentatively shifting towards the prospect of a voluntary coalition with the SDLP, the old anxieties resurfaced, loyalism was divided, and Paisley seized the day.

To Paisley, the political drama now unfolding had all the simplicity of a Morality play. It had been performed on countless occasions before, and its message was immediately discernable: concession spells appeasement, and appeasement ends in tears. The roles, too, had been rehearsed before – O'Neill had fallen, Chichester-Clark had gone, Faulkner had crumpled – with compromise each time ceding to righteousness. And now it was William Craig who was forced to act out the role of betrayer to Paisley's role of deliverer, true loyalist, and defender of the unionist cause.

In reality, though not in rhetoric, the idea that if one could manipulate the amenable centre of Northern Irish politics the confused stalwarts would ultimately follow had been the conviction of the British government in 1973.[70] But now there emerged the assumption, or better, perhaps, the hope, that it might be possible to educate the extremes of Ulster loyalism with the tools of parliamentarism – that under conditions favourable to dialogue the obduracy of the ultras would in the end relent, that boorish fundamentalism would finally abate in a world of political give and take. But this was a formula with no guarantee of success: the idea that immersion in political conversation was bound to lead to compromise proved more an honourable than a dependable presumption. Besides, the identification of the extreme had acquired an air of unreality now that the ideological extremes had come to occupy the political centre of decision-making in the Convention. Without the goodwill of loyalism, or at least its intelligent self-interest, the prospect of compromise would be eagerly awaited, but never actually realised.

Craig and Paisley had stepped forward as the political figureheads of loyalism – in unison it seemed, but really in competition.[71] Craig had gambled with the offer of a voluntary coalition with constitutional nationalism in the Convention – it need only last five years, and it would mollify the enemy, he reckoned: far better this, surely, than surrendering the initiative to the vipers of Republicanism. Did the situation not demand this much, was this not intelligent self-interest?

The gamble, however, did not pay off. Craig had upped the ante on numerous occasions with a studied recklessness in his public statements – 'We will fight back and fighting back does mean "shoot to kill",' he once insisted – and so for him the banality of routine politics was always bound to savour of pusillanimous retreat.[72] Like Paisley, he understood the competitive dynamic of unionist high politics but, under pressure from events, he was brought to violate one of its basic terms and conditions: the first to give ground in the battle for the soul of Unionism is sacrificed before the unyielding tribunal of loyalist hardliners. In essence, both Paisley and Craig had played the same game, but this time Paisley had won.

More than any other contender for the leadership of fundamentalist loyalism, Paisley was almost fated to win: dialogue, mediation, conciliation – these were so many vapid ecumenical nostra to the Reverend Ian Paisley. They were the stuff of parliamentarism, not the materials for a moral and spiritual crusade. Similarly, concession, tolerance, *rapprochement*: this was the stuff of decadent liberalism, not the values of besieged truth and embattled righteousness.

Craig, on the other hand, had begun his career as an orthodox Ulster Unionist – originally active in the Young Unionist movement, and later destined for ministerial office. An MP for Larne in 1960, he became Minister for Home Affairs in the O'Neill government of 1963 before moving to Health and Local Government for a year in 1964. After a successful stint in the newly created Ministry of Development, he returned to Home Affairs in 1966 and remained there until 1968 when he found himself at the heart of the escalating crisis associated with the rise of the Civil Rights Association.

Soon he was attracting a torrent of criticism over his handling of a delicate and deteriorating situation. In due course, he was advocating what O'Neill was to describe as 'almost' a policy of Ulster independence, openly criticising his Prime Minister with that 'fatal fluency of speech' which so distinguished him from the bulk of his colleagues, and he was swiftly removed from office.[73] From that point on, he began to launch a series of vitriolic attacks upon the reform programme foisted on the Northern Ireland government by Wilson and Callaghan, drifting ever more explicitly towards the option of a Unilateral Declaration of Independence for Ulster.

Indeed, it was that option which was to supply the Vanguard Movement with both its ideological identity and its strategic bottom line.[74] In 1972, the Movement published a pamphlet describing the Westminster administration as a 'jack-boot' government – William Whitelaw appearing variously as a 'satrap' and a 'gauleiter' – which had relegated the Province to the status of 'unwanted guest'.[75] This was Ulster's wake-up call: the old union of hearts and minds seemed irrecoverably distant now that the British establishment had turned their backs on generations of Protestant fidelity and sacrifice – 'They have called us back-woodsmen, barbarians and they have meant it.'[76]

The pamphlet invited its readership to reflect upon the fact that the Union with Great Britain 'was never an end in itself': 'It was always a means to preserving Ulster's British tradition and the identity of her loyalist people.'[77] British policy had unwittingly 'forged a nation' out of Ulster's 'blood and tears'. But the defence of this new nation could not be safely entrusted to a remote and uncommitted people whose only recent notable achievements had been the invention of 'rubber bullets and the anti-blood sports league'.[78] There was a right to survive and a right to be free, and consequently there was a right to resist where survival was imperilled and freedom undermined: 'The loyalists of 1912 were prepared to defy and did defy the Westminster government.'[79] Now that the sons of Ulster were at the mercy of an 'undemocratic and un-British regime', it was left to Vanguard to take up the challenge: its purpose was 'to mobilise all those moral forces of our breed, which have been hardened over generations of struggle'.[80]

In the next two years, Vanguard set about making good its promise. Mobilisation, in consequence, became the order of the day. Strikes were arranged and monster rallies called. At once deadly earnest and desperate to convince, Craig addressed the massed ranks of aggrieved spectators with meticulously crafted

ambiguities – always promising a showdown, and then prophesy-
ing victory. Nothing was left wanting from the perspective of
political theatre: prominent leaders from the Orange Order
mingled with the crowd, the Loyalist Association of Workers
offered its support, and the Ulster Defence Association stood in
uniform amidst banners, placards and a vast, imposing stage. Not
to be outdone, the Vanguard Service Corps arrived on motor-
cycles with outriders, exuding discipline and menace.

But now it was 1975, and Craig was exploring other options –
pitching deals with the enemy, he would soon be shaking hands.
His deputy leader, Ernest Baird, immediately jumped ship, allies
voiced their consternation, supporters turned their backs. As
defection mounted, Paisley stood his ground in the evangelical
style of a latter-day zealot. It is clear that over the decades he has
been the subject of the most hostile jibes and inexpensive parody,
but the description here is precise: evangelism after all was a duty,
and zeal a test of virtue.

This stance, of course, came easy to him. He had come from his
own Free Presbyterian Church in the Ravenhill Road area of
Belfast as a seeker into politics in the early 1960s, offering protest
against the lowering of the Union Jack upon the death of Pope
John XXIII in 1963, demonstrating against the raising of an Irish
Republican tricolour on Divis Street in west Belfast in 1964,
fulminating against the fiftieth anniversary commemorative
celebrations of the Republican Easter Rising in 1966. In that year
alone, twelve new congregations were formed within the Free
Presbyterian Church. The methods of the pulpit harangue had
served him well, and they were to serve him better still after 1968
when the Rome-ward trend of Ulster could at last be visibly
discerned in characters and speeches which the enthusiast could
identify with insurrectionary Republicanism.[81]

In fact and for the moment, insurrection, especially of a
Republican kind, remained *in partibus infidelium*. The IRA was all
but defunct, the Catholic population was effectively unarmed, and
the Civil Rights Association had designs no more extensive nor

deceptive than its stated aims. But Paisley, who had the pro-
foundest conviction in human frailty, was less moved by a sense of
the fallibility of his own judgement. The true nature of protest, he
knew, was legible in its tendency, and the tendency of civil rights
was towards the empowerment of Popery and, once minimally
gratified, it would urgently seek more. Conciliation, it seemed
obvious, would have to be stopped in its tracks.

This has all the appearance of a self-fulfilling prophecy – but
more certainly it had the power to persuade. Almost without effort,
Paisley's career had marched from one success to another. Having
founded the Ulster Constitution Committee and the Ulster
Protestant Volunteers as instruments of agitation, he had perfected
the techniques of the counter-demonstration. Later, launching the
Democratic Unionist Party in 1971, he began to apply his
intelligence to the development of wrecking tactics. Points of
order, the booming heckle, sit-ins and occupations: they all came
in for regular strategic employment.

At one point in the new Assembly in 1974, having occupied the
seats of the front bench, it took eight uniformed policemen to
remove his towering presence from the chamber. His character has
met with derision, and his actions have been regularly treated with
petulant disdain. On 23 May 1974, as the power-sharing initiative
looked set to fold, Merlyn Rees confessed in the House of
Commons that the Doctor's methods made him 'a little sick': 'The
honourable gentleman cannot have double standards and be a
democrat here and a demagogue in Northern Ireland.'[82] Most
usually, his politics, and also his profession, have been patronised
as risible, or as a wild anachronism. But the charge of anachronism
has always been wide of the mark, not least for the very obvious
reason that he has threatened, harried and sabotaged proceedings
in what can only be described as very much our own time, and
there is nothing even slightly comical about his conviction or
determination.

From early on, Paisley had grown quite impervious to the
influences of terrestrial shame, and he knew with certainty where

he wanted to go. His energy derived from looking inwards to the conscientious promptings of the Christian message, and his inspiration came from looking backwards to the example of the Protestant Martyrs.[83] The European, the American and the Scottish record of persecution, fortitude and resilience, of protest, secession and 'New Light', was a comfort and a solace. But the evident resurgence of ceremony, prelacy, Popery and heresy sounded a warning and extended an invitation to vigilance and resistance.[84]

For committed Ulster brethren, that memory of schism, disablement and recovery stretched back into the nineteenth, the eighteenth and the seventeenth centuries.[85] In the middle of the eighteenth, reflecting on the religious drama of the seventeenth century, David Hume had found something unaccountable in the operation of this 'religious spirit' which railed against the impositions of civil authority. It disregards, he had noted, 'all motives of human prudence'.[86] That judgement is not without its relevance today. To Ian Paisley, prudence was a kind of indulgence, an altogether mundane consideration in the face of a higher calling.[87] In 1975 and 1976 the voices of incorrigibility had spoken – not all of them, to be sure, as part of a religious chorus – but Paisley's role had been integral to the dynamic of recalcitrant opposition.

In the end the Convention's report – more or less endorsing the original Stormont system – received not so much as a moment's discussion in the British House of Commons. After the failure of the Convention's deliberations in 1975, one commentator, responding to eight years of discussion about intractable problems and possible solutions in Northern Ireland, offered the general view that 'the problem is that there is no solution'.[88] Optimism had always been low, but now, in 1976, it was facing extinction.

VIII

Reversals: 1976–1982

I

We have seen how the Convention ended in failure, passing out of existence on 5 March 1976. In the aftermath of failure, the politics of Unionism underwent a kind of reversal. But so too did British policy towards Northern Ireland. The attention of sections of the political establishment on the British mainland had been focused on Northern Ireland for eight continuous years now. They had been focused with varying degrees of intensity and purposefulness, it is true, but for those who had addressed themselves to finding a solution to the crisis, there was an emerging sense that the point of exhaustion was near.[1]

The latest effort to bring normality to a troubled situation had ended in acrimony, yet still the problem dragged on as if scarcely any effort had ever really been made to remedy it. The British Labour Party had by this time been in power for just over two years. Harold Wilson, however, was to call it a day in the middle of his term of office, announcing his resignation on 16 March, and he was replaced by James Callaghan at the beginning of April. Merlyn Rees hung on to his post as Secretary of State for Northern Ireland until the early autumn, handing over to Roy Mason, who until that point had been acting as Minister of Defence, in September. Mason concentrated his efforts on achieving a period of stability, as he saw it. In policy terms, however, this stability meant something of an about-turn: not exactly a revolution in strategy, to be sure, but nonetheless a significant reappraisal of the prospect of success in finding a way out of the Northern Ireland impasse in the short term.

Many of the changes associated with Mason's period in office had actually been initiated under Merlyn Rees. By the time that Rees quit the Northern Ireland scene, however, his name had become so intimately connected in the public mind with disorientation and indecision that a series of crucial developments which had occurred during his tenure of office have tended in retrospect to be identified with the Mason era.[2] The challenges that Rees encountered were undoubtedly enormous. He battled in the face of barely surmountable difficulties. The result was that he was forever chasing events, but never determining outcomes. 'Merlyn and I hadn't a clue where we were going,' an adviser later revealed.[3] But if Rees was somehow unequal to the task, if he seemed incapable of resolution, albeit in the face of an explosive situation, Mason at least created the illusion of executive determination. This he did with an attitude that looked like vaunting self-aggrandisement, and with an almost wilful boorishness.[4] But while he appeared all round to lack sensitivity and judgement, things nevertheless seemed to happen more or less in accordance with his designs. Despite this appearance, it was during the space of a year or so before Mason took up his post that the groundwork for a new departure had been laid.

It was decided, for instance, in November 1975, that persons convicted of terrorist offences should lose their 'special category' status, beginning in March 1976. From then on, paramilitary offenders would be classified as criminals – a classification that, as we have seen, was to have explosive consequences as the 1980s dawned. It was Rees who had drawn attention to the significance of the shift in policy when he referred in the House of Commons in June 1976 to violence in Northern Ireland as a security problem involving 'small groups of criminals'.[5] It was at this time also that the Bourne Committee was set up by the Northern Ireland Office to consider the question of police effectiveness.

Some effort was given to making the committee's work appear relevant to the nationalist community by including the issue of police 'acceptability' within the remit of the inquiry: security was to be acceptable to Roman Catholics as well. However, it was probably the case that both effectiveness and acceptability could not have been broached in any meaningful way at the same time. As things turned out, the former was indeed pursued with more vigour than the latter. But, as preparations for the reorganisation of the police reached an advanced stage, the implication that the role of the military would change accordingly seemed obvious.[6]

It will be recalled that the Provisional IRA truce had come to an effective end by the middle of 1975. Then, in December of that year, the policy of detention without trial was discontinued, clearing the way for a new judicial assault upon Republican insurgency. And now, in June of 1976, the policy of 'police primacy' was under way. Rees had announced this change of direction back in March, and by July the Bourne Committee was ready with its recommendations. First of all, the size of the RUC was to be significantly increased. Its reserve forces were to be given a larger role in security – especially in support of full-time officers when situations such as marches, riots and disturbances might occur. Members of the Constabulary were to be given greater flexibility in employment, Catholics were to be encouraged to join up, training facilities were to be expanded, and new specialised investigation teams were to be established. A paramilitary police force was being primed to take up position as the most prominent and direct line of defence against the IRA campaign of terror, with the military from then on lending its support.[7]

The purpose of this reversal was to quarantine the crisis. There was, however, a price to be paid. The RUC cannot readily be described as desperate and rampaging in its bigotry in the ordinary day-to-day conduct of its business, but it was predominantly Protestant in its composition, and potentially sectarian in its orientation. It was, after all, charged with holding the line against Republican sectaries in defence of a constitutional settlement which had not won the allegiance of the Catholic population. Under the conditions of a descent into unrestrained war, the presumption of RUC impartiality would be sorely disappointed, and the organisation would revert to incensed and belligerent partisanship. In effect, then, while Britain had sought to contain the conflict, it succeeded in engineering its entrenchment.

The British Army had originally been introduced into Northern Ireland to enforce the peace between two hostile communities. At that point, in 1969, the police and the paramilitary police – the RUC and the Ulster Special Constabulary – were in a position to act as the Protestant community's most effective means of visiting hostility upon their Catholic neighbours.[8] Now a reformed police force was to take the lead in imposing a peace after the Army had become a protagonist in the conflict. The element of reform had a somewhat cosmetic appearance from the perspective of Northern Ireland's Catholic community, especially from its Republican heartlands. It was from this vantage that the significance of the change in security tactics was particularly clear to see.[9] There were evident short term gains for Britain's political parties in unloading the burden of defence on to local security, but there were long term difficulties brewing also – difficulties which would emerge towards the end of the millennium when each community, together with the British and Irish governments, came to settle its differences with its enemy, and to establish a system of law and order, on a new agreed foundation.

When Roy Mason had been in office almost a year, the British Army's spearhead battalion was withdrawn, while the RUC was expanded. So too was the size of the Ulster Defence Regiment. The UDR had been established in 1970, after the disbandment of the Ulster Special Constabulary, and it was decided in 1977 that its numbers should be swollen to about 8,000 members.[10] The RUC grew from 3,500 men and women in 1970 to 7,500 in 1979, while the Army had been reduced from nineteen units in 1972 to thirteen by 1978.[11] What had begun under Rees was therefore taking on a discernible shape.

The IRA were to be criminalised and humiliated, and of course infiltrated and neutralised. At the same time, the RUC and the

UDR were to become a front line of attack in the war against terrorism, while the undercover attack fell to MI5, MI6 and the Special Air Services.[12] All this represented the culmination of developments which had started in 1975 at the latest. But, as a result of his own peculiarly unabashed pugnacity, Police Primacy, Ulsterisation and Criminalisation, as these developments came to be known, were perceived as Mason's own.[13]

Of course, it is also true that the very appointment of Mason seemed to mark a dividing line. Direct rule would continue indefinitely and, under the auspices of its semi-permanent status, the administration of justice was to be made more efficient through the extended use of 'Diplock' or juryless courts.[14] The IRA had been shaken, but its members were regrouping and digging in for a long war, and the British establishment was planning for a long haul. The time-scale within which resolution of the Northern Ireland problem had been anticipated was drastically expanded. Something of a vista had opened up, and attention was now focused on 'making direct rule work'.[15]

That focus was of course at least partly disingenuous. Direct rule was indeed to be made to work – but only minimally, until happier possibilities should emerge. It was not, in other words, to be made to work particularly well. No new initiatives were to be tried as far as returning government to the Province was concerned, but neither was any effort made to make the current situation comprehensively attractive to any section of the population in Northern Ireland. Mason wanted breathing space, and he wanted above all to minimise the impact of Northern Irish affairs on the British domestic scene.[16]

Such minimalism aptly captures the paradoxical position in which Northern Ireland had found itself from the collapse of Stormont in 1972 until the Good Friday Agreement of 1998. It remained an integrated part of the United Kingdom, yet not an integral part of its politics. It was directly under the control of British parliamentary authority, but that authority was not subject to the standard parliamentary procedures of scrutiny and debate.[17]

More than a paradox, the situation represented a stalemate in which Westminster could buy time whilst reducing to a minimum the impact of a Provincial civil war on routine political life in Britain. Society and politics in the Province calcified into bitterness – sectarian strife seethed, violence spluttered on, yet total war was averted. And, in the rest of the United Kingdom, while public opinion could be shocked into revulsion by repeated Provisional IRA 'spectaculars', the attitude remained one of disengaged bewilderment at a foreign conflagration. The bottom line was that Britain's established political culture could maintain its habitual procedures and dispositions relatively unscathed.

And so attention shifted to giving the appearance of normality to a highly precarious situation – which could, of course, degenerate still further. Accordingly, in September 1976, Mason made plain his ambition to alter the terms of debate. Improvements to the status quo would take precedence over grand political gestures: 'Unemployment, little new investment, too many businesses closing down, these are the questions that must receive priority.'[18] In fact, as it turned out, they did not receive any overwhelming priority. Attempts were certainly made to stimulate growth and reduce unemployment. Inward investment was encouraged, the public sector was expanded, and subsidies to manufacturers in decline were continued. Soon, leisure centres graced the desolate Belfast environs. But such endeavours did not in themselves harness the most purposeful executive energies concerned with Northern Ireland. In truth, political energy and skill had been effectively exhausted, and the little determination that remained was channelled into the expanding matrix of security. In the end, developments under Rees and Mason represented a holding measure, the purpose of which was perhaps inadvertently publicised in the *New Statesman* at the beginning of 1976: 'The Irish will have to be left to sweat it out for a while if they are to come to their sense.'[19]

The Mason project of normalisation continued until a change of government arrived in 1979. Before the general election of that year, the Conservative Manifesto had advertised the party's intention of supplementing direct rule with one or more regional councils charged with responsibility for a range of services at that time administered centrally. The implementation of the plan would fall to Airey Neave, then Opposition spokesman on Northern Ireland, and set to become Secretary of State in the event of a Conservative victory. Neave, however, was assassinated by the Irish National Liberation Army in March of the election year. His death has often been described as the most consequential political murder of the 'troubles'. In one sense, of course, it was. Its impact on Margaret Thatcher, a close ally of Airey Neave's, was both profound and lasting.[20] But, in the broader scheme of things, the plan for a regional administration, while it was greeted with enthusiasm across the spectrum of Unionism, represented a minor political adjustment within the established framework of policy rather than a serious change of course.

Neave had announced back in 1978 that power-sharing no longer looked like practical politics to him – but then it hadn't looked much like practical politics to Roy Mason either.[21] Conservative rhetoric gave some indication of the direction in which conciliatory gestures might be made, but not an example of how a method for comprehensive conciliation could be developed. Dismay and consternation at the ferocity of the IRA campaign had reached fever pitch within the ranks of the Conservative Party; at the same time, the general complaint of Catholic nationalism had grown shabby and unwelcome in the eyes of the British public; and so a tactical *rapprochement* between Conservatism and Unionism appeared the most expedient and palatable option to the incoming administration.

The honeymoon, however, did not last long. And neither could it have lasted for any significant period of time. The simple fact was that it made no practical sense to offer encouragement to a political faction in Northern Ireland in the expectation that its opponents would lie down defeated. Much like everywhere else, action was succeeded by reaction in Northern Ireland but, more than anywhere else, it had become impossible to neutralise any of the major players in the resulting drama. There was, consequently, no alternative to continued negotiation, however tedious and unfruitful this had proved to be in the past. Accordingly, after the Conservative victory, the new Secretary of State, Humphrey Atkins, embarked upon yet another initiative to restore a system of devolved government to the Province.

But by March 1980, the Atkins talks had failed, and politics drifted on into the autumn, when attention was turned to the awful prospect of political strife held out by the republican hunger strikes. That protest was to last for nearly a year, and by the time the hunger strikes came to an end with the death of ten republican martyrs, Sinn Féin had become a force to be reckoned with, nationalism had been both rocked and energised, and political accommodation generally had come to seem implausible in the extreme. At that point, in September 1981, Atkins was transferred out of Northern Ireland, and James Prior accepted the post of Secretary of State with a thinly disguised display of regret and disappointment.

Still, by his own estimate, having spent the winter months weighing up the options, Prior had arrived at his scheme for 'rolling devolution' by February 1982, bringing forward a government White Paper in early April.[22] The plan was to make use of the existing legislation which had brought the Northern Ireland Assembly of 1973 into existence – except this time, administrative power was to be transferred in stages, on a 'rolling' basis, depending on the measure of agreement achieved between the participating parties.

The Assembly itself would consist of seventy-eight members elected, as in 1973, under the single transferable vote system of proportional representation. It was to comprise a presiding officer elected to appoint chairmen and deputy chairmen who would convene statutory committees charged with monitoring the six Stormont departments of government. The committees were thus intended in the first instance to scrutinise but not to execute business. Even here the process of scrutiny was subject to various curtailments, and was ultimately dependent on the goodwill and co-operation of British government ministers.[23] Under the scheme, power would in the end be devolved either to individual departments or to the shadow executive as a whole, depending on how progress towards agreement proceeded. Agreement, in this instance, meant the ability to carry 70 per cent of the votes in the Assembly.

All things considered, the chances of success looked slim indeed. In London, the Northern Ireland Cabinet Committee, with the notable exceptions of Lord Carrington, Lord Hailsham, William Whitelaw, Francis Pym and Atkins, had given the proposals a singularly unenthusiastic reception.[24] Thatcher herself was in due course to describe the package with characteristic bluntness as 'a rotten Bill'.[25] Moreover, the publication of the White Paper coincided with the Falklands War, with the result that any discussion of its contents was obliged to proceed against a backdrop of national alarm and popular jingoism.

In Northern Ireland, the prospect of success was equally imperceptible. Sinn Féin still posed a threat to constitutional nationalism, having recently achieved its first electoral success since Bobby Sands' victory in the Fermanagh–South Tyrone by-election of April 1981: in May, Republican candidates standing under the 'Anti-H-Block' label had won 7.7 per cent of the vote in the District Council elections.[26] This hardly constituted a seismic shift in the distribution of votes in Northern Ireland – but to London, Dublin and the SDLP, the signs were depressing. SDLP members were themselves divided over both strategy and the overall direction of party policy. And Unionism, for its part, was in a state of disarray. As far as Prior's initiative went, the outlook could not have been much bleaker.

After the Bill had become law in July, with elections set for October, Sinn Féin was planning to stand on an abstentionist ticket.[27] So too was the SDLP. By now there was open dissension in their ranks, but unrest had been brewing since about 1977. It was at that time that the Irish Independence Party was formed to challenge the nationalist credentials of the SDLP, and in the same year Paddy Devlin, who had sat in the ill-starred power-sharing Assembly, was expelled from the party for his refusal to toe the line. Devlin had always been something of a maverick in Northern Irish politics. Gerry Fitt, however, was not, and his resignation as leader in 1979 did not bode well for party unity.[28]

Constitutional nationalism had been despairing of progress since the collapse of both Sunningdale and the Convention, with the result that a significant constituency within the SDLP had come to fix its gaze ever more intently beyond the frontier of an internal settlement. After Fitt's resignation, John Hume became leader, to the delight of the party's grass roots. He had been advocating a 'third way' between Republicanism and Unionism since 1978. The practicalities of this philosophy were obscure, but the language was effective – redolent with the promise of an 'agreed Ireland'.

The Irish problem since 1912 had not derived from nationalist aspiration, in Hume's judgement, but from the historical deformations produced by the 'British dimension'. But since this 'dimension' had by this point been reformed, it could obviously be used constructively to broker agreement and foster reconciliation.[29] That, of course, meant offering Unionism an ultimatum. But, despite Hume's rhetorical dexterity, competition for the heart and soul of nationalism continued unabated up until the election to Prior's Assembly. By then, Sinn Féin was waiting in the wings to exploit the expected capitulation of the SDLP. But the equivocation and uncertainty within nationalist ranks were matched by the complete fragmentation of the unionist cause.

2

Significant sections of the Ulster Unionist Party were by this time committed to a policy of complete political integration with the rest of the United Kingdom. The cause of integrationism was most notoriously espoused by Enoch Powell, Unionist MP for South Down since 1974, but it had also won the backing of his own party leader, James Molyneaux. It had the support of powerful advocates within Unionism like Robert McCartney, and it received encouragement from Tory allies in the House of Commons such as Nicholas Budgen, Sir John Biggs-Davidson and Julian Amery.[30] This integrationist alliance had from the start sought to frustrate the passage of Prior's Assembly Bill through Parliament in the spring of 1982. Procedural measures, points of order and a profusion of amendments obstructed progress at every stage. And while opponents of the Bill concerted to impede parliamentary business, the voices of acclamation were reduced to a faint murmur.[31]

The whole affair began to acquire the familiar characteristics of farce. Throughout the course of the second reading, not a single party leader contributed to the discussion, participation in general was derisory and, with media attention focused elsewhere, a motley crew of Tory dissidents gained every advantage. A succession of filibustering tactics through the Committee stage of the Bill ensured that after seventy-two hours of debate only its first three clauses had been addressed.[32] Political and constitutional argument did, of course, appear in various guises. But, as far as integration went, the central point of principle was supplied by Enoch Powell: 'The ultimate truth,' he declared, 'is that within the United Kingdom political purpose can only be dissolved and held in equilibrium, deprived of its dangers and given beneficence, force and the power of improvement, within the single parliamentary legislative structure of the United Kingdom.'[33] As Powell's meaning receded into splendid opacity, his speech grew animated with that devastating amalgam of passion and conviction which both his admirers and detractors had come to expect.

In essence, Powell's intervention amounted to a principled objection to the viability of devolution within the United Kingdom. Political purpose could only succeed harmoniously – be 'held in equilibrium' – on the basis of a complete and fully incorporating Union. The alternatives were the 'unparliamentary' method of direct rule currently in operation, under which legislation proceeded by Orders in Council, or the creation of a subordinate legislature. But either option, in Powell's account, spelt 'danger'. Each of them encouraged the subversion of goodwill or 'beneficence'. In the one instance it extinguished the goodwill of the government, and in the other the goodwill of the governed. This argument, of course, was by no means new. It had been wielded in opposition to the Liberal Home Rule bills of 1886, 1893 and 1912. Indeed, it had originally been advocated by William Petty some three centuries before as a means of securing Restoration policy in Ireland against rebellion.[34] But now it was being invoked as the surest way of disarming Republican strategy by depriving its ideologues of hope.

According to Powell, Sinn Féin and the IRA took comfort from the British effort to broker compromise as a sign of weakness. As he had put it back in 1980, 'when the United Kingdom starts to look for special institutions which in a part of itself will meet the wishes of those who do not want to be in the United Kingdom at all, that is a sure sign, seen as such by friend and foe alike, that Britain "wants out"'. It was apparently this perception that gave solace to Republican revolutionaries, and invested their designs with the expectation of success. Given an adversary such as Britain is made to appear in this account, is it any wonder, Powell asked, that the 'IRA is still in business after eight years packed with political encouragement that Britain itself has supplied?'[35] But while this position was being advanced once more in the House of Commons in 1982, Nicholas Budgen, despite his eagerness to lend support to Powell, revealed a flaw in the political logic of the integrationists' case. An incorporated Union had not, he observed, won anything like the unanimous backing of the Ulster Unionist Party.[36]

Powell's idea was that political integration would bring about a reversal of unionist fortunes. Certainly, when it appeared as the preferred option in the Ulster Unionist Party's Manifesto for the elections to the Prior Assembly, it represented a reversal of policy.

More than a reversal, it represented a revolution through 180 degrees back to the original nineteenth-century unionist agenda. That agenda ultimately met with defeat in the form of the 1920 Government of Ireland Act. However, the 1920 Act, promulgated in the midst of the Anglo-Irish War, was intended to settle the Irish Question in the best interests at once of Irish nationalism, Irish Unionism and British security. The Act was, in any case, not just a Home Rule settlement, but a Home Rule settlement twice over. It provided for the establishment of a subordinate parliament with jurisdiction over twenty-six counties in the South, and a subordinate parliament with jurisdiction over six counties in the North.

As we have seen, the agreement of 1920 was scuppered in the South in the face of ongoing hostilities between British and Irish Republican forces. It was then succeeded by the 1921 Anglo-Irish Treaty. But in the North, Unionism rallied to the defence of its hard won privilege. Since that privilege amounted to the establishment of a devolved Parliament, ultimately located at Stormont, the unionist defence of the 1920 provisions had since then been a defence of a Home Rule settlement. It was that settlement, and not the aspiration to an incorporated Union, which had won the allegiance of over 60 per cent of the population of Northern Ireland between 1920 and 1968. And it was that settlement which had called forth the desperate loyalty of the majority of Ulster Protestants to the institution of Stormont after the disturbances which began in 1968 and after the imposition of direct rule in 1972. But now Powell, with the support of Molyneaux, was making a case for the constitutional arrangements sought by Unionism prior to 1920. However William Ross, James Kilfedder and innumerable other Ulster Unionist MPs and activists remained committed, in effect, not to 'Unionism' in the strict sense, but to Ulster Home Rule. So too, indeed, did Ian Paisley's Democratic Unionist Party. But if the DUP favoured a Home Rule settlement in 1982, a decade earlier that party's position had been altogether different.

Paisley had outlined his preferences back in 1972. He had

predicted the demise of Stormont since the introduction of internment in 1971. Then, in early in 1972, in the British House of
Commons, he had appeared to lend his support to some form
of incorporative Union.[37] But by 22 March, in the Northern Ireland
House of Commons, without quite retreating from that position,
he sought at least to clarify his original intentions. Integration, he
explained, could be welcomed – but only as a policy of last resort.
Paisley was carefully setting out his stall in opposition to William
Craig, to the rising popularity of Vanguard, and to its advocacy of
Ulster independence in particular. The Democratic Unionist Party
had just been formed the previous October, Paisley's grip on the
rural Protestant community of small farmers was secure, but he did
not want to lose the support of urban skilled and unskilled labour
to Craig, and so it had to be made emphatically clear that
independence would be 'disastrous' – 'not only to this Province
but to the Protestant working classes who may today be deceived
and may think that this is the answer and a panacea to the ills of our
Province'.[38]

If attempts were made to coerce Northern Ireland into an all-
Ireland settlement, 'then probably every Member of this House,
even the Alliance Members, would be rebels', observed Paisley.
But faced instead with a diminution of the powers of Stormont, or
with the prospect of a 'community Government', then 'integration'
would appear as the best last option. 'As if we were like Rhodesia,'
he exclaimed: as if, in other words, a Unilateral Declaration of
Independence would meet with British resignation. Secession was
not an option, but integration was. Paisley's first loyalty was to the
Stormont parliament, 'as constituted under the 1920 Act'. But if
that Act were to be challenged, integration had to take precedence
over independence – the Union over autonomy for Ulster. After
all, 'Our fathers did not ask for this Parliament. They wanted to
remain under Westminster and this Parliament was forced upon
them.'[39]

In all this, Paisley was presenting his own perspective on what I
have described as the moment of crisis for Unionism. The political

structures of Northern Ireland were poised on the brink of transformation, yet the balance of forces was uncertain.[40] Choices
seemed to multiply, but the result of every course of action
appeared impossible to predict. Certainly the 1920 Government of
Ireland Act was under attack. Stormont's freedom of action had
been repeatedly reined in by Westminster over the preceding three
years, now direct rule loomed on the horizon, and the IRA was
prosecuting a war with a view to establishing a thirty-two county
Irish Republic, while Craig in opposition continued to promote the
goal of a six county Ulster Republic. Only four days before
Paisley's intervention, Vanguard had staged a massive loyalist
rally attended by over 50,000 protesters in Belfast's Ormeau Park.
The Ulster Defence Association, which had been formed in
September 1971, continued to recruit paramilitary volunteers in
their droves. Even the Ulster Volunteer Force, which dated back
to 1912, was enjoying a sort of rebirth.[41] But most pressing of all, as
Paisley rose to speak, Brian Faulkner was in London in conference
with Edward Heath over the future government of the Province.

'So in our crisis I say,' Paisley concluded, 'that the best thing for
us to do, if we have to do it — and please God we will not have to
do it — is to go back to first principles.'[42] That, of course, meant
Unionist first principles: the Union as salvation for the Protestant
cause, and the Crown-in-Parliament as the bond of Union. If
Northern Ireland were to be preserved from disaster, the principles
of Edward Carson, the original architect of unionist priorities,
could help to steer a course towards safety. Deliverance lay in
restitution — in a restoration of the old Union or Imperial
Parliament, dissolved under the Government of Ireland Act. By
implication, adopting the secessionist policy of Ian Smith, the
strategist behind Rhodesia's current difficulties, ensured the death
of British Ulster.

Direct rule arrived within days of Paisley's speech, but this was
not integration as he had originally envisaged it. The transfer of
powers was effected with blistering speed. A Secretary of State was
immediately appointed, together with two ministers of state and

three under-secretaries to execute the business of government. Between them, they would supervise the running of the former Stormont departments. The Northern Ireland Civil Service survived, but all initiative was ceded to the newly created Northern Ireland Office, based at Stormont Castle and Dundonald House, but with an office at Whitehall. The twelve Northern Ireland representatives were to sit in the British House of Commons, as more or less superfluous participants in the British legislative process. Legislation would be generated by Orders in Council, and therefore be exempted from parliamentary examination. Neither Labour, the Conservatives nor the Liberal Party would field candidates for election in Northern Ireland. This was evidently not the incorporated Union to which Paisley had come to reconcile himself, but an emergency dictatorship against which he would campaign over the course of the succeeding quarter-century.

In the elections to the Prior Assembly in 1982, the DUP lost out to Molyneaux' party, having kept a lead on their rivals since 1974. But Paisley was not easily discouraged. His centrality to the Northern Ireland scene had continued uninterrupted since the fall of the Convention in 1976. In one sense, his political successes had been few and far between. His failures, on the other hand, were legion. But his recovery rate was awesome. Back in 1977, Paisley and Ernest Baird, with the support of the UDA, attempted to seize the initiative and stage a recovery of unionist fortunes by calling a strike for 3 May. After so many reversals, a resurgence of the majority was eagerly awaited.[43] The Loyalist Association of Workers in 1973 and Ulster Workers' Council in 1974 had made their point – the latter to devastating effect – with concerted stoppages aimed at paralysing the Province. But neither effort succeeded in harnessing government policy to unionist purposes.

In 1977, with Vanguard and the Orange Order withholding their support, the outlook appeared even less favourable, and by 13 May the strike was called off, having failed to achieve its stated aim of forcing the government to implement the recommendations of the Convention Report from the previous year. Roy Mason, then only a few months in office, was jubilant. He later recalled circling above Paisley in a helicopter, surveying the Reverend's last stand below with the farmers of Ballymena : 'I took off in my helicopter from Stormont Castle that day, singing as I rose into the air "Don't Cry for Me Ballymena", and I went across the top of the city and there, looking down, like High Noon in the street were Paisley's men across the road.'[44] Paisley, however, was not to be written off. He had an unsurpassed ability to marry conviction with opportunism, and opportunities never failed to present themselves.

By 1980, Paisley's fortunes had recovered. In 1979, he topped the poll in the European elections, and during the period of the Atkins talks he was being fêted by an assortment of pundits as a man with whom the British could do business. Even Peter Jenkins in the *Guardian* conceded that the 'most striking change on the political scene' in Northern Ireland was the change in 'Dr Paisley himself'.[45] After the collapse of the talks, politics and the press reverted to their original assessments, and to the familiar characterisations of the pulpit politician. The *Daily Telegraph* was first to conclude that the Conservative flirtation with Paisleyite fundamentalism had been a mistake after all: 'It was a mistake to build up Mr Paisley in the pursuit of the chimera of devolved government on the assumption that given the chance he would be a force for moderation.'[46]

But before such analysis had even appeared in print, Paisley had embarked upon the campaign trail again. The campaign itself served the familiar cause of the rights of true-born Ulstermen, but the occasion was quite specific. This time the target was the appearance of co-operation between London and Dublin as indicated by the Haughey–Thatcher summit of December 1980. Here, once more, Paisley's tenacity of purpose was to prove so unrelenting that by 1982 his image within his own constituency as a dependable bulwark against any threat to the Union was virtually unassailable. But this time around, the Union denoted a form of Ulster Home Rule – not a recourse to the original 'first principles' of Unionism so deliberately adumbrated back in 1972.

3

And so it transpired that on the eve of elections to the Prior Assembly in October 1982, the UUP was divided between integrationists and Home Rulers, while the DUP was united on a majority-rule devolutionist platform. But the argument for independence had not yet gone away. In 1976, the Ulster Loyalist Central Co-ordinating Committee had published a document considering precisely that option.[47] The Co-ordinating Committee had been set up in the aftermath of the Ulster Workers' Council strike of 1974 as a forum for loyalist paramilitary organisations. It included both the major Protestant terror groups – the Ulster Defence Association and the Ulster Volunteer Force. But it also embraced a plethora of smaller organisations – the Red Hand Commandos, the Orange Volunteers, Down Orange Welfare – all similarly pledged to take the war to the Republican enemy.

That usually meant launching assassination attempts against arbitrarily selected members of the Catholic community, though bombing campaigns, like the massive Dublin and Monaghan explosions of 1974, were also undertaken. In due course, with assistance from the British security forces and the RUC, attacks were also launched against prominent Republicans.[48] By 1976, the UDA and Down Orange Welfare had withdrawn from the committee after suggestions that some of its members had been in discussions with the Provisionals about independence.[49] The problem here, however, had not been the issue of independence, but talks with the IRA. In the same year, a workshop was convened amid widespread publicity at Corrymeela in Co. Antrim to consider once again the viability of an Ulster state.[50] But, in the end, it was the UDA which gave the issue the most serious attention, publishing a proposed constitution for Ulster, together with an introductory essay, in pamphlet form in 1979.[51]

The prime movers behind this initiative included the prominent UDA activists, John McMichael and Andy Tyrie, together with the former Vanguard Deputy Leader, Glen Barr. 'Whilst there is

Constitutional disagreement between the two sections of our community,' the document proclaimed, 'there can never be political unity with any real meaning or purpose.'[52] Of course, there was nothing particularly startling in this analysis as such. But the document went on to propose a constitutional settlement for a sovereign Ulster, based on the principle of a separation of powers. A Prime Minister and his deputy would be chosen by popular election to appoint ministers with portfolios who would execute the business of parliament. Their work would be scrutinised by parliamentary committees whose composition would reflect the balance of forces within the Assembly. A Supreme Court would be invested with the judicial power to determine any alleged breach of Ulster citizens' political rights. Allegations could be brought via a Constitutional Preliminary Hearing Committee which would provide the necessary financial support.

But the key innovation, as the UDA saw it, was to come with the creation of a parliamentary Speaker to be elected by two-thirds of the members in the legislative chamber. The Speaker would set the calendar for debates, and appoint both committee members and their chairmen. In an interview conducted by Rob Mitchell in 1979, John McMichael explained the significance of all this: although power-sharing would not be enshrined as a constitutional imperative under these proposals, 'there will be Catholics in the executive because the Catholic-based parties will insist that if they're going to go along with the election of the speaker the executive must be non-sectarian, and it will come about'.[53] These recommendations represented the first concerted effort on the part of Protestant paramilitaries towards constitutional compromise in Northern Ireland. Their aim was not the oppression of their Catholic neighbours, but neither was it a defence of the historic British Union. For a unionist organisation, all this appeared a somewhat novel enterprise.

In the all-party negotiations of 1998 which brokered the Good Friday Agreement, the UDA was represented by the Ulster Democratic Party, led by Gary McMichael, John McMichael's son.

By then, John McMichael had been assassinated and independence was not high on the agenda. The UVF also found political expression at the negotiating table in 1998 through the Progressive Unionist Party, with David Ervine acting as its leader. By that time, both paramilitary organisations had been responsible for countless atrocities over a thirty-year period. But what their various commitments betray in 1976 and 1998, together with those of the main unionist parties, is the extent to which unity of purpose within Unionism had been shattered since 1968. Divisions within the unionist monolith began to appear during the premiership of Captain Terence O'Neill in the mid-1960s, and these had continued to subdivide as the Northern Ireland conflict escalated after 1969. However, in the midst of this proliferation of factional divisions there remained, at least in theory, a common unifying objective. That objective was declared by all to reside in the security of the Union.

But of course we have seen that the idea of a 'union' had now come to cover a range of political options for the settlement of Northern Ireland, not all of which were compatible with a British Union as such. Certainly, each option canvassed had excluded the resort to a union with the Irish State. But complete autonomy for Ulster implied no union other than Northern Ireland's unity with itself. By 1979, arguments for dominion status had been publicised much as arguments for independence had been explored. Devolution had been floated, and integration had been sought. In short, Unionism had come to encompass an extensive range of mutually incompatible constitutional preferences. This spirit of apparent innovation clearly sits uneasily with the declared positions of 'Not an Inch' and 'No Surrender'. However, the fact is that the need for innovation of some kind was presaged by events. Where the dynamic of events seemed to contribute towards a Republican outcome, as it invariably did in the eyes of the Republican movement's staunchest opponents, the result was a paralysing fear which disabled unionist initiative.

Consumed by fear, Unionism retreated behind its oldest

rhetorical figures: 'We are the People', 'Ulster will fight and Ulster will be right'. But even here, the situation of a new impetus behind an old rhetoric was not itself exactly new. The disappearance of constitutional debate within the Protestant community in Northern Ireland between 1925 and 1965 has tended to lend the appearance of novelty to the reversals within unionist polemic which began to intensify after 1976. But, of course, we know that a challenge to unionist security did not arrive without precedent in the latter part of the twentieth century – that a crisis had originally emerged around 1886, and that a series of reversals beset unionist aspirations from that date until 1920.

IX

Reversals: 1886–1920

I

It was during this original crisis that Albert Venn Dicey published his classic elaboration of the Unionist position, *England's Case against Home Rule*, in an effort to stem the tide of Gladstonian constitutional reform at the end of the nineteenth century. Dicey was acutely aware of the fact that Gladstone had been involved in various attempts to draw Irish support away from Republican militancy and towards constitutional politics ever since the Fenian uprising of 1867. The Fenian Brotherhood had been formed in 1858 as part of an attempt to carry over into a new generation certain of the ideals and principles which had fostered the Young Ireland movement and fed the abortive uprising of 1848. After the Fenians had staged their rebellion, Gladstone set about conciliating Irish Catholics with the disestablishment of the Church of Ireland in 1869 and the Land Act of 1870. The assumption was that religious disaffection, together with rampant agrarian discontent, fuelled political radicalism in Ireland. The disestablishment of Protestantism, followed by the provision of tenurial security to an impoverished peasantry, were therefore expected to drain support away from revolutionary politics.[1]

But still the demand for Home Rule could not be made to disappear. The 1801 Act of Union had been introduced to the consternation of sections of the Irish Protestant population, but in the absence of Catholic Emancipation it failed to win the allegiance of the mass of Catholic opinion either. When Emancipation came in 1829, under pressure from Daniel O'Connell's organisational and mobilisation skills, the attention of politically active sections of the Catholic population switched to agitation for Repeal of the Union. And now in 1870, as Gladstone's Land Act came on to the statute book, the Dublin Protestant barrister, Isaac Butt, was reviving the campaign for Repeal in the form of a design for Federal Home Rule in Ireland.[2]

Throughout the 1870s, Home Rulers were divided into radical and more moderate wings, while the Land League, and then the Irish National League, continued to focus attention on rural deprivation. Moderates rallied behind Butt, but radical sentiment after 1875 was attracted to the obstreperous determination of the MP for Meath, Charles Stewart Parnell.[3] In due course, agrarian agitation bore fruit with Gladstone's 1881 Land Act, which underwrote tenant rights, and the Ashbourne Act of 1884, by which sums for purchase were to be advanced to tenant occupiers. But, by January 1886, parliamentary agitation also looked set to steal a victory when the Irish Party emerged from the general election holding the balance of power between Lord Salisbury's Tories and Gladstone's Liberal Party.

Gladstone's conversion to Home Rule had been announced in the press the previous December, and now the way stood open for the introduction of a Home Rule Bill in February. The Bill was to provide for a parliament in Dublin invested with the power to legislate within its own designated sphere of competence, together with a responsible executive entrusted with the duty to carry parliamentary resolutions into effect. But it was a scheme, Dicey insisted, which provided less for a degree of constitutional compromise in Ireland and more for a 'fundamental revolution' within the United Kingdom as a whole.[4] The stage was set for a confrontation between Home Rulers, unionists and separatists which was to last until Easter 1998, and which would continue, of course, long beyond that date.

Dicey was happy to concede that the ingeniousness of the Bill lay in its subtle mix of Federalism and colonial self-government. The problem was that neither of these options was appropriate to the circumstances of Ireland, and that a mixture of the two would be fatal not only to the welfare of the Irish population but to the security of the United Kingdom. Dicey followed Gustave de Beaumont in discovering the source of Irish discontent in the historic existence of *'une mauvaise aristocratie'* whose privilege had been upheld in the midst of staggering rural impoverishment. De Beaumont was a friend of Alexis de Tocqueville who had himself toured Ireland in the mid-1830s. De Tocqueville had learned from Montesquieu that the success of aristocracies, much like the success of ancient republics, depended on the extent to which 'virtue' could be stirred to animate their proceedings, but that virtue in aristocracies took the specific form of 'moderation'.[5] However, it was precisely in moderation that *une mauvaise aristocratie* was likely to be found wanting. In Ireland in the nineteenth century, unlike England in the eighteenth, gross inequality was maintained in the absence of any principle of social accommodation. Deprived of the means of accommodation, the established division of ranks became virtually insupportable: mutual regard yielded to outstanding social hostility.[6]

The cry for Home Rule, Dicey contended, was a result of this inveterate system of social divisiveness. However, fundamental divisions could, with effort, be repaired. In the first place, improvement could be expected from an imaginative solution to the Land Question. But, ultimately, it would be necessary to promote a change in the 'spirit of Englishmen'.[7] It was to this last that Dicey looked to ensure the means of social accommodation within the United Kingdom. Once this had been achieved, one could expect the gradual alleviation of rural destitution and from this, in turn, the final elimination of political dissent. 'French peasants were Jacobins,' he commented, 'until the revolution secured to them the soil of France.'[8] But what was missing from Dicey's analysis was any account of how politics was currently conducted in regard to Ireland. He defended the principle of parliamentary sovereignty within the United Kingdom, and hoped for the development of harmonious political relations between

Britain and Ireland by at once modifying cultural attitudes and improving social conditions. But the question of how parliamentary sovereignty was actually exercised in the case of Ireland received virtually no attention in his work: while social manners and agrarian conditions were examined in some detail, the character of the existing government which managed Irish affairs barely registered in his treatment of the problem of Home Rule.[9]

The assumption that Irish ills could best be addressed by redeeming the 'spirit of Englishmen' had certainly been stated before. Four years earlier, in the Preface to his *Irish Essays*, Matthew Arnold had pointed out how 'English people keep asking themselves what we ought to do about Ireland'. It was, however, the 'great contention' of his *Essays* that 'in order to attach Ireland to us solidly, English people have not only to *do* something different from what they have done hitherto, they have also to *be* something different from what they have been hitherto'.[10] But, as with Dicey, the discussion of what Englishmen ought to *be* in relation to Ireland never focused on the practical question of how responsible government for Ireland might practically be organised. In fact, in Arnold, the concrete issue of the form of administration in Ireland had been even more drastically occluded than it was to be in Dicey since the treatment of political arrangements had been so thoroughly displaced by what was effectively an exclusive account of national manners and dispositions.

Arnold had launched himself upon this particular path of inquiry back in 1867 when he delivered his Oxford lectures on *The Study of Celtic Literature*. There he suggested that an appreciation of the nature and diversity of national characters represented the best way of beginning to effect harmony across the range of that diversity.[11] As he spoke, he advanced the claim that the greatest problem for reconciliation within the United Kingdom was posed by the Celtic national character, in particular by its peculiar brand of imagination and sentimentalism, which was permanently affronted by the insolence of its English rulers. While 'Celtic', for the purposes of Arnold's argument, was loosely synonymous with the Irish, 'English' comprised an unhappy mix of the characteristic defects of Normanism, Germanism and Celticism itself. As a result, Arnold commented, 'we have Germanism enough to make us philistines, and Normanism enough to make us imperious, and Celticism enough to make us self-conscious and awkward'.[12]

Such an amalgamation of attitudes was quite clearly, in Arnold's view, a recipe for conflict since philistinism, self-consciousness and imperiousness together confronted the more uniform emotionalism of the Irish Celtic sensibility with an attitude of scorn and rebuke. Of course, in the larger scheme of things, Arnold held that the severity and ignorance of the English middle classes threatened the stability of the Empire as a whole. The 'sympathetic and social virtues' of the French, he noted, 'actually repair the breaches made by the oppressive deeds of the Government'. In England, however, there was no 'vital union' between its people and 'the races they have annexed'.[13] The consequences for Ireland in particular were clear to see. Securing the Union had become one of the central tasks of statesmanship in the later decades of the nineteenth century, but that security required an effective reconstruction of the composition of English manners.[14]

Reconstruction, however, could not be tackled by storm. The general disposition of the English, Arnold claimed, would have to be 'suppled and reduced by culture'. This, in turn, would require 'a growth in the variety, fullness, and sweetness of our spiritual life'.[15] Arnold was to reiterate his point throughout the 1870s and 1880s as the Irish crisis mounted. It was his basic contention that, in the wake of the first two Reform Bills, English public life was set to undergo a process of democratisation. While that process was irreversible, it nonetheless threatened the Empire with dissolution much as it threatened the national polity with anarchy.[16] Imperial policy in its entirety would steadily fall to the grasping petulance of the Puritan middle classes whose imperfect civilisation stood in desperate need of the humanising agency of culture.[17]

2

While Dicey presented no such elaborate programme of reconstruction in 1886, he did accept that the collision between English
manners and Irish sensitivities had disabled effective government
in Ireland. But, he insisted, a revolution in politics, such as was
being advocated in the guise of self-government for Ireland, fell a
long way short of presaging a solution. It heralded, instead, the
impending death of the British constitution. That death would
follow fast upon the crisis in political subordination entailed by the
Home Rule Bill. The proliferation of arguments in favour of Home
Rule since the 1840s, and especially since Gladstone's conversion
to the cause in 1885, had apparently succeeded in obscuring the
inevitable consequences of any system of self-government
introduced into the United Kingdom. But the direst consequence
of all, Dicey anxiously predicted, would be an intensification of
political disputes leading to civil war.[18]

It was this very outcome that had been artfully concealed under
the existing layers of Irish disaffection. From the point of view of
the defenders of Home Rule, it seemed that things could hardly get
worse, as Dicey noted: the very depth of Irish resentment appeared
to require some form of radical redress.[19] Moreover, if history, as
it seemed to the advocates of self-government, had left no other
option, the prevalence of federations throughout the modern
world compounded the sense of the inevitability of Home Rule.
Canada, Hungary, the Swiss Cantons, Germany and the United
States all testified to the viability of self-government, dual
monarchy or federation in its various forms.[20] Why should not
Ireland, as Gladstonians argued, equally benefit from a constitutional settlement which would, as things then stood, happily
coincide with the general tendencies of the age?

Dicey's response revolved around the circumstantial nature of
constitutional arrangements in general. Their appropriateness, he
argued, was a matter of time and place. And so, there was no
inevitable virtue which attached to self-government in its many

forms. As an example, Dicey implored his readers to witness the suppression of Blacks in the Southern States of America. Social injustice of this kind could hardly stand as a recommendation for the devolution of powers from metropole to province or from Federation to member states.[21] But beyond this, there were certain conditions without which federations could not be made to survive. The principal condition, in Dicey's view, was the existence of loyalty, or a pre-existing desire for some form of political unity. Self-government could, for instance, safely be settled on a province like Victoria, first because its geographical distance reduced its strategic importance, but also because the bonds of allegiance which attached the Victorians to their mother country eliminated the possibility of political friction.[22]

If, on the other hand, friction could plausibly be expected from Deák's dual system for Austria-Hungary, it was worth recalling, as Dicey put it, that the Austro-Hungarian monarchy had the character of a 'permanent alliance' with a strong and unified executive concentrated in the hands of a single man. In both the Hungarian Diet and the Austrian Reichsrat, ministers were appointed by King and Emperor Franz Josef. The Federal Parliament, in turn, was composed of two delegated committees whose deliberations were independent of both the Hungarian and Austrian parliaments. Such arrangements, transposed to Britain, would entail the end of its parliamentary system and the demise of responsible government. All this, Dicey concluded, would mean exacerbation of the problem it was ostensibly designed to solve.[23]

The Swiss and American systems, Dicey continued, could offer little comfort to the Home Rule enthusiast either. In his *Law of the Constitution* of 1885, Dicey had argued that for a federation to work, its inhabitants must 'desire union' but not 'unity'.[24] Now, in 1886, he clarified his point. Federations involved a restraint upon power. In that sense they were not much given to 'unity'. But they evolved, nonetheless, from the principle of common nationality or allegiance. After all, it was German nationality which secured Bavarian autonomy against any drift towards independence. In

America and in Switzerland the same principle applied. Here federalism developed 'because existing states wished to combine in some kind of national unity'.[25] That wish, however, did not under-pin the Irish demand for Home Rule. The Irish demand, on Dicey's reckoning, was based on a claim to national difference, the Swiss federation on a will to national coherence.

On this analysis, a Dublin parliament would represent a concession to factionalism, while the American Union embodied the spirit of greater harmony. Irish aspirations were introverted and divisive, while the American and Swiss achievements were expansive and inclusive. As such, they encapsulated the 'tendency of modern civilisation' which was 'towards the creation of great states'.[26] The British Union was fully coincident with that modern tendency, and any derogation from the sovereignty of Parliament would for this reason imperil the progress of civilisation. A British federation made even less sense than an Italian, and Italy had naturally rejected that course: 'If Englishmen are to take lessons from foreigners,' Dicey concluded, 'they need not be ashamed of being instructed by Cavour.'[27]

Dicey's point here was that a federalisation of the United Kingdom offered the surest means of destroying the sovereignty of Parliament. It would require, at the outset, the establishment of a system of entrenched or fundamental law defining the principles of federation. This in turn would require the establishment of some means of determining alleged breaches in constitutional propriety. It would depend, in other words, on the creation of a mechanism for judicial arbitration. That would involve concocting a con-stitutional court with jurisdiction over both the confederacy and its members. At once, the legislative authority of statutes would be curtailed and undermined, Parliament would be divested of sovereign power, and government action would be weakened and dispersed.[28]

In such a revolution, however, sovereignty would not simply disappear. In federations, 'behind all the mechanisms and artifices of the constitution there lies, however artfully concealed, some sovereign power which must have the means both to support the principles of the constitution and, when occasion occurs, to modify its terms'.[29] Either that sovereignty would be based on a commonly acknowledged political power, in which case it was likely to revert to the Crown, or it would not, in which case it would be subject to dispute. But a dispute in this context could only mean war, and the spectre of war was the surest proof against the justice of a federal solution to the Irish problem.[30]

The advocates of Home Rule had been attracted to federalism, but they had been attracted to colonial self-government also, and here, in Dicey's opinion, the outlook was again quite hopeless. The foundation of self-government within the Empire had to rest on the simple principle of the 'complete and unquestioned supremacy of the British Parliament throughout every portion of the royal dominions'.[31] This principle might apply differently in Jamaica and at the Cape, or in Canada and New Zealand, according to the local organisation of social and political forces. But it could not logically be denied. Nor, in fact, was it denied throughout the colonial empire. However, it was precisely this supremacy which the Irish claim to nationality was likely to render contentious in the event of self-government being conceded.

In the end, it was Dicey's view that the establishment of colonial self-government in Ireland was preferable to any scheme for federalising the United Kingdom, but at the same time it was vital to recognise that, as circumstances then stood, self-government for Ireland would inevitably entail its eventual political separation from Great Britain. In a self-governing colony like Victoria, Dicey argued, the rights of the Colonial Governor were not disputed, the judgments of Victorian courts complied with the provisions of imperial statutes, and the legal authority of the Privy Council was not contested.[32] However, in Ireland it was precisely these manifestations of imperial authority that would be construed as burdensome impositions on national freedom. The Empire would gradually acquire the characteristics of tyranny in the opinion of Irish political activists, who would ultimately be drawn to assert the rightful liberty of their own institutions of government.

As it happened, the Home Rule Bill of 1886 did seek to bestow self-government upon Ireland. The independence of the Irish Parliament was, however, to be subject to various limitations, the most important of which were to be the Lord-Lieutenant's power of veto and the judicial authority of the Privy Council. These restrictions on Irish legislative freedom would, in Dicey's view, be the occasion for future bitter dispute. Under the Bill, Irish members would withdraw from the Imperial Parliament only to be recalled in the event of disagreements arising over the terms of the settlement. In that case, the Imperial Parliament would be reconstituted as a federal assembly. This federal component was, for Dicey, the most damaging part of the Bill.[33] However, it was his considered view that the potential for damage contained in the 1886 Bill paled into insignificance by comparison with the provisions contained in its sequel.

The first Home Rule Bill was defeated by thirty votes in the House of Commons on the morning of 8 June 1886, but in February 1893 Gladstone introduced a second Bill which in turn suffered overwhelming defeat in the House of Lords on 8 September. But before that outcome had been secured, Dicey had already come to the conclusion that Gladstone's second effort was more destructive than his first. In his polemical study of the 1893 Bill, *A Leap in the Dark*, the inevitability of civil strife was taken to reside in the Bill's more overtly federalist features, in particular its plan to retain a reduced number of Irish members in the Imperial Parliament. Were the Bill to be successful, Dicey wrote in May, the result would be a 'spurious federation' to be 'miscalled the United Kingdom'.[34]

Back in 1886, Joseph Chamberlain had been prepared to resign himself to the federalisation of the United Kingdom constitution as a bulwark against Irish independence. Independence, he thought, would inevitably follow the concession of colonial self-government to Ireland. The adoption of a scheme for 'Home Rule All Round', on the other hand, would guarantee the constitutional integrity of the Union.[35] This would involve the establishment at once of five subordinate legislatures – one in England, Scotland, Wales, and Ulster, and one for the three remaining Provinces of Ireland – together with an Imperial or Federal Parliament at Westminster responsible for defence, colonial affairs, customs and postal services.[36] The scheme was therefore intended as a complete, and not a partial, federalisation of the existing constitution. But in 1893 unionist polemic seized upon partial federalisation through the retention of Irish members in the Imperial Parliament as the most objectionable part of the Bill. Dicey himself commented that 'the retention at Westminster of eighty, or indeed of any Irish members at all, means under a scheme of Home Rule the ruin of Ireland and the weakness of England'.[37]

The Bill would be ruinous to Ireland chiefly because it had unwittingly provided for the simultaneous establishment of two irreconcilable systems of government within a single Irish jurisdiction. This, of course, was not a consequence of federation. It would come about instead because, while under the provisions of the Bill self-government would be conceded to Ireland, imperial supremacy would still be retained at Westminster. Since it was not possible to depend on Ireland's compliance with that supremacy either in the Irish legislature or in Irish courts, the moment that any contest arose the overriding authority of the Imperial legislature and the Privy Council would be obliged to decide the case.[38]

But, as Dicey put it, the 'moment that the British Government intervenes to support the judgement of the British Courts, we have in Ireland two hostile Executives. We tremble,' he went on, 'on the verge either of legal revolution or of civil war.'[39] But while such mayhem could be safely predicted for Ireland, in England the Bill would mean the effective destruction of Cabinet government by the creation of two disjointed Parliamentary majorities in the Imperial Parliament itself. There would, if the Bill became law, arise the immediate possibility of an Irish party constituting a majority on imperial affairs in coalescence with British Liberals in the lower House, while the Conservatives alone might constitute a majority on exclusively British matters.[40]

The Liberal expectation was that the presence of Irish MPs would ensure the attachment of Ireland to Britain, give Ireland a voice in imperial affairs, and leave the conduct of domestic politics to the British members alone.[41] In practice, however, such a scheme could only end in tears, in Dicey's estimate. It was not, in the first instance, so easy to effect a surgical separation between British matters and Imperial affairs. But beyond this, the Irish members, in concert with the Liberals, might find themselves in a position to erode the majority support enjoyed by the Cabinet in Parliament as debate shifted from domestic to foreign and colonial issues.[42]

It was in this sense that Gladstone's Bill had inadvertently provided for the creation of two potentially incommensurate majorities within a single legislative chamber. As Dicey put it: 'The Irish members and the English Liberals combined may put in office a Liberal Cabinet. On English matters, *e.g.* the question of Disestablishment, or of Home Rule for Wales, the British majority consisting of British members of Parliament only may constantly defeat the Gladstonian Cabinet, and thus force into office a Conservative cabinet which could command a majority on all subjects of purely British interest, but would always be in a minority on all matters of Imperial policy, *e.g.* on the conduct of foreign affairs. Which Cabinet would have a right to retain power? The sole answer is – neither.'[43] The whole scheme, in other words, guaranteed the institutionalisation of political conflict. It also contained within it the possibility that both the government of a subordinate legislature and the balance of power within the Empire would fall to the representatives of the Irish nation.

And so it emerges that the Home Rule Bill of 1893, like the Home Rule Bill of 1886, was seen by Dicey as destined to promote political strife in Ireland and constitutional subversion in Britain. But the third Home Rule Bill of 1912, which was finally placed on to the statute book in October 1914, appeared to him the final stage in an abysmal diminuendo, with each successive attempt to confer self-government upon Ireland exacerbating the folly of its pre-decessor.[44] The 1912 Bill was put before Parliament in April by a Liberal administration headed by Henry Asquith. The significant difference between 1912 and 1893 was that the new Bill was introduced in the wake of the Parliament Act of August 1911 by which the House of Lords had been deprived of its historic veto over all acts of parliamentary legislation. The probability of the Bill's success, by comparison with every previous attempt to devolve a Home Rule legislature upon Ireland, had consequently been increased by a very significant margin. Nonetheless, on terms set down by the Act, the Lords still retained the power to delay the implementation of laws until they had successfully passed through the House of Commons no less than three times in three successive sessions.[45] As the Bill made its advance through the Commons, Dicey set about championing the cause of the Union for the last time.

The result was his book, *A Fool's Paradise*, the title of which aptly summarises his approach to the Bill. It was in this work that he revealed, in the starkest terms to date, the precise order of preference in which he ranked the available options for a settlement of the Irish Question should the repeal of the Union be at hand. First came national independence for Ireland, and second came colonial independence on the model of New Zealand.[46] But as he wrote, events had rather overtaken his proposals and, for Andrew Bonar Law, then leader of the British Conservative and Unionist Party, and for Edward Carson, the chairman of the Ulster Unionist Council, both of *these* options now held out the prospect of civil war in Ireland – a civil war, moreover, from which Britain would not in any imaginable scenario be able to keep its distance.[47]

For both Carson and Law the inevitability of war was guaranteed by the position of Ulster. And so it was to the north of Ireland that the attention of Unionism was turned after the Parliament Act had effectively removed the House of Lords from the political equation. But, if all eyes were now fixed with peculiar intensity upon the fate of the northern counties, the question of Ulster as such was not in any sense new. Back in the 1840s Nassau Senior, the first Professor of Political Economy at Oxford, had written of Ireland as comprising in effect 'two countries' misleadingly comprehended under a single name.[48] The same argument, as is well known, was advanced to great polemical effect by John Bright, by Joseph Chamberlain, and not least by Randolph Churchill, on various occasions in opposition to the first Home Rule Bill.[49]

In a similar vein, in a speech against the second Home Rule Bill delivered at Limehouse in April 1893, Arthur James Balfour had spoken of the 'great Ulster minority' whom Britain could not abandon. He went on immediately to qualify his terms since the relevant minority was not 'confined to Ulster'. But in Stockport, in July, this delicate equivocation had virtually disappeared – now it was the duty of Britain to defend the more simple, more geographically compact 'Protestant minority in the North of Ireland'.[50] However, it was above all Edward Carson who, in 1912, seized upon the strategic significance of the northern Province as a weapon in the fight against Home Rule for Ireland: 'If Ulster succeeds,' he bluntly remarked, 'Home Rule is dead.'[51]

The strategy, however, was a sorry failure, and between April 1912 and the autumn of 1914, as the establishment of Home Rule became ever more certain, the question of Ulster became ever more involved. When the Home Rule Bill finally passed into law, it was accompanied by a suspending clause – intended to delay its implementation for the duration of the war – and by a pledge to secure special treatment for Ulster when the moment of decision was at hand.[52] After the war, and after the general election of December 1918, Lloyd George sat at the head of a coalition government obliged to settle the Irish Question at last. The result was the Government of Ireland Act of 1920 which repealed the Act of 1914 and provided for the extension of federal Home Rule at once to the North of Ireland and to the South, together with a Council of Ireland invested with the statutory right to negotiate the merger of the two Home Rule governments into a single legislature subordinate to the Imperial – or, as Dicey would have had it, the Federal – Parliament. The merger was to be negotiated on an equal and voluntary basis and, with that, the Council disappeared into history until its resurrection under the auspices of the Sunningdale Agreement of 1973 and again, when this had failed, the Good Friday Agreement of 1998 where it appeared in the guise of a 'North/South Ministerial Council'.[53]

3

The Northern Ireland Parliament at Stormont had, from an Irish and a British unionist perspective, been established by default as a subordinate and federated legislature within the Empire comprising six counties of Ulster – Fermanagh, Tyrone, Antrim, Down, Armagh, and Londonderry. The element of default, as we have seen, was to be emphasised by Paisley in 1972, as it had been by Carson after 1912. But it so happened that the default option set the terms of the political settlement – that Carson's strategy helped to defeat his own principle. The exceptionalism of Ulster, so broadly advertised in defence of the Union, inadvertently secured Home Rule for the North. This amounted, in effect, to the first great reversal to which Unionism had been subjected since the onset of crisis in 1886. And then, a century later, between 1976 and 1982, the unionist defence of the compromise settlement which had federated the Union in 1920 began in turn to unravel. Powell and Molyneaux became the disciples of Dicey, Paisley the defender of Ulster Home Rule, and the UDA the sponsors of Northern Irish independence.

In 1920, the exclusion of six counties from the jurisdiction of the South was effected *en bloc* and in perpetuity. This outcome, however, could scarcely have been anticipated at the beginning of 1912. Between then and 1920, there had been proposals for the exclusion of the nine Ulster counties from the remaining portion of Ireland – that is to say, including Donegal, Monaghan and Cavan in the excluded area. At the same time, there had been proposals for the exclusion of only four, with Fermanagh and Tyrone – both with Catholic majorities, according to the 1911 census – in that case coming under the authority of the South. Indeed, at one point in 1914 Lloyd George had suggested the exclusion of five and a bit counties, one part of Tyrone falling under the jurisdiction of a Home Rule Parliament in Dublin, and the other under that of a Home Rule Parliament in Belfast.[54]

Equally, temporary exclusion had been considered, with various time-scales projected, and permanent exclusion had been promoted on the basis of a range of legitimising principles. The exclusion of all nine counties had been defended in the light of the historic integrity of the Province, and the exclusion of four had been examined with a view to securing the safest Protestant majority. The exclusion of six had been sought on a clean-cut basis, together with the exclusion of whatever number it might be on the basis of a county by county plebiscite.[55] But the process of exclusion from the settlement in the South was at the same time a process of exclusion from the Union or, more properly, from the incorporated Union of Great Britain and Ireland, cemented by Pitt in 1801, and defended since then by the opponents of Home Rule down to 1920.

However, from 1920 to 1972, Unionism in Northern Ireland had been fighting to maintain a system of colonial self-government with federal links to the British Parliament. And yet the imposition of direct rule had inevitably altered the terms of the debate. Between 1972 and 1975 hopes for a settlement had been kept alive. Then the long war had begun in earnest. But in 1982, as the Prior Assembly was about to go into session, the legacy of British failure and Nationalist alienation, of Sinn Féin belligerence and Protestant desperation since 1976, began to be felt throughout the ranks of Ulster unionists. Unionism, accordingly, regrouped into a multi-faceted defence of positions whose pedigree can be traced back to the early days of the Home Rule crisis.

Those positions embraced an array of options ranging, as we

have seen, from a desire to effect an incorporated Union, to colonial self-government and federated Home Rule, and on to national independence. But whilst all of these positions had reappeared by 1982, there was a certain historical irony to the fact that they were actually now part and parcel of a unionist ideology whose original intention had been to rule each one of them – with the sole exception of an incorporated Union – out of court. However, this irony can readily be explained: in Ireland after 1911, Unionism, like Republicanism, began steadily to be converted into a doctrine of democratic sovereignty.[56] But popular sovereignty is compatible with an assortment of constitutional arrangements – at once with federation, devolution, and unitary statehood. By the time that Unionism had come to identify the precise bearer of this sovereignty – the Protestant population of the six Northern Irish counties – the question of the *means* by which that sovereignty was to be exercised had radically diminished in importance.[57]

It was this outcome, whereby Unionism became a vehicle for democratic sovereignty, that both Dicey and Matthew Arnold had sought tenaciously to avoid. The Union, for both of them, had come to represent the security of civil liberty against the egalitarian excesses of modern democratic aspiration.[58] But this commitment to the British Union was never supported by a demonstration of how liberty within the United Kingdom was protected under its existing powers of government. For Dicey, it was by means of the gradual accretion of judicial decisions that liberty had come to prosper under the British constitution.[59] The relation between legislative and executive power, especially as this operated with respect to the Irish electorate, was consequently afforded little scrutiny in his writings. For Arnold, on the other hand, it was by means of the redemption of national manners, through the humanising agency of culture, that political equality could ultimately be made compatible with such freedoms as had been the hallmark of aristocratic governments.[60] But throughout the series of analyses which Arnold put together over the course of his career, the actual operation of established political arrangements acquired no meaningful role in his thought.

Yet it was precisely the fact that Ireland was subjected to an administration which was not bound by any form of regular accountability that lent such a powerful sense of justice to the advocates of Home Rule.[61] The demand for self-government was rooted in the desire to render the form of government representative in Ireland. After that demand had failed on successive occasions between 1886 and 1906, and after the cause seemed badly compromised in the aftermath of 1914, the Irish electorate abandoned the goal of representative government and pledged itself instead to a representative state – or rather, it pledged itself to two representative states, one North and one South, which could separately embody the democratic wills of rival populations on the island.[62]

As the demand for democratic statehood burgeoned under the threat of civil war, debate about the character of democratic government moved rapidly down the agenda. This was substantially a result of the fact that the constituent populations of each of the two prospective Irish democracies could not readily be delimited. The various political options canvassed between 1916 and 1920 could, one way or another, have availed themselves of some kind of 'democratic' defence. That is, the assortment of proposals to resolve the Home Rule crisis could all have drawn support from relevant majorities to legitimise their particular claims. There was a majority opinion in the United Kingdom, a majority opinion in Ireland as a whole, and a majority opinion in the six northern counties which came to make up Northern Ireland.[63] There was a majority in the nine counties of the original Ulster Province opposed to a majority in the four at one time selected for partition – Londonderry, Antrim, Armagh and Down – and there was a majority in Belfast distinct from the majority in Fermanagh. Each opposing majority had a keenly preferred outcome. This fact, of course, immediately points to the question of whether the ability to muster majority popular acquiescence should unfailingly be taken as the defining feature of democratic legitimacy.

The argument of this book is obviously that it shouldn't: a democracy is a regime founded on equality, and not a political organisation belonging to a majority. Nonetheless, there was no overriding solution to the issue of partition once partition had become an entrenched demand on the part of a northern majority. There was no self-evident justice to the Southern refusal to countenance any form of Northern secession once secession had become a concerted project pursued by one million Ulster Protestants. Justice, in such a case, could only mean the common preference shared by all the parties concerned. It could only mean an agreed position, arrived at by consensus. But the brute fact is that political consensus was simply not available. There was no mean position between agreement and coercion, but only an unenviable choice between varying options for coercion. As it happened, the victims of the final decision were Northern Irish Catholics. But while there was always going to be a significant loser in the Anglo-Irish struggle, the sense of disadvantage among the Northern Irish minority which resulted from their raw deal in the aftermath of that struggle was compounded by the pretence that their experience of loss amounted merely to a begrudging complaint against the dictates of democracy.

After 1912, it was not possible to establish a Home Rule government in Ireland, encompassing the island as a whole, on the basis of a common allegiance embracing all sectors of opinion. Similarly, in 1920, it was not possible to establish a Northern Irish polity by democratic consensus. Nonetheless, it was possible to start with a majority allegiance, and then to build consensus. But consensus must be fabricated where it does not naturally grow: it requires political machinery to bring it into effect. The creation of such machinery in Northern Ireland in 1920 would have entailed, as a basic starting-point, ensuring that the majority who identified with the Ulster polity were not equally the beneficiaries of exclusive government control: it would have involved establishing an inclusive government which could offset the partiality of the state.

Of course, Northern Ireland after 1920 was not literally a state, but to Ulster Protestants it was nonetheless *their* country. But when a country is thus founded to represent a majority, its government should best be fashioned to represent the *common* interest if the regime aims to generate an equal democratic allegiance encompassing the population as a whole. The sorry reality was that debate about alternative forms of government had scarcely featured in Unionist polemic since 1886. Consequently, by the time that Unionism had converted itself into an Ulster Home Rule movement all attention had come to focus on securing Protestant consent, to the detriment of addressing how the government of the Province could be constructed on a representative basis.

The situation described here is still liable to confuse since the two issues it comprehends are habitually bundled into one. Democracies refer to states, but they also refer to governments. In relation to governments, democracy denotes the process of arriving at decisions, and the means of subjecting decisions to limitation and control. Processes of decision and mechanisms of control evidently come in a variety of forms, the choice between them providing ample scope for contention and debate. Such debate, however, would revolve around issues which are perfectly distinct from the issue of democracy in relation to states. This issue turns on the question of who it is that actually makes up a democracy.[64] It is this question which came to dominate the political agenda, North and South, after 1912. In the end, the issue was resolved, in regard to Northern Ireland, by resort to the principle of majority sovereignty: since Protestants in the Six Counties which constituted the new Ulster added up to the greater number of citizens, sovereignty over the affairs of the Northern Irish populace could plausibly be taken to reside in the majority.[65]

However, the sovereignty of the people is evidently distinct from the sovereignty of the majority. It was on account of the elision of this distinction in the public life of Northern Ireland that the institutions of government set up under the Government of Ireland Act were felt naturally to be the property of one portion of the population – the Ulster Protestants. Since Northern Ireland had been established with a view to enabling an Ulster majority to self-determine its exclusion from the jurisdiction of the South, it seemed to follow that the exercise of political power in the Province could be conducted in the interest of the majority thus established. That assumption, however, was exploded by developments in Northern Ireland towards the end of the 1960s. Nonetheless, the assumption had become such an integral part of the habitual defence of the British Union that it would take another generation to arrive at new terms of agreement that could hope to overcome the bitter legacy of the past.

X

Siege: 1982–1998

I

Crisis for Unionism meant a reversal of fortune, but a reversal of fortune brought a reversal of policy in its wake. After the Home Rule crisis of 1886–1912, Unionism rallied to the cause of devolution. After the suspension of Stormont in 1972, the defenders of devolution shifted ground again. However, this time around, they did not shift as one united body. Instead, Unionism split into a number of different factions. One faction, it is true, stayed loyal to the old Stormont system. But the remainder were divided into integrationists and Ulster nationalists – one group aiming at an incorporating Union, the other at an independent state.

Each of these positions was a defensive manoeuvre. They were stark indicators of a communal sense of siege, but they were not in any way compatible and neither were they united in a common defence of the Union. And so we come to recognise that the one unifying principle across the range of unionist opinion lay in a general appeal to the idea of democracy. Integration, independence, single-party rule: each of these was justified in terms of the broad and malleable tenets of democratic legitimacy.

So too were a host of further schemes, tirelessly advanced by unionists after 1982: there were arguments in favour of administrative devolution, polemics in defence of committee-style government, and belated apologias for power-sharing arrangements. There was even an appeal for a resuscitated Union of the British Isles.[1] But, one way or another, they were all supported with reference to the principle of self-determination. Indeed, as the

Ulster Workers' Council strike had shown, the same applied to popular insurrection: this too had been vindicated as a bold assertion of the right to self-determination, inherent in the will of the people. That will, it was maintained, had a right to dissent from the decisions of its government.[2] By extension, it was now argued, Northern Protestants had a right to incorporate themselves into the United Kingdom, but equally they had a right to establish themselves as an independent state.

However, the people to which this democratic right of self-determination seemed so naturally to be appended was only the bearer of an imagined unity of purpose.[3] In reality, this supposedly united populace was divided in its pursuit of a multitude of rival programmes, aspirations and objectives, ranging from integration to Ulster independence. Nonetheless, for Unionism, the imagined unity of the Protestant people provided the basis for democracy in Northern Ireland: it comprised a body of equals invested with the right to map out its political future in the light of its own best judgement.

The trouble was that this discrete democracy was opposed by another two competing democratic claims – the claim of Irish Republicanism on the one hand, and the claim of British parliamentary authority on the other. It was opposed, that is, by a Catholic minority and by a British majority. Since both of these were evidently out of harmony with Ulster Protestantism, they were presumed to lie outside the ambit of the democracy that mattered. Up until 1998, the best efforts of British and Irish political ingenuity had failed to match up these discordant minorities and majorities. They had failed, in other words, to establish general agreement about what should in practice constitute democracy in Northern Ireland.

I have been arguing that this amounted to an exemplary failure. Who counts in a democracy, and how those who count can make their relevance felt, are questions which lead us to the foundations of modern democratic society. The hope, of course, is that everybody counts in a democracy, and that everybody at the same time counts equally. But the expectation of democratic equality is open to serious disappointment on two particular fronts. It will most obviously be disappointed when a part of a democracy presumes itself to constitute an integrated whole – as when unionists claim to make up the total citizenship of Northern Ireland, or when Republicans see unionists as a deluded national faction against whom the majority on the island of Ireland should prevail.[4]

But while the expectations of modern political equality are readily thwarted by the advent of either factionalism or secession, they are likewise dashed by the requirements of political representation. Under a representative regime, the population does not count directly as the final arbiter of its welfare. To acknowledge this obvious fact about existing political arrangements is to challenge much that passes for a defence of democracy today. But to suppose otherwise, to suppose democracy to consist in explicit government by the people, is to allow the haziest ideology to play havoc with established practice. A hazy commitment to democracy involves the idea that 'the people' rule. But even under conditions of popular protest and insurrection, the sovereignty of the people is more a slogan than a fact.[5]

That much has been made apparent by our analysis so far: neither unionist nor Republican popular politics in Northern Ireland entailed equal participation in decision-making within each community. Instead, a process of radical politicisation was inaugurated, but this process soon required the most draconian control – in the one case by the Ulster Workers' Council, in the other by the Provisional IRA. We have seen what this involved inside the Republican community. In the same way, what the crises and reversals of Unionism reveal is a weak link in the assumptions pervading our ordinary democratic beliefs and aspirations as these have been handed down to us through generations of expectant political optimism. That optimism centres on the reassuring spectacle of a government by the people, of a democratic multitude freely determining its priorities and choices. The problem is that such optimism fails at the point of delivery.

Routine politics relieves us of any pressing concern with these discouraging realities. However, a crisis in the conduct of political affairs is likely to bring them home to us: radical politicisation in modern democratic societies does not facilitate the expression of the free choice of the people, but the coercive choice of popular representatives. Under circumstances of popular insurrection and resistance, solidarity and conformity are soon required by political leaderships: the exigencies of the situation encourage representatives to maximise uniformity across the demands of their constituents. Confronted with the impossibility of satisfying the demands which politicised civilians are apt to make, populist representatives are obliged to insist all the more belligerently upon the right of their own communities to make these choices: frustration serves to heighten the self-righteousness of the demands.

In other words, a right to choose never feels like the experience of the real thing, and in the absence of the genuine article Unionism confronted its antagonists in a state of siege. Besieged by rival claims to democratic legitimacy, the unionist majority was beset by a particular kind of fear. Fear can inspire a foresight of future harm, and encourage us to take precautions. In this sense, it can make us jealous of our interests, and intelligent about the maintenance of their long term security. When someone arrives to challenge that security, we strike a bargain. But fear can also appear in the guise of dread, and confine us within the limits of the present. It discourages all calculation of future profit: we turn our backs upon our enemy, and will not come to terms. So, while fear is capable of bringing about compliance, it can also bring about a refusal to give in.[6]

That refusal reached a crescendo of intensity three years after the Prior Assembly first went into session in 1982. It peaked, that is, around the time of the fallout from 15 November 1985, the day on which the Anglo-Irish Agreement was signed. That Agreement was the work of both the British and Irish governments. It had been negotiated in relative secrecy during the previous two years and it was to overwhelm Ulster Protestants with feelings of betrayal. It was to rekindle that mixed sense of panic and determination reminiscent of the crisis period of 1912 and, beyond this, it was to present the unionist position with its greatest single challenge since the prorogation of Stormont in 1972.[7]

Just three days after the Agreement had finally been concluded, the Ulster Unionist MP, Harold McCusker, rose in the British House of Commons to address its contents. 'I never knew what desolation felt like until I read this agreement last Friday afternoon,' he announced before the rows of awkward and embarrassed silence on either side of the chamber. 'Does the Prime Minister realise that, when she carries the agreement through the House, she will have ensured that I shall carry to my grave with ignominy the sense of injustice that I have done to my constituents down the years – when, in their darkest hours, I exhorted them to put their trust in this British House of Commons which one day would honour its fundamental obligation to them to treat them as equal British citizens? Is it not the reality of this agreement that they will now be Irish–British hybrids and that every aspect – not just some aspects – of their lives will be open to the influence of those who have coveted their land?'[8]

2

McCusker, on his own account, had sought to alleviate unionist fears. Now he could do no more than confirm his constituents in their dread. But that dread had been mounting since the beginning of the decade, in particular since Margaret Thatcher's visit to Dublin Castle for a summit meeting with the Irish premier, Charles Haughey, in December 1980. Haughey had travelled to Downing Street on a courtesy call the previous May, and Thatcher's return visit in the company of Humphrey Atkins, Lord Carrington and Geoffrey Howe was being billed as a significant diplomatic advance.

After the meeting between the two heads of state, their joint communiqué bore witness to the 'unique relationship between the two countries', and proceeded to reveal a plan to establish joint study groups to examine the 'totality of relationships within these islands'.[9] Within months Peter Robinson, the Deputy Leader of the DUP, gave his response: 'For almost half a century Ulster Unionists have viewed with grave suspicion any meetings their representatives had with Dublin politicians and with no less a degree of anxiety did they view the meeting between Mrs. Thatcher and Mr. Haughey.'[10]

Paisley's response was more dramatic still. Immediately after Christmas, in the bitter midnight cold, he trooped up an Antrim hillside with 500 men in military regalia bearing arms certificates and conniving at resistance. A smattering of bemused media reporters registered the gesture of defiance. But this gesture was no more than a taste of things to come: it acted as a prelude to the launch of a series of protest rallies to be staged across the Province. The following November, after the IRA's assassination of the Ulster Unionist MP, Robert Bradford, Paisley intensified his efforts, announcing the creation of a 'Third Force' to combat Republican terror: 'We demand that the IRA be exterminated from Ulster. The aim of the IRA is to destroy the last vestige of Protestantism in our island home. But there is one army the Republic fears and that every other enemy of Ulster fears and that is the army of armed and resolute Protestants.'[11] But, as he spoke, the joint British–Irish study groups promised by Haughey and Thatcher had already become a reality with all the implications for political traffic between London and Dublin that such an arrangement carried.

The aim of these joint study groups was to address the creation of new institutional structures between Britain and Ireland as a means of improving political relations within Northern Ireland. The final reports of the study groups were laid before Parliament on 11 November 1981, by which time Garret Fitzgerald had replaced Charles Haughey as Taoiseach. At that point it had been decided that existing patterns of contact between London and Dublin at ministerial and official levels should be formalised in an Anglo-Irish Intergovernmental Council.

The creation of this Council was recorded at the first summit meeting between Thatcher and Fitzgerald on 6 November 1981. In addition, it was suggested in the reports that an Anglo-Irish Ministerial Council might be established, together with a Secretariat, and that a complementary inter-parliamentary tier could also be set up.[12] However, it was the Intergovernmental Council itself that was to supply Anglo-Irish relations with some kind of forward dynamic. Although the Council had not been established as part of a formal international agreement, by the autumn of 1983 it was revealed that no fewer than twenty bilateral meetings had taken place within the Council's frame of reference, including the first meeting at Heads of Government level on 7 November 1983.

But all this political commerce did not imply any real progress. First of all, the intensification of contact between London and Dublin since the beginning of the decade had taken place against the background of two Republican hunger strikes staged back to back between 1980 and 1981. In addition, these contacts had to withstand the retarding influence of the Falklands War on Anglo-Irish relations, together with the political uncertainty created by three successive changes of government in the Republic between 1981 and 1983.

Beyond all this, the commitment of the British government never appeared convincing. Occasional pronouncements from the mouth of the junior Northern Ireland Minister, Lord Gowrie, promoted optimism in Irish political circles. For instance, in January 1980 he confided to reporters that direct rule was in his view quite 'unBritish': 'It is an absurdity that one has almost absolute power . . . I suppose that if I had my way I would have dual citizenship.'[13] Certainly the constitutional implications of such an arrangement received little elaboration from Lord Gowrie. But whatever solace the Dublin political establishment chose to derive from such tantalising remarks, they received not the slightest endorsement from Margaret Thatcher. Thatcher, in fact, was always anxious to defend her unionist credentials. She treated

Irish nationalist intentions with weary scepticism, and the enterprise of constitutional experiment with ill-disguised disdain.[14]

But, notwithstanding intermittent displays of scepticism and contempt from across the water, politicians in the Irish Republic, with encouragement from the SDLP, set about bringing fresh momentum to debate about the future government of Northern Ireland through the establishment of the New Ireland Forum in the summer of 1983. By May the following year, having taken evidence from a range of nationalist opinion throughout the island of Ireland, the Forum finally produced its summary Report. In tones of moral earnestness, and with a list of good intentions, the Report came up with three concrete proposals.

The first, and preferred, option was a 'united Ireland in the form of a sovereign independent Irish state to be achieved peacefully and by consent'.[15] This, of course, was very much the same old story, endlessly rehearsed in the South of Ireland since the advent of partition. But the Forum Report also gave due consideration to the possibility of creating either a confederal Irish state or a British–Irish form of joint authority. Thatcher, however, was quick to dampen any enthusiasm for the proposals on the British side. After her second summit meeting with Garret Fitzgerald in November 1984, she let her views be known: 'The unified Ireland was one solution – that is out. A second solution was the confederation of the two States – that is out. A third solution was joint authority – that is out.'[16] Irish ministers huffed with indignation, while British officials cringed.

Nonetheless, it was precisely after the second summit meeting between Thatcher and Fitzgerald that work began in earnest toward the establishment of a treaty of co-operation between Great Britain and the Republic of Ireland regarding the political and security problems afflicting both countries and Northern Ireland. Negotiations were to last for a further twelve months, with discussion restricted to senior ministers and diplomats in Britain and Ireland. Speculation about the shape of the proposed Agreement had been rife in the press throughout the period leading up to November, but when the document finally appeared its general purpose was easy to discern.

In general terms, the Agreement was to provide recognition, by both Britain and Ireland, for the 'legitimate aspirations' of both communities in Northern Ireland. But more specifically, its purpose was to underwrite the existing constitutional status of the Province while at the same time enabling the government of the Republic to represent the views of the Northern nationalist minority to the British government in the absence of devolved administration in Northern Ireland.[17]

In essence, the Anglo-Irish Agreement provided institutional machinery for the cultivation of a mature diplomatic rapport between Britain and Ireland.[18] A common understanding about the affairs of Northern Ireland was to be fostered between the two governments through the establishment of an Intergovernmental Ministerial Conference, serviced by a permanent Secretariat.[19] The Agreement's explicit purpose, for both the Southern Irish government and the SDLP, was to thwart the political advance of militant Republicanism. This, in Garret Fitzgerald's account, was to be achieved by 'seriously undermining its existing minority support within the nationalist community'.[20]

The Agreement also promised to supply a mechanism for circumventing the customary intransigence of unionist politicians. But both of these designs had evident advantages for Britain also. And the big prize, for the Thatcher government, lay in the anticipated improvement of cross-border security to be achieved by a tightening-up of extradition procedures between Britain and the Republic. 'I started from the need for greater security,' Thatcher later revealed. 'If this meant making limited political concessions to the South, much as I disliked that kind of bargaining I had to contemplate it.'[21]

For the unionist community of Northern Ireland, the principal threat contained in the Agreement related to the creation of the Intergovernmental Ministerial Conference itself, together with its Secretariat, to be established at Maryfield in County Down. The conference was to meet at ministerial and official levels to enable the Irish government to 'put forward views and proposals on matters relating to Northern Ireland within the field of activity of the Conference'.[22] But in the eyes of the Protestant population of Northern Ireland, these arrangements represented the most astonishing betrayal. They amounted, in the words of the Belfast *News Letter*'s editorial, to a 'recipe for bloodshed and conflict which has few parallels in modern history'.[23]

Despite the steady flow of soothing words and reassuring promises from London, Unionism rose in a chorus of dismay and agitation.[24] Eight days after the Agreement had been signed, between one and two hundred thousand Protestants descended on Belfast's City Hall in angry protest. Following the Commons debate on the Agreement on 28 November, unionist MPs withdrew from the House, and then resigned their seats in mid-December. 'Everything that I held dear,' declared McCusker, 'turned to ashes in my mouth.'[25]

The comprehensive attitude of despair which took hold of Protestant opinion in Northern Ireland should hardly have come as a surprise. Throughout the negotiations leading up to the Agreement, unionist politicians were kept firmly in the dark while a constant flow of vital information was transmitted from the Dublin government to the upper echelons of the SDLP. Even Thatcher's Cabinet was ignorant about progress and vague about the details up to the very last.[26] Tom King, Robert Armstrong and Douglas Hurd were the exceptions. The British view was for that reason represented by the Foreign Office and the Cabinet Office, with the key role in the discussions being left to Armstrong, Thatcher's Cabinet Secretary, whose capacity for political tact and practical conciliation appeared to be far in advance of her own.[27] The Northern Ireland Office, for its part, had its doubts about the wisdom of the Agreement, but for the most part kept its counsel.

Yet despite the wall of silence surrounding the negotiations, opinion within the leadership of Unionism was public knowledge. Its position could be gauged from its response to the proceedings of the New Ireland Forum, set out in a series of documents in 1984. Peter Smith, honorary secretary of the UUP, put forward the attitude of his party in the autumn of 1984. In clear and energetic prose, Smith insisted that what Irish nationalism had to accept if relations between the North and South were ever to improve was the principle of unionist consent. That principle ought by right to impose a duty on the Republic to acknowledge 'the consequences of conceding . . . self-determination to the people of Northern Ireland. Acceptance of . . . the right of self-determination necessarily means acceptance of the determination itself.'[28]

That statement came in November. The previous May, after the publication of the Forum Report, the Kilbrandon Committee had been established in the United Kingdom as an unofficial body to represent the main strands of British and Northern Irish political thinking as far as the government of the Province was concerned. A majority of the committee favoured the introduction of 'co-operative devolution' by which authority for the management of Northern Irish affairs would be shared at once by Great Britain and the Republic.[29] This, of course, was joint authority as envisaged by the New Ireland Forum, albeit presented in a somewhat different form, and sensitively packaged under a new name. But it was light years away from the perspective advanced by Peter Smith the following November: '"Joint authority",' he was to argue, 'is . . . one of the most ludicrous concepts to be put forward by any government.'[30]

The tone of rancour, and the disdain for nationalist complacency, were unmistakable. But earlier in the year, the previous April, just before the Forum Report was published, the Ulster Unionist Party's positive proposals appeared in print. These proposals centred on the prospect of subjecting Northern Ireland's 'basic services' to some kind of 'democratic control'. That meant transferring responsibility for local services – health, education, housing, the environment – from Westminster to a devolved administration in Northern Ireland. Power could indeed be shared on a cross-community basis in the Province, but only on the level of policy implementation. It could be shared, in other words, in those areas where conflict over the divergent political aspirations of Catholics and Protestants could be avoided: 'The present object, therefore, of those parties committed to devolution must be to obtain control of such powers as are not necessarily inconsistent with the two communities continuing to maintain their diverse constitutional policies.' Meanwhile, legislative authority would be retained by the British parliament, and a Bill of Rights could be introduced for the protection of the nationalist minority.[31]

Shortly after these proposals had appeared, the Democratic Unionist Party was ready to put its own principles and recommendations before the public. In *Ulster: The Future Assured*, the party made clear once more its opposition to institutionalised power-sharing, while pointing out that any parties who were committed to such an arrangement would be free, in the event of a devolved government being conceded to Ulster, to submit their argument to the judgement of the electorate. If the argument met with popular acclaim, a sharing of power would become possible without prejudice to the principle of majority rule: 'The vital element of democracy must be adhered to in any proposal if it is to last.'[32]

But the important point, for our present purposes, is that neither the DUP document, nor the UUP proposals, looked at all favourably upon the prospect of introducing an 'Irish Dimension' into any conceivable constitutional settlement. As the DUP put it, 'the people of Northern Ireland emphatically reject any institutionalised association or other constitutional relationship with the Republic of Ireland'.[33] From this contribution, one could conclude without much difficulty that the establishment of a British–Irish Ministerial Conference, such as was set up in November 1985, and through which the government of the South could put forward views concerning political and cultural matters affecting the nationalist minority in the North, would prove fundamentally unacceptable. Or, as Paisley himself was to put it, just over a year later, barely more than a week after the Anglo-Irish Agreement had been signed, 'Never! Never! Never!'[34]

When the Anglo-Irish Agreement had been ratified, both the Democratic Unionist Party and the Ulster Unionist Party resolved to channel their resistance through the Northern Ireland Assembly. The Assembly had by then been in existence for over three long, unproductive years. From the beginning, the SDLP had abstained from participation. The Ulster Unionist Party, for its part, had periodically boycotted its proceedings. And by the time that the Assembly was dissolved in June 1986, a succession of Secretaries of State for Northern Ireland had come and gone – first James Prior, then Douglas Hurd, and finally Tom King.

By that time also, each of the Assembly's scrutiny committees had published both their evidence and their arguments, and three reports from the Devolution Committee had been compiled. In practical terms, however, the situation in Northern Ireland had in no way been advanced. But on 5 December 1985, the Assembly took it upon itself to alter its terms of reference by establishing a Grand Committee on the Government of Northern Ireland 'to examine the implications of the Anglo-Irish Agreement for the government and future of Northern Ireland'.[35] The committee's deliberations were to result in the publication of three reports, the principal thrust of which, taken together, was to vindicate the democratic right to self-determination inherent in the people of Ulster.

The First Report of the Committee was finally published on 29 January 1986. It attempted to lay out the core unionist objection to the Anglo-Irish Agreement, and it did so by pointing to the consultative role regarding Northern Ireland's affairs conceded to the Irish Republic as tantamount to an 'encroachment on British Sovereignty'.[36] But that objection was never really going to make much headway in the relentless world of ideological counter-charge and political competition. Sovereignty, after all, refers to nothing less than the supreme right to bind the wills of those who happen to fall within its jurisdiction. In that sense, it is quite simply equivalent to a supreme right of self-determination. If Northern Ireland was to be understood as being in possession of an inalienable right to determine its destiny, it had to be seen as itself a sovereign body. Any encroachment upon British sovereignty would in that event be conspicuously beside the point. If, on the other hand, sovereignty was taken to reside in the United Kingdom parliament, the rights of Northern Ireland were entirely conditional upon the will of its superior and therefore hardly amounted to anything so unassailable as an ultimate right to self-determination.

This adds up to saying little more than is perfectly evident to common sense: namely, that genuine supremacy in politics – supreme acts of decision and final acts of arbitration – cannot be the property at once of two competing powers. Should a dispute arise as to which contender has the right to decide the case, the question is resolved by either conquest or agreement. Agreement, of course, is always preferable to conquest, but one can be sure that neither has been secured when ongoing dispute survives the effort to win acceptance for a single power. In that case, the issue can only finally be decided by continuing political struggle.

And so it happened that in Northern Ireland, in early 1986, the struggle was taken to the streets. But it was a struggle which the loyalist and unionist majority in the Province were inevitably going to lose. That inevitability had been ordained by the relative command of strength enjoyed by either side of the opposing forces. On one side stood a determined British government anxious to maintain its authority. On the other stood a stunned and beleaguered populace which had already shown its hand. The Ulster Workers' Council strike had brought the Province to the brink of disaster. But once that option had been driven to a conclusion, it became almost impossible to repeat the performance in the face of a fully resourced and resolute political administration.

And fully resourced and resolute the administration was. By this time the resources at the disposal of the British government included a substantial military machine, expert in the containment of civil disturbances, and an intelligence network which reached into the bowels of the Province. But they also included, crucially, the extensive array of forces at the command of the RUC. As the political temperature rose, and bitterness spread like a contagion, the Royal Ulster Constabulary stood firm, its loyalty intact. This was no mean achievement under the harsh and gruelling circumstances. It was, after all, the police who had borne the brunt of opposition to the Agreement from the first. Intimidation against their members had been rife since the early spring, and attacks on their houses had by now risen into the hundreds. By May, it had been reported that scores of members' families had been forced to move home. They were the final line of defence, besieged within the siege, and this when their allegiances were always less than certain.[37]

After all, the terms of the Agreement were never going to generate the ultimate in commitment within a predominantly Protestant force. But these terms were adequately vague, and their implications sufficiently remote, to keep the Constabulary loyal to established political authority. 'We are being asked to enforce the will of parliament against the will of the majority of the people,' commented one RUC officer in the early spring of 1986. 'But whatever their own views,' he went on to note, 'too many men have mortgages and family commitments to rebel.'[38] The issue was not decisive enough to provoke a mutiny within their ranks. Protestant paramilitary activity could in consequence be stifled, rioting in the streets was more or less contained, and the opportunities for insurrection were steadily closed down. Fear of a conflagration gradually died away.

Days and weeks and months passed. Then a year. Hopes for a return to the heady days of May 1974 had now all but receded. A unionist 'Day of Action' passed in precisely a single day. Membership of dissident organisations certainly grew apace: individuals flocked into the Ulster Resistance, they streamed into the Ulster Clubs. They were 'hoping for the best but preparing for the worst'.[39] However, the best was too much to hope for, and the worst case never obtained. By the time the third anniversary of the Agreement had arrived, resistance began to peter out into isolated skirmishes, and protest took the form of verbal bluster. But the enduring and palpable sense of grievance still managed to survive for another decade. 'It was like a bereavement,' as the leader of the Alliance Party put it, looking back in 1996: 'first of all there was a kind of numbness, then a sense of anger and blame.'[40]

What had been shattered was the sense of a common United Kingdom purpose – although this, in truth, might well be thought to have dissipated long before. Loss centred on a disparate collection of disappointed fantasies: stirrings of solidarity amongst the Protestant peoples of the Union, generous intimations of British fellow-feeling, an inherited nostalgia for the glory days of empire. The experience, however, was also one of treachery, and treachery registers its own peculiar pain. Unionism had been abandoned by the British parliament itself, the focal point of unionist affection. That abandonment, moreover, had been secured by stealth. The Agreement was planned over an extended tract of time, and it was devised in the very corridors of British rule. Worst of all, it had been plotted in concert with the Irish Republic, the implacable interloper in unionist demonology, in defiance of every expectation of trust which Unionism still managed to entertain.

3

Unionism after the Agreement went into a kind of free-fall. After the fall, the process of recovery began. That recovery started with an incremental reckoning, a gradual appreciation that the time to cut one's losses would arrive. What that dawning realisation entailed was a steady recognition of the fact that politics would not return full circle to those happier days before the autumn of 1968 when Stormont sat in magisterial splendour, when Orange marches filled the summers with the sound of Lambeg drums, and when politics still ministered to Protestant advantage.

Of course, most of this had already disappeared. But with so much already lost, how could Unionism countenance the departure of still more? By the early 1990s, Northern Irish politics had been subjected to a series of violent shocks administered over a twenty-five-year period of upheaval and disturbance. The Province had been overwhelmed by crisis and reversal, Unionism had been concussed by the experience of siege. The situation had teetered on the brink of revolution, but politics were now to be cast in another mould. What Unionism came to realise through the long period of disconsolate stupor which marked the aftermath of the Anglo-Irish Agreement was that there could be no going back, that no final restitution was at hand – that politics would never again be reconfigured on the basis of unionist first principles.

The Ulster Defence Association was quickest to recognise this fact. In 1987, the Association published its *Common Sense* document as a post-Agreement sequel to *Beyond the Religious Divide*.[41] This time, however, the UDA had moved even closer to accepting power-sharing arrangements, reiterating what the Northern Ireland Office had declared back in 1972: 'Majority rule in deeply divided societies is likely to be profoundly undemocratic.'[42] In the same year, there was also movement within both the DUP and the UUP towards some kind of new initiative. In February, the leaders of the two main unionist parties set up a 'task force' to look into the possibility of finding some alternative to the Anglo-Irish Agreement, and within five months the group was ready with its Report. 'Devolved-government is our objective,' the authors declared, and the power to be devolved should be controlled by a requirement for weighted majorities in the first period of any new Assembly's operation.[43] The Report, however, was promptly shelved. It was published in abridged form in the middle of June, but neither Paisley nor the leader of the UUP, James Molyneaux, gave it their seal of approval. Sentiment within Unionism had shifted, but it had yet to coincide with any meaningful political process.

That coincidence, in fact, would be a long time in the making. In September 1987, the then Secretary of State for Northern Ireland, Tom King, inaugurated a series of 'talks about talks' in the hope of introducing forward motion into the stalled engine of unionist high politics. That hope, however, was premature. It was not until after Peter Brooke succeeded King as Secretary of State in July 1989 that anything like progress began to appear. A bid for another talks process was launched in 1990. Procedures were then agreed in 1991. Negotiations were to be conducted along three determinate 'strands' – the first encompassing relations within Northern Ireland, the second relations with the Republic of Ireland, and the third relations between Britain and the Republic. 'Nothing would be agreed,' as the diplomatic jargon of the period had it, 'until everything was agreed.' Discussions began in June. They ended in early July. Nothing, as it turned out, was agreed. But Brooke, 'this courteous bumbling fellow' as the *Times* once put it, set out to try again.[44] Failure again. And then a general election. It was the middle of April 1992.[45]

For two years now, John Major had been acting as Prime Minister in Britain. After the election, he shuffled Peter Brooke into the Heritage Department, and installed Sir Patrick Mayhew as Secretary of State for Northern Ireland. Mayhew began where Peter Brooke left off, with a three-stranded process in which nothing would be agreed until everything was agreed. Talks began on 29 April. They ended in November: no new breakthrough, no seismic shift, no great leap forward. The talks had started out as a determined search for an 'historic agreement', but they became, as the *Irish Times* was to summarise the process, 'a search for heads of agreement, for elements of agreement, for a "soft landing" to allow for an early resumption of talks and, finally, for an "agreed statement"'.[46] A familiar road, from expectancy to disappointment, had been travelled. But the journey, for all that, was not completely futile. The unionist parties had in the process come face to face with the Irish government for the first time since 1973. Molyneaux' party even made an expedition to Dublin. The players had begun to limber up, and in the aftermath of failure events began to move.[47]

Three years into the new decade, and John Hume's dialogue

with Gerry Adams was beginning to produce results. The leaders had been in conference since 1988, and by 1993 they were ready with a statement showing unity of purpose.[48] A settlement was a matter for 'agreement', they announced: not, the subtext read, a matter for armed struggle.[49] A process of realignment had started, Irish nationalist energies were being progressively galvanised, and Britain was now obliged to make a definite response. That came in December, in the form of the Downing Street Declaration, a joint effort of the British and Irish governments, in which the principles for a settlement were presented. The truth was that, over the previous six years, off the public stage, soundings had been taken and conversations held to ascertain the position of Republicans. Hume had been speaking to prominent members of Sinn Féin, while the British and Irish governments' secretly parleyed with the IRA.[50] London and Dublin were now endeavouring to move together, and the result was the Declaration of 15 December 1993.

The Declaration pledged both the British and Irish governments to overcoming 'the legacy of history'. As part of that pledge, they committed themselves to working out 'a new political framework founded on consent and encompassing arrangements within Northern Ireland, for the whole island, and between these islands'.[51] The assumption was that the Republican movement had moved sufficiently to be able to live with these arrangements, that the promise to 'remove the causes of conflict' might draw them into a process of political negotiation.[52] Then, on 31 August 1994, a ceasefire was announced: the IRA, it seemed, had shifted ground. But would Unionism be able to shift also?

As it happened, in the face of rapid change, Paisley and Molyneaux stood their ground. Paisley, of course, had always thrived on an obdurate fixity of purpose. But James Molyneaux was himself no Talleyrand. He had been leader of his party since 1979; a cautious, dour, uninspiring figure, he found it difficult to rise to a political challenge. He was a committee man, a fixer, a steady pair of hands. But when the ground shifted, when larger opportunities arose, it was his instinct to retreat behind familiar formulations, and then refuse to budge. First the Declaration was 'comparatively safe', then it became 'a cause for some concern'. After the Provisional IRA ceasefire of 1994, exercising leverage over the Major government while the Conservative majority was dwindling in the Commons, he secured no long term, meaningful advantage. Nodding and winking, whispering in the corridors at Westminster, he had sought the inside track in the British political process only to find that he had been excluded from the race.[53]

Six months after the IRA cessation came the 'Frameworks' document. It was a lengthy, involved and detailed exposition of a possible Northern Ireland settlement. Once again, it was the work of both the British and Irish governments, and in its overall direction it seemed to pander to the proclivities and sentiments of Irish nationalism. The SDLP were delighted, Sinn Féin gave a guarded welcome. But Unionism winced, and Molyneaux was appalled: 'questions will be asked about the leader's judgement,' the *Belfast Telegraph* declared.[54] The remark was indeed prophetic. By 29 August 1995, Molyneaux had resigned, and leadership of the Ulster Unionists fell to David Trimble. The Irish, the British and the parties in Northern Ireland stood back, took stock and began to make predictions. Trimble had emerged from the Ulster Vanguard movement and the Ulster Clubs into the mainstream of unionist politics as a sharp, edgy, determined political operator. An academic lawyer by profession, he had a sure grasp of the larger constitutional issues at stake in the conflict, and a capacity for decisive political action. But would he do a deal? With Molyneaux now carping on the sidelines, Trimble prepared his party for full-scale negotiations.[55]

Talks began on 10 June 1996. It was a testing, nervous period in Northern Ireland. Sinn Féin, following the collapse of the IRA's 1994 ceasefire, was barred from entry. But the Ulster Unionist Party, the Democratic Unionist Party, Robert McCartney's United Kingdom Unionist Party, the Ulster Democratic Party under Gary McMichael, the Progressive Unionist Party under David Ervine, the Alliance Party, the Northern Ireland Women's

Coalition, and the SDLP. . . all showed up for the final chance, the last hard push for a solution, in Castle Buildings at Stormont under the chairmanship of Senator George Mitchell.

Progress, however, was considerably less than rapid. Procedural wrangling, haggling over the terms of reference for negotiations, and then debate over the agenda, dominated the talks for over a year. But, finally, substantive negotiations got under way in early October 1997. By this time Sinn Féin, after the IRA's second ceasefire of 21 July 1997, was admitted to the talks.[56] Straight away, the DUP and the UKUP walked out. Optimism rose, then optimism sank; everything was on, then everything was off. The media were swarming in glum anticipation, spectators gathered in eager hope. The deadline came, the deadline went – but then, on 10 April 1998, a deal was done. 'The telephone in my office rang at 4.45 p.m.,' recalled George Mitchell: 'David Trimble was on the line . . . "We're ready to do the business".'[57]

At five o'clock in a packed, rectangular conference room in Castle Buildings, with the parties present in plenary session and the atmosphere brimming with excitement, Mitchell addressed his audience: 'I'm pleased to announce that the two Governments, and the political parties of Northern Ireland, have reached agreement.' But what did this agreement, concluded at dusk on Good Friday 1998, after two years of negotiations and thirty years of war . . . what did it actually prove? George Mitchell was ready with an answer: it proved 'that democracy works', he confidently proclaimed.[58] But was everything really all that simple? Something, it was true, had finally worked. After more than a quarter of a century of devastation, of shattered hopes and ruined lives, a settlement had finally arrived. The bitterest hostility had been politically surmounted – old enemies were joined in a common pact, and something like consensus had emerged.

First of all, an Assembly had been agreed with a comprehensive range of legislative and executive powers. But how laws were to be enacted and resolutions put into effect was the central question. Sensitive legislation would be required to meet the test of 'cross-community support' and the composition of a new executive – the Northern Ireland arm of government – would reflect the range of parties in the Assembly. A First Minister, together with a Deputy First Minister, were to be created, and up to ten additional executive posts would be distributed according to the numerical strength of parties within the Assembly. A committee system would then scrutinise the executive departments, contribute to policy development and play a role in the initiation of legislation. Both committee memberships and committee chairs would again be allocated proportionately. A North–South Ministerial Council was to be established, a British–Irish Council would be set up, and a new British–Irish Intergovernmental Conference would be established. These bodies were to operate by consensus, and without infringement on the authority of each participating member.[59] This, then, was the fruit of the three-stranded process inaugurated by Peter Brooke in the spring of 1991. But in what sense are we entitled to call it 'democracy'?

The key to the whole Agreement was the Assembly itself, in particular the means by which it would arrive at its decisions. Under the provisions of the Agreement, the constituent parts would stand or fall together – 'all of the institutions and constitutional arrangements . . . are interlocking and interdependent'.[60] And so the success of each component would depend on the capacity of the Assembly to function effectively and harmoniously. That was to be achieved by manipulating the criterion for consensus which ordinarily obtains in democratic fora. At the first meeting of the Assembly, members were to register a designation of identity in terms of 'nationalist', 'unionist' or 'other', and assent was to be measured by the achievement of 'sufficient consensus'.[61]

In ordinary circumstances, decisions could still be taken by majority vote. But for standing orders and budget allocation, matters were to proceed in accordance with the Agreement's requirement for adequate consensus. That is, assent was to be measured in terms of cross-community support registered by either 'parallel consent' – a majority of both nationalist and unionist members – or by a 'weighted majority' of 60 per cent – including at least 40 per cent of each of the nationalist and unionist designations. Moreover, the requirement for sufficient consensus could be triggered in respect of any controversial piece of legislation by a Petition of Concern supported by at least thirty of the 108 members of the Assembly.[62]

This, then, was to be the government of Northern Ireland. In all its balance and complexity, it was intended as a mechanism for ending conflict. The requirement of an outright majority had given way to the principle of parallel consent, hostile factions had been transmuted into interlocking parties, and guerrilla commanders were now elevated into parliamentary partners. There could emerge, as a result, a new political balance of forces displacing the familiar dynamic of intractable confrontation: most of the political parties, and the main paramilitary factions, supported these arrangements for Northern Ireland. However, both the DUP and the UKUP would campaign in opposition.

But, on the positive side, neither of these was backed by a private army. There existed, therefore, a substantial majority standing in favour of the Agreement, opposed, as it happened, by a rump minority seeking to alter its terms by political means alone. In joint referenda held North and South on 22 May 1998, the Agreement, supported by the vast majority, was victorious at the polls. After so many years of agony and effort, after decades of outrage and recrimination, a charter for peace had arrived. Such, at least, was the hope: the Agreement promised finally to secure what had eluded so many previous initiatives – an end to division and armed rebellion, and the beginning of organised competition.

But, of course, the Agreement had this much in common with every other constitutional settlement devised by a mixture of luck and skill throughout the course of human history. A Roman peace was secured, in Gibbon's famous phrase, by 'an absolute monarchy disguised under the forms of a commonwealth'.[63] The religious wars of sixteenth-century France finally yielded, as Voltaire would come to describe the eventual peace, to a culture of placidity and politeness under the 'absolute power' of Louis XIV.[64] Peace, as the historical record amply testifies, is not the exclusive preserve of constitutional democracy. And so we come back to our earlier question: what, in the end, did the Agreement actually prove?

Mitchell's response, that it proved that 'democracy works', was the unanimous refrain uttered by a myriad of journalists and commentators in the aftermath of Good Friday. But the content of this utterance still remains opaque. Certainly the Agreement proved that a decision to end the war could bring about an end to all hostilities – that if political struggle succeeded the contest of arms in Northern Ireland, then civil administration would take the place of military confrontation. In the future, therefore, one could expect a system of organised political competition to replace the older pattern of insurrection and oppression which had character- ised the Northern Irish situation for more than a generation. But in what sense, we now need to ask, would this system of organised political competition amount to the advent of democracy?

We have already seen how democracy refers at once to states and to their governments. In relation to states, democracies are made of people united in agreement about their primary political allegiance to an established system of rule. As a result of that allegiance, they authorise a political process to act on their behalf. Under the Agreement, members of the Northern Ireland populace could continue to identify themselves as either British or Irish, but in practical terms they would authorise the newly established representative system for Northern Ireland to do their bidding, and thereby they would constitute its people.[65]

In fact, under the terms of the new accord, the newly devolved political system would remain under the jurisdiction of a sovereign British government and so, in authorising a system of adminis- tration in Northern Ireland, the people of the Province were indirectly authorising their political subordination within the United Kingdom. That subordination had one overriding practical consequence: should the Assembly and its government collapse, the exercise of political authority would revert to Westminster.[66]

But, short of that collapse, the system of rule in the Province was entrusted with the right to act upon its people as equally *one* people, and not, by implication, to act upon the populace in its more habitual pose of mutually hostile peoples – nationalists and republicans on one side, and unionists on the other – tilting their allegiance towards competitor regimes. But would the system thus established behave, as one might put it, democratically?

If democracy refers to states, as we have seen, it also refers to governments. In this sense, it refers at once to the mechanisms employed by ruling bodies for arriving at decisions, and to the character of the relationship between the government and the governed. We have seen how the new Northern Ireland Assembly was intended to arrive at its decisions by a process of generating cross-community consensus in lieu of the older requirement of majority consent. The democratic character of this political arrangement must be taken to reside in the way in which the system of cross-community rule answers sufficiently to the expectation of equality among the ruled. In simpler terms, it must be taken to reside in the relationship between the individuals who rule and those whom they are called upon to rule. Tyrannies rule in the name of single tyrants, and majorities in the name of the majority – but democracies rule in the name of equal citizens. But what does this formula entail?

Under the Good Friday Agreement, an Assembly was to be established to represent the people, an executive was to do the Assembly's business, and committees were to scrutinise the executive. The Assembly was to be composed of individual delegates, selected at the outset by popular vote, and delegates were to participate as members of political parties. Parties were to be designated as nationalist or unionist, and these were to be represented on the executive and the committees in proportion to their strength in the Assembly. Altogether, it was not significantly dissimilar from the Sunningdale Agreement of 1973. That Agreement, as we know, was brought down in 1974, but Good Friday looked set to succeed. What, we might ask, was the relevant difference? If democracy had at last succeeded in 1998, why then, at its earlier attempt, did it so obviously fail? Was Good Friday an expression of the actual will of the people and Sunningdale no more than a sorry betrayal? To answer this question we need to discover how, in each case, the popular will was actually represented.

When Sunningdale collapsed in 1974, there were three main political actors on the Northern Ireland scene – three antithetical political factions, each contending for supremacy as representatives of the will of the people. The supporters of Sunningdale in Northern Ireland were backed by the United Kingdom government, claiming to represent the people of that state. These were opposed by the Ulster Workers' Council, standing as the voice of the Protestant masses. And both were opposed by the Provisional IRA, acting in the name of the people of Ireland. But, in 1998, there was only one politically effective claimant to this representative status – namely, the Northern Ireland Assembly, represented in turn by the British government.

And so the acknowledgement, or authorisation, of one supreme representative system of government by the various protagonists in Northern Ireland was the specific achievement of the Good Friday Agreement. For Sinn Féin and the IRA, that acknowledgement was presented as a transitional commitment along the way to the establishment a sovereign united Ireland.[67] Consequently, the long term success of the Good Friday Agreement would depend on the extent to which that transitional commitment became a permanent allegiance or, alternatively, on the extent to which the IRA's preferred outcome was accepted in the end by their political enemies. It depended, in other words, on the long term durability of the acknowledged representative established under the terms of the Agreement. But, in the meantime, the achievement of peace in Northern Ireland was the result of a common pledge to a supreme representative body. But was this, then, a pledge to democracy? Representation, indeed, is a core component of modern democratic politics. It forges a link between government and people. But we need to know how it works.

In 1974 there were three representative political actors in Northern Ireland, each with a claim on the popular will. Not all of these claims were equally compelling, but neither were any of them above contention. That, in fact, is precisely the point. Each protagonist took its opponent to task for the principles underlying its particular claim to democratic legitimacy. But, unfortunately, we do not have available to us an overriding principle which can be invoked to settle our various disputes over particular discordant principles: despite the complacency which afflicts the standard political assumptions to which we are habitually exposed today, nowhere is this more the case than in disputes about democracy.

Such disputes can always arise because our modern attachment to popular representation has since the beginning been a somewhat uncertain affair. This uncertainty has impinged upon the politics of France – memorably after 1789 – much as it has impinged upon the politics of Germany – notoriously after 1918. The same goes for the United States since the very beginning of its career.[68] And, again, this same uncertainty pervades the Northern Ireland peace settlement of 1998. What is uncertain is the meaning of representation, and so it is this that we need to explore.

In France, in Germany, in the United States, and similarly in Northern Ireland, individual governments claim to act on the authority of their peoples, much as the IRA, the British government and the Ulster Workers' Council did, simultaneously and irreconcilably, in the North in 1974. Given the results of that year, it is overwhelmingly desirable, in the interest of peace and tranquillity, that the population of a given territory authorise a single representative system of government to secure its welfare. That result was not forthcoming in 1974 but, after a protracted and bloody detour, it was in 1998. To understand the true importance of that achievement, to understand its significance for democracy and representation, we need to grasp the nature of the authority which the people of Northern Ireland conferred upon their new regime in the aftermath of Good Friday. When people pledge themselves to a state by authorising a system of government, as occurred with the referenda on the Agreement held in May 1998, they do not in the process establish themselves as the arbiters of the system to which they are thus committed. However, it is precisely from this conclusion that theories of democracy tend to run shy when their exponents are called upon to explain the real operational content of democratic states.[69]

It must be remembered that a system of government was authorised in Northern Ireland as a means of resolving political dispute. That system comprises a legislative branch, an Assembly, and a ministerial branch, an executive, together with scrutinising and judicial functions. Scrutiny is the business of Assembly committees, justice the preserve of the judiciary. The whole edifice of government, so understood, acts as a means of adjudication. It acts, in other words, as a final arbiter, an ultimate court of appeal, and in that sense it acts as a representative will. It is in this capacity of representative of the people that it renders these acts of arbitration. But, in representing, it does not directly articulate the desires of the antagonists whose conflict it was intended to resolve. Instead, it seeks to patch up their fratricidal differences.

A representative regime, a democracy, is not the agent of its population's quarrels: it is not their delegate in this sense, not their tool – not a vehicle for their mutual hostility. From this perspective, it becomes clear that to see the populace as itself the arbiter of the mechanism for arbitration which it authorises is to commit the political order to a destructive circular process. The bearers of division and acrimony – the population at large – cannot logically be seen as submitting themselves to a process of arbitration whilst retaining the right to judge their adjudicator. If we take them to retain that right, in practice we confer upon them the right to wield the hostility and division whose political arbitration they have themselves already authorised.

Authorisation, in other words, confers authority, and one cannot retain what one has already conferred. What is authorised is a representative mechanism for composing hostile differences. And so it becomes obvious that the representative element in a democracy does not contain its populace in their collective individuality, it does not duplicate their multiple, conflicting purposes. Consequently, and this its point, it does not reproduce their political divisions. Representation, in other words, does not directly *represent*, it is not a literal standing-in-for the people in their manifold plurality.[70] A democracy is not deputised on sufferance, it does not act by the permission of its people. To assume that it does is to surrender analysis to the populist myth covertly advanced by the rhetoric of democracy. That rhetoric is of course entirely alluring since it encourages us in the belief that we are in fact the arbiters of our established systems of government. It promotes the almost irresistible idea that we are all now masters in our own domain – the ultimate governors of our state, in control of our own destinies: rulers, as we tend to believe, in the last instance. It appeals in the end to democratic vanity.

Vanity in the modern world takes the form of a belief in equality. When Tocqueville set out to explain the reasons behind the 'great democratic revolution' rising to power throughout all Europe in the nineteenth century, he found his explanation in 'the principle of equality' – a 'providential fact', as he put it, which the United States exemplified.[71] But equality, which comes in many forms, awakens many expectations. If these expectations are systematically disappointed, established politics risks being threatened by an assertion of equality through the direct power of the people. But in this direct intervention lies democracy's lethal potential. The lethal component derives from the appeal to popularity, from the implicit commitment to a system of rule controlled by the people themselves. When people claim the right to rule *their* country, they claim it as their common sovereign property. Yet when they claim the state as their own property, and endeavour to make good their sense of ownership, debate is liable to ensue about how that ownership ought properly to be used.

Such debates over the past two hundred years have had singularly unhappy consequences, leading, at their most extreme, to revolutionary war. The most notorious eruptions – in France after 1789, in Russia after 1917 – have usually been characterised in terms of ideological fanaticism.[72] But the 'fanaticism' in question was in each case nothing other than an assertion of democratic dignity, or vanity – the vain and seductive presumption that today, in the age of equality, we might all be equally rulers.[73]

It is this vanity which, as we have seen, inhabits our ordinary attachment to democracy. In its potency, throughout the twentieth century, it has frequently receded, but only to return. Now it slumbers, now it suddenly revives, and obviously it hasn't gone away. It haunted the dynamics of Northern Irish politics after 1968, and took thirty years to lay to rest. If it remains quiescent there into the distant future, it is still the case that the same struggle between peoples and their representatives, between popular self-determination and political authority, continues to consume world politics at the beginning of the new millennium. In this instance, like every other, we cannot simply call upon democracy to fix the situation since democracy itself is half of the problem.

The democratic ideal of a government by the people was conceived as a means of curbing the pretensions of political power. But that ideal has always been prone to serious misconception. In the settled democracies of today, the notion of a government by the people is a loose metaphorical construction. What democratic government actually denotes is government meaningfully conducted in the name of the people. That means government by proxy – by representation, and representation, as we have seen, does not amount to the political replication of popular ambition and desire. It amounts, instead, to the acknowledgement of representative adjudication. It entails the existence of an ultimate arbiter, or agreed procedures of decision: a sovereign agency.

This is not to suggest that people in a democracy are the passive recipients of decrees and directives. People, quite clearly, do themselves act, and they act to have their interests advanced. But that is not to say that they *rule*, if by rule we mean *decide*, and decide as a matter of entitlement, which of their various interests should in the end predominate. Governments today, then, are not restrained by a people taking into their hands the right to determine their destinies directly. Power, instead, is curbed by considerably more modest means.

It is curbed, in particular, by pragmatic restraints which the regular intercourse between rulers and ruled imposes on the activity of ruling. That intercourse has a myriad familiar forms: electoral processes, lobbying practices, media accountability, party machines and corporate interests, and the demands of apparent economic necessity. However, none of this amounts to the people as such determining its destiny as a matter of collective right. It amounts, instead, to an assortment of interests trying in their various ways to force the hand of government agents for better or for worse.

However, when one amongst those many interests claims to represent the popular will, to be the really existing popular component of the democratic state, it lays down a challenge to established democracy and threatens it with subversion. This was the substance of the Ulster Workers' Council's remark, publicised through its military wing, the Ulster Army Council, during the strike of 1974: 'If Westminster is not prepared to restore democracy . . . then the only other way it can be restored is by a *coup d'état*.'[74] But one rarely restores a democracy by means of revolution. More usually, one starts a civil war.

Epilogue: 1998–2003

I

At midnight on 14 October 2002, both the Northern Ireland Assembly and the power-sharing executive established under the Good Friday Agreement were suspended, and direct rule from Westminster was reinstated. It was the fourth time since the creation of the new Provincial government that control over the affairs of Northern Ireland had reverted from the devolved administration to the British parliament. The institutions created under the 1998 accord had been condemned to a precarious existence since their inception. Now, four years after the initial peace deal had been struck, the settlement itself seemed under threat. Sinn Féin had grown to doubt the dedication of Ulster Unionists to implementing the provisions of the original Agreement, while Unionism had lost faith in the determination of Republicans to abide by the standard protocols of democratic constitutionalism.

The misalignment had been developing since 1998. A year after the Good Friday negotiations had been concluded, a new government for the Province had yet to be established. Later again, in the summer of 1999, still without the executive in place, the British and Irish governments were forced to institute a review procedure to rescue the Agreement from the abyss. It was not until late November 1999 that an administration could be formed with the backing of the Ulster Unionist Party and its leader, David Trimble, together with the endorsement of the Ulster Unionist Council which decided on the policy of the party. But then by

February 2000 the executive was suspended amid fears that the Provisionals would fail to honour their commitments.[1]

However, shortly the Agreement's fortunes were to change: after the IRA agreed to have some of its arms dumps inspected by a group of international observers, power was devolved to the executive again. It was 30 May 2000. Two years had passed since the Good Friday settlement had been signed, and both participants and observers sighed relief. But in just over a year, another critical juncture in the peace process arrived as Trimble resigned his post of First Minister of the executive, and by 10 August 2001 the Assembly had been temporarily suspended once again. It was hoped that a start to the process of IRA disarmament might follow. But the hope was not fulfilled – actual decommissioning was not started until October and, in the meantime, John Reid, the successor to Peter Mandelson as Secretary of State for Northern Ireland, had been obliged to suspend the institutions of government yet again as a means of buying time for a resolution of the dispute about the handling of paramilitary weapons.[2]

On 26 October 2001, with the Northern Ireland Assembly facing imminent collapse, the IRA was reported to have destroyed some of its arsenal. The following April, another act of IRA decommissioning occurred. But suspicion between Republicans and unionists would not die down and, by the autumn of 2002, another critical showdown had appeared on the horizon: after allegations of a Republican spy ring operating at the heart of the Northern Ireland government had leaked into the public, the British Prime Minister, Tony Blair, held urgent talks with David Trimble to save the political process from a fateful, downward spiral. But the talks had failed by the middle of October, and the Assembly and the executive were brought down.[3]

Fresh elections to the Assembly had been scheduled for the spring of 2003. Anticipating their arrival, Tony Blair was openly calling for the disbandment of the IRA: Republicans were expected to embark on definite 'acts of completion' as a prelude to putting the Agreement on a more permanent foundation.[4] Intense negotiations among the Northern Ireland parties were conducted through the winter, and into spring. The elections to the Assembly, originally due for the start of May, were now deferred until the 29th of the month. But the impasse could not be surmounted, and the elections were again postponed – until the autumn of 2003.[5] When elections to the second Northern Ireland Assembly finally arrive – assuming that they will – Sinn Féin is expected to have become the largest nationalist party in Northern Ireland, and the Ulster Unionists might well have been overtaken by Ian Paisley's DUP: it can be anticipated that the struggle for advantage will continue.

2

From the beginning, the settlement in Northern Ireland had stumbled from one crisis to the next as the representative institutions, intended to defuse the conflict, buckled under pressure from popular distrust.[6] Fear had been most obvious among the Protestant community, whose commitment to the Agreement had never been as solid as the support which it enjoyed among the Catholic population. The fractious politics of antagonism, which had emerged into the open every summer during marching season since 1998, had only served to deepen pervasive Protestant suspicion: the annual stand-off surrounding an Orange march at Drumcree in Portadown continued to fuel political passion, confirming unionist sentiment that Good Friday signalled defeat.[7] A succession of Republican escapades increased the level of alarm: allegations of an IRA break-in at the special branch security complex at Castlereagh in east Belfast, evidence of a plot among Republicans to import hand-guns from Florida in the United States, and the charge of IRA involvement with Columbian guerrilla dissidents, encouraged unionist disbelief in the pacific intentions of Sinn Féin.

All the while, the supporters of the Republican movement noted the wrecking-tactics of the unionist parties, steadily convinced that they would never work the Agreement. In the absence of a conclusive unionist commitment to the accord, Republicanism was happy to flaunt its paramilitary origins, or to advertise what it took to be the 'transitional' nature of the arrangements which both Republicans and unionists had agreed under the accord. The devastation wrought by the republican splinter group, the 'Real IRA', in a bomb attack on Omagh town centre in August 1998, fortified the Provisionals against a return to armed insurrection. But they had still to be convinced of the merits of politics in Northern Ireland: the Good Friday pact was regularly represented as a stepping-stone to a united Ireland – as an interim arrangement along the road to something better.[8]

Consequently, since 1998, support for the Agreement among the parties in Northern Ireland has been far less than profound: Unionism has been unhappy with the composition of the new government, while Sinn Féin has shown no enthusiasm for the survival of the old state. In the autumn of 2001, hailing the first act of decommissioning on the part of the IRA, Gerry Adams could describe partition as an ongoing 'obscenity', despite the fact that both he and his party had voted for its continuance: it was, after all, the Good Friday Agreement which established Northern Ireland as a legitimate entity.[9]

Still, Gerry Adams' remark amounts to more than rhetorical bluster since, despite the current legitimacy pertaining to the existence of Northern Ireland, its status is indeed provisional under the terms of the current settlement: the signatories to Good Friday, it is vital to recall, recognised 'the legitimacy of whatever choice is freely exercised by a majority of the people of Northern Ireland with regard to its status, whether they prefer to support the Union with Great Britain or a sovereign united Ireland'.[10] With that formula, peace was secured for the present, but at the price of future dissent.

Commentators have been confused about the meaning of this formula, assuming that it provides for specifically *unionist* consent to the continuing existence of Northern Ireland as a political unit.

The confusion, however, is easily dispelled: the statement does not point to any particular political allegiance as the basis on which the status of Northern Ireland should be determined. The preference of neither 'nationalists' nor 'unionists' is decisive. Instead, the choice of a 'majority' is the crucial mechanism of decision. But, over time, a majority might be attained by Roman Catholics instead of Protestants. Despite this possibility, unionists are so attached to their historic rights as a majority that the term itself is assumed by them to refer to their own constituency.

Since obviously it does not, unionists should apply their intelligence to the consequences of this false assumption. In discussion in November 2002, the former chairman of the peace talks held in 1998, Senator George Mitchell, was at pains to point out that the requirement that a bare majority should act as the means of determining the status of Northern Ireland had been an ineliminable unionist demand since the start of the process. But he also added, ominously – this might yet prove to have been a 'strategic error' on their part.[11]

However, both the British and Irish governments, and indeed Sinn Féin itself, should also assess the potential long term fall-out from this provision. In an Annex to the Agreement, the basic reality was spelt out: Northern Ireland ought to retain its right of membership of the Union for as long as it can muster 'the consent of a majority'.[12] This clause has now been incorporated into British legislation. With its enactment, the Government of Ireland Act of 1920 was repealed. In fact, so too was the 1801 Act of Union, despite predictions to the contrary on the part of David Trimble.[13] There was, categorically, no right of secession, on any terms whatever, envisaged by the Act of 1801. In contrast, secession can now be triggered by any majority so minded in a plebiscite which can be called at the discretion of the British government.

This seems to suit Sinn Féin, but does it really? Are the Irish government content with this arrangement? Do they expect the incorporation of a dissident unionist minority to be achieved without a hitch, or even with Protestant facilitation? It is difficult to gain much insight into the expectations of the Irish government: up until now, it has only said that if it should face an eventuality of this kind, it would deal with the situation by holding negotiations in the spirit of mutual concord and respect.[14] This attitude has to rely on a remarkably sanguine set of predictions. But more astonishing, even the Ulster Unionists affect indifference on the subject. In fact, last winter they seemed prepared to advertise the stark reality of the problem, pushing for a border poll to be held with the Assembly elections.[15]

Unionists would clearly top the poll. But by how much? And here's the problem. Victory at a single poll, with the anxiety of the electorate newly focused on the future, hardly promises to soothe every aggravation in the Province, let alone to resolve the outstanding constitutional question.[16] Rather, it would only extend uncertainty, and it might foment dissent. One need only remember the words of Sinn Féin's northern chairperson, Mitchel McLaughlin, just before the Agreement. In an article for the *Irish Times* in October 1997, McLaughlin raised the issue of the 'demographic trends' which have haunted Northern Ireland since its inception. The results of the 1991 Northern Ireland census had been quite promising, in his view: they pointed to 'increasing tension and instability as the unionist community contemplates losing ever more political control and power in the six counties'. The next census, scheduled for 2001, would paint an even brighter picture in McLaughlin's estimation: it would show 'that the tide of history is eroding the ability of unionist politicians to exercise a veto over political change in our society'.[17]

The birth-rate of Northern Catholics has always darkened the imaginations of unionists forced to contemplate the long term prospects for their country. Premonitions of a critical shift in the demography of Northern Ireland might well be unsupported by the available statistical evidence. The results of the most recent census, published in December 2002, proved that the gap between the communities is less narrow than was predicted: Protestants now comprise 53 per cent of the population, while Catholics have only managed to climb to 44 per cent. Nonetheless, the trend is clear: it favours Catholics as an expanding component of the electorate. As a result, debate is beginning to home in on whether the advent of the crunch moment, when the Catholic population comes to stand at 51 per cent, will arrive in a single generation, or in another two.[18]

In a confidential draft proposal for a referendum to be held on the future status of Northern Ireland, prepared under the Labour government back in 1969, it was presumed that a Catholic majority was unlikely to emerge 'for, say, twenty years at the very earliest'. But it was still James Callaghan's view that 'if our present policies work in making opportunities more equal between Roman Catholics and Protestants, this would be likely to influence the rate of emigration of Roman Catholics and consequently bring forward the time by which Roman Catholics might form a majority of the population.'[19]

By the end of 2002, the advent of a nationalist majority had not quite yet come 'forward' into the present, as Callaghan had expected. But the real point is that no predictive calculus, since none can ever be quite certain, is likely to dispel the dark imaginings of Ulster's unionists while they watch Sinn Féin preparing for a nationalist majority. Currently, with the institutions of government in Northern Ireland in suspension, and all attention focused on the short term prospects for the Agreement, alarm about more distant trends is likely to be occluded. But when the current impasse over armaments and policing has been surmounted, the issue will re-emerge into the public for discussion. At that point, old enemies might position themselves for a collision in the coming struggle.

3

The crisis in Northern Ireland was born of a struggle over equality. Despite this, there has been a tendency to view the mayhem that has accompanied the contest as resulting from extraneous forces or anachronistic impulses – like 'tribal' hostility, or religious hatred.

But these perceptions offer testimony more to bafflement than to understanding.[20] Equality has come to constitute the core value of modern democracy, but the bloody turmoil that has come along with the various attempts at its realisation have been imputed to residual attitudes which long predate its apotheosis. The message here is clear: modernity is not responsible for its own particular forms of conflict.

The optimism behind this message is also easily understood. It was expected that the establishment of egalitarian values would facilitate social harmony to an extent that had been impossible under the rigorous division of ranks which modernity had abandoned in the aftermath of modern revolutions.[21] But in fact, equality has proved a fraught and acrimonious aspiration. In the eighteenth century, before the passion for equality had become an established political doctrine, David Hume could observe that it is not some conspicuous 'disproportion betwixt ourselves and another . . . but on the contrary, our [mutual] proximity' that inflames the dynamics of envy between individuals and groups.[22] Proximity provokes comparison, and comparison unnerves. But the desire for equality springs precisely from comparability, and not identity: we don't expect to be treated as somehow identical with other people – on the contrary, we hope that we might be favourably, or at least equitably, compared.

When the process of comparison in the world of political competition is affronted and undermined by the denial of equality, dissension is introduced into the vitals of the community. The difficulty is that political dissension looks both ways – towards eventual reconciliation on the one hand, and towards deepening disaffection on the other. In democratic societies, disaffection usually seeks redress by resort to that expedient most commonly associated with democracy itself: by resort, that is, to political weight in numbers. However, in Northern Ireland, disparity in numbers occupied the centre of the conflict as constituencies comprising rival minorities and majorities competed in a battle for legitimacy and recognition.

The recognition of Northern Ireland as the long term property of an exclusive majority ensures that bitter political contestation will survive for another generation. Everyone but the most ardent zealot must hope that the contest will be concluded without resort to a violent conflagration, although there can be no certainty that this hope will be fulfilled. While Republicanism threatens unionists with the dissolution of Northern Ireland, unionists will be slow to embrace the newly established government; yet while Unionism threatens Republicans with capsizing the new government, Republicans will harry Unionism with the prospect of a new state. It is still a matter of urgency that this cycle should be broken. Ultimately, the advantage will go to the party that is able to move first.

The commercial centre of Belfast is freely bustling today, in comparison with the agitated nervousness of the past. Even west Belfast is more peaceful than it has been for a generation. However, Portadown remains resentful, and the Ardoyne Road is still seething. The summer before last, in 2002, a republican tricolour had been hoisted over an abandoned Protestant church on the Whitewell Road in north Belfast. This summer, the Short Strand was still cramped by the fear of loyalist attacks. What could ignite these brittle materials, and spark dissidence into flame, if not the grimmest expectations of the future? By that stage, the struggle for equality between unionists and Sinn Féiners might be spirited back to life. An austere determination might reappear in the two communities, and the solidarities of the past undermine the appetite for peace.

Notes

Introduction

1 This global prediction is Francis Fukuyama's from 'The End of History', *The National Interest*, 16 (Summer 1989), p. 4. Brendan O'Leary, in his 'Comparative Political Science and the British–Irish Agreement', in John McGarry ed., *Northern Ireland and the Divided World: Post-Agreement Northern Ireland in Comparative Perspective* (Oxford: 2001), pp. 55–58, describes the Good Friday accord as 'perhaps unparalleled in its liberal democratic institutional detail', while conceding that the Agreement 'accepted the legitimacy of an irredentist aspiration'. The problem posed by this irredentism, however, is then passed over: namely, the fact that, under the terms of the 1998 accord, a cross-community agreement can be overturned by one of those communities alone – the numerically preponderant one. O'Leary side-steps this by equating the 'people of Ireland' with two concurrent majorities on the island, North and South. There can, however, be nothing 'liberal' or 'democratic' about the coercion of a prospective Northern Protestant minority. The reality of this possibility, as a right enshrined in the Agreement, is nonetheless usually occluded in the commentary on its provisions. See, for instance, Martin Mansergh, 'The Background to the Irish Peace Process', in Michael Cox et al. eds, *A Farewell to Arms? From 'Long War' to Long Peace in Northern Ireland* (Manchester: 2000), p. 23: 'the concept of mutual consent underlay the Agreement'. However there is, on the contrary, no mutuality involved in an arrangement whereby one entrusts one's political future to a potentially hostile majority. Similarly, Rick Wilford, 'The Assembly and the Executive', in Rick Wilford ed., *Aspects of the Belfast Agreement* (Oxford: 2001), p. 121, has commented that 'the Agreement left the future constitutional status of Northern Ireland contingent upon the popular will of its electorate'. However, as this book tries to argue, the 'popular will' cannot straightforwardly be identified with the majority will in a democracy.

313

2   On the first of these stipulations, see Robert A. Dahl, *Democracy and Its Critics* (New Haven and London: 1989), p. 3: 'Advocates of democracy . . . characteristically presuppose that "a people" already exists. Its existence is assumed as a fact . . . Yet the facticity of the fact is questionable. It is often questioned – as it was in the United States in 1861 when the issue was settled not by consent or consensus but by violence.' For the 'embarrassment' which this problem causes for democratic theory, see the 'Introduction' to Ian Shapiro and Casiano Hacker-Cordón eds, *Democracy's Edges* (Cambridge: 1999), p. 1. In the historical literature on this subject, the problem of co-ordinating democratic inclusion with the exercise of democratic power has most usually been discussed in terms of a reconciliation between 'nation' and 'state'. See, for example, Friedrich Meinecke, *Cosmopolitanism and the National State*, trans. Robert B. Kimber (Princeton, N.J.: 1970), p. 25, on the case of Revolutionary France: 'Carried along by the social movement of the third estate, the idea of the nation in France passed directly into the idea of national sovereignty and of the modern national state.' Most commentators follow the lead of John Plamenatz, 'Two Types of Nationalism', in E. Kamenka ed., *Nationalism: The Nature and Evolution of an Idea* (London: 1973) in treating the problems which have historically accompanied attempts at such reconciliation in terms of exclusive theories of 'ethnicity' or 'culture' employed to define nationality. See, for example, the 'Afterword' to Elie Kedourie, *Nationalism* (London: 1960, 1985), which takes the problem of nationalism to derive from ideas of national distinctness or uniqueness peddled by political ideologues in nineteenth-century Europe. Similarly, Liah Greenfeld, *Nationalism: Five Paths to Modernity* (Cambridge, Mass.: 1992), p. 11, has presented the spurious attachment to ideas about homogenous ethnic or cultural types as the key to nationalist chauvinism: 'nationalism may be distinguished according to criteria of membership in the national collectivity, which may be either "civic", that is, identical with citizenship, or "ethnic"'. But the contrast hardly clinches the point at issue since it is the question of 'membership' as such which poses the problem. Membership of modern democracies, which are known as nation-states, is determined by the criterion of 'equality'. The difficulties which attend satisfying this criterion are surely more illuminatingly described as a problem integral to democracy than vaguely as the problem of nationalism. On egalitarianism as pivotal to nationalist – i.e. democratic – struggle, see Ernest Gellner, *Nations and Nationalism* (Oxford: 1983, 1990), pp. 63–87.

3   See, however, Marianne Elliott, *The Catholics of Ulster: A History* (London: 2000), p. 481, on the existence of 16–30% Catholic support for the Union in the 1990s – although, at the same time, Elliott points out that Republicanism is capable of undermining this support.

4   *Agreement Reached in the Multi-Party Negotiations* (Dublin: 1998). 'Constitutional Issues', s. 1 (i): the parties to the Agreement 'recognise the legitimacy of whatever choice is freely exercised by a majority of the people of Northern Ireland with regard to its status, whether they prefer to continue to support the Union with Great Britain or a sovereign united Ireland'. Coupled with the demographic trend toward an increase in the Catholic population in Northern Ireland since 1922, it is difficult to square this provision with the claim advanced by Brendan O'Leary, 'The Character of the 1998 Agreement: Results and Prospects', in Rick Wilford ed., *Aspects of the Belfast Agreement*, p. 68, to the effect that 'The Agreement was designed to withstand major demographic . . . changes.' After all, as O'Leary himself puts it in ibid., p. 72: 'Northern Ireland has the right to secede, by majority consent, to unify with the Republic of Ireland.'

5   Emmanuel Joseph Sieyès, *Qu'est-ce que le Tiers-État* (Paris: 3rd edn, 1789), pp. 23–24n, for instance, remarked that democratic unity can be sustained only by a 'community of privilege': 'Il est sûr que la communauté des privilèges est le meilleur moyen de rapprocher les Ordres, & de préparer la plus importante des loix, celle qui convertira les Ordres en *une* Nation.' His remark was intended, of course, as a defence of the general interest against minority privilege. But John C. Calhoun, *A Disquisition on Government* in *The Works of John C. Calhoun*, ed. Richard K. Crallé (New York: 1861), I, p. 29, draws out the implications of this analysis in saying that it is a 'first and leading error . . . to confound the numerical majority with the people'. Majoritarian theory, on the other hand, finds its most powerful and influential advocate in Jeremy Bentham, 'Note by the Author, 1822' to *An Introduction to the Principles of Morals and Legislation* (1789), included in the 1823 edition of *A Fragment on Government* (1776), ed. J. H. Burns and H. L. A. Hart (1977; Cambridge: 1988), p. 58n, where 'the *greatest happiness* or *greatest felicity* principle' is presented as leading 'to the consideration of the *number*, of the interests affected'. In his '*Explanation, written July, 1822, relative to the above note*', p. 59n, Bentham clarifies his argument: it is 'a principle, which lays down, as the only *right* and justifiable end of Government, the greatest happiness of the greatest number'. However, as J. H. Burns has pointed out in 'Majorities: An Exploration', *History of Political Thought*,

XXIV, 1 (Spring 2003), pp. 66–85, Bentham had discarded this formulation by the summer of 1829: Bentham had by this stage come to the view that 'the reference to "the greatest number" could be used to justify the total sacrifice of a bare minority in the interests of a bare majority' (p. 82). However, it is the argument of 1822 that has come to be associated with Bentham. His influence, in terms of this earlier position, among British Philosophic Radicals like James Mill, and their influence on nineteenth-century democratic reform, is discussed at length by M. Ostrogorski, *Democracy and the Organization of Political Parties*, trans. Frederick Clarke (London: 1902), 2 vols, I, Part 1, Chs 2–4. However, the applicability of the 'utility' or 'greatest happiness' principle to democratic reform was rejected by John Stuart Mill, *Considerations on Representative Government* (1861; New York: 1991), pp. 133–45, where the majority principle is criticised as leading to 'a government of privilege in favour of the numerical majority': 'Suppose the majority Catholics, the minority Protestants, or the reverse: will there not be . . . danger?' For an account of Mill's employment of the Benthamite criterion of 'sinister interests' to undermine Bentham's own commitment to the utility principle, see Ross Harrison, *Democracy* (London: 1993), Ch. 6.

6   Robert A. Dahl, *A Preface to Democratic Theory* (Chicago: 1956), p. 133, argued that 'majority rule is mostly a myth'. Northern Ireland between 1920 and 1972, however, was a reality, and so an exception to Dahl's more general point. On 7 March 1972 the British Home Secretary, Reginald Maudling, remarked at a Cabinet meeting chaired by Edward Heath that 'Over 50 years, under an artificially constructed constitution, the Unionist party employed political domination at Stormont to the exclusion of the minority community' (Public Record Office, London [PRO] CAB 128/48). Ronald Dworkin, *Sovereign Virtue: The Theory and Practice of Equality* (Cambridge, Mass.: 2000), p. 358, has made a more recent case for democratic equality being incompatible with 'the "majoritarian" conception'.

7   The distinction here derives from Immanuel Kant, 'Toward Perpetual Peace: A Philosophical Project', in *Practical Philosophy*, trans. Mary J. Gregor, p. 324: 'The form of government (*forma regiminis*) . . . has to do with the way a state . . . makes use of its plenary power', while 'the form of sovereignty (*forma imperii*)' refers to that 'plenary power' itself.

8   Frank Millar, 'Northern Ireland Accord: Back to the Drawing Board?', *Irish Times*, 25 October 2002; Richard Bourke, 'The Good Friday Agreement's Built-in Flaw', *Financial Times*, 19 December 2002. As

Joseph Ruane and Jennifer Todd, 'The Belfast Agreement: Context, Content, Consequences', in Joseph Ruane and Jennifer Todd eds, *After the Good Friday Agreement: Analysing Political Change in Northern Ireland* (Dublin: 1999), p. 20, put it: 'while the Agreement makes the will of the majority the determinant of Northern Ireland's constitutional status, this principle does not apply to its mode of governance'. On the extent to which, despite these provisions, the Good Friday Agreement was seen by the Ulster Unionist Party as representing 'a final deal that secures the Union', see Norman Porter, *The Elusive Quest: Reconciliation in Northern Ireland* (Belfast: 2003), p. 220.

9 In this context, it is worth noting the remark made by the former Taoiseach, Albert Reynolds, to the effect that, in the wake of the 1993 Downing Street Declaration, 'British imperialist interest in Ireland [was] dead' (RTE 1, Six O'Clock News, 10 January 1994). However, for the ongoing strategic significance of the term, note Gerry Adams' advocacy of the decommissioning of IRA weaponry on 23 October 2001 in terms of saving 'the peace process' from those in the political establishment 'who think they still have an empire and we're it' (*Irish Times*, 24 October 2001).

10 For example, the Downing Street Declaration of 1993 was itself presented by John Major as a 'declaration for democracy' (BBC 1, Nine O'Clock News, 15 December 1993). But that Declaration contains the very principle that was to become central to the Good Friday Agreement: the principle of majority sovereignty.

11 See the relevant point made by John Dunn, 'Preface' to *Democracy: The Unfinished Journey, 508 BC to AD 1993* (Oxford: 1993), p. vi: 'the power and appeal of democracy comes from the idea of autonomy – of choosing freely for oneself . . . But in no modern state do its members . . . decide what is in fact done, or hold their destiny in their own hands. They do not, because they cannot.'

12 The colloquialism, of course, has a long intellectual pedigree that cannot be set out in detail here. But, typically, see James Bryce, *Modern Democracies* (London: 1921, 1929), 2 vols, I, p. 161: 'The Sovereignty of the People is the basis and the watchword of democracy. It is a faith and a dogma to which in our time every frame of government has to conform, and by conformity to which every institution is tested.' On the history of the doctrine of the sovereignty of the people, see Hugh Seton-Watson, *Nations and States: An Inquiry into the Origins of Nations and the Politics of Nationalism* (London: 1977), pp. 1–13; Bertrand de Jouvenel, *Sovereignty: An Inquiry into the Political Good* (Chicago: 1957), pp. 169–85; F. H. Hinsley, *Sovereignty* (Cambridge: 1986), pp.

214–35; Istvan Hont, 'The Permanent Crisis of a Divided Mankind: "Contemporary Crisis of the Nation State" in Historical Perspective', in John Dunn ed., *Contemporary Crisis of the Nation State* (Cambridge: 1995), pp. 166–231.

13   This tension is in fact apparent in rival accounts of what constitute the most essential of modern values as represented, on the one hand, by Isaiah Berlin, *Four Essays on Liberty* (Oxford: 1969), p. 165, who advocates the view that 'no power, only rights, can be regarded as absolute'; and, on the other hand, by Jürgen Habermas' attempt, in *Between Facts and Norms: Contributions to a Discourse Theory of Law and Democracy*, trans. William Rehg (Cambridge, Mass.: 1996), pp. 128–29, to reconcile individual freedom with 'democratic self-legislation'. For an assessment of the rival historical traditions on which these divergent evaluations are founded, see Philip Pettit, 'Republican Freedom and Contestatory Democracy', in Ian Shapiro and Casiano Hacker-Cordón eds, *Democracy's Value* (Cambridge: 1999). For an analytical account of the opposing theories of democratic justice on which the rival views are based, see Michael J. Sandel, *Liberalism and the Limits of Justice* (Cambridge: 1982, 1998), pp. 184–218.

14   The phrase here is John Rawls', from his *Political Liberalism* (New York: 1993, 1996), pp. 61–62: 'citizens as free and equal have an equal share in the corporate political and coercive power of society'.

15   For the classic treatment of the world-transforming significance of democratic equality, see Alexis de Tocqueville, *Democracy in America*, trans. Harvey C. Mansfield and Delba Winthrop (Chicago: 2000), p. 8: 'now ranks are confused; the barriers raised among men are lowered; estates are divided, power is partitioned, enlightenment spreads, intelligence is equalised; the social state becomes democratic, and fully the empire of democracy is peacefully established over institutions and mores.'

16   This fact constitutes the core complaint of Jean-Jacques Rousseau, *Du contrat social*, in R. Derathé et al. eds, *Oeuvres Complètes* (Paris: 1964), p. 368: 'le souverain . . . ne peut être representé que par lui-même' ('the sovereign . . . cannot be represented by anything but itself'). But the complaint has stoked more political problems than it has provided actual solutions. For a discussion of contemporary responses to these problems, see Ian Shapiro, *The State of Democratic Theory* (Princeton, NJ: 2003).

17   The competitive dynamic of modern democratic politics has been famously explored by Joseph Schumpeter in his *Capitalism, Socialism and Democracy* (London and New York: 1943, 1976).

18 For a more wide-ranging discussion of the point, see Adam Przeworski, *Sustainable Democracy* (Cambridge: 1995), p. 10: 'Democratic institutions can be consolidated only if they offer politically relevant groups the appropriate channels and incentives to process their demands within the framework of representative institutions.'

19 On the distance between ancient and modern expectations of democratic rule, see the contrast implicit in John Dunn, *The Cunning of Unreason: Making Sense of Modern Politics* (London: 2000), p. 279: 'What the modern republic is, in its own eyes, is simply a device for extending to every citizen, as far as it can, a full liberty to act as they choose, without thereby encroaching on the like liberty for any of their fellow citizens. It is a system of collective agency which is also at the same time a system of equitable mutual restraint.'

20 For a discussion of the transformation of voter preferences as integral to the deliberative process, see the 'Introduction' to Jon Elster ed., *Deliberative Democracy* (Cambridge: 1998); on the strictly unrepresentative character of decisions arising out of political representation, see Bernard Manin, Adam Przeworski and Susan C. Stokes, 'Elections and Representation', in Przeworski et al. eds, *Democracy, Accountability and Representation* (Cambridge: 1999).

21 For a challenge to this view, however, see Russell Hardin, *Liberalism, Constitutionalism, and Democracy* (Oxford: 1999), p. 36: 'In general, democracy works only on the margins of great issues. Indeed, it is inherently a device for regulating marginal political conflicts.' At the same time, on the practice of toleration in multinational empires, see Michael Walzer, *On Toleration* (New Haven and London: 1997), pp. 14–19.

22 Boutros Boutros-Ghali, for instance, made the point during his tenure as Secretary-General of the United Nations that 'democracy is one of the pillars on which a more peaceful, more equitable, and more secure world can be built' (Boutros Boutros-Ghali, 'Democracy: A Newly Recognised Imperative', *Global Governance* (Winter 1995), p. 3). The seeming plausibility of this sentiment can likewise be gleaned from its invocation by the members of the Organisation for Security and Cooperation in Europe in the 'Document of the Copenhagen Meeting of the Conference on the Human Dimension, June 29, 1990', in *International Legal Materials* (September 1990), p. 1307: 'the development of societies based on pluralistic democracy and the rule of law are prerequisites for progress in setting up the lasting order of peace, security, justice, and cooperation that they seek in Europe', or (similarly) from Misha Glenny, *The Rebirth of History: Eastern Europe*

in the Age of Democracy (London: 1990, 1993), p. 9: 'Political pluralism and democracy are essential if the peoples of Eastern Europe are to find solutions to the numerous nationalist conflicts in the area'.

23   In accordance with this diagnosis, modern political hatreds are habitually described as recidivist in nature: as Bill Clinton remarked, the aftermath of the Cold War 'lifted the lid from a cauldron of long simmering hatreds. Now, the entire global terrain is bloody with such conflicts' ('President Cautions on "Simplistic" Ideas in Foreign Policy', *Washington Post*, 26 May 1994). A similar assumption underpinned the majority of millennial forecasts which abounded in the political literature at the end of the last century: the problem besetting international peace was characterised as one of regressive ethnicity, as if ethnicity were not a problem for democracy as such – namely, the problem of which *demos* is entitled to self-determination. See Zbigniew Brzezinski, *Out of Control: Global Turmoil on the Eve of the Twenty-First Century* (New York: 1993) and Daniel Patrick Moynihan, *Pandaemonium: Ethnicity in International Politics* (Oxford: 1993).

24   Parliament of Northern Ireland House of Commons Debates (Hansard), vol. 16, col. 1091.

25   Herein lies the difficulty in presuming that political conflict will in the future be determined by what has been dubbed a 'clash of civilisations': are we retrospectively to account for this shortfall in Northern Irish politics by presenting the Province between 1968 and 1998 as a member of a distinct 'civilisation'? See Lester B. Pearson, *Democracy in World Politics* (Princeton: 1955) and Samuel P. Huntington, *The Clash of Civilisations and the Remaking of World Order* (London: 1997) on the modern cosmopolis as riven by specifically 'civilisational' conflicts.

26   James Callaghan, *A House Divided: The Dilemma of Northern Ireland* (London: 1973), p. 187.

27   Michael Walzer, *Just and Unjust Wars: A Moral Argument with Historical Illustrations* (New York: 1977, 2000), esp. pp. 21–33, argues powerfully against isolating the conduct of war from moral criticism on the familiar grounds of *inter arma silent leges*. Nonetheless, the fact of comparative moral deafness under conditions of human exigency and fear have to be factored into any strategy for bringing wars to an end.

28   *Agreement Reached in the Multi-Party Negotiations*, 'Declaration of Support', s. 1.

29   Ibid., s. 2.

30 Ibid., s. 5.
31 For the perception that the events of 11 September 2001 necessitated a war like no other, see the remarks of Vice-President Richard Cheney reported in *The Independent*, 22 October 2001; for comments on the expected solution to conflict in Afghanistan, see the remarks of the British Foreign Secretary, Jack Straw, reported in *The Times*, 23 October 2001. On George W. Bush's national security strategy, with its aim of 'Building Democracy', launched on 20 September 2002, see 'How US Will Lead "Freedom's Triumph"', *Financial Times*, 21 September 2002.

I Prologue

1 Gerry Adams, *Peace in Ireland: A Broad Analysis of the Present Situation* (Belfast: 1976), p. 1. The argument presented in this pamphlet was originally presented under the pen-name 'Brownie' in an article, 'Peace', in *Republican News*, 11 September 1976.
2 Richard Crossman, *The Diaries of a Cabinet Minister: Volume Three, 1968–1970* (London: 1977), p. 636.
3 Eamonn McCann, *War in an Irish Town* (Harmondsworth: 1974), p. 67.
4 Ibid. Conor Cruise O'Brien's remarks in *States of Ireland* (London: 1973), pp. 15–16, are worth quoting in this context: 'The Catholic–Protestant relationship and the relation of both communities in Britain have . . . been distorted or analysed out of existence, by various "Marxist" or post-Marxist interpretations adopted by some left-wing activists . . . and diffused by journalists and others in contact with those activists. These interpretations vary rather widely, but a common feature is the effort to trace the evils of Northern Ireland and the Republic, to a source in British imperialism.'
5 Bernadette Devlin, *The Price of My Soul* (London: 1969), p. 89.
6 Irish Republican Publicity Bureau Statement from January 1970, reported in *An Phoblacht*, February 1970.
7 Adams himself, of course, had occupied an uncertain position after the IRA split in December 1969, moving decisively over to the Provisionals only in March of that year. See Ciarán De Baróid, *Ballymurphy and the Irish War* (London: 1989), pp. 38–39, and David Sharrock and Mark Devenport, *Man of War, Man of Peace: The Unauthorised Biography of Gerry Adams* (London: 1997), pp. 68–71.
8 Gerry Adams, 'A Republican in the Civil Rights Campaign', in Michael Farrell ed., *Twenty Years On* (Dingle: 1988), p. 47.

9   See, for example, Ruairí Ó Brádaigh, 'What is Irish Republicanism?' *Irish Independent*, 9 December 1970: 'a Republican in 1970 . . . stands in a line of succession going back beyond Wolfe Tone to the Gaelic leaders of resistance to the Norman invasion.'

10   Such claims were integral to the analyses offered in the late 1960s in the *United Irishman* and, from 1970, in *An Phoblacht*. They also formed a part of the analysis offered by the Belfast-based Republican publicity organ, *Republican News*: 'Britain's economic policy is aimed at producing manufactured goods for export, and relying on cheap imported food. Ireland, in direct competition is permitted, or more accurately forced financially, to fill that need' (June 1971). For the developed thesis, see Gerry Adams, *The Politics of Irish Freedom* (Dingle: 1986), pp. 89–99: 'The British connection has lasted through several stages for many centuries . . . whether economic, political, territorial or cultural in substance . . . In recent decades [Britain's] strategic interest has been . . . for the maintenance of stability and social order in capitalist Europe.'

11   Gerry Adams, 'A Republican in the Civil Rights Campaign', p. 53. The same objective was advertised in *Republican News* as early as November–December 1970: 'the most basic right of all – the right of self-determination'.

12   Adams himself cites the works of James Connolly and Liam Mellows' *Jail Notes* as sources. In *The Politics of Irish Freedom*, p. 40, he writes that 'Mellows, like Connolly, possessed great clarity of political vision, and he spelt out what was happening [in 1922]: "Free State equals capitalism and industrialism equals empire . . . A political revolution in Ireland without a coincident economic revolution merely means a change of masters."' Mellows himself was indebted to an assortment of anti-capitalist arguments advanced from the mid-nineteenth to the early twentieth centuries by republican activists like Fintan Lalor and Michael Davitt, but the specific claims advanced by Adams to the effect that Ireland was a victim of 'neo-colonialism' are traceable through the Sinn Féin propagandist of the 1960s, Roy Johnston, to strains of European Marxist analysis which had themselves drawn on the work of the liberal advocate, J. A. Hobson. In September 1967, Roy Johnston had declared that imperialism was 'finding it increasingly difficult to maintain the huge profits it has been drawing from the neo-colonial exploitation of its former empire'. Britain, in consequence, had grown 'increasingly anxious to weld Ireland more tightly to her side as a secure neo-colony'. For this, see [Official] Sinn Féin, *The Lessons of History* (Dublin: 1970). By 1986, Adams, *Politics of Irish Freedom*, p. 39,

was offering the analysis that in 'the 6 counties we have a colonial situation. In the 26 counties we have a neo-colonial state in which the imperial foreign government was exchanged for a native one based on business interests.'

13   J. A. Hobson, *Imperialism: A Study* (London: 1902, 1988), p. 145.

14   Criticism of British foreign policy in the name of anti-imperialism had been mounting since 1898. The desire to stem the tide of negative publicity is already evident in J. Lawson Walton's article, 'Imperialism', which appeared in the *Contemporary Review*, 75 (March 1899), pp. 305–10. Nonetheless, ongoing disaffection with British 'imperialism' was made particularly explicit in the collaborative volume by F. W. Hirst, Gilbert Murray and J. L. Hammond, *Liberalism and the Empire* (London: 1900): imperialism's 'most poisonous' exemplification was now apparent', as Hirst put it, in 'the financial or speculative imperialism of Mr. Rhodes' (p. 4). By 1902, the activities of 'financial or speculative imperialism' had similarly incurred the wrath of the Irish Fenian, Michael Davitt, in response – once again – to developments in the southern African republics. See Michael Davitt, *The Boer Fight for Freedom* (London: 1902), pp. 588–89: 'England, by her money markets and press and commerce; by her howling hypocrisy in pulpit and Parliament; has successfully mammonized the world . . . she has enthroned the creed of human cupidity in the Temple out of which the gentle saviour of Nazareth . . . once banished the money changers.'

15   Hobson, *Imperialism*, p. 145.

16   Michael Davitt, *The Fall of Feudalism in Ireland* (London: 1904), p. 723. Davitt continued: 'The growth of military power, increasing armaments, aggressive politics which provoke international disputes, expeditions for the subjugation of so-called savage races, all mean a constant danger to social peace and true progress . . . I contend that Ireland independent of all English control and interference would be of far greater advantage to the working classes of Great Britain than an Ireland ruled and ruined under Dublin castle on the principles of imperialism – that is, for landlords, aristocrats and money-lenders.'

17   The point had, of course, already been made, but in more general terms, by F. W. Hirst et al., *Liberalism and the Empire*, p. 63: 'it is time to counterwork the busy, though unseen, agencies of international finance'.

18   W. F. Monypenny and G. E. Buckle, *The Life of Benjamin Disraeli* (London: 1910–20), 6 vols, V, p. 195. Criticism of Disraeli's departure had, however, been sounded almost since the beginning. See Robert

Lowe, 'Imperialism', in the *Fortnightly Review*, 24 (1878), pp. 453–65: 'What does Imperialism mean?' It means the assertion of absolute power over others' (p. 458).

19   On Richard Cobden in this context, see Miles Taylor, '*Imperium et Libertas?* Rethinking the Radical Critique of Imperialism during the Nineteenth Century', *Journal of Commonwealth and Imperial History* (January 1991), pp. 1–23. I am grateful to Andrew Fitzmaurice for this reference.

20   Richard Koebner and Helmut D. Schmidt, *Imperialism: The Story and Significance of a Political Word, 1840–1960* (Cambridge: 1964), p. 324. '*Imperialismus*' already carried this significance for Karl Marx by 1852: see his *Eighteenth Brumaire of Louis Bonaparte* (1852; London: 1934, 1984), pp. 104–19. But, ironically, by 1923 Carl Schmitt was identifying the imperialism of Napoleon III with the many manifestations of 'democracy' observable in the world since 1848 – 'all political tendencies could make use of democracy': see *The Crisis of Parliamentary Democracy*, trans. Ellen Kennedy (Cambridge, Mass.: 1985), p. 24. Schmitt's point here was developed from Max Weber's account of plebiscitary Caesarism, fully elaborated in his *Economy and Society*, ed. Guenther Roth and Claus Wittich (California: 1978), 2 vols, II, pp. 1125–30.

21   Hobson, *Imperialism*, p. 106. The historical viability of Hobson's account of continental partition in Africa has been questioned many times, most vigorously (and controversially) by Ronald Robinson and John Gallagher, with Alice Denny, *Africa and the Victorians: The Official Mind of Imperialism* (1961) (London: 1981), p. xiii: 'John Atkinson Hobson . . . transposed the early Victorian account of colonies of settlement anachronistically into an explanation of the late Victorians' tropical acquisitions.' For a recent neo-Hobsonian account of nineteenth-century imperialism, see P. J. Cain and A. G. Hopkins, *Imperialism, 1688–2000* (Harlow: 2002).

22   Hobson, *Imperialism*, p. 59. This assumption on Hobson's part has, however, long been a subject of intense dispute. For a comparatively recent critical account, see D. K. Fieldhouse, '"Imperialism": An Historiographical Revision', *Economic History Review*, 14 (1962), pp. 187–209: 'Hobson's sinister capitalists . . . were nothing more than a hypothesis, a *deus ex machina*, to balance an equation between the assumed rationality of mankind and the unreasonableness of imperial policies' (p. 209).

23   Hobson, *Imperialism*, p. 280: 'the phrases about teaching "the dignity of labour" and raising races of "children" to manhood, whether used

by directors of mining companies or by statesmen in the House of Commons, are little better than wanton exhibitions of hypocrisy. They are based on a falsification of the facts, and a perversion of the motives which actually direct the policy.'

24   The reputation of the *conduite perfide des Anglais*, within a more narrowly European context, had been revived by Frederick the Great at the close of the Seven Years' War, and resuscitated once again by Robespierre, and then Napoleon. See H. D. Schmidt, 'The Idea and Slogan of "Perfidious Albion"', *Journal of the History of Ideas*, 14 (1953), pp. 604–16. The first, great perfidious power was of course Carthage: in Livy's description, presented in *Livy in Fourteen Volumes*, ed. B. O. Foster (Cambridge, Mass.: 1919, 1988), 21, p. 4, Carthage is personified by Hannibal who possessed at once 'inhuman cruelty, a more than Punic perfidy [*perfidia plus quam Punica*], a total disregard of truth, honor and religion, of the sanctity of an oath and of all that other men hold sacred' (p. 26). Drawing on the tradition arising out of Livy's description, the identification of England with Carthage became commonplace in Irish Republican thinking by the late nineteenth century. But the identification was already conspicuous in Benjamin Constant's 'The Spirit of Conquest and Usurpation and their Relation to European Civilisation' (1814), in Biancamaria Fontana ed., *Political Writings* (Cambridge: 1988), p. 54: 'Carthage, struggling against Rome in Antiquity, was bound to succumb: the force of things was against her. But if the war between Rome and Carthage were fought now, Carthage would have the hopes of the entire world on her side; the customs of the day and the spirit of the times would be her allies.' It was Edouard Laboulaye who first observed in his commentary on the text that Carthage and Rome stood for London and Paris. See *Collection Complète des ouvrages sur le gouvernement représentatif et la constitution actuelle de la France*, ed. Edouard Laboulaye (Paris: 1861), 2 vols, II, p. 141n.

25   The equation is made diffusely in Gamal Abdul Nasser, *Egypt's Liberation: The Philosophy of Revolution* (Washington: 1957), but more deliberately in Kwame Nkrumah, *Africa Must Unite* (London: 1963), p. 7: 'colonial powers were guided primarily by economic, political and military considerations, probably in that order'. It also appears, confusedly, in Frantz Fanon, *The Wretched of the Earth* (1961; Harmondsworth: 1967, 1990): here, 'capitalism and imperialism' appear at once as conscious and concerted agents (p. 63). But, from early on, the Hobsonian thesis naturally had its prominent and vocal opponents. See, for example, Norman Angell, *The Great Illusion: A*

Study of the Relation of Military Power in Nations to their Economic and Social Advantage (London: 1910), p. 36: 'conquest would ensure to the conqueror no profit', from which he concluded that international trade ought properly to be seen as a means of civilising politics. The advance of Hobson's argument nonetheless proceeded undaunted. Henry Noel Brailsford tackled Angell's objections in *The War of Steel and Gold: A Study of the Armed Peace* (London: 1914), p. 42: 'The potent pressure of economic expansion is the motive force in an international struggle.' By 1920, it had won the approval of Fabians like Leonard Woolf, who was to argue in his *Economic Imperialism* (London: 1920), p. 101 that 'Economic imperialism is only the logical application of capitalism and its principles to internationalism.' In a more academic context, the Hobsonian line was resuscitated, with some modifications, after the Second World War by Hannah Arendt in Part Three of her *The Origins of Totalitarianism* (London: 1951), entitled 'Imperialism'.

26   Éamon de Valera, *Eamon de Valera States His Case* (Dublin: 1918), p. 2. The pamphlet is a transcript of a speech delivered in the United States, reprinted from the *Christian Science Monitor*, 15 May 1918.

27   The argument was expressed in this form by C. D. Greaves in *Reminiscences of the Connolly Association* (London: 1978), quoted in Henry Patterson, *The Politics of Illusion: A Political History of the IRA* (1989; London: 1997), p. 160. But the perspective was common within the ranks of the Wolfe Tone Society and the Connolly Association in the late 1960s.

28   The reference to 'economic imperialism' appears in Ruairí Ó Brádaigh, *Our People, Our Future: What Éire Nua Means* (Dublin: 1973), p. 18. Such forms of economic dependence as would survive the achievement of national independence were to be overcome, Ó Brádaigh explained in 'What Social and Economic System Would Serve Ireland Best' (*Irish Press*, 3 December 1970), by effecting the 'restoration of the means of production, distribution and exchange in Ireland to the Irish people'.

29   Ó Brádaigh, *Our People, Our Future*, p. 17. The idea that British policy had sought to advance itself by the method of 'divide and rule' had steadily gained ground within the ranks of Irish nationalism since the 1890s, but it became a theme within anti-imperialist polemic internationally in the 1950s and early 1960s. See, for example, Kwame Nkrumah, *Neo-Colonialism: The Last Stage of Imperialism* (London: 1965), p. 253: 'Thus far, all the methods of neo-colonialists have pointed in one direction, the ancient, accepted one of all minority ruling classes throughout history – *divide and rule.*' But a whole raft of

elaborations on this theme appeared throughout the 'troubles'. In the middle of the 1970s, the Revolutionary Communist Group could argue in their *Ireland: British Labour and British Imperialism* (London: 1976), p. 11, that 'bitter sectarianism' and 'discrimination' arose in Northern Ireland 'because the British ruling class needed an agent in Ireland to support its political domination of the whole island'. Four years later, the analysis was back again: the Irish socialist militant, Peter Hadden, argued in his *'Divide and Rule' – Labour and the Partition of Ireland* (Dublin: 1980), p. 1, that the 'partition of Ireland was a conscious act on the part of British Imperialism chiefly intended to divide the working class along sectarian lines'.

30 Ó Brádaigh refers to this generalised and undefined 'Imperial system' in 'What is Irish Republicanism?', *Irish Independent*, 9 December 1970.

31 Rudolf Hilferding, *Das Finanzkapital* (Vienna: 1910), Otto Bauer, *Grosskapital und Militarismus* (Vienna: 1911). Albert O. Hirschman, *Essays in Trespassing: Economics to Politics and Beyond* (Cambridge: 1981, 1984), p. 167, argues powerfully for the Hegelian provenance of the assumptions which they, and later Lenin, made: 'Hegel had an economic theory of imperialism when Marx did not.'

32 V. I. Lenin, *Imperialism: The Highest Stage of Capitalism* (1916; London: 1996), pp. 127–28.

33 Leonard Woolf, *Empire and Commerce in Africa: A Study in Economic Imperialism* (London: 1920), p. 364. By 1945, Woolf was calling for colonial disengagement. See his 'The Political Advance of Backward Peoples', in Rita Hinden ed., *Fabian Colonial Essays* (London: 1945), p. 85: 'Is it our intention to keep them permanently in a state of complete political tutelage or eventually to give them self-government?'

34 John Strachey, *The End of Empire* (London: 1959), p. 309. In the Preface, Strachey acknowledges the influence of James Callaghan and Richard Crossman on his thinking, before developing the argument that the 'end of empire', foreshadowed in the Durham Report, had been accelerated in the fifteen years since 1944: 'today, in 1959, little remains of the structure of world colonialism. In fifteen short years the whole edifice has almost disappeared' (p. 145).

35 Notably through the influence of two North American neo-Marxist economists, Paul A. Baran and Paul M. Sweezy on the New Left in Britain. Baran's *The Political Economy of Growth* (London: 1957), p. 15, pointed to recent global politics as a 'modern, more subtle and less transparent form of imperialism': imperialism, in this guise, no longer 'needed' colonial possessions to advance itself, but could maintain its strength by more indirect methods pursued on the part of multinational

corporations. See Baran and Sweezy's joint assessment, presented in 'Notes on the Theory of Imperialism', reprinted from the *Monthly Review* (March 1966) in Kenneth E. Boulding and Tapan Mukerjee eds, *Economic Imperialism: A Book of Readings* (Ann Arbor: 1972), p. 170: 'All the major struggles going on in the world today can be traced to this hunger of the multinational corporations for maximum *Lebensraum.'* The work of Baran and Sweezy was reviewed by James O'Connor in *New Left Review*, 40 (November–December 1966), pp. 38–50. But their influence was already in evidence in Michael Barratt Brown, 'Imperialism Yesterday and Today', *New Left Review*, 5 (September–October 1960), pp. 42–49.

36 Interview with the Director, Republican Press Centre, *Republican News*, 31 January 1976.

37 'Neo-colonialism' was made the subject of a resolution at the All-African People's Conference held in Cairo in 1961, which denounced 'the survival of the colonial system in spite of formal recognition of political independence in emerging countries which became the victims of an indirect and subtle form of domination by political, economic, social, military or technical means' (quoted in Colin Leys, *Underdevelopment in Kenya: The Political Economy of Neo-Colonialism, 1964–1971*, London: 1975, p. 26). By the mid-1960s, 'neo-colonialism' had become a key ingredient in the Republican analysis of Ireland, and by the early 1970s it was being adopted by the Provisionals. See 'Invitation to the U.D.A.', *Republican News*, 16 February 1973, where Britain's control over 'the wealth and therefore the politics' of the South is described as 'neo-colonialism'. In 'The North – Key to English Influence in Ireland', *Republican News*, 15 November 1975, the claim is again made that 'In 1922 we became Britain's first and the world's first neo-colony, in the South of Ireland . . . the 26-County State in the south of Ireland has even less economic independence than the neo-colonial countries of Africa and South America.'

38 Nkrumah, *Neo-Colonialism*, p. 256. For Gerry Adams' comments on Nkrumah, see his *Before the Dawn: An Autobiography* (London: 1996) p. 54: 'Nkrumah had become the first of a generation of African anti-colonialists.'

39 Nkrumah, *Africa Must Unite*, p. 174.

40 Michael Barratt Brown, 'Imperialism Yesterday and Today', p. 46n, presents post-colonial states as 'comprador' agents, in deference to the arguments of Baran and Sweezy. See also, on this, Ernest Mandel, 'After Imperialism', *New Left Review*, 25 (May–June 1964), pp. 17–25. On Ghana after the fall of Nkrumah, but with the composition of the

Convention People's Party in mind, see Jack Woddis, *Introduction to Neo-Colonialism* (London: 1967), p. 56: 'With the emergence of new states, the imperialists still utilise their old connections with feudalism and with tribal chiefs, as the experience of Nigeria, Ghana, Malaya, Indonesia and the Sudan indicate only too well.' More explicitly, see Roger Murray, 'Some Thoughts on Ghana', *New Left Review*, 42 (March–April 1967), pp. 25–39: 'The CPP leadership and cadres came preponderantly . . . from the *petty bourgeois salariat* . . . a mixed stratum which concentrated many of the political and cultural tensions of colonial society' (p. 29).

41 Joseph A. Schumpeter, 'The Sociology of Imperialisms' (1918) in *The Economics and Sociology of Capitalism* (Princeton, N.J.: 1991), p. 206 (italics in the original). The organising principles of Schumpeter's analysis can be traced to Benjamin Constant, 'The Spirit of Conquest', p. 53: 'War then comes before commerce. The former is all savage impulse, the latter civilized calculation.'

42 Éamon de Valera, *Eamon de Valera States His Case*, p. 3.

43 James Connolly, 'Labour in Irish History' (1910), in *Labour in Ireland* (Dublin: 1922), p. 168: past politics has effected a division of the people, but now, through the activities of social revolutionaries, 'North and South will again clasp hands'. However, it is worth noting that by 'The Re-Conquest of Ireland' (1915), in Connolly, *Labour in Ireland*, divisions in the north-east of Ireland are being ascribed by Connolly to indigenous factors, including the spirit of Protestant labour: 'If those poor sweated descendants of Protestant rebels against a king had to-day one-hundredth part of the spirit of their ancestors in question, the re-conquest of Ireland by the working class would be a much easier task than it is likely to prove' (p. 220). The assumption that Irish divisions are an externally imposed contrivance, however, is pervasive in P. S. O'Hegarty's writings, although the idea is most explicit in his *Ulster: A Brief Statement* (Dublin: 1919), p. 29: 'Unionism means division and manipulation'.

44 *United Irishman*, May 1969. The quotation obviously represents a strand of Republican analysis which circulated in the period before the split. The Provisionals, for their part, accepted the basis of the argument whilst rejecting the mode of redress which was to become Official Sinn Féin policy. In the same month, an editorial in the *New Left Review*, 55 (May–June 1969) declared that 'British capitalism has long exported its violence to its imperial possessions: it does so in full measure to its nearest vassal territory'(p. 1).

45 Mitchel McLaughlin, 'The Irish Republican Ideal', in Norman Porter

ed., *The Republican Ideal: Current Perspectives* (Belfast: 1998), p. 71.

46 Ibid., p. 75: 'In recent years it has become possible for British cabinet ministers to disclaim any selfish strategic or economic interest in Ireland. This is a most welcome statement, particularly if the present process of dialogue can be developed to the point where the British government also ends its political interest'. But, of course, as McLaughlin knew, the Downing Street Declaration of 15 December 1993 had conceded the final decision over Northern Ireland's sovereignty to a majority within the Northern Irish populace.

47 Nkrumah, *Africa Must Unite*, p. 173.

48 Jon Elster, in *Sour Grapes: Studies in the Subversion of Rationality* (Cambridge: 1983, 1996), pp. 101–3, provides this tendency to interpret intentions as a function of outcomes with an intellectual genealogy stretching back to the theodicy of Malebranche and Leibniz. However, as Elster further comments on p. 105, with the removal of providence from the picture, one is left postulating 'a diabolical plan to which there corresponds no devilish planner'.

49 McLaughlin, 'The Irish Republican Ideal,' p. 79.

50 Reported in *The Times*, 27 May 1955, and quoted in A. P. Thornton, *Doctrines of Imperialism* (New York: 1965), pp. 5–6.

51 Nasser, *Egypt's Liberation*, p. 103. Curiously, Nasser's anti-imperial solution was a new pan-African civilizing mission: 'We will never in any circumstances be able to relinquish our responsibility to support, with all our might, the spread of enlightenment and civilisation to the remotest depths of the jungle' (p. 110).

52 Nkrumah, *Africa Must Unite*, p. xvi.

53 See, for example, Constant, 'The Spirit of Conquest', p. 141: 'Commerce has brought nations closer together . . . monarchs may still be enemies, but peoples are compatriots.' On the contrast with Machiavelli, see John Dunn, 'Liberty as a Substantive Political Value', in *Interpreting Political Responsibility: Essays 1981–1989* (Cambridge: 1990).

54 Gore Vidal, 'The Enemy Within', *Observer*, 27 October 2002, provides a recent example of the phenomenon, especially in vogue since 11 September 2001: Vidal follows a host of others in citing Schumpeter as an authority on Roman policy – 'There was no corner of the known world where some interest was not alleged to be in danger or under actual attack' – despite the fact that the whole point of Schumpeter's analysis was to deny the equivalence between ancient policy and modern *raison d'état*.

55 Niccolò Machiavelli, *Discourses on the First Decade of Titus Livius*, in

The Chief Works and Others, trans. Alan Gilbert (Durham: 1989), 3 vols, I, p. 325.

56   The phrase here is Winston Churchill's, speaking in the House of Commons in 1922: 'we see the dreary steeples of Fermanagh and Tyrone emerging once again. The integrity of their quarrel is one of the few institutions that has been unaltered in the cataclysm which has swept the world.' The sentences are quoted in Richard Rose, *Governing Without Consensus: An Irish Perspective* (London: 1971), p. 359.

57   The image of a regime, headed by Captain Terence O'Neill, struggling to achieve significant reforms, has long been discredited. On this, see most recently Henry Patterson, *Ireland since 1939* (Oxford: 2002), p. 194: 'O'Neillism offered economic growth in exchange for collective amnesia on the part of the Catholic community about past and present grievances.'

58   Harold Wilson, *The Labour Government, 1964–1970: A Personal Record* (Harmondsworth: 1971), p. 693.

59   Wilson, *The Labour Government*, p. 693. The same alarm was registered by James Callaghan, *A House Divided: The Dilemma of Northern Ireland* (London: 1973), p. 23: reflecting on the confused situation in August 1969, he reported his own uncertainty – 'might both majority and minority communities turn on the British Army?' This was the particular worry of Denis Healey, as recorded at a Cabinet meeting on 19 August 1969: 'he wished to stress the importance of not pushing too hard and so alienating Protestant opinion'. And, at the same meeting, it was agreed by all present that 'Direct rule . . . would increase the risk of armed conflict with the Protestant community' (PRO, CAB, 128/46, 41st Conclusions, Confidential Annex). Later, having returned from a visit to Northern Ireland between 27 and 29 August, James Callaghan reported to Cabinet colleagues that 'There was indeed some danger of a Protestant right wing backlash' (PRO, CAB 128/46, Conclusions, 4 September 1969, Confidential Annex). By 16 September, it was noted in discussion that 'the use by the Army on a very small scale of CS gas against a Protestant crowd had produced a much more violent reaction than the expenditure of CS gas on a much larger scale by the Royal Ulster Constabulary against Catholics at an earlier stage' (PRO, CAB 128/46, 44th Conclusions, Confidential Annex).

60   Wilson, *The Labour Government*, p. 694. Eight years later, Joe Haines, in *The Politics of Power* (London: 1977), was still drawing the same conclusion: 'we have responsibility without power, the prerogative of the eunuch throughout the ages' (p. 121). But it was on 7 October 1968

that Wilson first employed the phrase in conversation with James
Callaghan: 'Pressure in the House of Commons for the United
Kingdom Government to take action in a situation where they had
responsibility without power' should be impressed upon Terence
O'Neill, advised Wilson (PRO, PREM, 13/2841, Memo of Meeting
Between Wilson and Callaghan).

61   PRO, CAB, 128/46, Conclusions, 4 September 1969, Confidential
     Annex.

62   Callaghan, *A House Divided*, p. 22: 'we knew little enough at first hand
     about what was going on, and [had] few reliable means of finding out'.
     In reality, the British political establishment was happy not to know,
     and not to avail itself of the means of finding out. Paul Rose,
     parliamentary private secretary to Barbara Castle in 1967, recounts the
     story – reported in Peter Taylor, *Provos: The IRA and Sinn Féin*
     (London: Bloomsbury, 1997) – of being asked by his minister 'Why is
     a young man like you concerned about Northern Ireland? What about
     Vietnam? What about Rhodesia?' (p. 2). On the British record of
     psychological disengagement, see also C. E. B. Brett, *Long Shadows
     Cast Before Dawn: Nine Lives in Ulster, 1625–1977* (Edinburgh: 1978),
     pp. 135–39: meetings between Brett, together with Northern Ireland
     Labour Party colleagues Tom Boyd and Sam Napier, and Roy Jenkins
     in 1966, and correspondence with Harold Wilson in 1968, produced
     little by way of engagement. 'A dozen times since [1969] I have been
     reproached by friends in the British Labour Party, one today a cabinet
     minister, with the words "Why ever did you not warn us of what was
     coming?" I have never yet succeeded in finding words adequate to
     reply to that question.'

63   Justin O'Brien, *The Arms Trial* (Dublin: 2000), pp. 152–86.

64   *Republican News*, July 1970. In autumn 1969, the Southern Irish
     sponsored republican publicity organ, *The North – The Voice of the
     People*, reminded its Northern Irish Catholic readership of the fears of
     the Ulster Protestant majority by quoting Lord Hamilton, Unionist
     MP at Westminster for Fermanagh–South Tyrone: 'There is a very
     real and genuine fear among the population of being outvoted and
     outbred into an All Ireland Republic.'

65   *Republican News*, 14 July 1972.

II Protest: 1968

1   Immediately after the 5 October march, the Royal Ulster Constabulary produced a report on the day's proceedings which was subsequently forwarded to Harold Wilson. The report stated that 'some 300 to 500 of those adjoining the Railway Square were, in fact, Protestant opposition. This was the very factor anticipated by the police and led to the advice tendered to the Minister to ban the parade in the sectors of the city where the ban was imposed' (PRO, CJ 3/30, 'Comments by the Inspector General of the Royal Ulster Constabulary'). These 'Comments' were, however, essentially designed to save face, and were couched as a response to 'The Eyewitnesses Report on Londonderry' compiled by the Westminster MPs Russell Kerr, Anne Kerr and John Ryan, which had been dispatched to the British Prime Minister on 8 October in order to confirm allegations of police brutality (PRO, PREM 13/2841).

2   The significance of international events, and of the student protest movement in particular, to developments in Northern Ireland in the late 1960s has long been acknowledged. The RUC itself made the connection in its 'Comments by the Inspector General of the Royal Ulster Constabulary' soon after the event (PRO, CJ 3/30). James Callaghan was again to make this point in *A House Divided: The Dilemma of Northern Ireland* (London: 1973), pp. 7–9: 'It was against this world problem of violence and revolt that the October 5 march in Londonderry should be seen.'

3   Despite the bitterness, the remnants of John Redmond's old Home Rule Party still survived in Northern Ireland. The persistence of constitutionalism can be explained in part in terms of the Catholic fear of reprisals from the Unionist regime, and the relative isolation of the north-east from developments in the rest of Ireland after 1918. See Enda Staunton, *The Nationalists of Northern Ireland, 1918–1973* (Dublin: 2001).

4   The situation faced by the Northern Ireland government in the 1930s – with the level of unemployment rising and poverty increasing, and with membership of the main Protestant fraternity, the Orange Order, declining – is described by David Fitzpatrick in *The Two Irelands, 1912–1939* (Oxford: 1998), p. 178. This is the context in which to assess Stormont's anxiety to maintain the sectarian allegiance of its Protestant population, and to bolster the majority's commitment to the need for Provincial security in the face of Catholic disaffection.

5   Michael Farrell, *Northern Ireland: The Orange State* (London: 1976), pp. 93–94.

6   Patrick Buckland, *A History of Northern Ireland* (Dublin: 1981, 1989), p. 65.

7   Internment was introduced in May 1922, and the military imposed a curfew in June. See D. W. Harkness, *Northern Ireland since 1920* (Dublin: 1983), pp. 29–30.

8   Civil Authorities (Special Powers) Act (Northern Ireland), 1922, s. 1, i.

9   The context for the Act is given by Henry Patterson in his *Ireland since 1939* (Oxford: 2002), p. 127: during the 1953 election in Northern Ireland, Protestant fundamentalism had begun to flourish, and 'Brookeborough's response was a substantial tack to the right . . . against the advice of the Inspector General of the RUC, a Flags and Emblems Act was passed.'

10   J. J. Lee, *Ireland, 1912–1985: Politics and Society* (Cambridge: 1989), p. 60, comments: 'By mid-1922 there was one armed policeman to every two Catholic families in Northern Ireland.'

11   Seán MacStiofáin, *Memoirs of a Revolutionary* (Edinburgh: 1975), p. 120.

12   J.H. Whyte, 'How Much Discrimination Was There Under the Unionist Regime, 1921–68?' in Tom Gallagher and James O'Connell eds, *Contemporary Irish Studies* (Manchester: 1983).

13   Speech to the Ulster Unionist Council, 5 April 1963, reprinted in Terence O'Neill, *Ulster at the Crossroads* (London: 1969), p. 41: 'Our task will be literally to transform the face of Ulster.'

14   *Belfast Telegraph*, 10 May 1969. On 2 March in the same year, the *Sunday Times* reprinted an advertisement from the *Belfast Telegraph* dated November 1959: 'Protestant girl required for housework. Apply to the Hon. Mrs T. O'Neill, Glebe House, Ahoghill, Co. Antrim'.

15   Terence O'Neill, *The Autobiography of Terence O'Neill* (London: 1972), p. 73.

16   Ibid., p. 47.

17   Ibid., p. 137.

18   Queen's Speech Debate, 13 December 1966, recorded in O'Neill, *Ulster at the Crossroads*, p. 123.

19   A typical example of this failure is recorded by Marc Mulholland in his *Northern Ireland at the Crossroads: Ulster Unionism in the O'Neill Years* (London: 2000), pp. 63–64: charged with having failed to appoint any Catholics to either the Northern Ireland Economic Council or the Lockwood Committee, O'Neill blamed the Catholic hierarchy for maintaining social divisions through its commitment to denominational education. Underlining the weakness of the Northern Ireland Prime Minister, within a year of O'Neill's having come to power, an

editorial in the Ulster daily, the *Belfast Telegraph*, was complaining that 'The crisis is that the Government, for all its brave new ideals, carries a millstone of old prejudices and fears and makes hardly an attempt to gain its intellectual freedom' (3 April 1964).

20 Parliament of Northern Ireland House of Commons Debates (Hansard), 15 October 1968, vol. 60, col. 1004.

21 David Bleakley, *Faulkner: Conflict and Consent in Irish Politics* (London: 1974), p. 78: 'Terence O'Neill's career was one of frustrated promise, during which he had created for Ulster people their own revolution in rising expectations; unfortunately, he was not able to satisfy the hopes he had raised.' O'Neill's willingness to pander to conservative forces in his own party in order to curtail the advancement of the Northern Ireland Labour Party is described by Peter Rose, *How the Troubles Came to Northern Ireland* (London: 2000), p. 41.

22 That O'Neill had sought to make some advance by means of the politics of gesture rather than by reform was later to become the official verdict of the British Secretary of State for Home Affairs. However, even as late as May 1969, James Callaghan was helping to prepare a Home Office Memorandum in which this approach was deemed to have been rather more unlucky than ill-conceived: 'While for many years the ruling Protestant majority had been accused of maintaining power by discriminating against the Roman Catholic minority, Captain O'Neill, during his tenure of office had made efforts, which showed every sign of promise, to remove sectarian bitterness in the Province arising from feelings of injustice on the one side and on the other, fear of absorption into a United Ireland . . . His policy was directed at the roots of communal bitterness rather than at reform in the fields where the specific complaints of injustice lay' (PRO, CJ 3/1, 'Northern Ireland: Historical Background').

23 Quoted in Bob Purdie, *Politics in the Streets: The Origins of the Civil Rights Movement in Northern Ireland* (Belfast: 1990), p. 92.

24 See the Campaign for Social Justice in Northern Ireland, *Northern Ireland: The Plain Truth* (Dungannon: 1964, 2nd edn, 1972), where the housing situation in Derry, Lurgan, Enniskillen and Dungannon, together with issues such as the franchise and unemployment, are associated with a policy of 'apartheid'. In addition, the Campaign set about embarrassing the Stormont government in *Northern Ireland: What the Papers Say* (Dungannon: 1964), which collected together an array of damning media commentary from *Le Monde* to the *Manchester Guardian*, with critical sentence being passed by pundits ranging from Alan Whicker to Charles Brett.

25 Nonetheless, by 1969 in Northern Ireland as a whole, Catholics occupied 31 per cent of local authority housing. See Graham Gudgin, 'Discrimination in Housing and Employment under the Stormont Regime', in P. Roche and B. Barton eds, *The Northern Ireland Question: Myth and Reality* (Aldershot: 1991), p. 103.

26 The significance of this occurrence was later underlined by the official inquiry into developments in Northern Ireland in 1968: *Disturbances in Northern Ireland: Report of the Commission Appointed by the Governor of Northern Ireland* (Cameron Report)(HMSO Belfast: September 1969) Cmd. 532, p. 14ff.

27 Conn McCluskey, *Up Off Their Knees: A Commentary on the Civil Rights Movement in Northern Ireland* (Galway: 1989), pp. 15–16.

28 *Irish News*, 18 January 1964.

29 Quoted in Campaign for Social Justice in Northern Ireland, *Northern Ireland: The Plain Truth*, p. 1.

30 Campaign for Social Justice in Northern Ireland, *Northern Ireland: Why Justice Can Not Be Done* (Dungannon: 1964), *passim*. In addition, the difficulty of securing redress in the Northern Ireland courts was exposed by the Campaign two years later in *Northern Ireland: Legal Aid to Oppose Discrimination – Not Likely!* (Dungannon: 1966).

31 PRO, PREM 13/2841, O'Neill to Wilson, 6 December 1968: 'Although ['one man, one vote'] is the slogan under which some people are demonstrating, we are convinced that the real issues underlying the current agitation are predominantly social.' Earlier, at a meeting of Northern Irish ministers with Wilson and Roy Jenkins on 12 January 1967, O'Neill had declared that the statutory provisions for the local government franchise – the absence of 'one man, one vote' – in Northern Ireland 'could be defended' (PRO, PREM 13/2266).

32 Government of Ireland Act, 1920, s. 75. As this same section makes clear, the Act applied to Southern Ireland also until it was effectively nullified and superseded by the creation of the Irish Free State under the Anglo-Irish Treaty of 1921. In Northern Ireland, however, the provisions of the 1920 Act remained in force.

33 The ruling, as given by Speaker J. H. Whiteley, appears in Parliamentary Debates (Hansard), House of Commons, Official Report, Fifth Series, vol. 163, cols 1623–25, 3 May 1923: 'With regard to those subjects which have been delegated to the Government of Northern Ireland, questions must be asked of Ministers in Northern Ireland and not in this House.' The issue is discussed in H. Calvert, *Constitutional Law in Northern Ireland: A Study in Regional Government* (London: 1968), p. 101. The use of the convention to Unionist

advantage is treated further in Paul Bew, Peter Gibbon and Henry Patterson, *The State in Northern Ireland, 1921–1996: Political Forces and Social Classes* (1979; London: 1996), p. 160.

34 Wilson's reluctance after 1966 to deviate from the arrangement described by the Convention, despite his publicly expressed irritation with the voting rights of Unionist MPs at Westminster, is presented in Rose, *How the Troubles Came to Northern Ireland*, pp. 55–56.

35 'The Ulster Problem', *This Week*, ITV (7 July 1966); 'John Bull's Political Slum', *Sunday Times*, 3 July 1966. It was also at this time that O'Neill came to advise Harold Wilson that any moves towards reconciliation would have to be put on hold. At a meeting inside 10 Downing Street on 5 August 1966, O'Neill is reported as having informed the Prime Minister that 'no other course was now open to him but to call a halt to progress [on community relations] for a period of six months or so. Any early movement towards reconciliation either internally or with the Republic would endanger him politically and could lead to his replacement by a more intransigent figure, or even to a "1912" situation' (PRO, PREM 13/2266, Minutes of Meeting between Wilson and O'Neill).

36 O'Neill, *Autobiography*, p. 76. See also p. 87: 'It was 1966 which made 1968 inevitable.' O'Neill's private secretary at the time, Kenneth Bloomfield, subsequently agreed. See his *Stormont in Crisis* (Belfast: 1994), p. 86: it was, he commented, 'a crucially difficult year which was to embrace the Malvern Street murders and the emergence of the Ulster Volunteer Force (UVF) murder gang, the commemoration of the fiftieth anniversary of the Somme and the Easter Rising, the Paisleyite disturbances . . . and that gentleman's subsequent imprisonment.'

37 Both the improved atmosphere and the latent factionalism within interdenominational relations were soon captured by Richard Rose in the 'Loyalty Questionnaire' of 1967–68 appended to his *Governing Without Consensus: An Irish Perspective* (London: 1971), pp. 474–510.

38 Bew, Gibbon and Patterson, *The State in Northern Ireland, 1921–1996*, p. 164.

39 See Marianne Elliott, *The Catholics of Ulster: A History* (London: 2000), p. 401, on the defunct nature of the Nationalist Party.

40 H. Calvert, *Constitutional Law in Northern Ireland*, Ch. 1; Sabine Wichert, *Northern Ireland Since 1945* (Harlow, Essex: 1991, 1999), p. 44.

41 Key to what was now termed the 'new departure' undertaken by the Goulding leadership were Anthony Coughlan, a young lecturer at

Trinity College, Dublin and Roy Johnston, a member of the Communist Party of Great Britain and the Connolly Association in London before he returned to Dublin. Both were members of the Wolfe Tone Society whose newsletter, *Tuairisc*, was to proclaim in an issue published on 31 August 1966 that 'we . . . oppose the domination of our national, political, economic, social or cultural life by British imperialism'. Such forms of domination were further characterised in the same article as 'manifestations of neo-colonialism': 'since 1920 [neo-colonialism's] aim has demanded a different strategy for each part of the divided country. In the North British troops plus discrimination to divide the people – in the South economic pressure.' The importance of Coughlan and Johnston to developments inside the Republican movement is recorded in detail by Henry Patterson, *The Politics of Illusion: A Political History of the IRA* (1989; London: 1997), pp. 96–110. Mike Milotte, in *Communism in Modern Ireland: The Pursuit of the Workers' Republic Since 1916* (Dublin: 1984), p. 265, has commented on the Connolly Association's assessment of Republican options in the aftermath on the border campaign: the IRA was 'advised to work through a broad alliance for the displacement of the Unionist regime and for political democracy in the North and for social progress . . . in the South. They were also advised to end their abstentionism and seek to work through parliamentary institutions.' By 1966, Sean Garland, Seamus Costello and Cathal Goulding, all members of the IRA Army Council, had accepted this new dispensation. Thomás MacGiolla, chairman of the Council at the time, was inclined to waver between this group and the remaining members of the Army Council disposed to reject such a 'newfangled' programme – Ruairí Ó Brádaigh, David O'Connell and Seán MacStiofáin. Later, Roy Johnston commented on the shift in direction to Kevin Kelley, as recorded in *The Longest War: Northern Ireland and the IRA* (Kerry: 1983), p. 87: 'The idea was that if links could be cultivated between the movement and the people, the roots would be firmly in the ground and a principled, political stand would be made, even in "illegal assemblies" such as Leinster House [the Dáil] without automatic corruption'. An example of the change in political rhetoric and substance can be glimpsed in the 'Bodenstown Oration' delivered in June 1966 by Seamus Costello: 'we must aim for the ownership of our resources by the people, so that these resources will be developed in the best interest of the people as a whole' (Linen Hall Library, Belfast: Northern Ireland Political Collection).

42 The *Sunday Times* Insight Team, *Ulster* (Harmondsworth: 1972), p.

26. The statement carries conviction if one compares the fortunes of the Republican movement in the mid-1960s with the strength of both the Provisional and the Official IRAs in 1972. But the real point was that Cathal Goulding was at this stage committed to reorienting Republicanism. Relevant here is the summary comment by Ed Moloney in *A Secret History of the IRA* (London: 2002), p. 58, on the new thrust: 'Gradually the emphasis of [the IRA's] activities shifted to social and economic agitation and away from the traditional goal of waging war against Britain. The IRA and Sinn Féin became involved in rural cooperatives, and in Dublin they set up a housing action committee that staged sit-ins to highlight poor living conditions and overcrowding.' As regards Northern Ireland, the immediate implication of this change in direction was that Republican energies would be directed to reforming the Stormont regime – in advance of a longer term socialist revolution, North and South. The logic behind that policy objective had been signalled in an article, 'Our Ideas', published in the Wolfe Tone Society newsletter, *Tuairisc*, on 31 August 1966: '*the old fashioned unionist intransigence which served Britain so well in the past will . . . be outdated and no longer so convenient to imperialism*'. The implication was that Britain now favoured Irish unity in the interest of economic union with Ireland. In response, socialist republicans should initially favour reform in the North, as opposed to the North's immediate unification with the South, as a bulwark against such 'imperialistic' integration.

43   See Ian McAllister, *The Northern Ireland Social and Democratic Labour Party: Political Opposition in a Divided Society* (London: 1977).

44   See Ian McAllister, 'Political Opposition in Northern Ireland: The National Democratic Party, 1965–1970', *Economic and Social Review* (April 1975), pp. 353–66.

45   Parliament of Northern Ireland House of Commons Debates (Hansard), 21 February 1968, vol. 68, col. 1444. The position of the Nationalist Party in the 1960s, and of Eddie McAteer in particular, in relation to the question of partition is discussed in Brendan Lynn, *Holding the Ground: The Nationalist Party in Northern Ireland* (Aldershot: 1997), p. 165. By November 1968 McAteer was introducing the question of Northern Ireland's status into the midst of the civil rights debate. See, for instance, his remark, quoted in Frank Curran, *Derry: Countdown to Disaster* (Dublin: 1986), p. 92: 'In the hopeful but still confused situation at this moment,' he commented at a meeting of the Derry Nationalist party at this time, 'we nationalists must do considerable rethinking . . . If Belfast is in Ireland, would it be

treasonable to work towards rule from Belfast rather than Dublin?'
However, his *actual* political preference was for an integrated British
Union, as he confided to Lord Stonham on 15 November: explaining
his previous comments as a result of circumstantial pressure, he is
reported as believing that 'there must be some form of union. If the
present causes of discrimination are abolished, it will allow Protestants
and Catholics to work side by side towards a political union. He did not
see any virtue in, nor did he desire, a unified Ireland' (PRO, CJ 3/30,
'Note of a Record of a Meeting between Lord Stonham and Mr
McAteer').

46 Bernadette Devlin, *The Price of My Soul* (London: 1969), p. 92.
However, despite this dawning realisation on Bernadette Devlin's
part, Paddy Devlin, a Republican activist from Belfast in the 1940s, but
chairman of the Northern Ireland Labour Party in 1967–68, could
later, in his *Straight Left: An Autobiography* (Belfast: 1993), comment
on the march: 'There was a strong feeling that . . . the civil rights
marchers represented both traditions' (p. 89).

47 Michael Farrell, 'Long March to Freedom', in Michael Farrell ed.,
Twenty Years On (Dingle: 1988), p. 57.

48 See Ian McBride, *The Siege of Derry In Ulster Protestant Mythology*
(Dublin: 1997).

49 The phrase had general currency among nationalists at the time, but
appears specifically in Bernadette Devlin's memoir, *The Price of My
Soul*, p. 143. On the conspicuousness of inter-communal antagonism in
Derry as compared with Belfast at the start of the 1960s, see Denis P.
Barritt and Charles F. Carter, *The Northern Ireland Problem: A Study in
Group Relations* (Oxford: 1962), p. 76. The extremity of the situation in
Derry was likewise highlighted in the Campaign for Social Justice in
Northern Ireland pamphlet, *Londonderry: One Man, No Vote*
(Dungannon: 1965).

50 Jonathan Bardon, *A History of Ulster* (Belfast: 1992, 2001), p. 648.

51 Martin Wallace, *Drums and Guns: Revolution in Ulster* (London: 1970),
p. 29.

52 *Disturbances in Northern Ireland* (Cameron Report), p. 13.

53 Ibid., p. 14.

54 Eamonn McCann, *War in an Irish Town* (Harmondsworth: 1974), p. 43.

55 *Disturbances in Northern Ireland* (Cameron Report), p. 43.

56 'Backs to the Wall', *World in Action*, ITV, 21 October 1968.

57 Wallace, *Drums and Guns*, p. 39.

58 Seamus Heaney, 'Old Derry's Walls', *The Listener*, 24 October 1968.

59 Ed Maloney and Andy Pollock, *Paisley* (Dublin: 1986), p. 163.

60 Sir Andrew Gilchrist, the British Ambassador in Dublin, clarified the Southern Irish position to the United Kingdom government by telegram on 13 November: 'The effects of the Londonderry disturbances continue to be felt in Dublin. Though it was the Taoiseach [Jack Lynch] who first raised the partition issue in connection with Londonderry, he did so in a gentlemanly way . . . but [Mr Blaney] has taken up the running with two strong statements' (PRO, CJ 3/30). By this time Neil Blaney, Minister for Agriculture in the Lynch government, had already been taken to task for his outburst by the *Irish Times* on 12 November in the following terms: 'What anyone inclined to carry Mr. Blaney's words much further must consider is this: the reiterated airing of the feelings of injustice which partition arouses leads inevitably to the gun. The middle-aged politician may play with words and leave them aside; it is otherwise with young, impressionable men and boys. Words kill, and it is the young men who die.'

61 Wilson continued: 'I have honoured the conventions that have hitherto governed our relationships. But we should have a fundamental reappraisal of the situation if these things are not dealt with. If it were necessary to resort to introducing legislation at Westminster, it would be wrong to conclude that legislation would necessarily be limited to a reform of the local government franchise' (PRO, PREM 13/2841).

62 Ibid.

63 PRO, CAB 128/44, Conclusions for 24 April 1969, Report from the Home Secretary. The minutes record more fully Callaghan's view that 'It was unlikely that the implementation of "one man, one vote" would now put an end to violence . . . The root cause of the unrest in Northern Ireland seemed to lie in the growing contrast, reminiscent of the situation in this country early in the century, between the relative prosperity of a section of the people and the continuing poverty of the majority.'

64 PRO, CJ 3/5, Memorandum, 'Northern Ireland: Political Summary for the Period 15th–22nd July 1969'. The beginning of the paragraph, which the sentence quoted concludes, reads: 'Most thoughtful comment on the most recent disturbances has regarded the ultimate cause as the chronic unemployment in Londonderry and the bitterness and frustration to which it leads. Traditional sectarian and political differences are recognised as relevant to the form which the disturbances took, but only to the extent of providing a natural and well-remembered channel . . .'

65 PRO, CAB 128/46, Conclusions for 4 September 1969, Confidential Annex.

66 Memorandum by the Prime Minister, November 1968: 'I have so far resisted demands from members of the House either to take advantage of the powers of Section 75 or to order an inquiry into the affairs of Northern Ireland preferring to exert pressure on the Northern Ireland Government through the medium of discussions with the Prime Minister of Northern Ireland . . . and his colleagues . . . [now we] must contemplate legislative action . . . We have introduced in the House of Commons a Representation of the People Bill . . . it would be possible at the same time to legislate as regards the local electoral franchise in Northern Ireland' (PRO, CJ 3/30).

67 PRO, PREM 13/2841.

68 PRO, CJ 3/30, 'Memorandum by the Prime Minister', November 1968.

69 On the continuing doubts and suspicions about the O'Neill reform programme within the Catholic community in Derry around December 1968, see Niall Ó Dochartaigh, *From Civil Rights to Armalites: Derry and the Birth of the Troubles* (Cork: 1997), pp. 31–33.

70 O'Neill, *Ulster at the Crossroads*, pp. 140, 145. Earlier, on the same day in which the 'Crossroads' speech was made, Andrew Gilchrist notified the Foreign and Commonwealth Office in London that 'It seemed likely that within seven days, unless [O'Neill] could achieve a miracle, of which he no longer felt at all confident, the present Government of Northern Ireland would break up, with unforeseeable consequences.' O'Neill himself had advised him that 'it is a miracle we have had no bloodshed. With a Reactionary Cabinet bloodshed could scarcely be avoided' (PRO, CJ 3/30, Telegram from British Ambassador in Dublin).

III Perfidy: 1969–1972

1 See the evidence of Fr. McLaughlin regarding the Clonard area of Belfast on the evening of 15 August 1969, recorded in *Violence and Civil Disturbances in Northern Ireland in 1969* (Scarman Report) (HMSO Belfast: 1972), Cmd. 566, 2 vols, I, p. 200: 'I was terribly agitated and worked up and terribly afraid there was going to be a holocaust and that the whole area was going to be wiped out.'

2 Quoted in David Sharrock and Mark Devenport, *Man of Peace, Man of War: The Unauthorised Biography of Gerry Adams* (London: 1997), p. 63.

3 Adams invoked the image of the perfidious English under his

'Brownie' pen-name in an article, 'Active Abstentionism', for *Republican News* on 18 October 1975, with the phrase 'the wily Sassanach [Englishman]'. The same phrase appeared in an anonymous article contributed to *Republican News* on 25 August 1972 concerned with 'the British method of conquest by fomenting suspicion and mistrust': this, we are told, is one of 'the tricks of the wily Sassanach'. Still earlier, in July 1971, *Republican News* described the constitutional parties in Northern Ireland as '"Albion's"' quislings. Then on 5 December 1971, in the same paper, we read that loyalists are less attached to 'perfidious Albion' than is commonly assumed. Finally, in an article – 'What Next?' – in the 10 March 1973 edition, we read that 'naked force has always been sufficient justification for Perfidious Albion'. But, according to Adams in *Before the Dawn: An Autobiography* (London: 1996), pp. 276–77, the 'key' to such republican 'feelings' and perceptions 'lay back in those first days when the troops had moved in but had chosen not to intervene when loyalists had burnt down Bombay Street'.

4 The phrase is Harold Wilson's as recorded in the minutes of a Cabinet meeting held on 24 April 1969: 'In the present situation, if it became necessary for the troops to intervene, they would be thought to be doing so in order to maintain the Orange faction in power' (PRO, CAB 128/44). Similarly, a month later, a Memorandum prepared for the Secretary of State for Defence, Denis Healey, records Whitehall's anxiety about being drawn in to prop up a 'repressive regime' (PRO, CJ 3/2). By the time the troops had intervened, however, the Defence Secretary gave his reasons for maintaining a faction in power: 'He agreed that they should aim to retain the Northern Ireland Government as an effective force, for in that way they stood more chance of being able to withdraw the troops' (PRO, CAB 128/46, 14 August 1969, 41st Conclusions, Confidential Annex).

5 Adams, *Before the Dawn*, pp. 110–11. Closer to these events, on the first anniversary of the August riots, the Belfast Republican, Jimmy Steele, had commented that the British government was itself 'responsible for the burning of homes': 'This is what British Occupation means' (*Republican News*, August 1970). Whatever the question of responsibility, however, the memory of this episode certainly seared deep: 'We need only . . . utter the phrase "August 1969" and this brings to mind the horrors that that fateful month brought to Nationalist people in the 6 counties' (*Republican News*, May 1971).

6 By 28 December 1969, the newly formed Republican Publicity Bureau of the Provisional IRA had declared its opposition to 'the forces of

British imperialism' unleashed 'last August' (Reprinted in Seán MacStiofáin, *Memoirs of a Revolutionary*, Edinburgh: 1975, pp. 142–43). See also MacStiofáin's own description – published after his stint as Chief of Staff for the Provisionals – of the political situation at 'the beginning of 1969', ibid., pp. 115, 92: Northern Ireland, for him, was the 'neglected colony of a decaying imperial power', while it was specifically 'British domination which had led to many of the abuses and injustices that called for social agitation'. Within a year, 'British domination' was to be described contemptuously as the 'vile rule of imperialism in Ireland' (*Republican News*, November–December 1970).

7 In the January–February edition of *Republican News* in 1971, it was already being argued that partition resulted from England having created 'a division' in the people of Ireland: this strategy, the article continued, is evident in 'different countries [which the British] occupied – India, Cyprus, Palestine'. In June 1971, another article – 'On Partition' – in the same paper insisted that 'England . . . decided on the policy of divide and conquer. This then was the starting point of partition. A policy born in the halls of Westminster, used the difference in religion to separate the Irish people.' The Easter edition of *Republican News* in 1972 returned once more to this theme, referring to 'that well tried and tested tactic so beloved of the British – *Divide and Conquer*'. 'Her methods have rarely changed down through history,' declared *Republican News* once more, on 24 September 1974: 'they included the old maxim of divide and conquer.' But the most extended meditation on this British imperial tactic appeared in an article, 'Why England Must Murder', *Republican News*, 8 September 1972: here it is alleged that a ready supply of counter-insurgency tactics are available in the 'bulky, dark files' which 'Britannia' has lodged in the Foreign and Commonwealth Office – 'just about any file will do, if they are seeking ideas about divide and conquer'. On this basis, a contributor to *Republican News* could argue, quoting Idi Amin, that Britain had engineered 'religious strife in Uganda', much as it had – since 1830 – in the Middle East: 'Political Zionism, the cause of the present strife in the Middle East, is a creation, not of Orthodox Jewry, but of British colonial policy' ('Rippon in Uganda, Whitelaw in Ulster', 25 August 1972).

8 Gerry Adams, *The Politics of Irish Freedom* (Dingle: 1986), p. 23.

9 Ibid.

10 Ibid., p. 54.

11 Ibid., p. 30.

12　Jimmy Steele, once again, made this guiding assumption plain in *Republican News*, August 1970, remarking on the fact that it took nearly twelve months for Catholics in the ghettos to consent more generally to the proposition: 'It took almost a year to bring it home to them and the weekend of the 3rd and 4th July in the Lower Falls Road area [i.e. the Falls Curfew] MUST surely give them the necessary food for thought – That there can be no peace whilst England occupies one inch of this land.' In *Republican News*, September–October 1970, the 'necessary' response to this situation was set out clearly: the aim of Republicanism must be 'total revolution, the success of which will inevitably demand a gradual transition from the current, practical, defensive tactics of today to that of, not too distant, direct offensive confrontation with the powers of imperialism in Ireland'.

13　Seán MacStiofáin himself was keen to assert in his *Memoirs of a Revolutionary* that, while the 'clouds of theory' (p. 113) which permeated debate among the more ideologically ambitious members of the IRA late in 1968 were a distraction, he too was armed with his own set of 'principles', and indeed with his 'own philosophy of revolutionary military activity' (p. 100). Nonetheless, 'ideas' were disingenuously associated by militarists within the IRA with the so-called 'politicos' inside the movement, an association promoted by Marxisant Republican intellectuals – Anthony Coughlan and Roy Johnston, in particular – who had been identified with the IRA Chief of Staff, Cathal Goulding, since the mid-1960s. The strategic preferences of the Gouldingite faction were captured by an editorial in the newsletter for the Wolfe Tone Society (Goulding, Coughlan and Johnston all belonged to the Society), *Tuairisc*, in June 1966: 'The obstacles to be overcome are . . . the illusion still current in some pockets of the Republican movement that a simple-minded armed struggle against the British occupation is alone sufficient to . . . complete the national revolution.' The pretensions of this strategy were then set out in an article, 'Our Ideas', published in the same newsletter, in August 1966: 'There is nothing stronger than an idea whose time has come.' The irony is that it was Provisional ideology which was soon to appear as 'an idea whose time has come'.

14　Adams, *Before the Dawn*, p. 101. In a similar vein, see Seán MacStiofáin, *Memoirs of a Revolutionary*, p. 111: 'it was the beginning of the end . . . Within hours October 5, 1968 could be clearly seen as a turning-point in Irish history.'

15　Adams, *Before the Dawn*, p. 83. For Kwame Nkrumah and James Connolly, see ibid., pp. 54, 64.

16   The more militant posture was adopted by veteran Republicans like Jimmy Steele and Billy McKee in Belfast, whose demands for 'action' were already evident in July 1969. As Peter Taylor, *Provos: The IRA and Sinn Féin* (London: 1997, 1998), pp. 45–56, reports: on 6 July, at an IRA commemorative event, Steele had addressed a 5,000-strong crowd, declaring that the Republican movement should employ 'the only methods that will ever succeed, not the method of the politicians, nor the constitutionalists, but the method of soldiers, the method of armed force. The ultimate aim of the Irish nation,' he concluded, 'will never emerge from the political or constitutional platform.'

17   Peter Taylor, *Provos*, pp. 60–61, records Billy McKee's account of the confrontation: 'I told them [i.e. Sullivan et al.] that they used the money that they got from subscriptions for their own political ends, not for weapons to defend the people.' In general terms, Jim Sullivan's defensive posture in Belfast resulted from the attempt to avoid an immediate escalation of conflict in the context of a perceived need on the part of Catholic enclaves for protection after the experience of August 1969. By contrast, the demand for 'defence' from McKee, Cahill and Steele – supported by MacStiofáin and O'Connell within the Southern leadership – was more a call for military preparations, in pursuit of which the possibility of escalating the conflict was countenanced. The difference in positions was already giving rise to tension during the months preceding the August débâcle. See the comment by Tomás MacGiolla, President of Sinn Féin in 1969, recorded in Patrick Bishop and Eamonn Mallie, *The Provisional IRA* (London: 1987), p. 94: 'What we were trying to do was to avoid getting involved in any campaign. That's why MacStiofáin was such an embarrassment. The objective was to avoid military confrontation and to avoid any appearance of sectarianism.'

18   See the comments by the veteran Republican Joe Cahill on the fallout from this, given in an interview with Patrick Bishop and Eamonn Mallie, reprinted in their book *The Provisional IRA*, pp. 122–23.: seeing the welcome received by the British Army on the Falls Road after 15 August 'it brought tears to my eyes . . . people were glad to see them because the IRA had betrayed them'.

19   See the relevant comments on this episode in Niall Ó Dochartaigh, *From Civil Rights to Armalites: Derry and the Birth of the Troubles* (Cork: 1997), p. 33: 'when the mainly Belfast-based students and left-wing activists of the People's Democracy decided they would march from Belfast to Derry in the first days of 1969 to maintain the pressure for reform, the DCAC was ambivalent about it'.

20 Terence O'Neill, *Ulster at the Crossroads* (London: 1969), p. 145.

21 The response of John Hume to the PD decision captures the tone of the dispute: 'the march would lead to sectarian violence', he contended. See Paul Arthur, *The People's Democracy: 1968–73* (Belfast: 1974), p. 38.

22 Michael Farrell, 'Long March to Freedom', in Michael Farrell ed., *Twenty Years On* (Dingle: 1988), p. 56. See also Bernadette Devlin, *The Price of My Soul* (London: 1969), p. 120: 'Our function in marching from Belfast to Derry was to break the truce . . . and to show people that O'Neill was, in fact, offering them nothing.'

23 Bowes Egan and Vincent McCormack, *Burntollet* (London: 1969), p. 2.

24 Ó Dochartaigh, *From Civil Rights to Armalites*, p. 39.

25 Eamonn McCann, *War in an Irish Town* (Harmondsworth: 1974), p. 47. In the Northern Ireland general election held on 24 February 1969, McCann stood as a People's Democracy candidate for the Foyle constituency in Derry, forfeiting his deposit by securing a mere 1,993 votes against John Hume (8,920 votes) and Eddie McAteer (5,267 votes).

26 Bernadette Devlin's verdict is instructive: 'Michael Farrell . . . and Eamonn McCann of Derry are the two people who are doing the thinking of the left in Northern Ireland and who will in the end create its political philosophy. Michael had, from October onwards, a tremendous impact on the PD . . . Second-in-Command of the Belfast left was Cyril Toman' (*The Price of My Soul*, p. 118). See also Arthur, *The People's Democracy*, pp. 36, 39: 'It was the decision to march from Belfast to Derry which finally separated the militants from a large group of students who were worried about a left wing take-over': the reversal of the original decision not to march was seen as 'the successful takeover of PD by the New Left'.

27 The *Sunday Times* Insight Team, *Ulster* (Harmondsworth: 1972), p. 76.

28 David McKittrick, Seamus Kelters, Brian Feeney and Chris Thornton, *Lost Lives: The Stories of the Men, Women and Children Who Died as a Result of the Northern Ireland Troubles* (London: 1999), p. 32: Samuel Devenny 'received multiple injuries, a possible fracture to the skull and damage to the eyes and mouth. He also suffered a severe heart attack . . . The inquest, after hearing medical evidence, attributed his death to natural causes . . . Later, a team of detectives from Scotland Yard was called in to investigate . . . Sir Arthur Young . . . announced later that there was a lack of evidence due to a "conspiracy of silence" among members of the RUC.'

29 McCann, *War in an Irish Town*, p. 57.

30 The headline is quoted in *Sunday Times* Insight Team, *Ulster*, p. 78. Responsibility for the bomb blasts is discussed in *Violence and Civil Disturbances in Northern Ireland in 1969*, I, pp. 20–24.

31 *United Irishman*, May 1969. The previous month, in response to the recent explosions in the Province, the British Home Secretary provided the Cabinet with a political assessment, on the evidence available, of both the IRA and NICRA: 'it was known that the Irish Republican Army (IRA) was now dominated by a Communist element and that the civil rights organisation contained a mischievous fringe of extremists' (PRO, CAB 128/44, Conclusions, 24 April 1969).

32 PRO, CJ 3/1, 14 May 1969, 'Note on Withdrawal of Troops': 'politically . . . we might be regarded as abrogating – in practical and moral, if not constitutional or legal terms – our responsibility for the preservation of law and order in Northern Ireland: and [we would need to take note of the] . . . effect of such a decision on opinion, particularly among the minority groups there'. At a Cabinet meeting on 1 May, the Home Secretary, James Callaghan, had insisted that there was 'no question of troops' – that is, of introducing more troops, or deploying them to deal with civil disturbances – at the present time (PRO, CAB 128/44). But throughout the month, the debate continued inside the government. A Memorandum by the Secretary of Defence, Denis Healey, written during this period, reads: 'At the Cabinet discussion on Northern Ireland on 7th May, it was suggested that the use of troops in sporadic disturbances of a relatively minor character might well tend to lead progressively to their use in more serious disorders, ending in full military intervention, and that the best course might be to withdraw our troops from Northern Ireland now'. However, the Memorandum continues, 'we would be accused of abandoning the minority' (PRO, CJ 3/2).

33 James Callaghan, *A House Divided: the Dilemma of Northern Ireland* (London: 1973), p. 90: the situation in Northern Ireland in 1969 'was a powerful indictment of the evil of the political control of the RUC and the urgent need for reform . . . Wolseley . . . told me that he wanted the RUC to be acceptable to the community but, given the present set-up, he had no ideas on how to achieve this. He said that the RUC as a State force – those were his words – was an obvious target for those who wished to attack the Government.' See, further, *Disturbances in Northern Ireland: Report of the Commission Appointed by the Governor of Northern Ireland* (Cameron Report) (HMSO Belfast: September 1969), Cmd. 532, p. 12: 'We would . . . draw attention here to two matters

which play an important part in the history and causes of the events we have to investigate. The first is the extent to which the Minister of Home Affairs is concerned with the administrative control of public meetings and processions and the wide powers and consequential responsibility conferred upon him in this regard . . . The second is the remarkable width of the powers given to the Royal Ulster Constabulary and Ulster Special Constabulary under the Civil Authorities (Special Powers) Act (Northern Ireland) 1922.'

34 There was criticism of the Northern Ireland regime in Whitehall and at Westminster at this time, but it was entirely unfocused: governments in Northern Ireland 'may even have been able to ignore the wishes of a large part of the population with impunity', concluded a document prepared by D. E. R. Faulkner for the British Home Office in July 1969 (PRO, CJ 3/5, Memorandum by the Secretary of State for the Home Department, 11 July 1969). The systematic nature of the difficulty, however, was not discussed, nor was a solution envisaged. As evidence for the pervasiveness of the problem, however, see O'Neill, *Ulster at the Crossroads*, p. 50: in a speech made before the Ulster Unionist Council back in April 1965, O'Neill himself effectively demonstrated the point by declaring 'The Ulster Volunteers, the Covenant, the Government of Ireland Act, and the Ireland Act of 1949: all are part of a coherent pattern – a demonstration of the will and determination of the people of Ulster to remain within the United Kingdom.' In fact, each of these episodes was evidence, not of the harmonious will of 'the people', but of the steadfast will of the majority. See also ibid., p. 48: comparison of the situation in Ulster in 1969 with a statement by O'Neill to the Queen's University Unionist Association in February 1964 indicates the extent to which the policies pursued during his own tenure of office helped to bring about what he had claimed he wanted to consign to the past – 'Where there is "apartheid" in our society it comes almost entirely from a voluntary separation from the mainstream of our public and social life.'

35 The British government's Home Office, struggling to understand the roots of the problem in the summer of 1969, prepared a document, 'Representation in the Northern Ireland Parliament', on 11 July 1969, which concluded that the electoral system for Stormont 'is not in itself less fair than the system in Great Britain', and that the problem lay instead with the 'special circumstances in Northern Ireland': 'a one party system, with all the dangers which that involves and all the penalties in terms of the quality of political argument and political life generally'. But since there was no electoral remedy in sight, no means

of improvement were considered possible, save 'in removing the issue of partition from the fore-front of Northern Ireland politics' (PRO, CJ 3/5).

36 *Sunday Times*, 27 April 1969.

37 Quoted in Martin Wallace, *Drums and Guns: Revolution in Ulster* (London: 1970), p. 52.

38 Brian Faulkner, *Memoirs of a Statesman* (London: 1978), pp. 50–51.

39 PRO, CJ 3/39, 'Draft of a Bill to make temporary provision for suspending the Parliament of Northern Ireland, and for purposes connected therewith', 5 February 1969.

40 PRO, CJ 3/39, 'Northern Ireland: General Appreciation', 3 February 1969.

41 PRO, CJ 3/39, 'Governor of Northern Ireland: Administrative Instrument in Emergency', February 1969.

42 A note of 28 April 1969 by a British Home Office official records the content of a telephone conversation in which O'Neill had conveyed both his intention to resign and his expectations for the future: 'Captain O'Neill ended by expressing the view that it would be unwise for the British Government to consider intervening at this juncture although he did not hide his view that the eventual outcome of continued disturbances might have to be direct rule from Westminster' (PRO, CJ 3/8).

43 PRO, CJ 3/1, 'Report of Officials on the Implications of Declaring Northern Ireland Independent', May 1969.

44 Ibid.

45 PRO, CJ 3/1, 'Memorandum by the Secretary of State for the Home Office', May 1969. 'Associated Status', which would have involved modelling a new Northern Ireland constitution on the West Indies Act of 1967, was ruled out for similar reasons.

46 Ibid.

47 PRO, CJ 3/1, 'Round Table Conference', May 1969.

48 PRO, CJ 3/1, 'Memorandum by the Secretary of State for the Home Office', May 1969.

49 Ibid.

50 See Ronan Fanning, 'Playing it Cool: The Response of the British and Irish Governments to the Crisis in Northern Ireland, 1968–69, *Irish Studies in International Affairs*, 12 (2001), pp. 57–85, on the details of divisions inside the Irish Cabinet which prevented the development of a coherent Northern Ireland policy.

51 See the comment of Max Hastings on this episode in his *Ulster 1969* (London: 1970), pp. 120–21: 'a dangerous precedent had been set. Any

chance of justice being done in respect of the Burntollet attackers or the April rioters had vanished . . . The trouble was, of course, that since October the police had been so wildly selective in their enforcement of the law and so erratic in their behaviour that their decisions had become almost meaningless.'

52 *Sunday Times* Insight Team, *Ulster*, p. 96: 'Violence had been mount-ing for the past three weeks: rival crowds, savage speeches, sporadic punch-ups. Yet Chichester-Clark and Inspector-General Peacocke were unworried. Orange marches, they said, never caused trouble. (This is an enduring myth in Ulster. Orange parades actually have a history of attracting disorders . . .)'. The diary entry for 15 July by the Secretary of State for Social Services, Richard Crossman, is also instructive in this regard: see *The Diaries of a Cabinet Minister: Secretary of State for Social Services, 1968–1970* (London: 1977), p. 570: in regard to 12 July he comments that 'There had been commotions [in Northern Ireland], on St. Patrick's Day, it may have been.'

53 Quoted in *Sunday Times* Insight Team, *Ulster*, p. 96.

54 'This Madness', exclaimed the *Times* editorial in a retrospective assessment on 14 August 1969: 'The folly of permitting the Apprentice Boys to trail their coats through Derry is now tragically apparent . . . when fears and animosities . . . are . . . awake in the province, the parade assumes the character of public exultation by a dominant caste and sect, and of public humiliation of their adversaries.' Conor Cruise O'Brien gave vent to the same sentiments in 'Holy War', *New York Review of Books*, 6 November 1969: 'When the Orange Order (in Belfast and elsewhere) and the Apprentice Boys (in Derry) commemorate the victories of 1690, as they do each year in elaborate ceremonies, the message they are conveying is that of their determination to hold for Protestants in Northern Ireland as much as possible of the privileged status which their ancestors won under William of Orange . . . The ritual is one of annual renewal of a stylised act of dominance.'

55 *The Times*, 11 August 1969.

56 *Violence and Civil Disturbances in Northern Ireland in 1969*, I, p. 68.

57 See the evidence of Father Mulvey, ibid., p. 74.

58 *The Times*, 14 August 1969: an 'astonishing intervention', commented the political editor, David Wood. At the same time, the head of the Irish delegation to the UN called on U Thant to inform the Secretary-General of a request made by the Republic of Ireland for a UN peace-keeping force in Northern Ireland. However, the current affairs magazine in Dublin, *Hibernia*, was unimpressed: 'the government . . . decided to play to the gallery' (29 August–11 September 1969).

59   *The Times*, 14 August 1969.

60   Hastings, *Ulster 1969*, p. 139. On the B Specials at this juncture, see ibid., p. 138: 'Chichester-Clark claimed privately that the situation was such that had the Specials not been officially mobilised, they would have mobilised themselves with even more disastrous results.'

61   The idea, pioneered by the RUC and the Stormont government, was that the IRA were fomenting and controlling the disturbances, although intelligence reports supporting this assessment have yet to be produced. Certainly the British government was quick to discount this assessment: 'there was little evidence to support the view of the Northern Ireland Government that the Irish Republican Army (IRA) was responsible' (PRO, CAB 128/46, Conclusions, 19 August 1969, Confidential Annex).

62   O'Neill, *Ulster at the Crossroads*, p. 201.

63   The text of the speech is reprinted in *Violence and Civil Disturbances in Northern Ireland in 1969*, II, pp. 34–37.

64   *The Times*, 14 August 1969.

65   As pointed out by the Cameron Commission – see *Disturbances in Northern Ireland*, p. 55: amongst the most fundamental causes behind the disturbances, from a Catholic perspective, was 'a sense of frustration at the failure of representations for the remedy of social, economic and political grievances . . . among the Protestants, equally deep-rooted suspicions and fears of political and economic domination by a future Catholic majority in the population'. For his part, Chichester-Clark, in the Northern Ireland House of Commons on Thursday, 14 August, had insisted that the disturbances in the Province, rampant since the previous Tuesday, should not be understood as 'the agitation of a minority seeking by lawful means the assertion of political rights' but as a 'conspiracy of forces to overthrow a Government democratically elected by a large majority'. (The speech is reproduced in Appendix V of *Violence and Civil Disturbances in Northern Ireland in 1969*, II, p. 34.) However, as the Scarman Tribunal stated, ibid., I, p. 10: 'there was no conspiracy to overthrow the Government or to mount an armed insurrection'. The Northern Ireland government had therefore not merely failed to enforce security, it had done battle with the minority community which it had conjured into a conspiracy.

66   At the time, however, the recidivist thesis kept gaining the upper hand. Even Harold Wilson, who was perfectly familiar with the structural peculiarities of Northern Irish politics, could lapse into offering this particular brand of explanation for Northern Ireland's difficulties. See

Harold Wilson, *The Labour Government, 1964–1970: A Personal Record* (Harmondsworth: 1971), p. 692: the events of August were 'the culmination of three centuries of atavistic intolerance'. Denis Healey, after an interval of time for thought and reflection, drew the same conclusion in *The Time of My Life* (London: 1989), p. 342: 'The conflict was expressed in terms of religious differences; but it was best understood as a form of tribalism.'

67 *Sunday Times*, 27 April 1969.

68 See the remark made by the Foreign and Commonwealth Secretary at a Cabinet meeting on 19 August 1969: 'Part of the frustration felt by the Catholic community arose from the fact that they had at present no hope of taking part in the Government' (PRO, CAB 128/46, Conclusions, Confidential Annex).

69 Wilson, *The Labour Government*, p. 692. James Callaghan, *A House Divided*, p. 10, also saw fit to remark that 'there was only the possibility of one-party government' in Northern Ireland. In like fashion, the lobby editor, John Bourne, of the *Financial Times*, having been briefed by the British government, referred diplomatically on 6 August 1969 to the Stormont government as 'rightly or wrongly . . . regarded as essentially Protestant in outlook'.

70 It was this situation, however, which the Defence Secretary had long sought to avoid. In planning for the withdrawal of British troops from the Province the previous May, the underlying rationale for the move was deleted from a Memorandum on the subject at the draft stage. The deleted sentence reads: 'this would relieve us of their [the troops] common Law obligation to assist the civil power on request' (PRO, CJ 3/2, 'Memorandum by the Secretary of State for Defence', May 1969).

71 Callaghan, *A House Divided*, p. 24.

72 Richard Crossman, on Tuesday, 19 August in *Diaries of a Cabinet Minister: Secretary of State*, p. 623. There were, of course, contingency plans, and schemes for maintaining security – but as yet there was no plan of action embracing Northern Ireland politics as a whole. Crossman goes on: 'It wasn't so much deciding what policy to have as being able to excuse it' that occupied the Cabinet on that day.

73 Callaghan, *A House Divided*, p. 21.

74 Adams, *Politics of Irish Freedom*, p. 33. While the allegation here is obviously being levelled long after the event, the claim had been established at the time, and it settled into a pattern of perception. See, for example, the Central Citizens' Defence *Barricade Bulletin*, 2, (1969): 'In the early hours of this morning shots were fired at the barricade at Ramoan Gardens . . . Despite the presence of a heavily

armed British Military patrol, the car was not intercepted. This reaffirms the C. D. C. contention that the defence of the liberated areas must come from the men of the district.' In recent Republican accounts, the point is usually made by insinuation and implication – see, for example, Ciarán de Baróid, *Ballymurphy and the Irish War* (London: 1989), p. 19: 'nationalist Bombay Street was razed to the ground in full view of British troops'.

75   See the evidence of Fr. Egan of Clonard Monastery in *Violence and Civil Disturbances in Northern Ireland in 1969*, I, p. 202: some time after 8 p.m., 'he had pointed to the Colonel [Napier] the stretch of Cupar Street where he thought soldiers should be positioned'. See also Desmond Hamill, *Pig in the Middle: The Army in Northern Ireland, 1969–1984* (London: 1985), p. 15, on 'the Orange–Green line' employed by the RUC to mark out the territorial divisions between Catholics and Protestants in Belfast: a senior Army officer in Belfast in mid-August 'had never heard of it'.

76   Tony Geraghty, *The Irish War: The Military History of a Domestic Conflict* (London: 1998), p. 25.

77   Hastings, *Ulster 1969*, p. 147; *Sunday Times* Insight Team, *Ulster*, p. 139. The poverty of Army intelligence cannot be doubted, but nonetheless it needs to be explained. After all, James Callaghan, *A House Divided*, p. 22, remarks that 'plainclothes soldiers appeared quietly on the streets in trouble spots to size up the situation' during the months before August; and Tony Geraghty, *The Irish War*, p. 24, reveals that around March 1969, Major Michael Mates – subsequently a Minister in Northern Ireland – arrived from his post in Berlin to assess the situation on the ground in Northern Ireland.

78   'Troops: When the Honeymoon Is Over', *Barricades Bulletin* (Young Socialists), 25 August 1969. Six days earlier, Denis Healey had commented at a Cabinet meeting in London that the troops 'had been welcomed by both sides; but there were already signs that the honeymoon period was ending' (PRO, CAB 128/46, Conclusions, 19 August 1969, Confidential Annex).

79   *Irish Times*, 8 October 1969. Related to this idiom, see Eamonn McCann's account of Bernadette Devlin's reaction to the arrival of British troops in the Bogside on 14 August 1969 in *War in an Irish Town*, p. 61: 'Bernadette Devlin, her voice croaking, urged "Don't make them welcome. They have not come here to help us", and went on a bit about Cyprus and Aden. It did not go down very well.'

80   See the account of one IRA activist – recorded in David Sharrock and Mark Devenport, *Man of Peace, Man of War*, p. 58 – who participated

in the rioting of 13 August 1969 in Belfast: 'Stones and petrol bombs were thrown and it was supposed to take the pressure off Derry . . . But this was really the beginning of the split. You had a handful of older guys outside the movement, older republicans. They were doing a bit of stirring with the younger lads.'

81   On militant Republicanism's war intentions at this time, see the record of Billy McKee's successful bid to encourage Martin Meehan back into the IRA in the wake of August 1969 as relayed by Peter Taylor, *Provos*, p. 63: 'He didn't indicate that there was going to be an immediate offensive against the British army. He said, "things take time. People have to be trained. People have to be motivated" . . . But the intention was there and it sounded good to me.'

82   'Troops: When the Honeymoon is Over', op. cit. See also the comment by the veteran IRA man, John Kelly, to Peter Taylor, recorded in *Provos*, p. 59: 'I have to say that we were relieved to see them arrive, yes.' Although he goes on: 'But we did not anticipate that they would stay on as an occupying force to maintain the established position of Unionism within the Six Counties.'

83   Quoted in Bishop and Mallie, *The Provisional IRA*, p. 112. The estimates of armaments available to the IRA in Belfast at the time vary – the calculation here is derived from ibid., p. 108 – but all sources agree that their quantity was derisory. See also J. Bowyer Bell, *The Secret Army: The IRA, 1916–1979* (Dublin: 1970, 1979), p. 363, on the state of the IRA in 1969: 'The IRA itself had practically given up maintaining the old military structure. Potential volunteers were turned away into more relevant organizations. Units were closed down.' Sharrock and Devenport, *Man of Peace, Man of War*, pp. 60–61, contend that the IRA weapons used at St Comgall's School, on the corner of Divis Street and the Falls Road, on 14 August 1969, had been moved in from Andersonstown, having been withheld from Sullivan and McMillen on the Lower Falls.

84   In March 1972, Cathal Goulding revealed that the failure to distribute weaponry in advance of August 1969 had in fact – as his opponents in the IRA suspected – been deliberate. 'We didn't give what guns we had. We hadn't thought there would be organised pogroms because of the worldwide publicity attracted by Derry. We miscalculated there.' The interview appeared in the journal *7 Days*, part of which is reproduced in Geraghty, *The Irish War*, p. 10. The faction that had offered armaments to Keenan in the Bogside has been identified as Saor Éire: see Ó Dochartaigh, *From Civil Rights to Armalites*, pp. 124–25.

85 John Diggera, 'Chaos in Dublin', *Action for Freedom*, Autumn 1969; Seamus O'Kane, 'The Seeds of the Current Struggle', ibid. See also the evidence given by Fr. Gillespie regarding events in the Ardoyne on Sunday, 17 August 1969, recorded in *Violence and Civil Disturbances in Northern Ireland in 1969*, I, p. 221: 'some residents "raided the houses of people who were supposed to be IRA men by repute and found nothing, and after the riots they called the IRA the 'I ran away' " '.

86 However, under pressure from events, they were not averse to inflaming a precariously sensitive situation with explicitly militant pronouncements. As the Ulster Unionist Party was to make plain in its own publication, *Ulster: The Facts* (Belfast: 1969), Goulding himself was prepared to declare in late August that 'Northern Units of the Irish Republican Army have played their part . . . We issue a warning to all young British soldiers now patrolling Irish streets and towns. You are in a very perilous situation. For this is not your country.' But the message was belied by the paucity of preparations.

87 *United Irishman*, September 1968.

88 Ibid., January 1969.

89 This combination was discussed at an Extraordinary Army Convention in the middle of December 1969. It led to the establishment of a National Liberation Front, through which Republicans were to enter into close co-operation with the organisations of the radical left, with the overall objective of achieving the 'reconquest of Ireland, shop by shop and factory by factory'. See Tim Pat Coogan, *The IRA* (London: 1970, 2000), p. 338.

90 The revolution would amount to a reconquest in stages: first the conquest of politics and society, North and South, and then the conquest of national wealth in tandem with national politics, in consequence of which political bureaucracy would disappear as socialism succeeded capitalist imperialism. The call for a reconquest goes back to James Connolly, 'The Re-Conquest of Ireland' (1915), in *Labour in Ireland* (Dublin: 1922), where the final demise of the existing political division of labour is connected to the advent of 'true' democracy: 'As Democracy enters, Bureaucracy will take flight' (p. 250). The Connollyite doctrine of 'reconquest' was transmitted to subsequent generations of Republican activists under the influence of nationalist radicals Peadar O'Donnell and Liam Mellows. For an account of the trajectory, see Patterson, *The Politics of Illusion, passim*. By the 1960s, however, the Republican advocacy of reconquest had been heavily larded with residues of European Marxism – hence the emphasis on 'monopoly capitalism' in the *United Irishman*, even as late as January

1969: 'The capitalist system is tottering on the brink of a crisis . . . the root cause of the problem is imperialism . . . Throughout the Western world there is a revolt against imperialism, capitalism and the rule of big business and international monopoly.'

91 MacStiofáin, *Memoirs of a Revolutionary*, p. 134. Opposition to the 'extreme' and unchristian socialism of the Goulding faction is also regularly cited as relevant to the divisions within the IRA. At the start of 1970, the caretaker [Provisional] executive of Sinn Féin was consequently pitching its own preferred form of socialism which, as *An Phoblacht*, May 1970 reports, was originally 'based on the native tradition of Comhar na gComharsam . . . founded on the right of worker-ownership and on our Irish and Christian values'.

92 As *Republican News* was later to put it, in April 1971, 'the true enemy' would thereby be made 'more "easily identifiable"'. Publicists for the Provisional IRA, however, were happy to draw on the Official IRA account of imperialism to bolster their own preferred strategic response. See *Republican News*, June 1971, for example, on the British system as 'being profit motivated'. By 24 March 1973, *Republican News* was admonishing: 'Let everyone be under no illusions, the B. A. [British Army] are here for one reason only, that is, to defeat all resistance to the continued domination and exploitation of the Six Counties by British capital and British imperialism.' Ultimately, an article in *Republican News*, 15 November 1975, could refer to 'Economic domination of both Northern Ireland and Southern Ireland by foreign monopolies'.

93 'Statement by the Prime Minister of Northern Ireland', 15 August 1969, Reprinted in Appendix V of *Violence and Civil Disturbances in Northern Ireland in 1969*, II, p. 38.

94 See *Republican News*, April 1971: 'Unionists realise that the beginning of direct rule is the beginning of their end . . . *Direct Rule* means the abolition of their [the Unionists'] position of privilege, patronage and power. It could mean the end of sectarianism since the patronage would not be any longer for transmission on a sectarian basis. And if sectarianism which Unionism nourishes itself on were eroded then Unionism is eroded and would crumble.'

95 MacStiofáin, *Memoirs of a Revolutionary*, pp. 135, 151.

96 Within a matter of months – in its Easter Commemoration Statement for 1970 – the Provisional Army Council would set out its stall: as reported in *An Phoblacht*, April 1970, the Provisional leadership announced that in 'the struggle for Civil Rights the abolition of Stormont would, as an interim measure, be a step forward. It would

bring us into direct confrontation with Westminster. English imperialism, both in its old and new forms, has been the root cause of Ireland's ills.'

97 *Sunday Times* Insight Team, *Ulster*, p. 204.

98 A British Home Office Memorandum for March 1970 reads: 'The Army have continued to deal completely successfully with the situation and retain a generally untarnished image, though antagonism against them is mounting on the Shankill Road. Their ready acceptance by Roman Catholics could, however, be imperilled at any time by a violent incident' (PRO, CJ 3/5, 'Northern Ireland, The Political Situation: Memorandum by the Secretary of State for the Home Department').

99 MacStiofáin, *Memoirs of a Revolutionary*, p. 146.

100 For the argument that political reform was incompatible with popular Unionist support, see, most importantly, Paul Bew and Henry Patterson, *The British State and the Ulster Crisis, From Wilson to Thatcher* (London: 1985), p. 33: 'Whilst a modernising and reforming Unionist party bereft of state power was a possibility, a Unionist regime with the double responsibility of reforming and reproducing mass support was not.' On the other hand, the case for political reform was being pressed by Fergus Pyle in 'Stormont: What Chance for the Future?', *Fortnight*, November 1970: 'Radical change would attempt to draw the community together. It would explore new kinds of government, such as an executive which would include members of the minority parties.'

101 Criticism of the original terms of engagement circulated as early as August 1969. See the *Times* editorial of 15 August 1969: 'the probability is that troops will be required in strength and for a longish period of time. That in turn necessitates some redistribution of political responsibility . . . The troops will of course remain within the military chain of command which terminates at the Ministry of Defence in Whitehall. They will not take their instructions from the present civil authorities in Northern Ireland; but in coming to the aid of the civil arm they will be taking part in operations, and confronting a situation, which are the responsibility of those authorities.' The political reality to which this arrangement gave rise was the establishment of the Joint Security Committee through which Provincial security was administered. The Inspector-General of the RUC, the General Officer Commanding of Northern Ireland, and the Stormont Home Affairs Minister all sat on the Security Committee. For their own part, British troops were licensed to act as common law officers of the peace, but

since this status soon proved useless for the purposes of riot control, the Army was forced to rely on the Special Powers Act.

102 The Address, delivered on 23 June, was recorded in the *United Irishman*, July 1968. The 'idea' cited was, of course, not Tone's, but Bentham's. In Garland it was intended as a defence of Irish socialism. Nonetheless, see Jeremy Bentham, *A Fragment on Government* (1776), eds J. H. Burns and H. L. A. Hart (1977; Cambridge: 1988), esp. the 'Explanation' to the 'Note by the Author, 1822', included in the 1823 edition of the *Fragment*, pp. 58–59n: 'the *greatest happiness* or *greatest felicity* principle . . . a principle, which lays down, as the only *right* and justifiable end of Government, the greatest happiness of the greatest number'.

103 MacStiofáin, *Memoirs of a Revolutionary*, p. 146.

104 *An Phoblacht*, April 1972. In a similar vein, see the *Andersonstown Bulletin*, 1972, n. d.: 'the sterile and hateful bigotry which divides the people in the interest of the MASTERS AND FOREIGN CAPITAL'.

105 See the moderate editorial account of deteriorating relations between Catholics and the British Army in 'Battling it Out', *Fortnight*, 19 February 1971: 'some soldiers have been guilty of provocative behaviour in the early stages of riotous behaviour. Relations between the Army and the residents of Ballymurphy for instance had already reached the stage where soldiers were reduced to touring round the estate and shouting sectarian slogans at the girls and youths . . . the verdict is that the blame for the escalation [to gunfire] lies fairly and squarely with the Provisionals and their supporters. But part of the blame for the initial confrontations must also lie with the Army, in its failure to deal openly and fairly with allegations of misconduct and in some instances of lack of discipline.'

106 Quoted in Jonathan Bardon, *A History of Ulster* (Belfast: 1992, 1996), p. 688.

107 See the statement of 'Sinn Féin Policy' included in *An Phoblacht*, September 1971: Britain 'considers it worth her while to pay out taxpayers' money to keep Ireland divided and safe for British investors to draw profits'.

108 'The Republican Solution', *An Phoblacht*, December 1972.

109 Patrick Pearse, 'The Spiritual Nation' (1916), in *Collected Works of Patrick Pearse* (Dublin: 1922), 3 vols, III, p. 343. An article entitled 'Patriotism' in *Republican News*, July 1971, commented in a similar vein: 'A nation is an association of people designed by God.' On 7 May 1977, another piece in *Republican News*, 'P. H. Pearse: Romantic or Realist', quotes extensively from Pearse's 'The Sovereign People' in

op. cit., seeking to illustrate the same point: 'The nation is the natural division, as natural as the family, and as inevitable. That is one reason why a nation is holy and an empire is not holy.'

110 See the Irish Republican Publicity Bureau statement, reported in *An Phoblacht*, September 1971: 'The root cause of foreign aggression is historically rooted in the unnatural division of our country and its domination by British imperialism.' See also the comment in 'Plain Speaking', *An Phoblacht*, October 1971: 'In 1918, five counties out of the nine counties in historic Ulster staked their claim democratically to a united Ireland. Twenty-seven counties in full, and large sectors of the remaining four, stated loudly – and, Dr Katanga O'Brien, democratically – that they wished a free, democratic, United Ireland.'

111 'South of the Border', *World in Action*, Granada Television (1971).

IV Perfidy: 1891–1923

1 The phrase 'essential unity' encompassed any arrangement which, in the judgement of Irish nationalism, would fall short of Ulster secession. For Griffith's sense, after the negotiations had been completed, that the Treaty had in fact delivered 'essential unity', see Arthur Griffith, *Arguments for the Treaty* (Dublin: 1922), p. 24.

2 Frank Pakenham, *Peace by Ordeal: An Account, from First-Hand Sources, of the Negotiation and Signature of the Anglo-Irish Treaty, 1921* (Cork: 1951), p. 161; Michael Laffan, *The Partition of Ireland, 1911–1925* (Dublin: 1983), pp. 80–83.

3 D. Macardle, *The Irish Republic* (Dublin: 1937), Chs 49–52.

4 The strategy pursued by de Valera during the negotiations is described in John M. Regan, *The Irish Counter-Revolution, 1921–1936* (Dublin: 1999), pp. 15–16, as amounting to a preparedness to push the British to the brink of war before intervening 'to strike the best possible compromise' himself in the form of 'external association' with the British Empire.

5 The leader of the Volunteers, Eoin MacNeill, explained the logic behind their foundation: the Ulster Volunteer movement represented at once a show of strength and a declaration of autonomy, and Irish nationalism should follow suit – 'the only solution now possible is for the empire to make terms with Ireland or to let Ireland go her own way . . . it is manifest that all Irish people, Unionist as well as Nationalist, are determined to have their own way in Ireland' (Eoin MacNeill, 'The North Began', *An Claidheamh Soluis*, 1 November 1913).

6 Michael Joseph O'Rahilly, *The Secret History of the Volunteers* (Dublin: 3rd edn, 1915) and Bulmer Hobson, *A Short History of the Irish Volunteers* (Dublin: 1918). See also the comment by P. S. O'Hegarty in *The Victory of Sinn Féin* (Dublin: 1924), p. 13: 'The Separatist movement of 1918 was the result of the seed sown by the I. R. B. and the *Gaelic League* and the *United Irishman*; but the I. R. B. was the parent and watcher.'

7 F. S. L. Lyons, *Ireland since the Famine* (London: 1973, 1985), p. 315.

8 Leon Ó Broin, *Revolutionary Underground: The Story of the Irish Republican Brotherhood, 1858–1924* (Dublin: 1926), pp. 167–69. See also the comment by Bulmer Hobson in his *Ireland Yesterday and Tomorrow* (Kerry: 1968), pp. 71–72: 'A small committee, of which McDermott and Clarke were the effective members, was appointed with instructions to examine the project [i.e. an insurrection], and to report back to the Supreme Council. They never reported back'; and p. 78: 'It was not the Supreme Council of the IRB who organised the insurrection, but a small junta inside the IRB, acting with the utmost secrecy and without the knowledge of the President and most other members of the Supreme Council.'

9 Paul Bew, in his *Ideology and the Irish Question: Ulster Unionism and Irish Nationalism 1912–1916* (Oxford: 1994), p. 150, collapses this development into a single moment with the result that 'the events in Easter week' are made to 'constitute a technical *coup*; a successful *coup* in the end, but none the less one lacking a substantive claim to democratic legitimacy'. But, of course, there was no actual coup in 1916 – instead there was a failed attempt at one. But the original existence of a failed coup does not cancel the legitimacy of the popular support for separatism which ultimately followed in its wake.

10 Arthur Griffith, *When the Government Publishes Sedition* (Dublin: 1916), p. 11.

11 Robert Lynd, *If the Germans Conquered England, and Other Essays* (Dublin and London: 1917), pp. ix–x. For a recent attempt to co-opt Lynd – 'a united Irishman, if ever there was one' – to the cause of post-ceasefire Provisional Republicanism, see Danny Morrison, *All The Dead Voices* (Cork: 2002), pp. 55–62.

12 For some of the key ingredients in the programme of Sinn Féin in the period, see Robert Lynd's comments in *The Ethics of Sinn Féin* (Limerick: 1912), pp. 4–5 on the 'duty' to 'de-Anglicise Ireland', to liberate oneself and one's country from 'the shame of foreign conquest and the ignominy of English rule'. On the mantle of revolution enveloping Sinn Féin after 1916, see A. De Blacam, *What Sinn Féin*

Stands For: The Irish Republican Movement; Its History, Aims and Ideals, Examined as to their Significance to the World (Dublin: 1921), p. 89: 'Indiscriminately, Gaelic Leaguers, Abstentionists, Republicans and Socialists were labelled Sinn Féin.'

13   William O'Brien, *The Irish Revolution, And How It Came About* (Dublin: 1923), p. 44.

14   It was over the influence of the Ancient Order of Hibernians, acting from Belfast as the Board of Erin, that O'Brien tendered his resignation from the Irish Parliamentary Party. See *Cork Accent*, 1 January 1910: 'It was only a knave would make, or a fool believe, the assertion that Home Rule was to be passed when the Lords' veto was abolished. Under the rule of the Molly Maguires [Board of Erin] no Protestant could be admitted into the National movement.'

15   The pervasiveness of the challenge to parliamentarism is implicit in the comments by the Home Rule MP, T. M. Kettle, in his Introduction to the English translation of L. Paul-Dubois' *Contemporary Ireland* (Dublin: 1908), p. ix: 'People speak as if the outcry against Parliamentarianism were a novel and unique thing . . . Today you can pick up anywhere in Paris or Brussels half-a-dozen pamphlets called "The Crisis of Parliamentarianism", "The Absurdity of Parliamentarianism", or "The End of Parliamentarianism".' In 1915, Eoin MacNeill displayed his own partiality for this ingredient of modern fashion: he despised – as he put it in his *Daniel O'Connell and Sinn Féin* (Dublin: 1915), p. 15 – the manner in which 'Ireland's representatives wheedled, fawned, begged, bargained and truckled for a provincial legislature'. On the revolt against parliamentarism among advanced nationalists in the period, see Tom Garvin, *Nationalist Revolutionaries in Ireland, 1858–1928* (Oxford: 1987), p. 95. See also his 'Great Hatred, Little Room: Social Background and Political Sentiment among Revolutionary Activists in Ireland, 1890–1922', in D. G. Boyce ed., *The Revolution in Ireland: 1879–1923* (Dublin: 1988) together with D. G. Boyce's *Nationalism in Ireland* (London: 1982, 1995), esp. pp. 295–338.

16   O'Brien, *The Irish Revolution*, pp. 81–2, 107, 167.

17   Ibid., p. 43. See also O'Brien's comments in the House of Commons in late 1916, reprinted in his *Sinn Féin and Its Enemies* (Dublin and London: 1917), p. 5: 'You [England] are fighting to put down militarism, as we know, in the interest of the small nations. Do you really expect anybody in America or in Europe could have any feeling except one of distrust . . . of the self-righteousness of that kind if your Censor would only allow them to learn what was happening in a

certain small nation called Ireland?' In like vein, see the remarks of Robert Lynd, on the period after 1914 generally, in *The Passion of Labour* (London: 1920), p. 175: 'Irishmen began to suspect that the promise of Home Rule was only "for the duration of the war" . . . The treatment of Irish men and women after the insurrection of 1916 confirmed them in their darkest suspicions. Meanwhile, they saw Home Rule movements turning into Republican movements all over the world – in the German, Austrian, and Russian empires. Finland abandoned Home Rulism for Republicanism. So did Poland. So did Bohemia.'

18 Oliver MacDonagh, *The Emancipist: Daniel O'Connell, 1830–1847* (London: 1989), p. 221; Conor Cruise O'Brien, *Parnell and His Party* (Oxford: 1957), p. 162.

19 Arthur Griffith, *The Resurrection of Hungary: A Parallel for Ireland [1904], With Appendices on Pitt's Policy and Sinn Féin* (Dublin: 3rd edn, 1918), p. xiv.

20 The 'Amended Constitution of the Irish Republican Brotherhood' is transcribed in Bulmer Hobson, *Ireland Yesterday and Tomorrow*, p. 103: 'The I. R. B. shall await the decision of the Irish Nation as expressed by a majority of the Irish people as to the fit hour of inaugurating a war against England.'

21 For a more detailed discussion, see Matthew Kelly, 'The End of Parnellism and the Ideological Dilemmas of Sinn Féin', in D. George Boyce and Alan O'Day eds, *Ireland in Transition, 1879–1923* (forthcoming).

22 O'Hegarty, *The Victory of Sinn Féin*, p. 162.

23 Griffith, *The Resurrection of Hungary*, pp. 5–6.

24 Ibid., p. 17: 'then came news that Schmerling had a policy which was infallibly to settle the Hungarian question and the Bohemian question and the Croatian question . . . Forty years later certain English statesmen rediscovered Schmerling's profound policy and labelled it "Home Rule All Round"'. See also Griffith's statement, ibid., p. 46n: 'Mr. Gladstone's second Home Rule Bill (1893) was mainly modelled on this Austrian proposal which the Hungarians unanimously rejected.'

25 Of course the Bill, as Griffith confided to George Russell, precipitated a day of reckoning: 'If a good Bill accepted by Ulster had been introduced I and my party would have disappeared from Ireland' (Richard P. Davis, *Arthur Griffith and Non-Violent Sinn Féin*, Dublin: 1974).

26 Griffith, *The Resurrection of Hungary*, p. 20.

27 Ibid., p. 70. See Arthur Griffith, 'Preface' to John Mitchel, *Jail Journal* (Dublin: 1913), p. xiv for the principle at work here: 'The right of the Irish to political independence was, is not, and never can be dependent upon the admission of equal right in all other peoples.'

28 Griffith, *The Resurrection of Hungary*, p. 60. The Hungarian tradition of physical force is represented in the *Resurrection* by the figure of Louis Kossuth who, standing on implacable Republican principle in 1849, invited Austrian arms to decide the matter and squandered in an instant the constitutional advances of 1848. 'In Mitchel,' as Griffith remarked, 'Ireland had a half parallel in Kossuth – she never had a Deak' (p. 72).

29 Ibid., p. 62.

30 Ibid., p. 82.

31 T. M. Kettle argued strenuously against Griffith's accounts of both Hungary and Ireland, together with his presentation of the similarities between them, in his 'Would the Hungarian Policy Work?', *New Ireland Review*, February 1905: Griffith's analysis, he insisted, 'reads like a fairy tale'. The example had, nonetheless, been bandied about since Gladstone. However, objections to the parallelism also long predate the publication of Griffith's book. See John Stuart Mill, *England and Ireland* (London: 1868), p. 34: 'the most favourable of all combinations of circumstances for the success and permanence of an equal alliance between independent nations under the same crown, exists between Hungary and Austria, least favourable between England and Ireland'. The viability of Griffith's Hungarian parallel has, however, been recently defended by Thomas Kabdebo, *Ireland and Hungary: A Study in Parallels* (Dublin: 2001).

32 Hobson, *Ireland Yesterday and Tomorrow*, p. 9; Laffan, *The Resurrection of Ireland*, pp. 20–40.

33 In *The Resurrection of Hungary*, pp. 56–57, Griffith elaborates this point under cover of the Hungarian response to the imminence of the *Ausgleich*: 'Every deputy was ready with a scheme for the final settlement of the Hungarian question, and with a speech upon it, and between the Republicans, the Radicals, and Conservatives – all agreed that the status quo was impossible, but all differing as to what New Hungary should be – only Deak could have saved Hungary from playing into Belcredi's hands.'

34 Griffith, *The Resurrection of Hungary*, p. 85: 'England renounced her claim to govern this country [in 1783], awed by the bayonets of 200,000 Irish Volunteers. Though her divide-et-impera policy subsequently succeeded in riving the union of the people of Ireland, the memory of

Dungannon she can never eradicate.' Similarly, in June 1971, an article in *Republican News* was to declare that we have to 'go back to men like Sir William Pitt, British Prime Minister' to discover the origin of partitionist policy.

35 The argument is once again exemplified by Griffith in the *Resurrection* using the case of Hungary: 'From the day the Constitution of Hungary was restored, the fullest equality reigned, and sectarian intolerance is utterly unknown in the kingdom' (p. 70).

36 William O'Brien, 'Toleration in the Fight for Ireland', in *Irish Ideas* (London: 1893), p. 115.

37 Arthur Griffith, 'The Sinn Féin Policy', reprinted in *The Resurrection of Hungary*, Appendix II, p. 163.

38 Ibid., p. 144.

39 *Sinn Féin*, 4 August 1906.

40 Griffith, 'The Sinn Féin Policy', p. 149. The theme was to be a persistent one in the history of Republican argument and perception. *Republican News*, July 1971, was to contrast the fact that 'Mother England now casts herself in the role of benefactor' with the reality of the 'wiles and guiles of her diplomats'. The English are, the article continues, 'the most able and accomplished political schemers the world has ever had to witness'. The object of that scheming was described in familiar terms by Michael MacNaolain, an internee in Cage 10 at Long Kesh prison camp, in *Republican News*, 15 November 1975: 'The primary characteristic of the National Struggle is the struggle by imperialism to control and dominate the Irish people in order to exploit their resources and rob them of their wealth.' Republicanism, by contrast, is given the role of exemplifying selflessness and Spartan rigour. As Gerry Adams put it, under the pen-name 'Brownie', in 'Why Died the Sons of Rosín Dubh', *Republican News*, 10 January 1976: 'there is more to life than material affluence'. Another internee, Pat Shannon, spelt the implication out in 'Social Republicanism', *Republican News*, 21 February 1976: 'The Republican Movement is the highest concentrate of selfless, courageous dedication to National Service in the country.' In fact, the second issue of *Republican News*, July 1970, had already dwelt on these characteristics as a requisite for the success of the movement: 'We need to cultivate the following qualities in the members of our movement: Patriotism, Loyalty, Courage, Determination, Confidence, and Efficiency.'

41 Griffith, 'The Sinn Féin Policy', pp. 144, 149.

42 Ibid., p. 149.

43   Friedrich List, *The National System of Political Economy*, trans. Sampson Lloyd (London: 1885, 1904), p. 293. In describing imperial policy, List's complaints usually refer to the British, Griffith's to the English, but neither is perfectly consistent on this score.

44   Arthur Griffith, 'Pitt's Policy: Imperialism and Ireland', reprinted in *The Resurrection of Hungary*, Appendix I, p. 100.

45   Ibid., p. 108.

46   'Declaration and Resolutions of the Society of United Irishmen of Belfast' (October 1791), reprinted in *Life of Theobald Wolfe Tone*, ed. Thomas Bartlett (Dublin: 1998), p. 299.

47   Griffith, 'Pitt's Policy: Imperialism and Ireland', pp. 105–14. See the comments by 'Brownie' [Gerry Adams] on this period in relation to current IRA strategy in 'Active Republicanism', *Republican News*, 1 May 1976: 'We may not be able to bomb an unwilling group of people into our Republic, into their Republic, but they cannot deny us the right to use force against those [i.e. the British] preventing or withholding our freedom . . . We must remember, as William Thompson said in the 1820s . . . "It was only after the repression of the '98 Rebellion that the antagonism between the Orangemen and Papists was deliberately fostered by the Castle as a means of maintaining power . . . There was Profit in it for the Castle you see."'

48   List, *The National System of Political Economy*, p. 293.

49   Thus, following List, Griffith declares that *The Wealth of Nations* 'was, is and will remain the best example of a subtle scheme for English world-conquest put forward under the guise of an essay on political economy flavoured with that love of man which hooks in sentimentalists of all countries' ('Pitt's Policy: Imperialism and Ireland', p. 122).

50   List, *The National System of Political Economy*, pp. 296–97.

51   Ibid., p. 297. Griffith cites this conclusion in 'Pitt's Policy: Imperialism and Ireland', p. 122.

52   List, *The National System of Political Economy*, pp. 339–40.

53   Griffith, 'Pitt's Policy: Imperialism and Ireland', p. 120.

54   Ibid., p. 137.

55   Ibid., p. 138.

56   Ibid.

57   Norman Angell, *The Great Illusion: A Study of the Relation of Military Power in Nations to their Social and Economic Advantage* (London: 1910), pp. 103, 108, 204, 257.

58   P. S. O'Hegarty, *A Short Memoir of Terence MacSwiney* (Dublin and London: 1922).

59 Terence MacSwiney, *Principles of Freedom* (Dublin: 1921), pp. 191, 197–98.

60 Ibid., pp. 202, 25.

61 For the idiom, see Quentin Skinner's treatment of 'neo-roman' elements in the thought of Milton and Harrington deriving from the *sententiae* of such Roman historians and moralists as Livy and Seneca in *Liberty before Liberalism* (Cambridge: 1998). Patrick Maume, in *The Long Gestation: Irish Nationalist Life, 1891–1918* (Dublin: 1999), p. 50, has situated elements of Griffith's teaching within this same 'classical republican ethos of self-sacrifice.'

62 MacSwiney, *Principles of Freedom*, pp. 26–27, 34.

63 Ibid., p. 111.

64 It is worth recalling in this context that the editorial to the first issue of *Republican News*, June 1970, read: 'We shall preach the Gospel of Tone in seeking to unite all our people, Protestant, Catholic and Dissenter in the common cause of our Nation's unity and independence.' Again, in the August 1970 edition, Jimmy Steele refers to the casualties of 14 and 15 August 1969, as 'victims of the senseless sectarian outlook fostered by those whom Wolfe Tone described as the cause of all our political evils – the evils of British rule and British Imperialism'.

65 See the remarks of Seamus Loughran, 'Long Kesh Prison Camp', *Republican News*, 13 October 1972, the typicality of which is by this stage well-established: the British Army in Northern Ireland since 1920 is presented as ensuring that 'one end [was] attained, and the end was the division of the Irish people, following the "divide and conquer" policy that Britain has maintained all over the world'.

66 MacSwiney, *Principles of Freedom*, p. viii.

67 Ibid., p. 198.

68 Niccolò Machiavelli, *The Prince*, in *The Chief Works and Others*, trans. Alan Gilbert (Durham: 1989), 3 vols, I, pp. 12–16.

69 MacSwiney, *Principles of Freedom*, p. 199. In fact, in the passage under review, Machiavelli is considering the options open to an opportunistic and powerful intruder upon a scene of conquest for turning the situation to his own advantage and, in general terms, he actually cautions against the method of 'divide and conquer' – as he wrote at XX, iii: 'I do not believe that divisions ever do any good; on the contrary, when the enemy approaches, divided cities are lost at once; because the weaker party always takes the side of the foreign troops, and the other cannot resist' (p. 78).

70 MacSwiney, *Principles of Freedom*, pp. vii–viii.

71 Ibid., p. viii.

72   For recent discussion of the 1798 Rebellion, see in particular Ian McBride, *Scripture Politics: Ulster Presbyterians and Irish Radicalism in the Late Eighteenth Century* (Oxford: 1998); Roy Foster, 'Remembering 1798', in Ian McBride ed., *History and Memory in Modern Ireland* (Cambridge: 2001). For the view that the Rebellion momentarily transcended established sectarian divisions, see Kevin Whelan, *The Tree of Liberty: Radicalism, Catholicism and the Construction of Irish Identity, 1760–1830* (Cork: 1996). For a review of the literature since then, see Ian McBride, 'Reclaiming the Rebellion: 1798 in 1998', *Irish Historical Studies* (May 1999), pp. 395–410.

73   Theobald Wolfe Tone, *Journals, Notes, Letters, Memorandums, 1789–1795*, in Bartlett ed., *Life of Theobald Wolfe Tone*, p. 236. The position outlined here is, of course, a revision of Tone's original public statement on the subject as presented in 1791: in his *Argument on Behalf of the Catholics of Ireland* (ibid., p. 270) the 'disgrace' of Ireland's situation is traced to 'our evil government' as its 'proximate cause', but the 'remote one' is said to be 'our own intestine division which, if once removed, the former will be instantaneously removed'.

74   *Two Memorials on the Present State of Ireland, Delivered to the French Government, February 1796*, ibid., pp. 604–5.

75   Ibid., p. 605.

76   Wolfe Tone, *An Argument on Behalf of the Catholics of Ireland*, ibid., pp. 284, 296: 'a nation governed by herself will pursue her interests more steadily than if she were governed by another', while the national interest is only to be secured by 'an honest and independent representation of the people'.

77   Thomas Paine, *The Rights of Man, Part II*, in Bruce Kuklick ed., *Political Writings* (Cambridge: 1989), p. 168.

78   Ibid., pp. 173, 168.

V Politics: 1972–1998

1   Bobby Sands, 'Diary', 1 March 1981, in *Writings from Prison* (Cork: 1998), p. 219.

2   As Seamus Deane, 'Civilians and Barbarians' (1983) in *Ireland's Field Day* (London: 1985), p. 42, was later to comment: 'for a time it seemed as if [the hunger strikes] might change everything'. For prisoners' reactions in the aftermath of 1981, see Laurence McKeown, *Out of Time: Irish Republican Prisoners, Long Kesh 1972–2000* (Belfast: 2001); Brian Campbell, Laurence McKeown and Felim O'Hagan eds, *Nor*

Meekly Serve My Time: The H-Block Struggle, 1976–1981 (Belfast: 1998); Padraig O'Malley, *The Uncivil Wars: Ireland Today* (Belfast: 1983).

3   Quoted in Peter Taylor, *Provos: The IRA and Sinn Féin* (London: 1997, 1998), p. 243. However, on the other side, Sands himself had displayed an altogether more thoroughgoing confidence. See his comment, recorded in *One Day in My Life* (Cork: 1983), p. 118: 'They have nothing in their entire imperial arsenal to break the spirit of one single Republican Political Prisoner-of-War who refuses to be broken.'

4   Quoted in David Beresford, *Ten Men Dead: The Story of the 1981 Hunger Strike* (London: 1987), p. 138.

5   Quoted in Patrick Bishop and Eamonn Mallie, *The Provisional IRA* (London: 1987), p. 301.

6   Interview with Jim Gibney: http://www.pbs.org.

7   Interview with Seán MacStiofáin, recorded in Rosita Sweetman, *On Our Knees: Ireland 1972* (London: 1972), p. 156. See also the assessment by Maria Maguire in *To Take Up Arms: A Year in the Provisional IRA* (London: 1973), p. 32: 'MacStiofáin . . . was visibly bored by the arguments for the need of a political campaign.' This, however, did not so much make MacStiofáin anti-political as an ideological fundamentalist in politics. As the veteran Belfast Republican, John Kelly, commented: MacStiofáin 'was difficult to distract from an objective once he saw his way towards an objective. He always believed that every military operation should have a political objective' (Interview with John Kelly, http://www.pbs.org).

8   Interview with Jim Gibney, op. cit.: 'it was probably one of the high points in terms of convincing Republicans of the merits of electoral politics'.

9   Interview with Seamus Kerr: http://www.pbs.org.

10 Jim Gibney, in an interview with the author, commented that the party had not yet 'internalised' the opportunities opened up by the hunger strike elections (February 2003).

11 Kevin Kelley, *The Longest War: Northern Ireland and the IRA* (Kerry: 1983), pp. 300–20.

12 See Gerry Adams, *Before the Dawn: An Autobiography* (London: 1996), pp. 283, 284, on electoralism and the politics of the 'struggle'. Ed Moloney, *A Secret History of the IRA* (London: 2002), p. 202, has claimed that it was Bernadette Devlin's candidacy in the European elections of June 1979 that acted as 'the spur' for Adams' own 'turn-around on electoral politics'. However, no such turn-around in fact occurred: Devlin achieved electoral success despite a small share of the

vote, and – according to Jim Gibney – the result, if anything, 'reinforced opposition' to electoralism within the Republican movement (Gibney Interview with the author, February 2003). Those who were committed to the idea of an electoral strategy had committed themselves before 1979, and they included Gerry Adams, Danny Morrison, Jim McGivern, Francie Molloy and Jim Gibney. But these figures were, in terms of the whole movement, 'out on their own', as Gibney put it (ibid.). Danny Morrison has claimed that he first seriously considered the merits of electoral politics in 1977 (Interview with the author, February 2003). While both he and Jimmy Drumm spoke against a motion at the 1980 Sinn Féin Ard Fheis brought by McGivern and Molloy favouring participation in electoral contests, he had been 'disciplined' to do so: together with other associates of Adams, he was keen to make the transition to electoralism, but they 'didn't know how the transition could be made' (Morrison, ibid.). For Adams' open-mindedness, as far back as 1975, on the issue of Republican participation in electoral politics, see 'Brownie' [Gerry Adams], 'Active Abstentionism', *Republican News*, 18 October 1975. There, Adams' keen awareness that Republicanism had lost vital ground to the SDLP through its political passivity and its opposition to electoralism is ventriloquised in the form of a fictional dialogue between a Long Kesh inmate and the 'man-in-the-street': 'sez Mr. Man-in-the-street [i.e. Adams] . . . "while the SDLP and other unionists monopolise elections I'm afraid the ordinary Nationalist will always opt for the lesser of two evils offered and plump for the SDLP"'.

13   As the recently amalgamated *An Phoblacht–Republican News* commented on 27 October 1979: 'Conditions placed by the republican movement in the past, for political campaigns to also support the armed struggle, no longer apply.'

14   An assortment of pamphlets were produced around this time from the various sections of the National H-Block/Armagh Committee. *Trade Unions and the H Block* (Belfast: 1980), p. 2, was typical of the attempt to achieve a broad, humanitarian appeal: 'the prisoners in the H-Blocks are far from being the psychopathic thugs which they are portrayed as by the propaganda of the British government's Northern Ireland Office'.

15   Quoted in Beresford, *Ten Men Dead*, p. 255.

16   Quoted in Brendan O'Brien, *The Long War: The IRA and Sinn Féin* (Dublin: 1993, 1999), p. 111.

17   The merger was launched with an article, 'Out of the Ashes', printed

in *An Phoblacht–Republican News*, 27 January 1979, which announced: 'One paper, one message . . . we the nationally dispossessed . . . are in the business of achieving power and establishing a real democracy.'

18   The message, crafted in 1975 and put into operation by 1978, was being skilfully disseminated through *Republican News*, between 1976 and 1977, under the editorship of Danny Morrison. See, for instance, the comments by an 'Andersonstown POW' in 'For a Nation's Freedom', *Republican News*, 21 August 1976: 'the Republican Movement can only succeed under the direct revolutionary leadership of the Republican Army and also with the full support of the working class people . . . the members of the Republican Movement not only belong to the people – they are the people . . . the Irish Republican Army is a people's Army'. Within six months, the argument was being more programmatically espoused by 'Vindicator' [Gerry Brannigan] in 'Power to the People', *Republican News*, 15 January 1977: '1977 must be the year of consolidation and politicisation within the Nationalist ghetto areas.'

19   In other words, IRA operatives would be militarily isolated while the dissemination of Republicanism would ensure that they were politically supported. The 'British government's attempt to depoliticise the Republican Movement during the period of the bi-lateral truce [i.e. through 1975] is now seen to have failed,' declared 'Vindicator' [Gerry Brannigan] in 'Peace Movement: Kitson in Action', *Republican News*, 21 August 1976. In the same year, back on 21 February, in an article, 'Social Republicanism' in *Republican News*, Pat Shannon 'POW' had insisted that 'physical force alone was insufficient' to secure victory: 'But, notwithstanding our magnificent achievements over the past five years, we often fail to activate the mass backing which alone could make the struggle more effective.' This, Shannon claimed, had been the position advanced originally by Liam Mellows 'who PROPHETICALLY claimed that a revolutionary situation cannot be judged in terms of men and guns alone . . . Mellows considered everything within a political context.' The following month, on 27 March, Peter Arnlis [Danny Morrison], in 'Nature of Strategy, Politics, Revolution, British Withdrawal', printed in the same organ, was already claiming progress in this regard: 'Above all, we have the people. This is the substance of real power.' 'Brownie' [Gerry Adams], in 'The National Alternative', *Republican News*, 3 April 1976, then focused on the long term strategic possibilities created by popular politicisation. As was frequently the case with Adams, the argument is again ventriloquised: '"Your man" speaks: "as the Brit seeks to isolate us, we instinctively become immersed with the local people"'. But this

immersion was to be pursued as a political, and not a military exercise.

20   *Republican News*, 9 December 1978.

21   Some of the details of the overhaul of the Republican movement were made public in an interview with a 'Senior Member of the IRA Leadership' which originally appeared in *Magill* magazine and was reprinted in *Republican News* on 5 August 1978: '[Last year] we undertook a massive reorganisation of the movement in which we displaced the old locally-based pyramid structure of the IRA and set up a cell system . . . We don't have as many volunteers as we did five or six years ago and this is no bad thing. People were joining for all the wrong reasons . . . Now we have a much more politicised volunteer corps.' Much of this detail, however, had already been publicised since a document discovered in the possession of Seamus Twomey was released after his arrest at the end of 1977. As quoted in Liam Clark, *Broadening the Battlefield: The H-Blocks and the Rise of Sinn Féin* (Dublin: 1987), p. 253, a part of the document reads: 'Sinn Féin should come under Army organisers at all levels. Sinn Féin should employ full-time organisers in big republican areas. Sinn Féin should be radicalised (under army direction) and should agitate about social and economic issues which attack the welfare of the people.'

22   The Revolutionary Council came into existence in the period around 1976–77. It was intended by Ivor Bell that this organ of revolution replace the established Army Council by acting as a mini-Army Convention, but it was the Revolutionary Council that was the first to expire after the 'Young Turks' from Belfast and Derry had gained an effective ascendancy over their opponents in the movement. The fullest account of the military reconstruction of the IRA after 1976 is given in Moloney, *A Secret History of the IRA*, pp. 152–62.

23   For an account, see Liam Clarke and Kathryn Johnston, *Martin McGuinness: From Guns to Government* (Edinburgh: 2001, pp. 95–98.

24   The following sequencing is alleged by Moloney, *A Secret History of the IRA*, Appendix V: Seán MacStiofáin, Chief of Staff, December 1969–November 1972; Joe Cahill, Chief of Staff, November 1972–March 1973; Seamus Twomey, Chief of Staff, March 1973–June 1973; Eamon Doherty, Chief of Staff, June 1973–June/July 1974; Seamus Twomey, Chief of Staff, July 1974–December 1977; Gerry Adams, Chief of Staff, December 1977–February 1978; Martin McGuinness, Chief of Staff, February 1978 to autumn 1982; Ivor Bell, Chief of Staff, autumn 1982 to September 1983; Kevin McKenna, Chief of Staff, September 1983–October 1997; Tom Murphy, Chief of Staff, October 1997– .

25　The Provisional IRA's Army Council is a seven-person committee that decides on Army policy, while the executive is a thirteen-person body that elects the Army Council.

26　It should be recalled that the proposal to end the policy of abstention back in the late 1960s had been one of the principal reasons for the IRA split of December 1969 and the formation of the Provisionals.

27　A General Army Convention is a delegate meeting of the IRA membership constituting the supreme authority over the organisation entitled to revise its constitution and elect the Army Executive.

28　Quoted in Brian Feeney, *Sinn Féin: A Hundred Turbulent Years* (Dublin: 2002), p. 332.

29　Adams, *Before the Dawn*, p. 318.

30　PRO, CJ 3/98, 'Record of a Meeting between the SDLP and UK Representative in Northern Ireland', 11 April 1972.

31　PRO, PREM 15/1009, 'Note of a Meeting between John Hume and Paddy Devlin, and William Whitelaw', 15 June 1972. The transcript of a secret conversation held in early May 1972 between the Southern Provisional, Myles Shevlin, and R. J. C. Evans of the British Embassy in Dublin, records Shevlin delivering pretty much the same message: 'The end of internment in the North would be the best thing for the British and the worst thing for us' (PRO FCO, 87/2).

32　PRO, PREM 15/1011, 'Memorandum on Preventive Detention for Terrorist Offences', July 1972: 'Any action we take must be such as not to alienate the minority community as a whole: a consideration which must rule out the further use of internment in the arbitrary form which it now takes under the Special Powers Act.' Of course, there had been doubts from the very start in both the British government and the Army about the wisdom of Faulkner's resort to internment without trial. Nonetheless, on 16 August, a week after internment had been put into operation, it was being argued in the British Cabinet that the 'arrests had achieved a large measure of success, and about half the leaders of the Irish Republican Army had been apprehended'. However, regrets about the measure were in evidence at an early stage. On 21 September 1971, the Secretary of State for Defence reported to the Cabinet that it was 'too early to say that internment had failed'. But, at a Cabinet discussion on 29 September in the same year, the view was expressed that there would 'be obvious political advantages if further IRA suspects could be charged with offences rather than interned' (PRO, CAB 128/48).

33　PRO, CAB 128/48, 2 March 1972.

34　Ibid., 3 February 1972.

35 Ibid., 2 September 1971: 'The Prime Minister, summing up the discussion, said that the Government's fundamental purpose must be to secure a situation in which the objective of participation by the minority in the life of the community could be pursued by reasonable and constructive discussion.' What participation 'in the life of the community' might mean had been floated at a Cabinet meeting held in the aftermath of internment: on 16 August 1971 it was being argued that representatives from Unionism and nationalism should meet with the Home Secretary 'to devise further means of giving representatives of the minority, as well as the majority, an active and prominent role in the processes of government and administration' (ibid.).

36 Ibid., 3 February 1972. There was still, however, a degree of dissent within the Cabinet: on 7 March 1972, it was argued 'in discussion' that '"Community Government", with statutory allocation of Cabinet portfolios according to the representation of Parties in the Northern Ireland House of Commons could not be reconciled with the democratic concept of responsibility to a Parliamentary majority' (Ibid.).

37 Even nine months earlier, there is evidence that sections of the Provisional movement were anxious about the level of public support they enjoyed, especially in the South. In May of that year, after the opposition to joining the European Common Market in the Republic of Ireland had succeeded in garnering only 17 per cent of the vote despite Sinn Féin's own publicly expressed antipathy to the EEC, Ruairí Ó Brádaigh's disappointment was made all too apparent in a private conversation with the independent Stormont Unionist MP Tom Caldwell, a transcript of which was forwarded to the British government. 'This has been a bad week for Sinn Féin,' Ó Brádaigh admitted: a better result, he went on, 'would have given us political respectability; it would have stalled [Jack] Lynch . . . Had we achieved a respectable result we could have emerged as a political party in the South as well as in the North. We had hopes of entering the Local Government elections in the North this autumn. I would say that's completely out now' (PRO, FCO 87/2, 'Transcript of Conversation between Tom Caldwell M. P. and Ruairí Ó Brádaigh', May 1972).

38 The assessment by the British Commander of Land Forces in Northern Ireland, Major-General Robert Ford, of the attitude prevailing within the Provisional IRA at this time is entirely fanciful: 'Their morale at the moment is very low,' he was happy to report, although Derry still remained 'an intolerable problem' (PRO, FCO 87/2, R. C. Ford, 'The Campaign against the IRA: An Assessment of the Current Operational Situation', 20 March 1972).

39   More precisely, 'special category status' had been granted since, as P. J.
      Woodfield (representing William Whitelaw) had explained to Gerry
      Adams and David O'Connell at a secret meeting in June, 'political
      status' 'was not a concept known to the law' (PRO, PREM 15/1009,
      'Note of a Meeting with Representatives of the Provisional IRA', 21
      June 1972).

40   William Whitelaw, *The Whitelaw Memoirs* (London: 1989), p. 100. A
      confidential report of the meeting sent to the Prime Minister's Office
      recorded that Whitelaw 'was clearly depressed at the outcome of the
      meeting' (PRO, PREM 15/1011). After all, a meeting held on 21 June
      1972 between a senior Northern Ireland Office official, P. J.
      Woodfield, and David O'Connell and Gerry Adams, resulted in a note
      to Edward Heath's office declaring that 'these two at least genuinely
      want a cease fire and a permanent end to violence' (ibid., 15/1009). A
      message delivered from Whitehall to the British Ambassador in
      Dublin in the wake of the talks with the IRA delegation gives a clear
      impression of the British intelligence assessment of the key players in
      the Provisionals at this time: 'You should urge that the Irish govern-
      ment use every effort to arrest those hardliners who can think only in
      terms of violence . . . e.g. Stephenson [i.e. MacStiofáin], Cahill,
      Twomey, Meehan . . . by our appreciation of the personalities
      involved, O'Connell may still have reservations about violence, and be
      prepared to shift to peaceful political action . . . the hawks must be
      removed if the doves are to exercise their influence' (PRO, FCO 87/2,
      Sir John Crawford to Sir John Peck, 13 July 1972). The reaction of the
      IRA negotiating team to the talks is presented in Taylor, *Provos*, pp.
      140–47.

41   PRO, PREM 15/101, Letter from the Taoiseach to Edward Heath, 11
      August 1970. It is, however, notable that real fear underlay the hard-
      line public stance put forward by the Irish government. The previous
      month, a telegram from the British Embassy in Dublin to the Foreign
      and Commonwealth Office communicated 'the strongest impression'
      on the part of R. J. C. Evans that 'Lynch and Hillery . . . are terrified
      that the worsening of the situation in the North caused by the imminent
      Orange Order Parades would topple the Dublin Government through
      pressure of public opinion in the South and that Civil War would
      follow' (PRO, PREM 15/100, 6 July 1970).

42   PRO, CAB 128/48, Cabinet Meeting of 9 September 1971: Heath is
      reporting the substance of his meeting with the Irish premier at
      Chequers on 6 and 7 September.

43   Ibid., 3 February 1972: Heath reports that after Bloody Sunday such

optimism as had been displayed by Jack Lynch had now been overtaken by events, but that up until then the Taoiseach had held the view that the best time to push for an agreement was when the strength of the Belfast Provisionals was depleted 'but the Protestant community were [*sic*] still sufficiently apprehensive of violence to be prepared to offer a measure of compromise'.

44   PRO, PREM 15/1011, Telegram from John Peck, originally sent to the Foreign and Commonwealth Office in London, 31 July 1972: Lynch's answer to a question about the importance of Irish unity 'amounted to saying that he could not care less. As far as he was concerned, he wanted peace and justice in the North and close friendship and cooperation with us.'

45   'What Next', *Republican News*, 10 March 1973. 'This sort of fight', the article went on, 'it lost in Palestine, Cyprus, Aden and elsewhere.'

46   PRO, CAB 128/48, 7 March 1972.

47   'Brownie' [Gerry Adams] was to concede as much a little later in 'A Review of the Present Situation — Past, Present and Future', *Republican News*, 14 August 1976: 'We have seven years of war behind us and perhaps another seven years before us, that is if we are not defeated before then.'

48   The most detailed account of the British and the IRA positions during the truce is given in Taylor, *Provos*, pp. 177–97. But whatever the insistence on the part of the old-guard leadership of the Provisionals to the effect that 'structures of disengagement' had been productively discussed between the United Kingdom government and Republicans during the truce, the negative verdict passed on the ceasefire by the generation of younger IRA militants was soon clear. Peter Dowling's [Phil Shimeld's] response in 'Open or Closed', *Republican News*, 9 July 1977, was typical: 'The following question needs to be asked. How many people were confused about the 1975 Truce? What about the frustrating questions in the visiting cubicles of the Kesh [i.e. Long Kesh prison camp]. Was it enough to say, "Well, someone must know?"' A month earlier, during the annual Bodenstown Oration, delivered by Jimmy Drumm but written by Gerry Adams and Danny Morrison, and reprinted in *Republican News*, 18 June 1977, the public criticism was more emphatic still: 'The British Government is NOT withdrawing from the 6 counties and the substantial pull-out of business and the closing down of factories were due to the world recession though mistakenly attributed to symptoms of withdrawal. Indeed the British Government is committed to stabilising the 6 counties.' In this vein, a 'Senior Member of the IRA Leadership'

commented in an interview reprinted in *Republican News* on 5 August 1978 that there 'is absolutely no question of another ceasefire or truce. In my opinion the last one went on far too long . . . It appears that the British intention [during the truce] was to "educate" the representatives of the Republican Movement in the "realities" of their "very difficult" situation in the north of Ireland.'

49   The success enjoyed by the Peace Movement provoked an agitated response from 'Brownie' [Gerry Adams] in 'Peace', *Republican News*, 11 September 1976. Much of the article was republished verbatim in pamphlet form in his *Peace in Ireland: A Broad Analysis of the Present Situation* (Belfast: 1976). The pamphlet was subsequently reviewed in *Republican News*, 9 October 1976.

50   A recent account of these developments is given by Chris Ryder, *Inside the Maze: The Untold Story of the Northern Ireland Prison Service* (London: 2000, 2001), pp. 147–67.

51   On these developments, see Martin Dillon, *The Dirty War* (London: 1990); Mark Urban, *Big Boys' Rules: The Secret Struggle against the IRA* (London: 1992); Toby Harnden, *'Bandit Country': The IRA and South Armagh* (London: 1999).

52   R. G. McAuley, 'Republican Movement Alive to Importance of Political Status', *Republican News*, 12 June 1976. The same connection between Republican politicisation and 'Political Status' had already been made by 'Brownie' [Gerry Adams] through the character of 'Cedric' in a mock-prison debate presented in 'The National Alternative', *Republican News*, 3 April 1976: 'Like we don't really need to make that distinction [between politics and war] here 'cos we're all Volunteers claiming *political* status because of our *military* actions.'

53   R. G. McAuley, 'Political Status', *Republican News*, 4 December 1976.

54   Solon, 'Naked Colonialism', *Republican News*, 18 June 1977. Frank Kitson, who had served in the British Army in Northern Ireland in the early 1970s, had conceded as much in a book which Republicans regularly consulted in the prisons – *Low Intensity Operations: Subversion, Insurgency, Peace-Keeping* (London: 1971). See, for example, p. 29: 'no campaign of subversion will make headway unless it is based on a cause with a wide popular appeal'. But the point was already platitudinous in 1971. See Richard Clutterbuck, *The Long Long War: The Emergency in Malaya, 1948–1960* (London: 1966), p. 4: 'Counter-insurgency has been headline news for so long that such phrases as "winning hearts and minds" and "separating the guerrillas from the people" have become platitudes.'

55   See 'Vindicator' [Gerry Brannigan], 'Ulsterisation', *Republican News*,

29 May 1976: 'We must realise that the real political initiative lies with us . . . By giving the people a platform from which they can launch their own affairs, with a positive and constructive role to play . . . we can ensure that the people will develop that political awareness which will prevent their exploitation by British imperialism.' The same author put the same case again in 'Politics Means People', *Republican News*, 22 January 1977: 'The success of any revolutionary struggle depends on the revolutionary's ability to "mobilise" the people on the issues on which the war is being fought.'

56 'Brownie' [Gerry Adams], 'The Republic: A Reality', *Republican News*, 29 October 1975. Adams underlined the point by repeating it in a call for a 'complete fusing of military and political thinking' through the persona of 'Cedric' in 'The National Alternative', *Republican News*, 3 April 1976. The same strategy had been proposed by Amilcar Cabral, *Revolution in Guinea: An African People's Struggle* (London: 1969, 1974), pp. 82, 118: 'the only effective way of definitively fulfilling the aspirations of the people, that is to say of attaining national liberation, is by armed struggle . . . The political and military leadership of the struggle is one: the political leadership.' In 'Solidarity Brothers', *Republican News*, 2 October 1976, Adams had written that 'while persisting in resistance against the Brits, Republicans could do worse than to listen to Amilcar Cabral'. Cabral's argument was, however, a standard example of militant national liberation strategy in parts of Africa and South America in the 1960s. See Carlos Marighela, *For the Liberation of Brazil* (Harmondsworth: 1971), p. 59: 'We do not have a separate military policy subordinated to the political. Our policy is a total revolutionary policy combining military and political policy as a single entity.' But Adams had certainly read Marighela too. See ibid., p. 89, 'The work of armed propaganda really means the sum total of the actions achieved by urban guerrillas', and compare with Gerry Adams, *The Politics of Irish Freedom* (Dingle: 1986), p. 64, 'in effect, the armed struggle becomes armed propaganda'. By 1980, a pamphlet issued by Republican prisoners in the Maze – *The H-Blocks: The New Internment* (Belfast: 1980) – supplied its own bibliography of literature on guerrilla warfare and political strategy, listing the following as essential reading: Charles Foley, *The Memoirs of General Grivas* (London: 1964); Charles Foley, *The Legacy of Strife: Cyprus from Rebellion to Civil War* (London: 1962); Mohamed Amin and Malcolm Caldwell eds, *Malaya: The Making of a Neo-Colony* (London: 1977); Donald L. Barrett and K. Njama, *Mau Mau from Within* (London: 1966); and Anthony Clayton, *Counter-Insurgency in Kenya, 1952–1960*

(Nairobi: 1976). Testimony to the importance of Grivas to Provisional strategy in the early 1970s is given by a Republican representative in an interview conducted in 1971: see 'The Provos' Tactical War', *This Week*, 12 March 1971.

57 'Brownie' [Gerry Adams], 'The Republic: A Reality', *Republican News*, 29 October 1975.

58 Peter Arnlis [Danny Morrison], 'Nature of Strategy, Politics, Revolution, British Withdrawal', *Republican News*, 27 March 1976.

59 'Brownie' [Gerry Adams], 'Active Abstentionism', *Republican News*, 18 October 1975. Adams went on to elaborate on the 'implementation policy' itself: 'In Belfast alone, could not the three or four big nationalist areas be organised into community councils . . . And could these three or four completed councils not then unite into a City Council?' Adams was conscious of the precedent set by Arthur Griffith and Sinn Féin between 1904 and 1919. In the same article, writing with reference to British plans to establish a Northern Ireland Convention in 1975, Adams recalled the situation in Ireland between 1917 and 1919: 'In June 1917 the Brits held an "Irish Convention". Sinn Féin boycotted it – the Convention failed! In January 1919 Sinn Féin established Dáil Éireann as an alternative with Republicans in the overwhelming majority.' A month later, in 'The Republic: A Reality', *Republican News*, 29 October 1975, Adams was pointing to the ceding of political initiative on the part of the irregular Irish Republican Army after 1922 to the Free State forces as one of the most significant reasons for the defeat of Republicans in the Irish Civil War: 'the fact that the Free State established their institutions of Government and forced the Republicans into an "irregular" position cannot be ignored as a major reason for the defeat of the Republic'.

60 The need for a 'rallying point' was proposed by 'Brownie' [Gerry Adams] in 'The Republic: A Reality', *Republican News*, 29 November 1975. The sentence is a modification of a plea from Liam Mellows, which Adams quotes: '"Where is the Government of the Republic? It must be found. Republicans must be provided with a rallying point and the Movement with a focussing point" . . . Today [1975] that position remains unchanged.' In 'Active Abstentionism', *Republican News*, 18 October 1975, Adams had put his case in the following terms: 'We need an alternative to the British (and Freestate [*sic*]) Administrations in our country, especially now in the 6 counties and when the Republican Movement has control to some degree in all the Nationalist areas. So why not cement this into a local Government structure?' The People's Councils idea was still being floated two years later. See Peter

Dowling [Phil Shimeld], 'The Road to People's Assemblies', *Republican News*, 19 February 1977; 'Scopoli', 'People's Assemblies', *Republican News*, 5 March 1977; 'Thoughts on Eire Nua', *Republican News*, 5 November 1977. The argument that Republicanism must be based upon the 'understandings and needs' of the 'people of no property' was set out by 'Brownie' [Gerry Adams] in 'Conscience', *Republican News*, 21 February 1976, where a quotation from Liam Mellows once again sets the terms of the debate: 'the "stake in the country" people were never with the Republic', as Mellows put it in Adams' citation. 'They are not with it now and they will always be against it – until it wins! We should recognise that definitely now, and base our appeals on the understandings and needs of those who have always borne Ireland's fight.' The identification of 'ordinary people' and the 'people of no property' as the natural constituency of Provisional Republicanism is likewise proposed in 'Solon', 'The Men of No Property', *Republican News*, 26 March 1977; and 'Easter Message from the Republican Movement', *Republican News*, 16 April 1977.

61 'Brownie' [Gerry Adams], 'A Review of the Present Situation', *Republican News*, 14 August 1976. The previous spring, in 'Active Republicanism', *Republican News*, 1 May 1976, Adams had been hammering away at the same theme: 'They [the people] are our fight, and our fight must be based among them . . . Their enemy must therefore be our enemy, their needs must be our needs, our Republicanism.'

62 PRO, PREM 15/1011, 'Briefing to the Prime Minister by Burke Trend', 31 July 1972: 'A high level of control has been established in the former "no-go" areas of Belfast and Londonderry, and in other major trouble spots throughout the Province . . . The IRA appear to have gone to ground.'

63 'Interview with the Director, Republican Press Centre [Tom Hartley]', *Republican News*, 31 January 1976: 'The I.C.s [incident centres] symbolised something for the common people: they were turning to Incident Centres as local Parliaments.'

64 'Brownie' [Gerry Adams], 'The National Alternative', *Republican News*, 3 April 1976. The various ingredients of Provo power were itemised in the article by assorted characters in a semi-fictionalised Cage 11 dialogue: in particular, by 'Your Man' 'Joe' and 'Cedric', all of whom are presented as ultimately converging around the Adams line.

65 PRO, CAB 128/46, 19 August 1969, Confidential Annex. Part of Chichester-Clark's statement, delivered at a press conference on Sunday, 17 August 1969, reads: 'I am not rejecting . . . means of

achieving a broadly-based support for a return to peace and a resumption of progress' ('Statement by Chichester-Clark', Appendix V, *Violence and Civil Disturbances in Northern Ireland in 1969*, Scarman Report, HMSO Belfast: 1972, Cmd. 566, 2 vols, II, p. 41).

66 PRO, CJ 3/98, Frank Kitson, 'Future Developments in Belfast', Submitted to the Office of the UK Representative in Northern Ireland, 4 December 1971.

67 PRO, PREM 15/100, 'Notes by Burke Trend for a Meeting with the Chiefs of Staff', July 1970.

68 See the description supplied by Simon Winchester, *In Holy Terror: Reporting the Ulster Troubles* (London: 1974), p. 253: on their television screens, viewers 'saw a man – or rather, a heavy, bloody chunk of dirty meat – being shovelled . . . into a polythene bag . . . Gerry O'Hare, the IRA's chief press man . . . wept openly himself that day, as he confronted Twomey, the hatchet-faced bookie who had organised the affair. "What the hell am I going to tell them now?", O'Hare cried at the commander.'

69 PRO, PREM 15/1011, 'Memorandum to PM by Burke Trend', 26 July 1972, confirms that Operation Motorman was 'designed to take advantage of the mood of public opinion generated by the bombing atrocities of Friday, 21st July'. But up until the last there was debate about whether to proceed with the operation and, if the go-ahead was given, about how extensive the British occupation should be. As Trend put it, 'The first thing which ministers need to decide is whether this advantage should in fact be taken – or whether we should try to regard "Bloody Friday" as a hiccough in the middle of the détente deriving from the ceasefire.' Then, he advised, it had to be decided whether to concentrate on the Bogside and Creggan, or whether to include Belfast, 'especially Ballymurphy and Andersonstown'.

70 'Brownie' [Gerry Adams], 'Active Abstentionism', *Republican News*, 18 October 1975.

71 PRO, FCO 87/3, 'Handout issued by Oglaigh na hEireann [IRA] B Coy 2 BN, Ballymurphy' June 1972: 'Today we require the absolute assistance of the Irish people. In the district there will be mobile foot patrols . . . These patrols will be particularly vigilant throughout the night. In the affected areas the administering body [i.e. the IRA's B Company, Second Battalion] will coordinate law and order . . . An information and complaint centre will be established. By employing such tactics we become an administration reaching back to the Provisional Government of [the] Irish people which we have always [laid] claim to. Now it can be tested overtly.'

72 'Brownie' [Gerry Adams], 'Frank Stagg', *Republican News*, 10 January 1976.

73 Adams, *Politics of Irish Freedom*, p. 86.

74 Adams, *Before the Dawn*, p. 315.

75 Danny Morrison himself describes the Republican attitude of the 1970s and 1980s as 'purist' and 'fundamentalist' (Interview with the author, February 2003).

76 For the extent to which the 1981 hunger strikes confirmed Republicans in their established commitments, see the 'Statement issued by the Republican Prisoners in the Maze' on 3 October 1981 in the *Irish Times*, 5 October 1981: 'nationalist pacifism in the Northern Ireland context dooms the nationalist population to subservience, perpetuates partition and thwarts the quest for a just and lasting peace in Ireland'.

77 Standard accounts of the trajectory of the Irish peace process trace its origins to the key moment at which the Provisionals turned 'political'. See, for example, M. L. R. Smith, *Fighting for Ireland: The Military Strategy of the Irish Republican Movement* (London: 1995, 1997), pp. 148–68; Deaglán De Bréadún, *The Far Side of Revenge: Making Peace in Northern Ireland* (Cork: 2001), p. 5; Jeremy Smith, *Making the Peace in Ireland* (London: 2002), pp. 119–39. For a more sceptical approach, see Malachi O'Doherty, *The Trouble with Guns: Republican Strategy and the Provisional IRA* (Belfast: 1998), pp. 201–11. But the standard resort to this stark antithesis between 'war' and 'politics', with the latter somehow acting as a means to tame the former, is so blunt as to invite the most extreme misdiagnosis. See, for instance, Moloney, *A Secret History of the IRA*, pp. 149 and 245, who, on the basis of this schematic representation, discovers the 'seeds' of the Irish peace process back in 1976 and its advent in discussions between Gerry Adams and a Redemptorist priest in 1982.

78 An editorial in *An Phoblacht*, March 1970, set out the Provisionals' stall: 'We see a nation (and the people are the nation) asking for a new leadership which will put the interests of the people first.' What *actual* people 'the people' was intended to encompass were identified in an article for *Republican News*, January–February 1971: 'When making reference to the position here [in Northern Ireland] the British Government and the Stormont Government both in the last year use words such as Minority, Majority and Democracy when after 50 years they support Stormont's constitutional position financially and reinforce it with a show of arms to keep in existence a state formed undemocratically against the wishes of the majority of the Irish people.' For an appreciation of the 'political' nature of Republican

militarism, see Richard English, *Armed Struggle: A History of the IRA* (London: 2003), pp. 126–33.

79 For an articulation of this rival perspective, see the argument set forth in the Paisleyite pamphlet by Louis Gardner, *Resurgence of the Majority* (Belfast: 1970), p. 8: 'it is not possible to conceive the position of Irish Loyalists as anything other than a garrison, culturally and spiritually, divorced from a numerically superior and relentlessly hostile populace'. The embattled status of a majority besieged by a 'numerically superior' population is presented as the organising principle of 'Loyalist populism' (p. 31).

80 The attempt to explain Republican fundamentalism in terms of a fusion of religion and nationalism in Ireland has been the prime polemical objective of Conor Cruise O'Brien's numerous treatments of insurrectionary violence in Northern Ireland. See, for example, *States of Ireland* (London: 1972), p. 229; *Herod: Reflections on Political Violence* (London: 1978), p. 57; *Passion and Cunning: Essays on Nationalism, Terrorism and Revolution* (London: 1988), *passim*; and *Ancestral Voices: Religion and Nationalism in Ireland* (London: 1994), *passim*. A fusion of mysticism, heroism and ideas of sacrifice does indeed appear in the armoury of Irish nationalist rhetoric, as the literary careers of W. B. Yeats and Patrick Pearse amply testify. See, in particular, Patrick Pearse, *The Spiritual Nation* (1916), in *Collected Works of Patrick Pearse* (Dublin: 1922), 3 vols. In turn, Pearsean themes did make an appearance in *Republican News* in its early years. See, for example: 'We assert the authority of God from whom all social power comes and our belief in democracy is based on this' (23 June 1972). Or, more strikingly, see the reference to 'a country sanctified by the memory of brave and holy lives, whose history is one long record of noble and unselfish sacrifice, whose heart, even in the hour of her greatest sorrow, thrills at the thought of the love that has been given to her by saints and scholars and soldiers' (29 September 1972). These sentiments are, however, pretty much the exception in both *Republican News* and *An Phoblacht*. And in any case, they were, in the words of Danny Morrison, 'utterly unrepresentative' of the views of Northern Provisional operators on the ground (Interview with the author, February 2003). They certainly fail to explain the attitude of secular Republicans like Brian Keenan, Ivor Bell, and a host of others. More pointedly, the young militants who seized control of the Republican movement after 1976 – Adams, McGuinness, Hartley, Gibney, Morrison, et al. – explicitly opposed what they termed the 'theology' of Republicanism. O'Brien's thesis is therefore founded on an entirely

doubtful assumption. That assumption was driven by the idea that, since consensus is a standard feature of modern secular democracy, the failure of consensus can only be explained in terms of archaic, essentially religious, residues within modern culture. Nonetheless, on the devoutness of Gerry Adams, see Marcus Tanner, *Ireland's Holy Wars: The Struggle for A Nation's Soul, 1500–2000* (New Haven and London: 2001, 2003), p. 278. Also, on the general tendency 'to see society *sub specie consensus*' as a characteristically 'liberal' disposition, see Raymond Geuss, *History and Illusion in Politics* (Cambridge: 2001), p. 4.

81 By early 1970, a Whitehall civil servant was describing the IRA as 'split between the official leadership, which is Marxist in attitude and believes in political action, and the traditionalist believers in the gun'. The Report continues: 'There is strong support for the traditionalists in Northern Ireland and they are almost certainly better armed and more numerous now than they were last August' (PRO, CJ 3/5, Confidential Notes by A. J. Langdon, 10 March 1970). A year later, the British Ambassador in Dublin, John Peck, was informing the Foreign and Commonwealth Office in London that 'the Bradyites [i.e. Provisionals] appear to have little interest in the state to be set up after their triumph' (PRO, FCO 33/1593, 'Sinn Féin and the IRA', 16 February 1971). However, the actual position of the Provisionals can be gleaned from the fact that they had *every* interest in 'the state to be set up' in the wake of victory, but 'little interest' in how a newly established government would represent this new state.

82 Quoted in Brendan Anderson, *Joe Cahill: A Life in the IRA* (Dublin: 2002), p. 167. Evidently this 'theory' was successfully disseminated. See the comments by 'Dustin' in 'The Necessity of a Military Campaign', *Republican News*, 10 April 1976: 'Many of us now involved in the Republican Movement were, even in 1969–70, either totally uninterested in what had been going on [since 1962] . . . or we just didn't understand the situation . . . [until] we came to realise that "Northern Ireland" was an artificial state . . . Contrary to British propaganda, we are motivated by political ideology – Republicanism.'

83 'Socialism without National Liberation is a Farce', *Republican News*, 13 October 1972. Earlier in the same year, immediately following pro-rogation, a former Adjutant-General of the IRA, Myles Shevlin, had explained the implications of the IRA position in a comment to a British official in Dublin: 'The majority of the Irish people want a united Ireland and it is their will which must prevail' (PRO, FCO

87/3, 'Transcript of Secret Conversation', May 1972). Somewhat earlier still, the same argument had been presented by Frank Card [aka Proinsias MacAirt] in 'The Irish Question', *Republican News,* June 1971: 'If a minority of our whole national population can not accept the will of the majority where is Democracy?'

84   Recent assessments of Republican orientation in the wake of 1969 have missed precisely this point in insisting that the Provisionals were more a product of either exigent circumstances or of visceral sectarianism. See, for instance, Henry Patterson, *Ireland since 1939* (Oxford: 2002) p. 236: 'The cutting edge of the armed campaign was being provided by young working-class Catholics in Belfast, whose republicanism was more a product of the conflict with Protestants and the security forces since 1969 than any ideological commitment to a united Ireland or identification with the martyrs of 1916.' Similarly, Moloney, *A Secret History of the IRA*, p. 80, argues: 'the recruits who flocked to the ranks of the Provisionals were a new breed, motivated by an atavistic fear of loyalist violence and an overwhelming need to strike back'. Both authors are following the lead set by Anthony McIntyre, 'A Structural Analysis of Modern Irish Republicanism, 1969–73', DPhil, Queen's University (Belfast: 1999). Moloney quotes the former Belfast Commander, Brendan Hughes, to underline the point about exigency and defence: Catholics were 'being attacked by Loyalists, by B Specials, by the RUC, by the British Army, and there was a need to hit back. I mean I was in Bombay Street the morning after it was burned out' (p. 81). In addition, he quotes a former IRA prisoner, Micky McMullen, to suggest that for many Provisionals the incentive to 'strike back' was at base sectarian: 'a lot of my friends would have been trying to join the IRA and the rationale would be just to get stuck into the "Orangies" you know' (p. 81). However, the inescapable fact is that doctrine gave direction to popular responses on the ground, defining the objective and informing the strategies adopted by the movement as a military organisation.

85   Anderson, *Joe Cahill*, p. 169. In this context, it is worth noting that Republicans had launched petrol bomb attacks in the spring of 1969, and that grenade and bomb attacks by members of the IRA predated the assaults on Catholic enclaves in August 1969. For the petrol bombing of police stations in Belfast on 20 April 1969, see above, Chapter III. For the resort to gun and grenade attacks on Leeson Street in Belfast on 13 August 1969, see David Sharrock and Mark Devenport, *Man of Peace, Man of War: The Unauthorised Biography of Gerry Adams* (London: 1997), p. 58. For the attempt to explode nail

bombs on 14 and 15 August 1969, see 'Brownie' [Gerry Adams], 'The Firing Party', *Republican News*, 27 November 1976: 'He [i.e. Adams, remembering his escapades with fellow Republican, Liam McParland] thought of August 14th/15th, only a few months past. Cursed nail-bombs without detonators . . . An RUC Shorland car drove over one. Nothing happened.' Beyond this, the Provisionals went on the offensive early in 1970 without actually announcing this to their members. See Anderson, *Joe Cahill*, p. 190: 'the main body of volunteers would not have known about this'.

86   See Robin Evelegh, *Peace Keeping in a Democratic Society: The Lessons of Northern Ireland* (London: 1978), p. 17: 'In the Ulster troubles since 1969, the Army has acted as the instrument of Central Government rather than as independent officers of the law aiding the local civil authorities.'

87   Gibney, Interview with the author, February 2003.

88   'Brownie' [Gerry Adams], 'An Ard Fheis', *Republican News*, 18 September 1976.

89   'Brownie' [Gerry Adams], 'Agitate, Educate, Liberate', *Republican News*, 22 May 1976.

90   Jimmy Drumm, 'Bodenstown Oration', *Republican News*, 18 June 1977.

91   Morrison, Interview with the author, February 2003.

92   'Army Council Declaration', *Republican News*, 28 January 1978.

93   Feeney, *Sinn Féin*, pp. 322–23: the words are those of Jim Gibney.

94   Eamonn Mallie and David McKittrick, *Endgame in Ireland* (London: 2001), pp. 70–83.

95   In prison in 1991, the Provisional IRA member, Anthony MacIntyre, confronted Danny Morrison with the proposition that the 'war was over'. Morrison denied this by citing what he termed 'the party line' – implying that the decision to end the war had indeed been made, presumably some time before this, but that the official position remained otherwise (Morrison, Interview with the author, February 2003).

96   The text of the interview is reprinted in *Republican News*, 30 November 1974.

97   Paul Bew and Gordon Gillespie, *Northern Ireland: A Chronology of the Troubles, 1968–93* (Dublin: 1993), p. 240.

98   The *Northern Star*, August 1992, reported a statement from Jim Gibney that Sinn Féin expected a settlement to arise out of 'negotiations'.

99   'Presidential Address by Gerry Adams', Sinn Féin Ard Fheis, 18 April 1998.

100 'Brownie' [Gerry Adams], 'Why Died the Sons of Rosín Dubh?', *Republican News*, 10 January 1976.

101 'Brownie' [Gerry Adams], 'A State of Emergency', *Republican News*, 4 September 1976. For a similar verdict on the South, see 'Vindicator' [Gerry Brannigan], 'Internal Counter-Revolution', *Republican News*, 16 October 1976.

102 'Brownie' [Gerry Adams], 'The National Alternative', *Republican News*, 3 April 1976.

103 'Brownie' [Gerry Adams], 'Active Republicanism', *Republican News*, 1 May 1976: 'We, as Volunteers of the Republic, must become servants of the people. We must bring them with us because they are our Republic and it will only be as complete as they are'; 'Brownie' [Gerry Adams], 'The National Alternative', *Republican News*, 3 April 1976: 'The OC is the representative in the area and his duty therefore is to establish a "mini-republic" in his area and to coordinate, direct and push all Republican activity there.'

104 'Brownie' [Gerry Adams], 'Clearing the Decks', *Republican News*, 8 January 1977. See the comparable analysis offered by 'Vindicator' [Gerry Brannigan], 'Politics Means People', *Republican News*, 22 January 1977.

105 'Presidential Address by Gerry Adams', Sinn Féin Ard Fheis, 18 April 1998.

VI Prologue

1 Margaret Thatcher, *The Downing Street Years* (London: 1993, 1995), p. 384.

2 Back in the early 1970s, by comparison, informed opinion in Great Britain had been altogether less confident. See James Callaghan, *A House Divided: The Dilemma of Northern Ireland* (London: 1973), p. 100: 'I was brought up to believe that democracy's foundations and civilization's roots were embedded like rocks in our society. But I do not believe that any more.' Nonetheless, the extent to which Northern Ireland was seen by the British government as some kind of democracy after 1969 remains unclear. Preparing for the possible prorogation of Stormont in January and February 1969, a Home Office document talks about clearing the way 'for a return to fully democratic government and institutions in Northern Ireland', but without specifying whether this 'return' would involve introducing institutions of government different from those which had already been in

existence in Northern Ireland (PRO, CJ 3/39, 'Governor of Northern
Ireland: Administrative Instrument in Emergency', 15 January
1969–18 February 1969). Adding to this confusion, a year and a half
later Burke Trend was to comment in a brief for Edward Heath that
'Northern Ireland is . . . a Parliamentary democracy' (PRO, PREM
15/100, 'Background Brief for PM by Burke Trend', 23 June 1970).

3 In a pamphlet published at the start of the 'troubles' by the Ulster
Unionist Party, *Ulster: The Facts* (Belfast: 1969), p. 10, it was pointed
out that 'it is often not realised that the Northern Ireland government
has all along been supported by overwhelming majorities of votes at
successive elections'. But, five years later, another unionist organisation, the Ulster Workers' Council, identified one of its aims in a
Broadsheet (May 1974) as involving the attempt to seek a 'N. I.
Government which reflects democratically the hopes and aspirations
of all citizens in N. I. who believe in traditional democracy' (Linen
Hall Library, Belfast: Northern Ireland Political Literature). Twenty-
four years later, just four months before the negotiations for the Good
Friday Agreement were concluded, the liberal unionist, Basil McIvor,
Hope Deferred: Experiences of an Irish Unionist (Belfast: 1998), p. 154,
was looking forward to the re-establishment of what had been
disestablished in 1974: 'the 1973 powersharing experiment will be
reintroduced in one form or another, replacing direct rule from
Westminster. This will permit true democracy to work.' On the other
side, the Republican preoccupation with democracy was presented in a
lengthy article, 'Democracy in the New Ireland', *Republican News*, 19
January 1973, as 'taken and used by all politicians according to their
own particular preferences and methods'. For this writer, however,
modern democracy had to be a 'REPRESENTATIVE OR INDIRECT
DEMOCRACY' such as would 'cater for the greatest good for the
greatest possible number of people' on the island of Ireland. What this
meant for unionists was set out in an article for *Republican News*, 2
February 1973: 'democracy demands that the Unionists take their
rightful place in the New Irish State. Justification and precedent for
this can be found in the writings of Irish patriots, and also in French
history . . . The idea is found . . . in Article 3 of the Declaration of the
Rights of Man where it is formulated that sovereignty and authority
reside and originate in the nation, not any section of it.'

4 Ed Moloney, 'Opinion Divided over Decommissioning', *Sunday
Tribune*, 12 April 1998. See also Frank Millar, 'Trimble Remains in
Ditch over Arms', *Irish Times*, 29 December 1998: 'Mr Trimble's
difficulty, as Gerry Adams once put it, is that he seeks to reintroduce

the precondition Mr Donaldson failed to get on Good Friday. Most parties to the Agreement, and most commentators (this one included), agree that – on a literal and legalistic read – Sinn Féin has it right. Decommissioning is not stipulated as a precondition for the party's entry to the Executive. Nor, as Mr McCartney would argue, is there even a defined penalty exclusion clause if decommissioning has not happened over a two-year period.' On unionist consternation regarding decommissioning during the 1998 negotiations, see Henry Sinnerton, *David Ervine: Uncharted Waters* (Kerry: 2002).

5   Frank Millar, 'Pressures on Trimble Present Strong Challenge to Sinn Féin', *Irish Times*, 29 June 1998; Suzanne Breen, 'Anti-Pact Side Now Sure They Can Put Kibosh on Assembly's Key Decisions', *Irish Times*, 29 June 1998.

6   On the running of the referendum campaign in the North, see Quentin Oliver, *Working for 'Yes': The Story of the May 1998 Referendum in Northern Ireland* (Belfast: 1999).

7   'Lundy' is a reference to the Governor of Derry who, in 1689, had been prepared to negotiate the surrender of the city to the Catholic forces of James II.

8   *Irish Times*, 29 June 1998.

9   *The History-Makers*, BBC Radio Ulster, 22 January 1989. See also Paisley's comments, recorded in Padraig O'Malley, *The Uncivil Wars: Ireland Today* (Belfast: 1983), p. 196: 'I happen to be a democrat. I believe in the rule of the majority.'

10   On the details of Paisley's changing views of the Union, see below Chapters VII and VIII. The attitude of Paisley's Democratic Unionist Party to the talks process after the entry of Sinn Féin into the negotiations was outlined in its document, *Democracy – Not Dublin Rule* (April 1997). The party's assessment of the Agreement itself was presented in *Step by Step Guide to the Trimble/Adams Deal* (May 1998).

11   Robert McCartney, *What Must Be Done* (Belfast: 1986), pp. 1, 3. McCartney's position had been set out more fully the previous year, in *Liberty and Authority in Northern Ireland* (Derry: 1995), pp. 25–26: 'The true and essential Union is not an exclusive union of loyalists or protestants, but a union between peoples who believe in liberal democracy and civil and religious liberty for all in the fullest sense of a pluralist society.' McCartney was following what he took to have been the arguments of John Stuart Mill and Isaiah Berlin in defending the Union as a bastion of 'negative liberty' against Romantic nationalism. His meditations on this and similar themes are collected in his *Reflections on Liberty, Democracy and the Union* (Dublin: 2001). His

opposition to the Good Friday Agreement was presented in 'Yes There is an Alternative', *Parliamentary Brief* (May/June 1998). For a more academic attempt to identify the Union, rather than the Republic, with liberal democracy, see Arthur Aughey, *Under Siege: Ulster Unionism and the Anglo-Irish Agreement* (Belfast: 1989), pp. 146–57. For an attempt to retrieve McCartney's core political intuitions in the face of criticism, see Arthur Aughey, 'McCartney in the Wings', *Fortnight* (June 1995). For an analysis of the occlusions evident in McCartney's and Aughey's theses, see Norman Porter, *Rethinking Unionism: An Alternative Vision for Northern Ireland* (Belfast: 1996, 1998), pp. 127–68. For the philosophical foundations of Porter's own criticism of McCartney and Aughey, see Charles Taylor, 'What's Wrong with Negative Liberty', in Alan Ryan ed., *The Idea of Freedom* (Oxford: 1979); for a reconstruction of the historical parameters of debates about 'types' of liberty, see Quentin Skinner, 'The Idea of Negative Liberty: Machiavellian and Modern Perspectives', in *Visions of Politics: Renaissance Virtues* (Cambridge: 2002).

12 John Dunn, *Western Political Theory in the Face of the Future* (Cambridge: 1979, 1993), p. 2.

13 Thucydides, *The Peloponnesian War: The Complete Hobbes Translation*, ed. David Grene (Chicago and London: 1989), Bk. I, 21, 23. The word 'harm' in Hobbes' translation appears in Thucydides as *pathêmata* – sufferings, ordeals. On the special claims which Thucydides makes for the Peloponnesian War as 'greater' (*meizón*) than any previous Greek conflict, see A. W. Gomme, 'The Greatest War in Greek History', in *Essays in Greek History and Literature* (Oxford: 1937), together with Simon Hornblower, *A Commentary on Thucydides* (Oxford: 1991–96), 2 vols, I, pp. 62–63.

14 *The Histories of Polybius*, trans. E. S. Shuckburgh (London: 1889), 2 vols., Bk. I, §1.

15 Ibid., Bk. 1, §3. F. W. Walbank, *A Historical Commentary on Polybius* (Oxford: 1970–79), 3 vols., I, p. 43, points out that 'universal history' in Polybius' text contrasts with the episodic accounts of past events characteristic of 'scattered' (*sporades*) – typically uncivilised – communities.

16 *Fortnight*, May 1998.

17 The prospect of a civil war in Northern Ireland engulfing the South, which was the generally expected outcome of a British withdrawal, was nonetheless a matter of persistent strategic concern for Britain since, as Burke Trend put it to the British Chiefs of Staff in 1970, in the event of all-out war in Ireland, 'other people might try to fish in those troubled

waters' (PRO, PREM 15/100, 'Notes for a Meeting with Chiefs of Staff', 9 July 1970).

18 For the analysis of Northern Ireland in comparative international perspective, see Frank Wright, *Northern Ireland: A Comparative Analysis* (Dublin: 1987); Adrian Guelke, *Northern Ireland: The International Perspective* (Dublin: 1988); Ian Lustick, *Unsettled States, Disputed Lands* (Ithaca, N.Y.: 1993). For the comparative analysis of the Irish peace process, see Adrian Guelke, 'The Peace Process in South Africa, Israel and Northern Ireland: A Farewell to Arms?' *Irish Studies in International Affairs*, 5 (1994), pp. 93–106; Adrian Guelke, 'Comparatively Peaceful: The Role of Analogy in Northern Ireland's Peace Process', *Cambridge Review of International Affairs*, (Summer/Fall 1997), pp. 28–45; Fred Halliday, 'Peace Processes in the Late Twentieth Century: A Mixed Record', in Michael Cox et al. eds, *A Farewell to Arms? From 'Long War' to Long Peace in Northern Ireland* (Manchester: 2000).

19 Niccolò Machiavelli, *Discourses on the First Decade of Titus Livius* in *The Chief Works and Others*, trans. Alan Gilbert (Durham, N.C.: 1989), 3 vols, I, p. 191.

20 Martin van Gelderen and Quentin Skinner eds, *Republicanism: A Shared European Heritage* (Cambridge: 2002), 2 vols, gives a wide range of recent scholarly opinion on the diverse traditions of Republican thought from early modern Europe to the French Revolution. For an account of the pedigree of Unionist argument, see John Robertson, 'Empire and Union: Two Concepts of the Early Modern European Political Order', in John Robertson ed., *A Union For Empire: Political Thought and the British Union of 1707* (Cambridge: 1995).

21 Alexis de Tocqueville, *The Ancien Régime*, trans. J. Bonner (London: 1988), p. 110.

22 Its ultimate modern intellectual provenance, however, is to be found in Thomas Hobbes. In his *Elementorum philosophiae sectio tertia de cive* (1642), ed. Howard Warrender (Oxford: 1983), VII, v–xi, Hobbes declares that every polity derives its power (*potestas*) from the people (*populi*), and that 'Qui coïerunt ad ciuitatem erigendam, pene eo ipso quod coïerunt, *Democratia* sunt' (those who came together for the purpose of establishing a state, were, by their very congregation, a *democracy*). On the adaptation of the Hobbesian doctrine of popular sovereignty in the eighteenth century, see Istvan Hont, 'The Permanent Crisis of a Divided Mankind: "Contemporary Crisis of the Nation State" in Historical Perspective', in John Dunn ed.,

Contemporary Crisis of the Nation State (Cambridge: 1995), pp. 166–231. For Hans Kohn, *The Age of Nationalism: The First Era of Global History* (1962; Westport, Conn.: 1976), pp. 3–38, the transition to self-determination as a politically active doctrine begins with the French Revolution, whose inspiration lay in Rousseau and whose core principles were articulated by Kant. Kohn's account involves some serious distortions, but for our purposes it is nonetheless worth noting the relevant point made by Richard Tuck, *The Rights of War and Peace: Political Thought and the International Order from Grotius to Kant* (Oxford: 1999), p. 197: 'Rousseau and Kant, it can be said, were the eighteenth century's two most perceptive and interesting readers of Hobbes, both of them able to see past the vulgar denunciations of his views found in most modern writers and willing to incorporate important elements of his theories in their own.'

23 *The Messages and Papers of Woodrow Wilson*, ed. Albert Shaw (New York: 1924), 2 vols, I, p. 355. On the intellectual roots of Wilson's commitment to self-determination, see Arthur S. Link, *The Higher Realism of Woodrow Wilson* (Nashville, Tenn.: 1971); on the tensions inherent in the Wilsonian doctrine, see Kalevi J. Holsti, *Peace and War: Armed Conflicts and International Order, 1648–1989* (Cambridge: 1991, 1992), pp. 175–89; for criticism of the impact of the doctrine after 1918, see F. H. Hinsley, *Power and the Pursuit of Peace: Theory and Practice in the History of Relations between States* (Cambridge: 1963, 1967), p. 282.

24 For discussions of self-determination in this period, see Alfred Cobban, *National Self-Determination* (London: 1944), pp. 64–65, for whom Rousseau acted as the sponsor of such unrealisable democratic expectations as underlie the concept of self-determination; and Harold S. Johnson, *Self-Determination within the Community of Nations* (Leyden: 1967), p. 27, for whom the 'blend of democracy with nationalism became the basis for a claim for national self-determination'. More recently, see Russell Hardin, 'Fallacies of Nationalism', in Ian Shapiro and Stephen Macedo eds, *Designing Democratic Institutions* (New York: 2000), p. 186: 'what undermines the notion of self-determination as a conceptual matter is the difficulty or impossibility of saying who the relevant self is'. On the problem of majorities and minorities in the context of disputes about self-determination, see John McGarry, '"Orphans of Secession": National Pluralism in Secessionist Regions and Post-Secession States', in Margaret Moore ed., *National Self-Determination* (Oxford: 1998).

25 See, for example, Brendan O'Leary and John McGarry, *The Politics of*

Antagonism: Understanding Northern Ireland (London: 1993), *passim*; and Michael Ignatieff, *Blood and Belonging: Journeys into the New Nationalism* (London: 1993, 1994), p. 164. Joseph Ruane and Jennifer Todd, *The Dynamics of Conflict in Northern Ireland: Power, Conflict and Emancipation* (Cambridge: 1996, 2000), p. 307, are more expansive, but still elusive: 'The conflict [in Northern Ireland] rests on sharp and overlapping differences in respect of religion, ethnicity, settler-native status, notions of progressiveness and backwardness, national identity and allegiance.' For more general attempts to trace modern political conflicts to the tribulations of ethnicity, see Donald L. Horowitz, *Ethnic Groups in Conflict* (Berkeley, LA: 1985, 2000); Anthony D. Smith, *The Ethnic Origins of Nations* (Oxford: 1986, 1991).

26   The term itself derives from the Greek, as the standard accounts of the phenomenon of ethnicity are quick to point out. See, for instance, Elisabeth Tonkin, Maryon McDonald and Malcolm Chapman, *History and Ethnicity* (London: 1989), pp. 11–17. H. G. Liddell and R. Scott eds, *An English-Greek Lexicon* (Oxford: 1843, 9th rev. edn, 1940, 1951), 2 vols, I, p. 480, give 'a number of people living together, company, body of men' for *ethnos*, citing '*ethnos hetairôn*' in Homer, *Iliad*, Bk. 3, l. 32. But a Homeric band of companions can offer little guidance to attempts to understand specifically modern forms of sociability, since the terms and conditions of Homeric social interaction are notable for being conspicuously distinct from our own. See M. I. Finley, *The World of Odysseus* (1954; London: 1999); A. A. Long, 'Morals and Values in Homer', *Journal of Hellenic Studies*, 90 (1970), pp. 121–39. Simon Hornblower and Anthony Spawforth eds, *The Oxford Classical Dictionary* (Oxford: 3rd rev. edn, 1996), pp. 558–59 supply the following gloss on fourth-century BC usage: 'They [*ethnê*] are characterised by the fact that by contrast with *poleis* (which retained total autonomy), individual communities surrendered some political powers (usually control of warfare and foreign relations) to a common assembly.' The later Greek usage thus points to peoples in league – quite the reverse of peoples in conflict.

27   William MacKnight, *Ulster As It Is, Or Twenty-Eight Years' Experience as an Irish Editor* (London: 1896), 2 vols, II, p. 380. MacKnight was the author of a monograph on Edmund Burke which sought to claim the authority of Burke for the cause of the Union. The problem, however, as MacKnight saw it, was that the Union was under attack from Jacobin principles imported into Ireland throughout the nineteenth century. 'The Ulster Unionists . . . now disclaim exceptional privileges. But having abolished one ascendancy, they maintain that [the Imperial]

Parliament can have no moral, no constitutional right to virtually substitute another, which would really be an ascendancy of ignorance, poverty, and disaffection' (p. 381). The problem for Unionists having renounced exceptional privileges – 'ascendancy' – was that they were vulnerable, not to an indeterminate 'ethnic' onslaught, but to the tyranny of the majority which was seen as accompanying egalitarian democracy and thus at the same time as rendering liberal democracy impracticable: 'To maintain that a majority of the House of Commons, no matter how chosen or how small, has a right to deprive any portion of the Queen's subjects in the United Kingdom of their inherited privilege as British citizens to remain under the direct control of the Parliament at Westminster, would at any other time have been considered monstrous. This is to subject the loyal Ulster people to the tyranny of a virtually disloyal majority. It is to act directly contrary to the principle laid down by Charles [James] Fox, that the tyranny of a majority was the worst of all tyrannies, because it rendered the case of the minority hopeless. The supremacy of a majority, which is now by many people regarded as an unquestionable truth, is only conventional. It is not in the nature of things. Even in the modern Republics something more than a mere majority in a single Chamber is required to alter the Constitution on any important point' (p. 379).

28   Frank Wright, *Two Lands On One Soil: Unionist Politics before Home Rule* (Dublin: 1996), p. 510, traces the dynamic leading to this situation back to the 1880s, describing it as having generated an 'ethnic frontier' in the north-east of Ireland. However, he correctly links this development to the process of democratisation: 'The North of Ireland was becoming during the 19th century an ethnic frontier between the British and the Irish nations. As the settlement colonial structure decayed, the two communities became opposed national peoples in conflict for the same land . . . Normally, democratisation tended to pull all citizens of a modern society on a plane of formal equality . . . In ethnic frontier societies, by contrast, democratisation meant that the ethnic antagonism became increasingly difficult to restrain.' James Bryce, *England and Ireland: An Introductory Statement* (London: 1884), p. 17, had indicated the extent to which the demand for Home Rule sprang from the sentiment of nationality which had itself become an ineliminable feature of modern democratic politics: 'The sentiment of nationality, which was comparatively new and feeble in 1832, has wonderfully developed itself since then under the example of its successful assertion not only in Italy and Germany, but even in small peoples like the Bulgarians or Roumanians, or in remote regions like

Iceland.' In Ireland, after the 1867 Reform Bill and the 1872 Ballot Act, the sentiment of nationality was given expression by precisely those parliamentary representatives chosen by a newly enfranchised Irish electorate. Further franchise reform in 1884 only consolidated that process. In Ulster, the impact of democratisation on politics became especially significant after 1905. See Alvin Jackson, *The Ulster Party: Irish Unionists in the House of Commons, 1884–1911* (Oxford: 1989), p. 320, on the transformation by 1911 of Ulster Unionism from a parliamentary movement 'into an army of resistance'. At the same time, for the response of advanced British liberals like J. A. Hobson to Unionism as a species of 'sedition' intended to 'frustrate democracy and social reform', see G. K. Peatling, *British Public Opinion and Irish Self-Government, 1865–1925: From Unionism to Liberal Commonwealth* (Dublin: 2001), p. 76.

29 Ronald McNeill, *Ulster's Stand for Union* (London: 1922), p. 15. McNeill tried to advance his argument by citing Sir Henry Summer Maine, *Popular Government* (1885; London: 1909), p. 28, to the effect that 'Democracies are quite paralysed by the plea of nationality. There is no more effective way of attacking them than by admitting the right of the majority to govern, but denying that the majority so entitled is the particular majority which claims the right.' McNeill commented: 'This is precisely what occurred in regard to Ulster's relation to Great Britain and to the rest of Ireland respectively. The will of the majority must prevail, certainly. But what majority? . . . Ulster, whilst agreeing with the general Unionist position, contended ultimately that her own majority was as well entitled to be heard in regard to her own fate as the majority of Ireland as a whole' (p. 15).

30 See Joseph Schumpeter, *Capitalism, Socialism and Democracy* (London and New York: 1943, 1976), pp. 250–69; Bernard Manin, *The Principles of Representative Government* (Cambridge: 1997), pp. 161–92; Bernard Manin et al., 'Introduction' to Adam Przeworski et al. eds, *Democracy, Accountability and Representation* (Cambridge: 1999), esp. pp. 1–5.

VII Crisis: 1972–1976

1 Of course, as we have seen, the British government was always on the verge of a major reassessment of its position, but without ever actually moving toward a definite decision. For instance, Roy Hattersley has claimed in *Fifty Years On: A Prejudiced History of Britain since the War* (London: 1997), pp. 204–5, that 'For six months [after December 1970]

the Army and the RUC did their best to prevent the outbursts of sporadic violence from turning into civil war . . . But there was no real peace in the Bogside and the Ardoyne or along the Shankill and Falls roads. A lasting settlement depended on a major constitutional initiative which Jim Callaghan looked forward to promoting after the Labour government was re-elected – a prospect which most commentators took for granted. The new Labour government would rewrite the Northern Ireland constitution.' But, of course, Labour was not re-elected, and so whatever plans there might have been for constitutional reform could not progress even if they had already reached an advanced stage, for which there is no evidence. Similarly, on 22 July 1971, the Prime Minister, Edward Heath, had reported to his 'Northern Ireland' Cabinet Colleagues that the situation in the Province was such 'that we now had seriously to contemplate the possibility that we might be compelled to institute direct rule in Northern Ireland if Mr. Faulkner's administration was unable to retain its authority and was replaced by a regime whose policies we could not accept'. However, at the same meeting, it was suggested in discussion that 'the institution of direct rule should be regarded as a policy of last resort and that before it was adopted it might well be right to agree that the Northern Ireland Government should invoke their powers of internment'. But, as evidenced by the minutes of a Cabinet meeting held on 3 February 1972, the government's determination to arrive at a political settlement had grown altogether more fierce after Bloody Sunday: now a 'Community Government' for Ulster, together with the possibility of some kind of 'constitutional association between the two parts of Ireland', was being openly entertained. A month later, on 2 March, when the government had settled on a policy of fundamental constitutional reform for Northern Ireland, it was announced by the Home Secretary, Reginald Maudling, that for such reform to succeed, 'it would be necessary to make a break with the past and to arrange for the United Kingdom Government to exercise direct responsibility for the administration of Northern Ireland for an interim period' (PRO, CAB 128/48).

2   Quoted in Richard Deutsch and Vivien Magowan, *Northern Ireland: A Chronology of Events, 1968–1974* (Belfast: 1973–75), 4 vols, IV, p. 163. The context for the remark is given by David McKittrick and David McVea in *Making Sense of the Troubles*, p. 80: 'Part of the message here was a warning to Britain not to bring down Stormont, but Heath was undeterred.'

3   The suspension of Stormont was enacted by the Northern Ireland

(Temporary Provisions) Act 1972, s. 1 (3): 'the Parliament of Northern Ireland shall stand prorogued'. Its dissolution was provided for under the Northern Ireland Constitution Act 1973, Part V, s. 31 (1): 'The Parliament of Northern Ireland shall cease to exist.' Jennifer Todd, 'Unionist Political Thought, 1920–1972', in D. George Boyce, Robert Eccleshall and Vincent Geoghegan eds, *Political Thought in Ireland since the Seventeenth Century* (London: 1993), p. 207, presents the 1972 Act as a turning-point: 'With the fall of Stormont in 1972 the cause was lost . . . In reaction, unionist political thought at once splintered and developed.' On 1972 as a watershed, see also Gordon Gillespie, 'Loyalists since 1972', in D. George Boyce and Alan O'Day eds, *Defenders of the Union: A Survey of British and Irish Unionism since 1801* (London: 2001), p. 251: in the wake of the prorogation of Stormont, 'fear and isolation' become the key to unionist responses. Equally, see the verdict of Alvin Jackson in 'Irish Unionism', in D. George Boyce and Alan O'Day eds, *The Making of Modern Irish History: Revisionism and the Revisionist Controversy* (London: 1996), p. 121: 'The broadening of political debate since 1972 has made ideological and strategic demands for which the Unionist movement, schooled disastrously at Stormont, has had no response.'

4   Parliamentary Debates (Hansard), House of Commons, Official Report, Fifth Series (London: 1968–1992), vol. 826, col. 1586, 25 November 1971. The 'aspirations' to which Wilson was referring comprised the provision made in the Government of Ireland Act 1920, ss. 3 (1)–(3), for the establishment of a parliament for the whole of Ireland to replace both the Council of Ireland, and the parliaments of Northern and Southern Ireland, set up under the 1920 act: 'The Parliaments of Southern Ireland and Northern Ireland may, by identical Acts agreed to by an absolute majority of members of the House of Commons of each Parliament at the third reading . . . establish, in lieu of the Council of Ireland, a Parliament for the whole of Ireland . . . There shall also be transferred to the Government and Parliament of Ireland, except so far as the Constituent Acts otherwise provide, all powers and duties of the Parliaments and Governments of Southern Ireland and Northern Ireland.'

5   Thus 1972 had been billed as the 'Year of Decision' by the Provisionals in *An Phoblacht*, January 1972. But the dissolution of Stormont had long been presented as a first step along the road to a final reckoning: see Chapter V above.

6   Quoted in Conor O'Clery, *Phrases Make History Here* (Dublin: 1986), p. 144. This sentiment was to be endlessly repeated in loyalist

publications down to 1974: on 19 May of that year, the Ulster Workers'
Council *Strike Bulletin*, no. 1, declared that 'Ulster is nobody's colony'.
Five days later, Stanley Orme, the Northern Ireland Minister of State,
was being derided in *Strike Bulletin*, no. 5, as an aspirant 'colonial
administrator' who believed, ironically, that Northern Ireland was 'a
colony [waiting] to be freed' (Linen Hall Library, Belfast: Northern
Ireland Political Collection).

7   Northern Ireland Office, 'Foreword' to *The Future of Northern Ireland:
     A Paper for Discussion* (London: 1972).

8   Ibid., §12.

9   Ibid., §14. It is of course clear that a competitive system of party govern-
     ment is not simply a characteristic of British political arrangements, but
     is a common feature of democratic politics more generally. On this, see
     Albert O. Hirschman, *Exit, Voice, and Loyalty: Responses to Decline in
     Firms, Organisations and States* (Cambridge, Mass.: 1970) and Adam
     Przeworski, *Democracy and the Market* (Cambridge: 1991). On the
     model of consensual – or 'consociational' – government, intended for
     circumstances where party competition is liable to become zero-sum
     and lethal, see Arend Lijphart, *Democracies* (New Haven: 1984). For a
     general appraisal of such consensual arrangements, see Robert A.
     Dahl, *Democracy and its Critics*, Ch. 15. For a discussion of the intrinsic
     fallibility of electoral accountability, see John Dunn, 'Situating
     Democratic Political Accountability', in Adam Przeworski et al. eds,
     Democracy, Accountability and Representation (Cambridge: 1999),
     although the author does point to one of the chief benefits of successful
     party competition relevant to the discussion here: prospective victory
     in the future 'assuages the bitterness of political defeat' (p. 332).

10   On the changing attitudes within, and conflicting pressures upon, the
     Ulster Unionist Party since the 1930s, see Henry Patterson, *Ireland
     since 1939* (Oxford: 2002), p. 5, beginning with Northern Ireland's first
     Prime Minister, James Craig: the latter's 'failure to deliver on his early
     non-sectarian rhetoric [was] . . . a product of . . . the regime's fear of
     divisions in the Protestant community and a resultant propensity to
     indulge grass-roots Loyalism . . . The other factor was . . . the failure
     of the IRA to abide by . . . a cessation of armed activity in the North.'
     By the early 1960s, many of the elements feeding that dynamic
     remained intact. See ibid., p. 182, on the closing period of Viscount
     Brookeborough's premiership of Northern Ireland: 'a government
     immobilized by fear of schism and unable to respond to a real oppor-
     tunity to develop a better relationship with the minority community'.

11   British proposals to hold a 'Round Table Conference' at which

'different political opinions in Northern Ireland' would be represented
had been circulated around the Home Office as far back as May 1969.
At that point, James Callaghan was arguing that 'it is for us to take
whatever steps we can to encourage reconciliation. This is the purpose
of my proposal that we should consider a Round Table Conference of
Northern Irish political leaders under U. K. Government chairmanship' (PRO, CJ 3/1, 'Memorandum' by the Secretary of State for the
Home Office, May 1969). The proposal, however, was never acted
upon, although it was taken up again in the autumn of 1970, except this
time negotiations were to take the form of a tripartite conference –
including, in other words, the government of the Irish Republic. The
plan, however, was deemed not to be 'propitious' under the circumstances of the time (PRO, CJ 3/25, 'Relations with the Irish Republic:
Proposals for Tripartite Discussions', September–November 1970).
Then, in February of 1972, the plan to hold tripartite talks was
resuscitated by the British Cabinet: 'The acceptance by Roman
Catholics of any political settlement . . . depended in large measure on
its endorsement by the Government of the Republic. The long term
solution might therefore have to involve some kind of constitutional
association between the two parts of Ireland, while permitting the Six
Counties of Northern Ireland to form part of the United Kingdom'
(PRO, CAB 128/48, 3 February 1972). Suggestions for the reform of
the Northern Ireland government itself, however, were altogether
slower in being produced. It was recognised by Michael Stewart at a
Cabinet meeting in August 1969 that the Catholic community had no
hope of participating in the government of Northern Ireland under
current arrangements, prompting him to suggest that 'the Commission
on the Constitution might be asked to consider means of remedying
this situation' (PRO, CAB 128/46, Confidential Annex, 19 August
1969). The suggestion, however, was never implemented. Indeed, in
due course, the British government was actually moving in the
opposite direction: at a meeting of the British 'Northern Ireland'
Cabinet, convened soon after the Conservatives' victory in the general
election of 1970, the determination to 'take every opportunity of
building up the authority and position of the Northern Ireland
Government' was recorded (PRO, PREM 15/100, 22 June 1970). But,
as we have seen, soon after the introduction of internment, minority
representation in the Northern Ireland government was being
proposed by sections of the British government (PRO, CAB 128/48,
16 August 1971), and by early 1972 it had become British government
policy.

12 New Ulster Movement, *The Reform of Stormont* (Belfast: 1971), p. 3. Precisely the same point had been made in the autumn of 1970 by Fergus Pyle: see 'Stormont: What Chance for the Future', *Fortnight*, November 1970. The issue was raised again by Calvin MacNee in 'The Question Why', *Fortnight*, 19 February 1971, in defence of 'minority participation in government by Stormont'. However, the earliest, and most searching, attempt to advocate such a course of action was made by R. J. Lawrence who, in *The Times* on 10 January 1969, protested that 'A permanent minority cannot alter the rules in its own favour.' Acknowledging this reality, Jack Lynch is reported by Edward Heath in September 1971 to have been pushing for the replacement of Stormont 'by a Commission in which the minority groups would have authority equally with the majority' (PRO, CAB 128/48, 9 September 1971). In response to mounting pressure for major constitutional reform, the British Defence Secretary reported to Cabinet two weeks later that 'Some speculation appeared to be current about the possibility of an alliance between extreme Protestant and extreme Roman Catholic factions. This might not be wholly unrealistic; but, if so, it must emerge as an arrangement made by Irishmen themselves, not as an artificial creation imposed on them by the Government of the United Kingdom.' The British government itself, consequently, had no definite plan of action at this time. As the Defence Secretary went on to argue at the same meeting: 'It was possible to believe that the only solution of the problem which would ultimately prove to be realistic would lie in a physical separation of the Protestant and Roman Catholic factions or in some transfer of population from the Province to the Irish Republic. But an arrangement of this kind would prove impracticable in a city such as Belfast, where the two communities were closely intermingled; and it would encounter the most bitter opposition' (PRO, CAB 128/48, 21 September 1971).

13 Government of Ireland Act 1920, ss. 3 (1)–(3).

14 Ibid., s. 1 (2).

15 Ireland Act 1949, s. 1 (1). The Act, coming so soon after the Second World War, was intended to offer permanent security to Ulster Unionism since the position of the Province, in light of the events of 1939–45, was seen by the post-war Labour administration as a strategically vital concern. The view that Britain could not afford to allow Northern Ireland to quit the jurisdiction of the United Kingdom 'even if the people of Northern Ireland desired it' was expressed in an official report dispatched in a memorandum by Clement Attlee to the Cabinet in January 1949. But the fact remains that any long term

guarantee to Ulster depended on the will of the British political establishment which, already by 1954, is not what it had been in 1949: in that year, both Patrick Gordon Walker and George Brown were discussing the possibility of an end to partition in exchange for the Irish Republic accepting membership of NATO. On both of these developments, see Peter Rose, *How the Troubles Came to Northern Ireland* (London: 2000), pp. 5, 9.

16   PRO, CJ 3/30, Letter from Terence O'Neill to Harold Wilson, 6 December 1968.

17   PRO, PREM 15/100, Minutes of Northern Ireland Cabinet Meeting, 22 June 1970. PRO, PREM 15/100, Letter from James Chichester-Clark to the Home Secretary, 12 July 1970.

18   PRO, CJ 3/28, 'Proposal to Change 1 (2) Ireland Act 1949', 1 December 1969. The notes were prepared by A. J. Langdon.

19   Downing Street Declaration (London: 1969), Cmd. 4514, §1.

20   Wilson made clear that this had been his own understanding of the Downing Street Declaration of 1969 on 25 November 1971: see Parliamentary Debates (Hansard), Fifth Series, vol. 826, col. 1585.

21   PRO, CJ 3/28, 'Referendum to Decide the Constitutional Position of Northern Ireland', 1 December 1969.

22   PRO, CAB 128/48, 3 February 1972.

23   Ibid., 7 March 1972.

24   Ibid.

25   Ibid.

26   Ibid.

27   Northern Ireland Constitution Act 1973, Part V, s. 31 (1).

28   Northern Ireland Constitution Act 1973, Part I, s. 1: 'It is hereby declared that Northern Ireland remains part of Her Majesty's dominions and of the United Kingdom, and it is hereby affirmed that in no event will Northern Ireland or any part of it cease to be part of Her Majesty's dominions and of the United Kingdom without the consent of the majority of the people of Northern Ireland voting in a poll held for the purposes of this section in accordance with Schedule 1 of this Act.'

29   PRO, CAB 128/48, 23 March 1972. On this, see Mark Garnett and Ian Aitken, *Splendid! Splendid! The Authorized Biography of William Whitelaw* (London: 2002), p. 112: 'The idea that plebiscites in the North would be held at regular intervals suggested that British ministers wanted to keep open the possibility of reunification in the future.'

30   PRO, CJ 3/28, 'Referendum to Decide the Constitutional Position of Northern Ireland', 1 December 1969.

31   See Barry White, 'Counting the Days Ahead', *Belfast Telegraph*, 21
      December 2002, on the Northern Ireland census results of the previous
      year.

32   Northern Ireland Act 1998, Part I, ss. 1–2: 'It is hereby declared that
      Northern Ireland in its entirety remains part of the United Kingdom
      and shall not cease to be so without the consent of a majority of the
      people of Northern Ireland voting in a poll held for the purpose of this
      section in accordance with Schedule 1. But if the wish expressed by a
      majority in such a poll is that Northern Ireland should cease to be part
      of the United Kingdom and form part of a United Ireland, the
      Secretary of State shall lay before Parliament such proposals to give
      effect to that wish as may be agreed between Her Majesty's
      Government in the United Kingdom and the Government of Ireland.
      The Government of Ireland Act of 1920 is repealed; and this Act shall
      have effect notwithstanding any other previous enactment.'

33   The motto appears emblazoned on the front cover of the *People's Press*,
      27 August 1969. The basic political assumption which the motto
      invoked was quite specific, and powerfully influential: if it was
      legitimate for majorities to select governments, then it was proper for
      a majority to control the constitution. Under such an arrangement, it
      was tempting to take the whole polity as in fact constituted for the
      exclusive benefit of the majority. The Loyalist Association of Workers'
      Rules, drafted in 1972, just before the prorogation of Stormont,
      embodied this assumption in its stated 'Objectives': 'To uphold and
      maintain the constitution of Ulster . . . in its present form' (Linen Hall
      Library, Belfast: Northern Ireland Political Collection). However,
      two years later, in the midst of the Ulster Workers' Council strike,
      loyalist protesters attempted to grapple further with the principle that
      'the will of the majority' is entitled to determine, not simply a par-
      ticular government's policies, but the actual form of the government in
      general. Such an argument would extend the principle of majority rule
      beyond the familiar practice of majorities competing to form govern-
      ments by turns: it would encompass instead the principle of
      majoritarian democracy more broadly. A commitment of this kind
      would amount to suggesting that Northern Ireland as a whole ought to
      cater to the ruling majority. This position was indeed advanced by the
      loyalist ultra, Kennedy Lindsay, in his 'Eight Point Plan for Ulster', 25
      October 1972, reprinted in the *Loyalist Association of Workers*, 1, no. 29:
      'The British Government must state clearly that it has set aside all [*sic*]
      intention of endeavouring to impose unwanted constitutional arrange-
      ments which are not common to other regions of the United Kingdom.'

34 Ulster Vanguard, 'Declaration of Intent and Covenant to Act', February 1972 (Linen Hall Library, Belfast: Northern Ireland Political Collection). The notice was actually prepared by the Loyalist Association of Workers, chaired by Hugh Petrie and Billy Hull, which had been formed out of the Workers' Committee for the Defence of the Constitution back in 1971. For the relations between these organisations, see Sarah Nelson, *Ulster's Uncertain Defenders: Loyalists and the Northern Ireland Conflict* (Belfast: 1984), pp. 101–7.

35 Ulster Vanguard, 'Declaration of Intent', op. cit. This stipulation was not, however, a bottom line for all organisations grouped at one time or another under the Vanguard umbrella. While the *Loyalist Association of Workers*, 2, no. 49, could declare in an editorial from 1973, issued immediately after the spring publication of a British government White Paper on future political arrangements in the Province, that the introduction of power-sharing would mean the imposition of 'alien rule' in the sense that 'British democracy [would] no longer . . . govern the essential command structure in the country', the Ulster Workers' Council *Strike Bulletin*, no. 1, declared on 19 May 1974 that 'Power-sharing has been shown to work', adding that a 'Council of Ireland is not necessary to power-sharing'. In *Strike Bulletin*, no. 2, 21 May 1974, this point was specifically emphasised: 'Many of the strikers' representatives will say they are against "Sunningdale". This enables it to be said that the strike is against power-sharing. But there are two elements in "Sunningdale": power-sharing and the Council of Ireland. It is the Council of Ireland that is the issue in the strike' (Linen Hall Library, Belfast: Northern Ireland Political Collection). The same view was expressed in the *Loyalist News*, 1 June 1974: 'we believe that the Loyalist people given a fair crack of the whip, would not be opposed to power-sharing with their Roman Catholic countrymen'.

36 Ulster Vanguard, 'Declaration of Intent', op. cit. The provenance of this emphasis on 'consent' was originally traced by David W. Miller in his *Queen's Rebels: Ulster Loyalism in Historical Perspective* (New York: 1978) to Whig political argument in the seventeenth and eighteenth centuries, although he cautions, pp. 5–6: 'Ulster Protestants do not, of course, regulate their political conduct by copies of Locke's *Second Treatise*, or even the Solemn League and Covenant, somehow lovingly preserved in their families since the seventeenth century. They often do, however, think in terms reminiscent of those documents.' The extent to which Locke himself actually sought to discipline the principle of consent is discussed in John Dunn, 'Consent

in the Political Theory of John Locke', *Political Obligation in its Historical Context: Essays in Political Theory* (Cambridge: 1980), esp. p. 31: 'consent denotes the occasion of incurring political obligations. To suppose that it must therefore constitute the ground of these obligations is to make the error of confusing the occasion of incurring an obligation with the general ground of the duty of honouring it.' In this context, it is worth recalling that majoritarian democracy has been associated with the argument of Locke's *Two Treatises* by Willmoore Kendal, *John Locke and Majority-rule* (Urbana, Ill.: 2nd edn, 1959). However, Kendal's thesis has been effectively challenged in John Dunn, *The Political Thought of John Locke: An Historical Account of the Argument of the 'Two Treatises of Government'* (Cambridge: 1969), pp. 127–30. In the first place, Locke's concern is not with decision-making procedures for established governments, but with the theoretical foundations of political obligation. Consequently, each individual's submission to the majority does not entail submission to majority rule, and submission to the majority is only advanced in the absence of 'any number greater than the majority'. See John Locke, *Two Treatises of Government*, ed. Peter Laslett (Cambridge; 1960), II, §99. This passage is discussed further in James Tully, *An Approach to Political Philosophy: Locke in Contexts* (Cambridge: 1993), p. 33. Having said all this, there is in any case no reason to associate Locke with any kind of specifically democratic theory. The departure from characteristically Lockean forms of political argument during the century succeeding the publication of the *Two Treatises* is dealt with by John Dunn, 'The Politics of Locke in England and America in the Eighteenth Century', *Political Obligation in its Historical Context*, and again by J. G. A. Pocock, 'The Varieties of Whiggism from Exclusion to Reform: A History of Ideology and Discourse', in *Virtue, Commerce and History: Essays on Political Thought and History, Chiefly in the Eighteenth Century* (Cambridge: 1985). The debt to Hutcheson, rather than Locke, in Irish Presbyterian political argument is traced by Ian McBride, 'The School of Virtue: Francis Hutcheson, Irish Presbyterians and the Scottish Enlightenment', in D. George Boyce, Robert Eccleshall and Vincent Geoghegan eds, *Political Thought in Ireland since the Seventeenth Century*.

37 The association in unionist polemic of majority consent with democratic consent was made explicit in a broadsheet issued in the name of the Executive Committee of the Ulster Workers' Council in May 1974 (Linen Hall Library, Belfast: Northern Ireland Political Collection). The 'Aims' of the Council were presented in the following terms: '1.

To bring about constitutional change resulting in a government which will reflect normal democratic procedure. 2. To see a N. I. Government which reflects democratically the hopes and aspirations of all citizens in N. I. who believe in traditional democracy.' The point here is made clear by the fact that by May 1974 only members of the majority community were seeking to credit this 'traditional democracy'.

38 The point is made in Jean-Jacques Rousseau, *Du contrat social*, in R. Derathé et al. eds, *Oeuvres Complètes* (Paris: 1964), p. 440, that an aggregate of individuals can only contract into a sovereign people (a popular state) by an act of 'consentement unanime' (*unanimous* consent). Thereafter, the establishment of the form of regime (or government) is properly secured by the vote of the majority. Likewise, legislation is ratified by majority vote. But, in each of these two cases, the aim is not to discover the majority will, but the general will. To determine this, provision has to be made for an acceptable proportion between the majority and minority, as Rousseau makes clear on p. 441: 'La différence d'une seule voix rompt l'égalité, un seul opposant rompt l'unanimité; mais entre l'égalité et l'unanimité il y a plusieurs partages inégaux, à chacun desquels on peut fixer ce nombre selon l'état et les besoins du corps politiques.' Whilst Rousseau's theory of democratic sovereignty, as presented here, was designed for regimes based on direct popular participation, and so can hardly stand as a model for modern representative democracy, the basic principle of unanimous popular consent was nonetheless adopted into French Revolutionary theories of popular representation which came to be employed as benchmarks of modern democratic practice. See, for example, Emmanuel Joseph Sieyès, *Qu'est-ce que le Tiers-État?* (Paris: 3rd edn, 1789), pp. 122–23, where it is argued that, in the making of political society, 'une volonté commune représentative' ought to be understood as having been deputed by a 'volonté commune *réelle*': here again, a 'common will', not a majority will, is taken to be key. On this basis, majority sovereignty ought to be seen not as a democratic, but as a pleonocratic principle of state.

39 Northern Ireland Office, *The Future of Northern Ireland*, op. cit.

40 See New Ireland Forum, *Report* (Dublin: 1984), Ch. 7. See also B. O'Leary et al., *Northern Ireland: Sharing Authority* (London: 1993), *passim*. For conflicting opinions in the theory of British constitutional law, see H. W. R. Wade, 'The Basis of Legal Sovereignty', *The Cambridge Law Journal* (1955) pp. 172–97, and H. W. R. Wade, 'Sovereignty – Revolution or Evolution', *Law Quarterly Review* (October 1996) pp. 568–75, opposed by T. R. S. Allan, 'Parliamentary

Sovereignty: Law, Politics and Revolution, *Law Quarterly Review* (July 1997), pp. 443–52. In neither Wade nor Allan, however, is the idea of 'joint' sovereignty accorded any analytical credibility: supremacy can be modified as regards its mode of exercise, or reconstitute itself as a new 'unity', but distinct political bodies cannot be jointly supreme.

41 See T. C. Barnard, *Cromwellian Ireland: English Government and Reform in Ireland, 1649–1660* (Oxford: 1975, 2000), pp. 16–25. On the doctrine of sovereignty in historical perspective, see J. G. A. Pocock, 'A Discourse of Sovereignty: Observations on the Work in Progress', in Nicholas Phillipson and Quentin Skinner eds, *Political Discourse in Early Modern Britain* (Cambridge: 1993); Richard Bourke, 'Sovereignty, Opinion and Revolution in Edmund Burke', *History of European Ideas*, 25 (1999), pp. 99–120.

42 Ulster Unionist Party, *Towards the Future* (Belfast: 1972), ss. 4, 5. A weaker version of this proposal had been agreed upon by the Northern Ireland Cabinet at Stormont back in the summer of 1971: 'Ministers were agreed that there was no evident initiative open to them beyond the Parliamentary Committee system which when proposed had met with wide approval and which must remain the principle initiative to be pursued' (Bloody Sunday Tribunal, Planning and Intelligence Core Bundle, 'Conclusions' to a Meeting of the Northern Ireland Cabinet, 10 August 1971, G 7a.60.1.1–4).

43 The Alliance Party Proposals are presented in *The Future of Northern Ireland*, Annex 5.

44 Social Democratic and Labour Party, *Towards a New Ireland* (Belfast: 1972), s. F.

45 *The Future of Northern Ireland*, §§60, 76, 79.

46 *Northern Ireland Constitutional Proposals* (London: 1973), Cmnd. 5259, §§35, 51.

47 The Provisional Sinn Féin office on Kevin Street in Dublin produced its own plan for a United Ireland, together with suggestions for the revolutionary reconstruction of both the North and the South in *Proposals for Peace in a New Ireland* (Dublin: 1972): community councils were to replace local government authorities in both parts of the island, regional assemblies were to be introduced as a new tier of popular representation, and four provincial assemblies were to be brought under the authority of a federated national parliament. This was, in essence, the Éire Nua policy concocted by Ruairí Ó Brádaigh and then torpedoed under the Adams leadership of Sinn Féin in the early 1980s.

48 Back in October 1971, Faulkner had informed Edward Heath that he 'could not contemplate leading or serving in a Government of Northern Ireland which included Republicans, whether or not they eschewed the use of violence in bringing about a unified Ireland'. In fact, he went further: 'Nor would he serve in a Ministry composed according to proportional principles. In neither case could a workable Government be formed since its component parts would be too disparate' (Bloody Sunday Tribunal, Planning and Intelligence Core Bundle, 'Record of a Discussion with the Prime Minister of Northern Ireland', Downing Street, 7 October 1971, G 16.92–118).

49 Northern Ireland Assembly Act 1973, s. 1 (1–2); Northern Ireland Constitution Act 1973, Part II, ss. 4 (1)–11 (3).

50 On this episode, and its background, see Peter Clarke, *Hope and Glory: Britain 1900-1990* (Harmondsworth: 1996, 1997), pp. 329–39.

51 Brian Faulkner, *Memoirs of a Statesman* (London: 1978), p. 252.

52 For an account of the events of the strike, see Don Anderson, *Fourteen May Days: The Inside Story of the Loyalist Strike of 1974* (Dublin: 1994).

53 Quoted in Robert Fisk, *The Point of No Return: The Strike Which Broke the British in Ulster* (London: 1975), p. 81.

54 Quoted in ibid., p. 49.

55 Garret Fitzgerald, *All in a Life: An Autobiography* (Dublin: 1991), pp. 222–24.

56 Conor Cruise O'Brien, *Memoir: My Life and Themes* (London: 1998), pp. 350–53.

57 Faulkner, *Memoirs of a Statesman*, pp. 260–86. Faulkner's verdict, however, has to be understood as a description of what had cost *him* most: the North-South Council arrangements appeared to him to be of little account. However, constitutional change in Northern Ireland is something he had steadfastly resisted since coming into office. See the assessment of Faulkner given by the United Kingdom Representative, Howard Smith, to Reginald Maudling in May 1971: 'He is a short-term thinker and if he assumes, as I think he does, that the problem of the minority is first and foremost a problem of weeding out the violent elements, that is to say at present primarily a security problem, the main political pressure which he feels is the threat to his own position from Mr Paisley. He is therefore tempted to see his policy in terms of countering this political threat, and in this lies the danger that he will fall down on reform' (PRO, CJ 3/98, Telegram from UK Representative Office to Maudling, 10 May 1971).

58 'Press Statement from the Ulster Workers' Council', 15 May 1975

(Linen Hall Library, Belfast: Northern Ireland Political Collection).

59   The phrase was uttered by Harry Patterson of the Ulster Workers
     Council. See Fisk, *The Point of No Return*, p. 40.

60   Merlyn Rees, *Northern Ireland: A Personal Perspective* (London: 1985),
     p. 83. See also the verdict of Harold Wilson, *The Labour Government,
     1974–1976: The Final Term* (London: 1979), p. 78: 'It was an extra-
     Parliamentary defeat for the combined efforts of the major parties at
     Westminster, a defeat for law and order, with all this meant for Britain,
     not least in our overseas relationships. For centuries no external attack
     had been successfully made on the authority of Parliament. Now it
     had. The bully boys had won.'

61   The phrase was originally that of Seamus Mallon, deputy leader of the
     SDLP during the negotiations leading to the Good Friday Agreement.
     But Peter Mandelson was to try to cast doubt upon this judgement. See
     Peter Mandelson, 'The Good Friday Agreement – A Vision for a New
     Order in Northern Ireland', in Marianne Elliott ed., *The Long Road to
     Peace in Northern Ireland* (Liverpool: 2002), p. 116, where it is claimed
     that the later deal was 'a broader, deeper, fairer Agreement' than
     Sunningdale had been.

62   Max Weber, 'Parliament and Government in Germany under a New
     Political Order: Towards a Political Critique of Officialdom and the
     Party System', in Peter Lassman and Ronald Spiers eds, *Weber:
     Political Writings* (Cambridge: 1994), pp. 209–33, examines
     plebiscitary acclamation under mass democracy, but is concerned in
     that instance with its 'Caesarist' manifestations.

63   *The Northern Ireland Constitution* (London: 1974), Cmnd. 5675, §50.

64   Rees, *Northern Ireland*, p. 106.

65   An anonymous British Civil Servant commented revealingly on the
     rationale for discussion at the time: 'The paramilitary figures of today
     are the politicians of tomorrow.' See 'Murder at Bogus Checkpoint',
     The Times, 26 August 1975.

66   The rumours date from the aftermath of the Ulster Workers' Council
     strike which brought down the Sunningdale Agreement. As early as 2
     November 1974, the *Irish Times* was commenting that 'The word
     "withdrawal" may not be said in the corridors at more than a whimper
     but of the certitude [regarding the constitutional status of Northern
     Ireland] of which [Enoch] Powell speaks there is none.' See also the
     view expressed by the headline in the *Loyalist News*, 9 August 1975,
     after the arrest of Seamus Twomey: A DEAL HAS BEEN DONE.

67   The comments of Republican leader David O'Connell after the
     breakdown of the truce reveal part of his own rationale for action: 'The

overall feature of that truce was a statement by the British government that it was committed to disengage from Ireland but it could not say so publicly' ('Ulster 1968–78: A Decade of Despair', *Sunday Times*, 18 June 1978). That withdrawal, together with re-partition, were both discussed and rejected by a Cabinet sub-committee on Northern Ireland from the summer of 1974 through to 1975 is revealed in 'Labour Thought of Ulster Pull-Out', *Guardian*, 19 July 1983. As far as a British victory over the IRA goes, Martin McGuinness' comments in interviews given in 1985–86 make the point with perfect clarity: the ceasefire marked 'the most critical stage in the last sixteen years and if changes had not taken place in a short time then the IRA would have been defeated'. See Patrick Bishop and Eamonn Mallie, *The Provisional IRA* (1987; London: 1994), p. 275. On Harold Wilson's attitude to withdrawal at this time, see Philip Ziegler, *Wilson: The Authorised Life of Lord Wilson of Rievaulx* (London: 1993), p. 466: 'he devised his own plan, which involved British withdrawal over a period of five years, but . . . was so alarmed by the implications of what he called his "Doomsday Scenario" that he discussed it with only a few senior officials' [after May Strike 1974]. See also Bernard Donoughue, *Prime Minister: The Conduct of Policy Under Harold Wilson and James Callaghan* (London: 1987), p. 128.

68 'Want RUC to be Loyalist "Soldiers"', *Irish Times*, 28 August 1975.

69 Parliamentary Debates (Hansard), Fifth Series, vol. 874 , col. 183, 21 May 1974.

70 On this, see Paul Dixon, *Northern Ireland: The Politics of War and Peace* (Basingstoke: 2001), pp. 130–31.

71 An example of the divisions between Paisleyism and Vanguard is illustrated by the defensive strikes against Vanguard contained in Irene K. Brown's pamphlet, *Consistent or Inconsistent* (Newtownards: 1972).

72 'Secret Ulster Talks on Craig Move', *The Times*, 15 September 1975.

73 Terence O'Neill, *The Autobiography of Terence O'Neill, Prime Minister of Northern Ireland, 1963–1969* (London: 1972), pp. 107–8.

74 This was the position, as it were, in print. In general terms, members were attracted more by the avowed militancy of Vanguard than by any neatly worked out platform. See Nelson, *Ulster's Uncertain Defenders*, Ch. 9. But for the official Vanguard stance see Ulster Vanguard, *Spelling It Out* (Belfast: 1973), and William Craig, *The Future of Northern Ireland* (Belfast: 1973). For a similar diagnosis, though not exactly Vanguard's, see Kennedy Lindsay, *Dominion of Ulster?* (Belfast: 1972).

75 Ulster Vanguard, *Ulster – A Nation* (Belfast: 1972), pp. 3, 12, 9.

76   Ibid., p. 7.

77   Ibid., p. 9.

78   Ibid., pp. 7, 12.

79   Ibid., p. 9.

80   Ibid., p. 13.

81   See the arguments put forward by the Paisleyite pamphlet, Louis Gardner, *Resurgence of the Majority* (Belfast: 1970), p. 11: 'In 1968 Ireland's failed rebels adopted a new strategy designed to compel Westminster to intervene decisively on their behalf. Their tactics were temporarily to suspend sallies in armed terrorism in favour of the methods of the fashionable international protest industry.'

82   Parliamentary Debates (Hansard), Fifth Series, vol. 874, cols. 616, 618.

83   See Ian Paisley, *Northern Ireland: What Is the Real Situation?* (1969), pp. 5–17. See also Ed Moloney and Andy Pollak, *Paisley* (Dublin: 1986), pp. 215–60.

84   For the tone and direction of these sentiments, see the statement from Paisley in the *Revivalist* (July 1963) enjoining protest against the lowering of the Union Jack in Belfast upon the death of Pope John XXIII quoted in Steve Bruce, *God Save Ulster: The Religion and Politics of Paisleyism* (Oxford: 1986), p. 73: such gestures were 'lying eulogies . . . being paid to the Roman anti-Christ by non-Romanist Church leaders in defiance of their own historic creeds'.

85   For a generalised historical account, see Peter Brooke, *Ulster Presbyterianism* (Dublin: 1987); for the complex developments in the 1790s, see Ian McBride, *Scripture Politics: Ulster Presbyterians and Irish Radicalism in the Late Eighteenth Century* (Oxford: 1998); for the interplay between politics and 'cosmic' forces in New Light Protestant thinking, see David W. Miller, 'Presbyterianism and "Modernisation" in Ulster', in C. H. E. Philpin ed., *Nationalism and Popular Protest in Ireland* (Cambridge: 1987).

86   David Hume, *The History of England* (Indianapolis: 1983), 6 vols, V, pp. 67, 80.

87   See Ian Paisley, *United Ireland – Never* (Belfast: 1976), p. 6: 'there's no politician – no party or no organisation that could extract us and pull us out of the mess that we're in. We need the intervention of Almighty God.'

88   Richard Rose, *Northern Ireland: A Time of Choice* (London and Basingstoke: 1976), p. 139.

VIII Reversals: 1976–1982

1 On the attitude of the Labour government, and of Harold Wilson in particular, after the collapse of Sunningdale and the Convention, see Harold Wilson, *The Labour Government, 1974–1976: The Final Term* (London: 1979), p. 78: 'the Government inevitably had no new proposal for the future of the Province'.

2 The planning behind many of the Rees reforms themselves naturally date back even earlier, to the middle of Heath's term of office. See PRO, PREM 15/1011, 'Memorandum on Preventive Detention for Terrorist Offences', July 1972, discussed above, Chapter V.

3 Paul Bew and Henry Patterson, *The British State and the Ulster Crisis* (London: 1985), interview with Bew and Patterson, p. 108, n. 72.

4 See the verdict on Mason offered by the Northern Ireland Civil Servant Maurice Hayes in *Minority Verdict* (Belfast: 1995), p. 235: 'Roy Mason . . . had the insecurity of many small men, the over-compensating aggressiveness and the ignorance of the truly uneducated. He was a small man in every respect, probably the worst secretary of state in my time (apart of course from the totally invisible and lazy Humphrey Atkins)'.

5 Parliamentary Debates (Hansard), Fifth Series, vol. 913, col. 50.

6 On the change in Army tactics around this time, see Lieutenant-Colonel Michael Dewar, *The British Army in Northern Ireland* (London: 1985), pp. 147–64.

7 On these developments, see Chris Ryder, *The RUC: A Force Under Fire, 1922–2000* (London: 1989, 2000), pp. 139–57; Tony Geraghty, *The Irish War: The Military History of a Domestic Conflict* (London: 1998), pp. 74–77.

8 The conduct of security before the arrival of the British Army in 1969 first came in for official criticism in the Cameron Commission's *Disturbances in Northern Ireland in 1969* (Cameron Report) (HMSO: 1969). The *Report of the Advisory Committee on Police in Northern Ireland* (Hunt Report) (HMSO: 1969), Cmd. 535, brought the existing enforcement of law and order into further question by recommending disarmament of the RUC – the RUC 'fulfils a military as well as a civilian role', the Report commented (p. 21) – and the replacement of the Ulster Special Constabulary (USC) by a new part-time force under the British Army's General Officer Commanding (GOC). The fundamental difficulty with the RUC, according to Lord Hunt's findings, centred at once on the Force's political character, its lack of community accountability, and its problematic relationship to the

Secretary of State for Home Affairs in Northern Ireland. See *Report of the Advisory Committee on Police*, pp. 21–22: 'The law about the relationship between the Government of Northern Ireland and the Royal Ulster Constabulary . . . defines the relationship in a vague and unsatisfactory way, but in general it indicates that the Minister of Home Affairs is responsible for law and order, but that the Inspector-General is responsible for operational control and for the enforcement of the law. In fact the Inspector-General is not accountable to anyone for his operational policies; yet he and his force are held by many to be closely associated with the Government, which has since the setting up of the Government of Northern Ireland been formed from the same party. The position is unsatisfactory on both grounds . . . We are entirely in favour of the idea that the Inspector-General and the Force should not be subject to political pressures; yet we believe that it is equally important that there should be some body, representative of the community as a whole, to which he can be accountable, and through which the wishes and fears of the community can be expressed. It would be best if this body could consist of elected representatives; but in the political circumstances of Northern Ireland, at present, [there is no mechanism by which to] represent the minority parties and communities.' The contribution made by the Ulster Special Constabulary in heightening tension during the disturbances of August 1969 was highlighted in detail in Lord Scarman's *Violence and Civil Disturbances in Northern Ireland in 1969* (Scarman Report) (HMSO: 1972), published three years after the Hunt Report. The USC's lack of discipline in riot management, and in their use of firearms, also came in for criticism in the Scarman Report – as did the activities of the RUC, particularly their use of Browning machine gunfire in Belfast on 14, 15 and 16 August 1969, together with their failure to intervene impartially in the face of Protestant assaults on Catholic districts around the same time. A highly critical, and avowedly partial, account of the RUC was compiled by Denis Faul and Raymond Murray in *The RUC: The Black and Blue Book* (Tyrone: 1976).

9 Provisional activists on the ground during the truce, like Danny Morrison, have subsequently claimed that they, at the time, unlike the leadership of the movement, were operating under the assumption that British forces were regrouping rather than seriously negotiating a withdrawal (Interview with the author, February 2003). For the Republican reaction to Ulsterisation, see 'Vindicator' [Gerry Brannigan], 'Ulsterisation', *Republican News*, 29 May 1976.

10 A 'new force' to replace the Ulster Special Constabulary, and to be

called the Ulster Defence Regiment, was announced by the British Secretary of State for Defence to Cabinet colleagues in November 1969: 'The new force was needed to counter the threat from the Irish Republican Army, for which purpose an unacceptably large garrison would otherwise be needed.' At the same time, the force was designed to be acceptable to Protestants so that the Ulster Special Constabulary would 'transfer to it' (PRO, CAB 128/48, 6 November 1969). A commemorative volume celebrating the record of the Ulster Defence Regiment's predecessor was produced by the Ulster Special Constabulary Association under the title *Why?* (Belfast: 1980).

11 For these figures, see Sydney Elliott and W. D. Flackes, *Northern Ireland: A Political Directory, 1968–1999* (Belfast: 1999), pp. 638–59.

12 The SAS were first introduced into Belfast in 1970, although they were first dispatched to South Armagh in an official capacity in 1976. On their original deployment, see Roger Faligot, *The Kitson Experiment: Britain's Military Strategy in Ireland* (London: 1983), pp. 24–56. On the circumstances surrounding their introduction into South Armagh, see Raymond Murray, *The SAS in Ireland* (Cork: 1990), pp. 163–84; Mark Urban, *Big Boys' Rules: The Secret Struggle against the IRA* (London: 1992), pp. 3–78.

13 Elements of what was to become the new British security programme had been recommended as far back as 25 October 1972 by none other than the loyalist ultra, Kennedy Lindsay, in his 'Eight Point Plan For Ulster', reprinted in the *Loyalist Association of Workers*, 1, no. 29: 'There must be an "Ulsterisation" of the war. The RUC, UDR and Police Reserve must be greatly expanded and the Ulster regiments brought home immediately. Ulster personnel must be used to the full at all levels, but especially in intelligence and planning.' The British did not, of course, delegate either intelligence or planning. In other respects also, Lindsay went much further in his scheme for Ulsterisation than the British government were prepared to go – including recommending the incorporation of loyalist terror organisations into the security establishment: 'The UDA, LDV [Loyalist Defence Volunteers] and related organisations should be reorganised officially into the security system on the model of town and village guards in the Malayan emergency.' The same view was still being argued in Richard Cameron, *Self-Determination? The Question Ulster Must Answer* (London: 1993), p. 38: 'Only when Ulster people are once again in charge of their own security will there ever be peace in this Country.'

14 Juryless trials were introduced into Northern Ireland on the

recommendation of Lord Diplock in 1973. For an account of their impact on the criminal justice system in the Province, see Richard Harvey, *Diplock and the Assault on Civil Liberties* (London: 1980); John Jackson and Sean Doran, *Judge Without Jury: Diplock Trials in the Adversary System* (Oxford: 1995). The use of the judicial system for counter-insurgency purposes later developed further with the resort to 'supergrass' witnesses in 1981. On this, see Steven Greer, 'The Supergrass System', in Anthony Jennings ed., *Justice Under Fire: The Abuse of Civil Liberties in Northern Ireland* (London: 1988). On the development of emergency provisions for the management of civil unrest since 1973, see Tom Hadden, Kevin Boyle and Colm Campbell, 'Emergency Law in Northern Ireland: The Context', in ibid.; C. A. Gearty and J. A. Kimbell, *Terrorism and the Rule of Law: A Report on the Laws Relating to Political Violence in Great Britain and Northern Ireland* (London: 1995). On the allegations of a 'shoot to kill' policy operated by the security forces, see Anthony Jennings, 'Shoot to Kill: The Final Court of Justice', in Anthony Jennings ed., *Justice Under Fire*.

15 For an account of the development of British policy during this period, see Michael Cunningham, *British Government Policy in Northern Ireland, 1969–2000* (Manchester: 2001), pp. 20–30.

16 See Roy Mason, *Paying the Price* (London: 1999), pp. 160–61, on security as his top priority, with employment coming second.

17 On the details of the constitutional arrangements under direct rule, see Derek Birrell and Alan Murie, *Policy and Government in Northern Ireland: Lessons of Devolution* (Dublin: 1980), pp. 68–89.

18 *The Times*, 28 September 1976.

19 *New Statesman*, 14 January 1976. The disengagement of the British political establishment was to continue during the premiership of Margaret Thatcher: under Thatcher's leadership, Northern Ireland was regularly exempted from policy initiatives undertaken throughout the rest of the United Kingdom. See Frank Gaffikin and Mike Morrissey, *Northern Ireland: The Thatcher Years* (London: 1990), pp. 199–208.

20 Thatcher's comment in her memoirs about the Brighton bomb attack of 1984 which claimed the lives of political friends and associates resonates with the memory of Neave's fate. See Margaret Thatcher, *The Downing Street Years* (London: 1993, 1995), p. 415: 'for some reason the death of a friend or family member by violence leaves an even deeper scar'.

21 Paul Bew and Gordon Gillespie, *Northern Ireland: A Chronology of the Troubles, 1968–1993* (Dublin: 1993), p. 126.

22 James Prior, *A Balance of Power* (London: 1986), pp. 190–98.

23 *Northern Ireland: A Framework for Devolution*, Cmnd. 8541 (London: 1982), §36: 'Ministers and their departments will co-operate closely with the Assembly and its committees, although the Assembly will not have a formal power to summon Ministers responsible to Parliament, or their officials, or have access as of right to departmental papers.'

24 Lord Hailsham's open-mindedness on the issue of federalism within the United Kingdom was presented in his *The Dilemma of Democracy: Diagnosis and Prescription* (London: 1978), pp. 167–69.

25 Prior, *A Balance of Power*, p. 199. For a sceptical analysis of the legislation providing for 'rolling devolution', see Brigid Hadfield, 'The Northern Ireland Act 1982 – Do-It-Yourself Devolution?' *Northern Ireland Legal Quarterly* (Winter 1982), pp. 301–25.

26 Sydney Elliott and R. A. Wilford, *The 1982 Northern Ireland Assembly Elections* (Strathclyde: 1983).

27 In the event they secured 10% of the vote, a significant incremental increase on the elections of the previous year. See ibid., p. 73.

28 On strains within the SDLP at this time, see Paul Routledge, *John Hume: A Biography* (London: 1997), pp. 148–54.

29 *Irish Times*, 16 February 1978. Hume was to repeat the position *ad nauseam* for the next twenty years. For a representative formulation of the argument, see his *Personal Views: Politics, Peace and Reconciliation in Ireland* (Dublin: 1996), Ch. 4.

30 John Biggs-Davison had set out his own views on the proper method of progress in Northern Ireland as requiring 'the partnership of two sovereignties, the United Kingdom of Great Britain and Northern Ireland and the Irish Republic' in *This Hand is Red* (London: 1973), p. 153. On 18 April 1972, in a speech delivered at Ballynahinch, he had addressed the possibility of political integrationism in a positive light; however, he had strongly opposed the prorogation of Stormont in a speech delivered to the House of Commons on 28 March 1972. See ibid., pp. 199–202.

31 On the instruction in parliamentary tactics which opponents of the Assembly Bill received from Enoch Powell, see Robert Shepherd, *Enoch Powell: A Biography* (London: 1996, 1998), p. 461.

32 Cornelius O'Leary, Sydney Elliott and R. A. Wilford, *The Northern Assembly, 1982–86: A Constitutional Experiment* (Belfast: 1988), p. 73.

33 Parliamentary Debates (Hansard), Sixth Series, vol. 25, col. 240, 9 June 1982. For one of Powell's earliest statements of the position, see his 'Speech to a Meeting in the Ulster Hall', Belfast, 18 April 1974, in Rex Collings ed., *Reflections of a Statesman: The Writings and Speeches*

of Enoch Powell (London: 1991), pp. 496–502. For the details of his opposition to the rolling devolution scheme, see Simon Heffer, *Like the Roman: The Life of Enoch Powell* (London: 1998), pp. 857–60.

34   William Petty, *The Political Anatomy of Ireland* (1672) in Charles Henry Hull ed., *The Economic Writings of Sir William Petty* (New York: 1986), p. 159: 'if both Kingdoms, now two, were put into one, and under one Legislative Power and Parliament, the members whereof should be in the same proportion that the Power and Wealth of each Nation are, there would be no danger such a Parliament should do any thing to the prejudice of the *English* interest in *Ireland*; nor could the *Irish* ever complain of Partiality, when they shall be freely and proportionately represented in all Legislatures'. Fourteen years later, in 'Of Reconciling the English and Irish and Reforming Both Nations' (1686), reprinted in *The Petty Papers: Some Unpublished Writings of Sir William Petty* (New York: 1967), pp. 59–63, Petty was again recommending a Union of 'the two Kingdomes' to succeed the introduction of his elaborate schemes for the transplantation of large sections of the Catholic population. On the Irish context of Petty's arguments, see Nicholas Canny, *Kingdom and Colony: Ireland in the Atlantic World, 1560–1800* (Baltimore and London: 1988), pp. 108–16; on the broader context of Petty's thought, see David Armitage, *The Ideological Origins of the British Empire* (Cambridge: 2000), pp. 149–69.

35   Enoch Powell, 'The Test of Britain's Will To Be A Nation' in the *Guardian* Special Issue on *Ulster '80: Year of Decision*, February 1980.

36   Parliamentary Debates (Hansard), Sixth Series, vol. 25, col. 356, 9 June 1982.

37   Sarah Nelson, *Ulster's Uncertain Defenders: Loyalists and the Northern Ireland Conflict* (Belfast: 1984), p. 103.

38   Northern Ireland Parliamentary Debates, 22 March 1972, vol. 84, col. 23. Compare the response of the Vanguard supporting *Loyalist News*, 8 April 1972, to such arguments: ' "Integration" – that last but one step to Hell and an Irish Republic . . . freedom and an independent Ulster we demand. Mark this well, the Fenian enemy is secondary. They do not control us. The English are the Political masters of Ulster. They have the bullet-power to present us gift-wrapped to the Fenian foe; and intend to. They must be seen as our Primary enemy. If we break Westminster's stranglehold the way will be open to freedom and the Fenian lines.'

39   Northern Ireland Parliamentary Debates, 22 March 1972, vol. 84, col. 23.

40 See, for instance, the response of the *Official UDA News*, no. 32, 1972, to the publication of the British government's Green Paper on the future of Northern Ireland: 'London has cast us into Limbo'.

41 See David Boulton, *The UVF 1966–1973: An Anatomy of Loyalist Rebellion* (Dublin: 1973); Jim Cusack and Henry McDonald, *UVF* (Dublin: 2000), pp. 73–100.

42 Northern Ireland Parliamentary Debates (Hansard), 22 March 1972, vol. 84, col. 23.

43 Ed Moloney and Andy Pollak, *Paisley* (Dublin: 1986), pp. 363–80.

44 Interview conducted for *The View from the Castle*, BBC Northern Ireland 1988. See also Mason, *Paying the Price,* pp. 173–98, for a lengthy account of his experience of the Paisley Strike.

45 'Patience on the Way Forward' in the *Guardian* Special Issue on *Ulster '80: Year of Decision*, February 1980.

46 *Daily Telegraph,* 20 April 1981.

47 John McKeague, *Your Future? Ulster Can Survive Unfettered* (Belfast: 1976). For a more recent consideration of this arrangement as the optimal solution to Northern Ireland's difficulties, see Paul A. Fitzsimmons, *Independence for Northern Ireland: Why and How* (Washington, D.C.: 1983).

48 The widely reported allegations of collusion between the Security services and loyalist terror groups are still under investigation by Sir John Stevens. A preliminary report of his findings, substantiating the allegation of collusion in general terms, was published in April 2003.

49 Such discussions had been ongoing within loyalism since 1975. See the *Conference Report* (1975) on the conference held by the Ulster Defence Association between 27 and 29 March 1975 at Hotel Frommer: 'In contrast to the definite goal of the I. R. A. the U. D. A. had no clear cut objective . . . Experience of the strike of May, 1974, led to the belief that it was important for the U. D. A. to take an initiative because manifestly they could not depend either upon their own politicians or upon Westminster . . . While the objective of the U. D. A. is to promote a Northern Ireland identity based on British traditions, it was nevertheless agreed that it might prove necessary to give some consideration to the possibility of some form of independence for Ulster' (Linen Hall Library, Belfast: Northern Ireland Political Collection).

50 *A Critical Look at Independence: Papers from a Weekend Workshop at Corrymeela* (1976). Corrymeela is an inter-denominational community centre at Ballycastle, Co. Antrim. For a vehement statement of the opposing view, see Brendan Clifford, *Against Ulster Nationalism* (1975; Belfast: 1992).

51 New Ulster Research Group, *Beyond the Religious Divide* (Belfast: 1979).

52 Ibid., p. 2. For a developed version of this thesis within a comparative framework, see Anthony Alcock, *Understanding Ulster* (Belfast: 1994), esp. pp. 140–50, where comparison is made with Finland, Cyprus and South Tyrol.

53 Interview in *Dawn: Independence for Ulster?* (Belfast: 1976), p. 13.

IX Reversals: 1886–1920

1 On Gladstonianism as a response to Fenianism, see R. F. Foster, *Modern Ireland, 1600–1972* (London: 1988), pp. 395–99; on the social and political context of the Fenian movement, see R. V. Comerford, *The Fenians in Context: Irish Politics and Society, 1848–1882* (Dublin: 1985); on agrarian discontent and attempts to defuse it, see Paul Bew, *Land and the National Question, 1858–1882* (Dublin: 1979); on the changing organisation and structure of Irish politics through the key reforms of the nineteenth century, see Theo Hoppen, *Elections, Politics and Society in Ireland, 1832–1885* (Oxford: 1984).

2 The fullest version of Butt's proposals for Irish self-government was set out in his *Irish Federalism: Its Meaning, Its Objects, and Its Hopes* (London: 3rd edn, 1871). On Butt generally, see David Thornley, *Isaac Butt and Home Rule* (London: 1964); on the context of Butt's attempts at constitutional reform, see Alvin Jackson, *Ireland, 1798–1998* (Oxford: 1999, 2000), pp. 109–17; on the development of Catholic disaffection under the Union, see Oliver MacDonagh, *Ireland: The Union and Aftermath* (London: 1977), pp. 53–71; on Daniel O'Connell's agitation for Repeal, see Oliver MacDonagh, *O'Connell: The Life of Daniel O'Connell, 1775–1847* (London: 1991); on Catholic Emancipation itself, see Fergus O'Ferrall, *Catholic Emancipation: Daniel O'Connell and the Birth of Irish Democracy* (Dublin: 1985).

3 On Parnellism, see F. S. L. Lyons, *Ireland since the Famine* (London: 1971, 1973), pp. 178–201; Foster, *Modern Ireland*, pp. 400–28.

4 A. V. Dicey, *England's Case against Home Rule* (London: 1886), p. 197.

5 Charles Louis de Secondat, Baron de Montesquieu, *Spirit of the Laws*, eds, Anne Cohler, Basia Miller and Harold Stone (Cambridge: 1989), p. 25: 'Therefore, moderation is the soul of these governments. I mean the moderation founded on virtue . . . ' On *public* virtue, or patriotism, as the moving principle of ancient republics and democracies, see ibid., p. 22: 'in a popular state there must be an additional spring, which is

VIRTUE'. Adam Ferguson was later to make use of the same argument in an effort to explain the precariousness which pervaded the achievement of moderation in aristocracies. See his *An Essay on the History of Civil Society* (Edinburgh: 1767), p. 103: 'The elevation of one class is a moderated arrogance; the submission of the other a limited deference . . . When this moderation fails on either side, the constitution totters.' It was this failure which, according to Edmund Burke, characterised the immoderately aristocratic government of eighteenth-century Ireland up to 1792. See his 'Letter to Sir Hercules Langrishe' (1792), in R. B. McDowell ed., *The Writings and Speeches of Edmund Burke: The Revolutionary War and Ireland* (Oxford: 1991), p. 600, where he describes the constitution of Ireland as amounting to a 'plebeian oligarchy' pretending to supply the advantages of aristocratic government: 'The Protestants of Ireland are not *alone* sufficiently the people to form a democracy; and they are *too numerous* to answer to the ends and purposes of an aristocracy. Admiration, that first source of obedience, can be only the claim or the imposture of the few.' In other words, the Protestant 'few' in Ireland could not plausibly stake a claim to popular acclamation, the Protestant 'many' were too numerous to constitute the few, and the many were in any case less admirable than the few. For Burke's diffuse impact on nineteenth-century British thought, see Stefan Collini, Donald Winch and John Burrow, *That Noble Science of Politics: A Study in Nineteenth-Century Intellectual History* (Cambridge: 1983, 1987), pp. 19–20; for his influence on A. V. Dicey, see Stefan Collini, *Public Moralists: Political Thought and Intellectual Life in Britain, 1850–1930* (Oxford: 1991), p. 293; for his importance to that section of the British liberal establishment that was to commit itself to Home Rule, see John Morley, *Burke* (London: 1879).

6   Gustave de Beaumont, *L'Irlande sociale, politique et religieuse* (Paris: 1839), 2 vols, II, p. 228. For Dicey's reference to de Beaumont see *England's Case against Home Rule*, p. 80. For attempts to explain the mechanisms of social accommodation both generally and with reference to eighteenth-century Britain, see Adam Smith, *The Theory of Moral Sentiments*, ed. D. D. Raphael and A. L. Macfie (Oxford: 1986), pp. 50–66, and John Millar, *Observations concerning the Distinction of Ranks in Society* (London: 1771), pp. 185–89. Smith traces the survival of social co-operation in the midst of inequality to the human 'disposition to admire' the fortunate (p. 64). But, as Burke saw, having studied Smith's *Moral Sentiments*, this disposition was scarcely infallible, and its failure, according to the 'Letter to Sir Hercules

Langrishe', was immediately observable in eighteenth-century Ireland, as the passage from the 'Letter' already cited makes plain: 'Admiration, that first source of obedience, can be only the claim or the imposture of the few.' On Burke's debt to Adam Smith, see Richard Bourke, 'Edmund Burke and Enlightenment Sociability: Justice, Honour and the Principles of Government', *Journal of the History of Political Thought*, 4 (2000), pp. 623–56.

7   Dicey, *England's Case against Home Rule*, pp. 70–80.

8   Ibid., pp. 137, 139.

9   For a later analysis of this omission as part of a general tendency, see G. F.-H. Berkeley, 'The Present System of Government in Ireland', in Basil Williams ed., *Home Rule Problems* (London: 1911), p. 35: 'One still meets Englishmen who do not yet realise that we already possess in Ireland a separate government, organised for Irish purposes, working, so to speak, within the ring-fence of Irish affairs and problems and entirely outside the circle of English interests, whether home or foreign. It deals with questions which are usually unknown to the English voter; it is paid for its services out of "Irish Expenditure".'

10 Matthew Arnold, Preface to *Irish Essays* (1882), in R. H. Super ed., *The Complete Prose Works of Matthew Arnold* (Ann Arbor: 1960–77), 11 vols. Arnold thought he had learned this piece of seeming wisdom from Edmund Burke. In the preface to his edition of Burke's *Letters, Speeches and Tracts on Irish Affairs* (London: 1881), p. x, he remarked that 'In general, our Governments, however well informed, feel bound, it would seem, to adapt their policy to our normal mental condition, which is, as Burke says, an unthinking one. Burke's paramount and undying merit as a politician is, that instead of accepting as fatal and necessary this non-thinking condition of ours, he battles with it, mends and changes it; he will not rest until he has "put people in a mood a little unusual with them", until he has "set them on thinking".' But under Arnold's direction, unlike Burke's, we are not encouraged to rethink Irish politics so much as Irish and British sensibilities – an integral part of Irish politics, certainly, but hardly sufficiently all-encompassing to instruct in isolation. Ultimately, Arnold was motivated to correct such forms of wanton prejudice as had found their consummate expression in J. A. Froude's *The History of the English in Ireland in the Eighteenth Century* (London: 1872–74). But this did not lead him towards an investigation of the realities of the political organisation of Ireland within the United Kingdom. Instead, in advertising the case for Irish cultural or racial particularity, he contributed, much like J. S. Mill before him, more to the development of

separatist arguments than to the defence of the Union whose necessity they had both avowedly been seeking to recommend. On this, see R. F. Foster, 'History and the Irish Question', *Transactions of the Royal Historical Society*, 1983, p. 179: 'Matthew Arnold's belief in Celtic qualities, though part of an argument for bringing Celtic culture fully into the Anglo-Saxon cultural and political system, reinforced a view of early Irish history and an interpretation of Celticism which strengthened irreconcilable ideas of separatism.' As evidence for this, over the longer term, one need look no further than W. B. Yeats' 'The Celtic Element in Literature' (1902), in *Essays and Introductions* (London: 1961, 1980). On the *mode* of argument adopted by Arnold, but duly promoted by rival political persuasions, see F. S. L. Lyons, *Culture and Anarchy in Ireland, 1890–1939* (Oxford: 1979), pp. 57–73; Margaret O'Callaghan, 'Denis Patrick Moran and "The Irish Colonial Condition", 1891–1921', in D. George Boyce, Robert Eccleshall and Vincent Geoghegan eds, *Political Thought in Ireland since the Seventeenth Century* (London: 1993), pp. 146–60; Patrick Maume, *The Long Gestation: Irish Nationalist Life, 1891–1918* (Dublin: 1999), pp. 1–13.

11 On the context of Arnold's *On the Study of Celtic Literature*, see J. V. Kelleher, 'Matthew Arnold and the Celtic Revival', in H. Levin ed., *Perspectives on Criticism* (Cambridge, Mass.: 1950), pp. 197–221; on the significance of his argument in the history of Irish cultural politics, see Seamus Deane, *Celtic Revivals: Essays in Modern Irish Literature* (London: 1985), pp. 17–27.

12 Arnold, *On the Study of Celtic Literature* in *Irish Essays*. Arnold's employment of literary history as a means of pointing up the deficiencies of contemporary political reality is broadly indebted to French and German cultural histories of the late eighteenth and nineteenth centuries. On the post-French Revolutionary attempt, in Britain and France in particular, to advance cultural theories of the development of 'national character', see Seamus Deane, *The French Revolution and Enlightenment in England, 1789–1832* (Cambridge, Mass.: 1998), esp. Ch. 2 and the discussion of Germaine de Staël. De Staël's argument received its most refined expression in *Des Circonstances actuelles qui peuvent terminer la révolution et des principes qui doivent fonder la République en France* (1798) (Paris: 1979). Here she argues that the modern republican spirit in France after 1793 had grown to dominate politics without the moderating influence of a 'public opinion' educated by literature: 'il leur manque l'art de captiver une nation' (p. 93). In due course, she explored the theme more fully in

De la Littérature, considérée dans ses rapports avec les institutions sociales (Paris: 1801), 2 vols, I, p. xvii: 'Dans l'état actuel de l'Europe, les progrès de la littérature doivent servir au developpement de toutes les idées généreuses.' The identification of literature and philosophy as formative agents in the history of modern French civilisation was taken up by François Guizot, at the close of *The History of Civilization in Europe* (1828) (London: 1997), pp. 242–43, where, however, their very independence from practical life is deemed to have posed a problem for political judgement: 'in France, in the eighteenth century, you find the human spirit exercising itself upon all things, upon ideas which, connecting themselves with the real interests of life, seemed calculated to have the most prompt and powerful influence upon facts. Nevertheless, the leaders and actors of these great discussions remained strangers to all species of practical activity – mere spectators, who observed, judged, and spoke, without ever interfering with events ... never before had philosophy aspired so strongly to rule the world, never had philosophy been so little acquainted with the world.' This argument was, of course, to become the core thesis advanced by Alexis de Tocqueville in Ch. 13 of *The Ancien Régime and the Revolution* (1856). Arnold, who, like so many other British publicists of his generation, was strongly influenced by Tocqueville, effectively inverted the Tocquevillian thesis, proposing instead the line first advocated by de Staël. In 'Democracy', which appeared in *The Popular Education of France* (1861), Arnold quotes Tocqueville on the corrupt manners of aristocracies; but his proposal for a solution consists in the promotion of 'high ideals' through the medium of culture (see Arnold, *Works*, II, pp. 9–18).

13 Matthew Arnold, *On the Study of Celtic Literature*. Inside a generation, this argument was taken up by J. R. Seeley, but with the reverse end in view: the failure of cultural cohesion – of a common principle of nationality – became grounds for a dissolution of the British Empire in the east. In *The Expansion of England* (1883; London: 1909), p. 54, Seeley was arguing that 'when the State advances beyond the limits of the nationality, its power becomes precarious and artificial. This is the condition of most empires; it is the condition for example of our own empire in India.' A decade later, William Edward Hartpole Lecky was coming to the same conclusion in 'The Empire: Its Value and Growth' (1893), reprinted in his *Historical and Political Essays* (London: 1910), p. 61: 'It is probable ... that the true tie that must unite the different portions of the Empire must be mainly a moral one ... the cohesion can only be permanently maintained by the wide diffusion of a larger and

Imperial patriotism, pervading the whole like a vital principle . . .' The diffusion of this patriotism, Lord Milner came to explain in *The Nation and the Empire* (London: 1913), p. xxxiv, was the 'difficult, but by no means impossible task' which imperialists of his generation had set out to achieve.

14   In pursuing this venture, Arnold was indirectly drawing on the procedures of eighteenth-century Scottish social and political analysis, but shorn of the more ambitious scope which had informed the original Scottish project. William Robertson, Adam Ferguson and John Millar had all sought to build on the arguments of David Hume and Adam Smith, both of whom had in turn emphasised their debt to Montesquieu's pivotal achievement, by connecting manners to morals and ultimately to laws. In *The History of the Reign of Emperor Charles V, With a View of the Progress of Society in Europe, from the Subversion of the Roman Empire, to the Beginning of the Sixteenth Century* (Dublin: 1862), 2 vols, I, p. 24, William Robertson, for instance, had argued that 'human society is in its most corrupted state [between the 6th and 11th centuries in Europe] when men have lost their original independence and simplicity of manners, but have not attained that degree of refinement which introduces a sense of decorum and propriety in conduct, as a restraint on those passions which lead to heinous crimes.' But the progress from rudeness to refinement in Robertson's account proceeds from the joint operation of the spread of chivalry (I, pp. 62–63), the expansion of commerce (I, p. 71), and the moderation of European governments (I, p. 140) – not by the simple and comparatively free-standing education of the passions advocated by Arnold. On the survival and modification of eighteenth-century Scottish historical and political argument in nineteenth-century Britain, see Collini et al., *That Noble Science of Politics*, pp. 23–62. For one channel by which this school of thought was popularised in nineteenth-century Ireland, see Marilyn Butler, 'Irish Culture and Scottish Enlightenment: Maria Edgeworth's Histories of the Future', in Stefan Collini, Richard Whatmore and Brian Young eds, *Economy, Polity and Society: British Intellectual History, 1750–1950* (Cambridge: 2000).

15   Matthew Arnold, *On the Study of Celtic Literature*.

16   On Arnold's understanding of the anarchy which threatened modern British politics, see Stefan Collini, *Arnold* (Oxford: 1988), pp. 69–92; on his proposed remedy, see the chapters on Arnold in David J. DeLaura, *Hebrew and Hellene in Victorian England: Newman, Arnold, Pater* (Austin, Tex.: 1969), and in John Holloway, *The Victorian Sage:*

Studies in Argument (London: 1953); for the broader European context of Arnold's thought and criticism, see Lionel Trilling, *Matthew Arnold* (1939; Oxford: 1982). On A. V. Dicey's nostalgia for British political culture in the period prior to 1867, see Richard Cosgrove, *The Rule of Law: Albert Venn Dicey, Victorian Jurist* (London: 1980), p. 30.

17   Arnold, 'Irish Catholicism and English Liberalism' (1878) and 'The Incompatibles' (1881), in *Irish Essays*. But see also *Culture and Anarchy*, ed. Stefan Collini (Cambridge: 1993), pp. 85–87.

18   The prospect of civil war as the alternative to Union had been keenly envisaged by unionists immediately before the 1801 Act of Union. See, for instance, the assessment advanced by Josiah Tucker in *Four Letters on Important National Subjects, Addressed to the Right Honourable The Earl of Shelbourne* (London: 2nd edn, 1773), p. 87: 'The destructive Civil Wars of 1641, to 1648, which ended in the Tyranny of a single Despote, set many Persons on considering the Nature, and Ends of Government. But they could agree in nothing, except in one Point; namely, that Aristotle's *Political Animal*, the People, was such a capricious, restless, thoughtless, and unreasonable Animal, that it must be governed and controuled by some superior Power, for the sake of preventing it from doing Mischief to itself, and to other Beings.' But this 'superior Power', as Tucker explained three years later, could not readily be reconciled with the devolution of legislative power to dependent colonies, since it is almost in the nature of colonies to strike for independence: between full incorporation and complete separation, there was little room for manoeuvre. As he put it in *The True Interest of Great Britain, Set Forth in Regard to the Colonies* (Philadelphia: 1776), p. 13: 'I believe (and if I am wrong, let the history of all Colonies, whether ancient or modern, from the days of THUCYDIDES down to the present time, confute me if it can; I say, till that is done I believe) that it is the nature of them all to aspire after Independence, and to set up for themselves as soon as ever they find that they are able to subsist, without being beholden to the Mother-Country.' By comparison with the American colonies, the case for Irish legislative independence was stronger, but still fatally flawed, in Tucker's view. In *The Respective Pleas and Arguments of the Mother Country and of the Colonies, Distinctly Set Forth* (Gloucester: 1775), pp. 15–16, Tucker claimed that 'Of all the Pleas for independence . . . the Claims, which were so artfully urged by the famous Mr. Molineux (another Disciple of Mr. Locke's) for the Independence of *Ireland*, seemed the most plausible. And yet even these amounted to nothing, when examined to the bottom.' But when American colonial independence had become a fact, and especially in

the aftermath of the 1798 Rebellion, Tucker turned his attention more deliberately to Ireland in order to recommend an incorporative union on the grounds that federalism within free states – as opposed to under monarchies – was a recipe for civil discord leading to separation since the spirit of party, and ultimately of faction, prospered under precisely the conditions of political liberty. As he put the case in T. B. Clarke, *Dean Tucker's Arguments on the Propriety of an Union Between Great Britain and Ireland* (Dublin: 1799), p. 47: 'Parties, however, should not be confounded with Factions; and, of the latter, Ireland has long been too productive. They have been its bane; but Incorporation [i.e. a full incorporative union] is the antidote . . . such bodies [i.e. factions] are always influenced by private, not public ambition: . . . their leaders would raise themselves upon the management of individuals and the fall of their country: because it is the very spirit of faction to have division and competition in the State, and not union in the Empire, not integrity in its parts.'

19 Dicey, *England's Case against Home Rule*, p. 73.

20 See above, Chapter IV, on the use to which the Austro-Hungarian example was put by both nationalist and federalist publicists after 1867. Butt, in *Irish Federalism*, p. 22, had himself invoked the example: 'Austrian statesmen rose to the necessity of giving to Hungary the free constitution which has made that country the strength, instead of the weakness, of the Austrian Confederation.' The other familiar examples were also deployed by Butt, p. 16: 'From the formation of the Achaean League to the incorporation of the North American Provinces into one dominion of Canada, the principle has forced itself upon nations. The Germanic Confederation, established at the Congress of Vienna, recognized it. For centuries each of the Swiss Cantons has preserved its perfect independence – while differing as they do in religion, language, and in race, they have found unity and security in one general confederation, and one general diet of them all.'

21 Dicey, *England's Case against Home Rule*, p. 109. As Dicey was aware, the argument for Southern Confederation against the American Union had been weakened by this objection. Lord Acton, in following the lead of John C. Calhoun's defence of the Confederate cause, as evidenced by his *Reports on the Civil War in America*, July 1862, reprinted in J. Rufus ed., *Essays in the History of Liberty by John Emerich Edward Dalberg-Acton* (Indianapolis: 1986), p. 319, had been forced to concede that, in his view, 'Slavery in the Southern States is less opposed to the first principles of political morality than are the Northern ideas of freedom.' The grounds for Acton's opposition to

American Unionism were most clearly set forth in his letter to General Lee, 4 November 1866, reprinted ibid., p. 363: 'Without presuming to decide the purely legal question, on which it seems evident to me from Madison's and Hamilton's papers that the Fathers of the Constitution were not agreed, I saw in State Rights the only availing check upon the absolutism of the sovereign will, and secession filled me with hope, not as the destruction but as the redemption of Democracy.'

22 Dicey, *England's Case against Home Rule*, p. 53.

23 Ibid., pp. 59–65.

24 A. V. Dicey, *Lectures Introductory to the Study of the Law of the Constitution* (London: 1885), p. 129.

25 Dicey, *England's Case against Home Rule*, p. 54.

26 Ibid., p. 66. On the extent to which this perception was widespread in nineteenth-century Europe, from Mill to Mazzini, see E. J. Hobsbawm, *Nations and Nationalism since 1870* (Cambridge: 1990), Ch. 1.

27 Dicey, *England's Case against Home Rule*, p. 66.

28 Ibid., p. 172.

29 Ibid., p. 165. This point had, again, been forcefully made by Josiah Tucker, *The Respective Pleas and Arguments*, p. 12: 'In all Societies there must be a dernier Resort, and a *Ne plus ultra* of ruling power.' On this, of course, Tucker was in agreement with Edmund Burke, with whom he was more generally in dispute over the fate of the American Colonies. Since there was no long term viable alternative between separatism and Unionism, and since at the same time circumstances favoured the former option over the latter in the case of America, Tucker felt confident, as he put it in *The True Interest of Great Britain*, p. 49, that 'a separation from the northern Colonies, and also another right measure, viz. a complete union and incorporation with Ireland (however unpopular either of them may now [in 1776] appear) will both take place within half a century'. In his 'Speech on Conciliation with the Colonies' (1775), in *Speeches and Letters on American Affairs* (London: 1908, 1945), p. 104, Burke had likewise conceded that, 'though every privilege is an exemption (in the case) from the ordinary exercise of the supreme authority, it is no denial of it. The claim of a privilege seems rather, *ex vi termini*, to imply a superior power.' Tucker's complaint about Burke, set forth in *An Humble Address and Earnest Appeal to Those Respectable Personages in Great Britain and Ireland . . . Whether a Connection With, or a Separation From, The Continental Colonies of America, Be Most For the National Advantage, and the Lasting Benefit of These Kingdoms* (London: 3rd rev. edn, 1776), turned not on the doctrine of sovereignty, but on the theory of empire,

as advanced by Burke, which sought to balance the privileges of dependencies against the supremacy of the seat of sovereignty: this scheme, Tucker insisted, 'had a tendency to sow Jealousies and Dissensions both at Home and Abroad, in the Mother-Country and in the Colonies' (p. 44). On Burke's theory of British imperial sovereignty, see Richard Bourke, 'Liberty, Authority, and Trust in Burke's Idea of Empire', *Journal of the History of Ideas* (Summer 2000), pp. 453–71.

30 Dicey, *England's Case against Home Rule*, pp. 165–70.

31 Ibid., p. 201.

32 Ibid., pp. 215, 201–3.

33 Ibid., pp. 232–33.

34 A. V. Dicey, *A Leap in the Dark: A Criticism of the Principles of Home Rule as Illustrated by the Bill of 1893* (London: 2nd edn, 1911), p. 118.

35 On nineteenth- and early twentieth-century debate about 'Home Rule All Round', see David Harkness, 'Ireland', in R. W. Winks ed., *The Oxford History of the British Empire: Historiography* (Oxford: 1999). For an indication of the persistence of Chamberlain's legacy, see 'Pacificus' [F. S. Oliver], *Federalism and Home Rule* (London: 1910). For the United States as a model for thinking about Imperial Federation, see F. S. Oliver, *Alexander Hamilton: An Essay in American Union* (London: 1906). The key text influencing opinion here had been James Bryce, *The American Commonwealth* (London: 1888), 3 vols. For a defence of the principle of 'Imperial Federation', whereby an imperial legislature would be distinguished from the United Kingdom legislature without federating the Union along the lines of Home Rule All Round, see L. S. Amery, 'Home Rule and the Colonial Analogy', in S. Rosenbaum ed., *Against Home Rule: The Case for the Union* (London: 1912).

36 J. L. Garvin, *The Life of Joseph Chamberlain* (London: 1932–34), 3 vols, II, p. 63.

37 Dicey, *A Leap in the Dark*, p. 33.

38 Ibid., p. 91.

39 Ibid., p. 96.

40 Ibid., pp. 43–48. Dicey was pleased to be able to point out that this criticism had been made by the liberal Home Ruler, John Morley, back in 1886, in a defence of the first Home Rule Bill – a criticism that should surely undermine his ardent defence of the second Bill, which he was nonetheless happy to recommend. Morley's original position was set out in *The Times*, 22 April 1886.

41 *Annual Register*, New Series (1893); *The Times*, 10 May 1893.

42 Dicey, *A Leap in the Dark*, p. 44.

43 Ibid., p. 45.

44 On the development of Dicey's views in response to the succession of Home Rule bills between 1886 and 1912, see Hugh Tulloch, 'A. V. Dicey and the Irish Question, 1870–1922', *Irish Jurist*, 15 (1980), pp. 137–65.

45 For these developments, see Paul Bew, *Ideology and the Irish Question*, Chs 1–2.

46 A. V. Dicey, *A Fool's Paradise, Being a Constitutionalist's Criticism on the Home Rule Bill of 1912* (London: 1913), p. viii.

47 For a treatment of these events, see A. T. Q. Stewart, *The Ulster Crisis: Resistance to Home Rule, 1912–1914* (London: 1967), Chs 1–5.

48 Nassau Senior, *Journals, Conversations and Essays Relating to Ireland* (London: 1868), 2 vols, I, p. 22.

49 Nicholas Mansergh, *The Irish Question, 1840–1921* (London: 1965), pp. 182–95. For a typical, but powerful subsequent use of the argument, see W. F. Monypenny, *The Two Irish Nations: An Essay on Home Rule* (London: 1913).

50 Arthur James Balfour, *Aspects of Home Rule* (London: 1912), pp. 55, 141.

51 E. Marjoribanks and I. Colvin, *The Life of Lord Carson* (London: 1932–36), 3 vols, II, p. 104.

52 On these events, see Foster, *Modern Ireland*, pp. 461–76.

53 *Agreement Reached in the Multi-Party Negotiations* (Dublin: 1998), Strand Two, s. 1: 'Under a new British/Irish Agreement dealing with the totality of relationships, and related legislation at Westminster and in the Oireachtas, a North/South Ministerial Council to be established to bring together those with executive responsibilities in Northern Ireland and the Irish Government, to develop consultation, co-operation and action within the island of Ireland . . . on matters of mutual interest within the competence of the Administrations, North and South'. See also above, Chapter VII , and below, Chapter X.

54 Nicholas Mansergh, *The Unresolved Question: The Anglo-Irish Settlement and Its Undoing, 1912–1972* (New Haven: 1991), p. 76.

55 Jackson, *Ireland, 1798–1998*, pp. 215–44. The intractable difficulties experienced in deciding between these arrangements exposes the vacuity of the remark by Ernest Renan in his 1882 lecture, 'What is a Nation', reprinted in Homi K. Bhabba ed., *Nation and Narration* (London: 1990), to the effect that a 'nation' is 'a daily plebiscite'.

56 See, on one side, Erskine Childers' defence of Home Rule in terms of democratic entitlement in *The Framework of Home Rule* (London:

1911), p. xiii: 'So long as one island democracy claims to determine the destinies of another island democracy, of whose special needs and circumstances it is admittedly ignorant, so long will both islands suffer.' On the other side, see The Marquis of Londonderry, 'The Ulster Question', in Rosenbaum ed., *Against Home Rule*, p. 164: 'Opposition to Home Rule in Ulster . . . has destroyed all differences between parties and classes. I doubt if there are any more democratic organizations than those of the Ulster Unionist Council, the Unionist Clubs, and the Orangemen . . . It is an uprising of a people against tyranny and coercion; against condemnation to servitude; against deprivation of the right of citizens to an effective voice in the government of the country.' For the view that the durability of modern empires is complicated by the emergence of modern democracy, see the 'Introduction' by C. P. Lucas to George Cornewall Lewis, *An Essay on the Government of Dependencies* (1841; Oxford: 1891), p. viii, where the requirement 'to adapt a system which was born in a despotic age to a time of democratic equality' is underlined. For the principle of nationality as an integral feature of modern democratic sentiment, see L. T. Hobhouse, 'Irish Nationalism and Liberal Principle', in J. H. Morgan ed., *The New Irish Constitution: An Exposition and Some Arguments* (London: 1912), p. 361: 'Successive generations hoped and feared, wept and rejoiced with the rebels of Greece, of Italy, of Hungary, of Poland, of the Balkans. Their successes and failures were events of moment in the calendar of British Liberalism, for they were recognised as essential parts of the democratic movement, and the democratic cause was in that century looked upon as one all the world over.'

57   This development was already evident in P. Kerr-Smiley's *The Peril of Home Rule* (London: 1911), p. 143: 'Irish Unionists hope that Great Britain in its wisdom will not establish a Parliament in Dublin; but if the worst comes to the worst, then they will confidently defy it, and one thing is certain, that the descendents of the men who held Londonderry, in the face of pestilence, fire, and sword, will never submit to be ruled by their hereditary enemies.' See also Anon., *Is Ulster Right?* (London: 1913), p. 248, where the case of Ulster is aligned at once with the cause of Empire and the right of 'self-preservation'.

58   For Arnold's commitment to the Union, see his *On Home Rule for Ireland* (London: 1891). For his scepticism about democracy, see 'Ecce, Convertimur ad Gentes' (1879), in *Works*, IX, pp. 15–17: 'The state is just what Burke very well called it . . . *the nation in its collective and*

corporate character. To use the state is simply to use cooperation of a superior kind . . . The middle classes cannot assume rule as they are at present, – it is impossible . . . they have lived in a narrow world of their own, without openness and flexibility of mind . . .' The political nation after 1867, not to mention after 1884, was therefore not, in Arnold's view, sufficiently humanised to generate an acceptable corporate character: the British state was consequently not yet ready for democracy. Dicey's defence of the Union against the spread of democratic sentiment is evident in *England's Case against Home Rule*, p. 43: 'For the first time in the course of English history, national policy has passed under the sway, not so much of democratic convictions, but a far stronger power – democratic sentiment.' His alarm about the dogmatic spread of egalitarian ideas in the context of debates about Home Rule was again trenchantly expressed in *A Leap in the Dark*, pp. 121–22. On the suspicion of democracy among public moralists of Dicey's generation, see Ernest Barker, *Political Thought in England, 1848–1914* (1915; London: 1947), and Collini, *Public Moralists*, pp. 251–307. On 1848 as a watershed, see Henry Summer Maine, *Popular Government* (1885; London: 1909), p. 88: 'by 1848 the word ['democracy'] had come to be used very much with its ancient meaning, the government of the commonwealth by the many'. On the importance of Tocqueville as a key reference for anxieties about egalitarianism in the earlier part of the century, see David P. Crook, *American Democracy in English Politics, 1815–1850* (Oxford: 1965); for Tocqueville's enduring significance, see J. W. Burrow, *Whigs and Liberals: Continuity and Change in English Political Thought* (Oxford: 1988), pp. 45–46. For the expression of these anxieties in the context of Irish politics, see William Edward Hartpole Lecky, *Democracy and Liberty* (1896; Indianapolis: 1981), 2 vols, II, pp. 1–13.

59 Dicey, *Law of the Constitution*, pp. 216–17.

60 In 'Equality', originally delivered as a lecture to the Royal Institution in February 1878, reprinted in Stefan Collini ed., *Culture and Anarchy*, Arnold made plain that while equality was the foundation of modern sociability – it explains why France had managed 'to attach so ardently to her the German and Protestant people of Alsace, while we have been so little able to attach the Celtic and Catholic people of Ireland' (p. 226) – it had first to be civilised if it was not to deteriorate into grasping selfishness.

61 See G. F.-H. Berkeley, 'The Present System of Government in Ireland', pp. 35–36: 'In England each separate department is represented by a Cabinet Minister . . . Should he make mistakes, he will at

once be checked either by popular clamour or by his own ministerial colleagues . . . But in Ireland the case is exactly the contrary. All the boards are represented in Parliament by one man, the Chief Secretary. He can utterly disregard popular clamour because he depends, not on the Irish taxpayer who pays him, but on the English taxpayer. Similarly, he is not tied to the Parliamentary majority of Ireland. He is in the position of Prime Minister, but of one entirely independent both of the people whom he rules and of any kind of Cabinet appointed by him.' See, by comparison, the expectation held out for devolution as described by Lord MacDonnell of Swinford, 'Irish Administration Under Home Rule', in J. H. Morgan ed., *The New Irish Constitution*, p. 79: 'responsibility for every agency engaged in the administration of public business in Ireland will attach to a particular Minister, responsible to the Irish Parliament . . . interest in Irish public business will be enormously stimulated in Ireland, and . . . a salutary public control will be effectively exercised.'

62 Of course, the South claimed that it had in fact pledged itself to an island state *de jure* on the principle of majority sovereignty, although the claim was subsequently withdrawn with the signing of the Anglo-Irish Agreement in 1985.

63 Dicey had himself already pointed to the dilemmas which would accompany the attempt to apply the democratic principle of majority choice to the determination of democratic sovereignty in *England's Case against Home Rule*, p. 69: 'the principle that the will of the majority should be sovereign cannot, whether true or false in itself, be invoked to determine a dispute turning upon the enquiry which of two bodies is the body the majority of which has a right to sovereignty. The majority of the citizens of the United States were opposed to Secession, the majority of the citizens of the Southern States were in favour of Secession; the attempt to determine which side had right on its side by an appeal to the "sovereignty of the majority" involved in this case, as it must in every case, a *petitio principii*, for the very question at issue was which of two majorities ought, as regarded the matter in hand, to be considered the majority.'

64 Amongst the earliest discussions of the problem appears in Lord Acton, 'Nationality' (1862), reprinted in Rufus ed., *Essays in the History of Liberty*. According to Acton, the 'theory of nationality' was the most 'powerful auxiliary of revolution' in modern times (p. 414); but he also understood the demand for nationality to be part of a modern movement of thought which embraced socialism and the doctrine of sovereignty of the people too: 'Rousseau proclaimed the

first, Baboeuf the second, Mazzini the third' (pp. 411–12). It is clear that the common denominator between all three is the principle of equality, and that therefore, without actually stating the fact, he grouped nationality, along with popular sovereignty and socialism, under the general heading of 'democracy'.

65 It is evidently the case that, in technical terms, Northern Irish sovereignty resided at Westminster; but, regarding matters devolved to the competence of the Stormont parliament, Northern Irish politics after 1920 nonetheless endeavoured to operate on the principle of majority sovereignty. See above, Chapters II and VII.

X Siege: 1982–1998

1 All of these positions were canvassed in unionist pamphlet literature between 1982 and 1998. A common refrain can be found in James Allister's *Irish Unification Anathema* (Belfast: 1982), p. 9: 'Irish unification could only occur by a suppression of Northern Ireland's democratic right of self-determination ... the most fundamental constitutional right people can enjoy – the right of freely choosing their own destiny.' During the same period, David Trimble wrote in support of 'an Executive formed in the usual way [i.e. by majority vote] and a committee system with various powers to check the Executive' in *Options: Devolved Government for Northern Ireland* (Belfast: 1982), p. 16; John Biggs-Davidson set out the argument for a United Ireland that was 'part of Islands United once again' in *United Ireland, United Islands? A Conservative and Unionist Approach to the New Ireland Forum* (September 1984); Robert McCartney spelt out the case for integration in *The Case for Integration* (Belfast: 1986); and Alistair Cooke supported power-sharing without an 'Irish dimension' in *Ulster: The Unionist Options* (London: 1990).

2 See *Combat: The Voice of the Ulster Volunteer Force*, vol. 2, no. 5, 1975: the UVF 'acknowledges that rebellion against lawful government is a grievous sin against God; nevertheless, when a government becomes so radically and incurably corrupt that it ceases to respect the democratic wishes of its subjects', then rebellion by the people is justified.

3 On nationalism as founded upon a fictitious or 'imagined' community, see Benedict Anderson, *Imagined Communities: Reflections on the Origin and Spread of Nationalism* (London: 1983). The argument, however, has an extended pedigree. For its elaboration in Thomas

Hobbes, see the latter's claim in *The Elements of Law*, ed. J. C. A. Gaskin (Oxford: 1994), p. 120, to the effect that a political community is a 'fictitious body'. For Hobbes' subsequent modification of the view in *Leviathan*, where 'personated' is substituted for 'fictitious', see Quentin Skinner, 'Hobbes and the Purely Artificial Person of the State', in *Visions of Politics: Hobbes and Civil Science* (Cambridge: 2002).

4   This perception, it seems, still underwrites Sinn Féin policy today. See the Sinn Féin 'Position Paper', presented to the then British Secretary of State for Northern Ireland, Mo Mowlam, at Stormont, 7 August 1997: 'The route to peace in Ireland is to be found in the restoration to the Irish people as a whole of our right to national self-determination . . . We believe that the wish of the majority of the people of Ireland is for Irish Unity. We believe that an adherence to democratic principles makes Irish unity inevitable.' By 27 February 2002, in a Keynote Address by Gerry Adams to a Sinn Féin Special Conference in Dublin, it was still the case that 'Self-determination for the people of this island has yet to be achieved.' Both statements appear on http://cain.ulst.ac.uk.

5   The argument that the rhetoric of modern democracy masks the reality of oligarchical organisation was pervasively advanced in the early twentieth century. See, for example, Robert Michels, *Political Parties: A Sociological Study of the Oligarchical Tendencies of Modern Democracy*, trans. Eden Paul and Cedar Paul (New York: 1962). The point being advanced here, however, is not that modern democracies are disguised oligarchies, but rather that power is not exercised by populations inside contemporary democracies by direct political means, but by indirect social means: its direct exercise is an instrument of revolution, not of democracy, and the 'direct' revolutionary power of the people is in any case in reality directly exercised by their political leaders under circumstances which require the most rigorous political control. On the fraught relationship between revolutionary propaganda and actual revolutionary practice, see John Dunn, *Modern Revolutions: An Introduction to the Analysis of a Political Phenomenon* (Cambridge: 1972, 1989); Theda Scocpol, *States and Social Revolutions* (Cambridge: 1979); John Dunn, 'Understanding Revolutions', in *Rethinking Modern Political Theory* (Cambridge: 1985).

6   On the political significance and character of fear, see Thomas Hobbes, *Elementorum philosophiae sectio tertia de cive* (1642), ed. Howard Warrender (Oxford: 1983), I, §ii, where fright, diffidence, distrust, suspicion and precaution are all presented as constituent

elements of the passion. Hobbes' interest in the dynamics of fear derives, at least in part, from his study of Thucydides. See Thucydides, *The Peloponnesian War: The Complete Hobbes Translation*, ed. David Grene (Chicago and London: 1989), Bk. I, §23: the truest cause of the Peloponnesian war 'I conceive to be the growth of the Athenian power, which putting the Lacedaemonians into fear necessitated the war'.

7   This reaction, moreover, had been anticipated in advance. See the expectation expressed by Ken Bloomfield, head of the Northern Ireland Civil Service on the eve of the signing of the Anglo-Irish Agreement, that the Agreement would 'drive Ulster Unionism deeper and deeper into a laager of dangerous resentment', in his *Stormont in Crisis* (Belfast: 1994), p. 254.

8   Parliamentary Debates (Hansard), Sixth Series, vol. 87, col. 29.

9   For the text of the joint communiqué issued after the summit, see Martin Mansergh ed., *The Spirit of the Nation: The Speeches and Statements of Charles J. Haughey, 1957–1986* (Cork and Dublin: 1986), pp. 406–14. For discussion of its impact, see Anthony Kenny, *The Road to Hillsborough: The Shaping of the Anglo-Irish Agreement* (Oxford: 1986), p. 37. On the meeting held the previous May, see Bruce Arnold, *Haughey: His Life and Unlucky Deeds* (London: 1993), pp. 167–69: 'Privately, Haughey was both pleased and puzzled. He was pleased at the superficial success of the encounter . . . At the same time he was puzzled about what she might do about Northern Ireland in the future.' On the December summit, see ibid., pp. 172–73: 'He [Haughey] oversold the encounter . . . the communiqué did, however, indicate some important achievements.'

10 Peter Robinson, *Ulster in Peril: An Exposure of the Dublin Summit* (Belfast: 1981), p. 5.

11 Quoted in Peter Taylor, *Loyalists* (London: 1999), p. 177.

12 *Possible New Institutional Structures*, Cmnd. 8414 (London: 1981).

13 *Belfast Telegraph*, 13 January 1980.

14 See, however, Margaret Thatcher's recent comments on nationalism and 'the national interest' in regard to Montenegro in her *Statecraft: Strategies for a Changing World* (London: 2002), p. 318: 'the European Union has been warning Montenegro against breaking away from Serbia. One really might have thought that international diplomats would have learned by now the lesson of trying to tell other people what is in their own national interest. Montenegrins are inevitably tempted by the thought of a modestly prosperous life without being bullied or bled by Serbs. It is for Serbia – not us – to try to persuade

them to stay, by offering suitably favourable terms.'

15 New Ireland Forum, *Report* (Dublin: 1984), ss. 5.4, 5.5.

16 *Belfast Telegraph*, 20 November 1984.

17 The Anglo-Irish Agreement 1985 in Tom Hadden and Kevin Boyle, *The Anglo-Irish Agreement: Commentary, Text and Official Review* (London: 1989), Part B: The Intergovernmental Conference, pp. 22–30.

18 For an early recommendation that the British government should move in this direction, see the proposals set down by the former British Ambassador to Dublin, John Peck, in his *Dublin from Downing Street* (Dublin: 1978), p. 220. For the most probing assessment of its long term success as a strategy, see Paul Arthur, *Special Relationships: Britain, Ireland and the Northern Ireland Problem* (Belfast: 2000), pp. 179–221. For an analysis of the international significance of the 1985 Agreement, see Clive R. Simmons, 'The Anglo-Irish Agreement and International Precedents: A Unique Experiment in Inter-State Co-operation on Minority Rights', in Jon Hayes and Paul O'Higgins eds, *Lessons From Northern Ireland* (Belfast: 1990).

19 For the long term impact of the Anglo-Irish Agreement on the Southern Irish grasp of Northern realities, and on the British grasp of Irish 'sensitivities', see the view expressed by the one time Conservative Minister in Northern Ireland, Richard Needham, in his *Battling for Peace* (Belfast: 1999), pp. 78–79: 'the work of the conference did start to give Southern politicians and Southern policy-makers a much better feel for the intractable division between the two communities in the North . . . On the British side, the Anglo-Irish Agreement led to the NIO [Northern Ireland Office] taking greater account of Southern sensitivities and of the need for more consultation and discussion.' See also the similar verdict of W. Harvey Cox, 'From Hillsborough to Downing Street – And After', in Peter Catterall and Sean McDougall eds, *The Northern Ireland Question in British Politics* (London: 1996), p. 185.

20 Garret Fitzgerald, *All in a Life* (Dublin: 1992), p. 532.

21 Margaret Thatcher, *The Downing Street Years* (London: 1993), p. 385.

22 The Anglo-Irish Agreement 1985, Part B, Article 2 (b).

23 *Belfast News Letter*, 16 November 1985.

24 The range and character of that dismay can be gleaned from a selection of pamphlets from the period: Anon., *Government Without Majority Consent: A Unionist View of the Anglo-Irish Agreement, 1985* (Surrey: 1987); E. Haslett, *Ulster Must Say No: A Commentary on the Anglo-Irish Agreement* (Belfast: 1986); Ian Gow, *Ulster After the Agreement*

(London: 1986); John Biggs-Davison, *Ulster Catholics and the Union* (London: 1986), Conor Cruise O'Brien, *Addresses to the Friends of the Union* (London: 1988).

25   Parliamentary Debates (Hansard), Sixth Series, vol. 87, col. 29.

26   Nigel Lawson, *The View From No. 11: Memoirs of a Tory Radical* (London: 1992), p. 699.

27   The central, and fateful, role played by Robert Armstrong in the negotiations leading up to the Anglo-Irish Agreement is captured by John Oliver, former Northern Ireland Civil Servant, in his *Headway in Ulster: Some Practical Ideas* (London: 1987). See Geoffrey Howe, *Conflict of Loyalty* (London: 1994), p. 426–27, on his own comparatively relaxed attitude to the arrangements established under the Anglo-Irish Agreement as compared with Margaret Thatcher's: 'her head was persuaded, her heart was not'. See also Mark Stuart, *Douglas Hurd, The Public Servant: An Authorised Biography* (Edinburgh and London: 1998), p. 149, on Hurd's contribution to persuading Thatcher to sign up to the Agreement.

28   Peter Smith, *Opportunity Lost: A Unionist View of the Report of the Forum for a New Ireland* (Belfast: 1984), p. 3.

29   Kilbrandon Committee, *Northern Ireland: Report of an Independent Inquiry* (London: 1984).

30   Ibid., p. 15.

31   Ulster Unionist Party, *The Way Forward* (Belfast: 1984), pp. 3, 4, 6–8.

32   Democratic Unionist Party, *Ulster: The Future Assured* (Belfast, 1984), p. 2.

33   Ibid., p. 5.

34   *Belfast Telegraph*, 24 November 1985.

35   Committee on the Government of Northern Ireland (Northern Ireland Assembly), *Report, Proceedings and Appendices* (Belfast: 1986), Part I, s. 8.

36   Ibid., Part I, s. 52.

37   On uncertainty about how the RUC would react at this time, see Arwel Ellis Owen, *The Anglo-Irish Agreement: The First Three Years* (Cardiff: 1994), p. 19.

38   *Fortnight*, 24 February – 9 March 1986.

39   Paisley established the Ulster Resistance on 10 November 1986 in an effort to bring down the Anglo-Irish Agreement. The Ulster Clubs were established by Alan Wright, in imitation of Carson's anti-Home Rule trail-blazing activities, but again with the Anglo-Irish Agreement as the target for resistance. 'Hoping for the best but preparing for the worst' became the official slogan of the Ulster Clubs.

40 Interview with John Alderdice MP, in Feargal Cochrane, *Unionist Politics and the Politics of Unionism since the Anglo-Irish Agreement* (Cork: 1997, 2001), p. 28.

41 The UDA pamphlet, *Beyond the Religious Divide*, had been published back in 1979. See above, Chapter VIII, for a discussion.

42 *Common Sense* (Belfast: 1987), p. 9. On the emergence of the Ulster Democratic Party, the political wing of the UDA, in the aftermath of the *Common Sense* document, see Gary McMichael, *An Ulster Voice: In Search of Common Ground in Northern Ireland* (Dublin: 1999), pp. 24–37.

43 Harold McCusker, Peter Robinson and Frank Millar, *The Task Force Report: An End to Drift* (Belfast: 1987), p. 7.

44 *The Times*, 21 January 1992. Few nationalists concurred with this assessment.

45 Nonetheless, on the importance of the Brooke initiative as slowly inching unionists 'out of their blind alley', see David Bloomfield, *Political Dialogue in Northern Ireland: The Brooke Initiative, 1989–1992* (Basingstoke: 1998).

46 *Irish Times*, 11 November 1992.

47 See David Bloomfield, *Developing Dialogue in Northern Ireland: The Mayhew Talks, 1992* (Basingstoke: 2001), p. 141, on the determination on the British side to make sure that the door 'remained open for future' negotiations after the collapse of the Mayhew initiative.

48 An account of the talks between the SDLP and Sinn Féin since 1988 is given in Brian Rowan, *Behind the Lines: The Story of the IRA and Loyalist Ceasefires* (Belfast: 1995), pp. 7–18. For Sinn Féin's response to discussions with the SDLP in 1988, see Gerry Adams, *A Pathway to Peace* (Cork and Dublin: 1988), pp. 73–76. For the original Sinn Féin and SDLP positions c.1988, see the *Irish Times*, 7 September 1988, and the *Irish Times*, 19 September 1988.

49 *Irish News*, 26 April 1993.

50 See David McKittrick, *Endgame: The Search for Peace in Northern Ireland* (Belfast: 1994), p. 310; Jack Holland, *Hope Against History: The Course of Conflict in Northern Ireland* (London: 1999), pp. 225–62; Thomas Hennessey, *The Northern Ireland Peace Process* (Dublin: 2000), pp. 67–114. For John Major's account of his government's discussions with the IRA, see *John Major: The Autobiography* (London: 1999), pp. 442–47. See also Anthony Seldon, *Major: A Political Life* (London: 1997), pp. 415–18. For the claim that both the British and the Irish governments' dealings with the Sinn Féin leader stretch back at least as far as 1987, see Ed Moloney, *A Secret History of the IRA* (London: 2002), pp. 248, 277.

51   Downing Street Declaration, 15 December 1993, §§1, 2.
52   The inevitability of compromise was publicly signalled in a letter from
      Danny Morrison to Gerry Adams in 1991, reprinted in Morrison's
      Then the Walls Come Down: A Prison Journal (Cork: 1999), p. 91. The
      private recognition of this inevitability dates back, however, to the
      aftermath of both the Anglo-Irish Agreement and the IRA Libyan
      arms shipments when Provo arguments in favour of a 'nine month'
      blitz from which '200 or 300 or 400' deaths might result lost out to
      plans to intensify political engagement with Irish nationalism (Danny
      Morrison, Interview with the author, February 2003).
53   Ann Purdy, *Molyneaux: The Long View* (Antrim: 1989), sets out the
      case for the UUP leader's calculating prescience in the context of
      political stalemate. But when the stalemate was disturbed, Molyneaux
      was flummoxed.
54   *Belfast Telegraph*, 22 February 1995.
55   On Trimble's journey from Vanguard to the leadership of the UUP,
      see Henry McDonald, *Trimble* (London: 2000).
56   On the build-up to Sinn Féin's joining the negotiations, see Mo
      Mowlam, *Momentum: The Struggle for Peace, Politics and the People*
      (London: 2002), pp. 110–14.
57   George Mitchell, *Making Peace: The Inside Story of the Making of the
      Good Friday Agreement* (London: 1999), pp. 3–4. For the period
      between the 'Frameworks' Document and the Good Friday
      Agreement, see Paul Bew and Gordon Gillespie, *The Northern Ireland
      Peace Process, 1993–1996: A Chronology* (London: 1996); Henry
      Patterson, *Ireland Since 1939* (Oxford: 2002), pp. 325–43.
58   George Mitchell, *Making Peace*, pp. 181–82.
59   On these provisions altogether, see *Agreement Reached in the Multi-
      Party Negotiations* (Dublin: 1998), 'Strand One: Democratic
      Institutions in Northern Ireland'; 'Strand Two: North/South
      Ministerial Council'; 'Strand Three: British–Irish Council, British–
      Irish Intergovernmental Conference'. For a detailed account of these
      proposed arrangements, see Brendan O'Leary, 'Comparative Political
      Science and the British–Irish Agreement', in John McGarry ed.,
      *Northern Ireland and the Divided World: Post-Agreement Northern
      Ireland in Comparative Perspective* (Oxford: 2001).
60   *Agreement Reached in the Multi-Party Negotiations*, 'Declaration of
      Support', s. 5.
61   Ibid., 'Strand One', ss. 5, 6.
62   Ibid., 'Strand One', ss. 5, d (i)–(ii).
63   Edward Gibbon, *The History of the Decline and Fall of the Roman*

Empire, ed. J. B. Bury (London: 2nd edn, 1900–2), 7 vols, I, Ch. 2.

64   Voltaire, *Le Siècle de Louis XIV* (Berlin: 1751). 2 vols, II, p. 138. The point is not that Voltaire's claim was uncontroversially true – it was anything but – but rather that a constitutional settlement does not have to be a democratic settlement.

65   On this understanding, a democratic state is a union of equals under a representative system. Executive action within that system is carried out by the government, staffed again by representatives. A properly functioning democracy is therefore doubly representative: the *system* of rule must be representative in the sense that it must answer to the popular expectation of equal treatment under that system, and individual representatives governing the community (MPs, Ministers, and so on) must be answerable to the popular expectation of fair competition for power.

66   *Agreement Reached in the Multi-Party Negotiations*, 'Constitutional Issues', s. 1 (v) and 'Validation, Implementation and Review', s. 7.

67   In a Statement issued by Gerry Adams on 18 October 1999, the implication that the Good Friday Agreement was a transitional settlement on the way to an island democracy was made perfectly apparent: 'We recognise the fears of the unionist section of our people. We want to make peace with you. We want to share the island of Ireland with you on a democratic and equal basis' (http://cain.ulst.ac.uk). But for an analysis of the Provisionals as having capitulated to partition, see Anthony MacIntyre, 'Republicans Acknowledging a Democratic Basis to Partition', *The Blanket*, 10 February 2002.

68   For competing claims about the character of representation in Revolutionary France, see Istvan Hont, 'The Permanent Crisis of a Divided Mankind: "Contemporary Crisis of the Nation State"' in Historical Perspective', in John Dunn ed., *Contemporary Crisis of the Nation State?* (Oxford: 1995), p. 204 and *passim*: 'Sieyès' definition of the popular political community ... Robespierre claimed, was the most odious despotism ever invented because it allowed no recourse to the people against their own representative.' On the conflict between competing theories of representation in early twentieth-century Germany, see Max Weber, 'Parliament and Government in Germany Under a New Political Order', in Peter Lassman and Ronald Spiers eds, *Weber: Political Writings* (Cambridge: 1994). On the character of representation in the American federation as proposed by James Madison, see *The Federalist Papers*, ed. Isaac Kramnick (London: 1987), p. 373: 'The true distinction between [ancient and American

representation] ... lies *in the total exclusion of the people in their collective capacity*, from any share [in the American government].' For discussion of the historic shift in the theory of representation in America between 1776 and 1787, see J. R. Pole, *Political Representation in England and the Origins of the American Republic* (New York: 1966), pp. 537–38. For this theme in its wider context, see Hanna Fenichel Pitkin, *The Concept of Representation* (Berkeley, LA: 1967); Bernard Manin, *The Principles of Representative Government* (Cambridge: 1997).

69 See, however, in opposition to the populist presumption, Emmanuel Joseph Sieyès, *Qu'est-ce que le Tiers-État?* (Paris: 3rd edn, 1789), p. 7: 'It is a false and dangerous idea to presume the existence of a contract between a People and its Government. The Nation does not contract with its mandatories, she *authorises* them to exercise their powers.'

70 This does not, of course, imply that individual representatives within the representative system have no relation to the constituencies for which they stand and neither, by implication, does it imply that the system deliberates and decides in isolation from the pressures of public opinion. Instead, it implies that the intensity of popular political senti-ment is moderated by the participation of individual representatives in a political process which curtails their liberty to advance their optimal demands. By these means, successful democratic representation progressively depoliticises democratic civilians – it is not an instrument of populist political control.

71 Alexis de Tocqueville, *Democracy in America*, trans. Harvey C. Mansfield and Delba Winthrop (Chicago: 2000), pp. 3, 6.

72 The argument that the democratic doctrine of the 'rights of man' is a species of fanaticism derives from Edmund Burke. See the remark contained in his 'Letter to Richard Burke, Esq.' (19 February 1792), in Paul Langford et al. eds, *The Writings and Speeches of Edmund Burke* (Oxford: 1981–), IX, p. 647: 'It is the new fanatical Religion, now in the heat of its first ferment, of the Rights of Man, which rejects all establishments, all discipline, all Ecclesiastical, and in truth all Civil Order, which will triumph, and will lay prostrate your Church; which will destroy your distinctions, and which will put your properties to auction, and disperse you over the earth.' It is, however, entirely questionable whether modern egalitarian struggle derives from a fanatical expression of the religious spirit. In the twentieth century, populist 'fanaticism' has been typically identified, in neo-Burkean fashion, with Messianism: see, for example, J. L. Talmon, *The Origins of Totalitarian Democracy: Political Theory and Practice During the French Revolution and Beyond* (London: 1952), pp. 249–55.

73   On democratic equality in relation to vanity or, in Rousseauian parlance, *amour-propre* – see John Rawls, *The Law of Peoples* (Cambridge, Mass.: 1999), pp. 34–35: 'amour-propre ... shows itself in a people's insisting on receiving from other people a proper respect and recognition of their equality'. This, of course, leads Rawls' argument in directions which it might prefer not to go.

74   Quoted in Robert Fisk, *The Point of No Return: The Strike Which Broke the British in Ulster* (London: 1975), p. 49.

Epilogue: 1998–2003

1   Eamonn Mallie and David McKittrick, *Endgame in Ireland* (London: 2001, 2002), pp. 291–335; Deaglán De Bréadún, *The Far Side of Revenge: Making Peace in Northern Ireland* (Cork: 2001), pp. 332–62.

2   Dick Walsh, 'Setback to High Hopes of Three Years Ago', *Irish Times*, 10 August 2001; Rosie Cowan, 'General Testifies to IRA Arms Destruction', *Guardian*, 27 October 2001.

3   David McKittrick, 'Assembly Politicians Bow to the Inevitable', *Independent*, 15 October 2002.

4   John Murray Brown, 'Blair Challenges IRA Commitment to Peace', *Financial Times*, 18 October 2002.

5   The postponement was described by Steven King as 'the most blatant demonstration of British sovereignty over Northern Ireland since Peter Mandelson suspended the Assembly for the first time in February, 2000', in 'Some Unionists Must Stop Seizing Defeat from the Jaws of Victory', *Belfast Telegraph*, 9 May 2003.

6   This was in fact the verdict of the Joint Declaration, published by the British and Irish governments in April 2003: 'A key impediment to completing the evolution' towards an inclusive settlement 'is that both major traditions have lacked confidence and trust in each other'.

7   David McKittrick, *Through the Minefield* (Belfast: 1999), pp. 165–68; Ruth Dudley Edwards, *The Faithful Tribe: An Intimate Portrait of the Loyal Institutions* (London: 1999), pp. 410–30. More generally, for an account of post-Agreement Protestant disaffection, see Susan McKay, *Northern Protestants: An Unsettled People* (Belfast: 2000), *passim*.

8   Jim Gibney, in an interview with the author in February 2003, declared specifically that Sinn Féin were now keen to look at 'federal arrangements' for a new united Ireland.

9   *Irish Times*, 24 October 2001.

10   *Agreement Reached in the Multi-Party Negotiations* (Dublin: 1998), 'Constitutional Issues', s. 1 (i).

11   Senator George Mitchell, Interview with the author, November 2002.

12   *Agreement Reached in the Multi-Party Negotiations* Annex A, s. 1 (i).

13   *Parliamentary Brief* (Summer 1994).

14   Martin Mansergh, 'Is Consent Sufficient for a United Ireland?', *Sunday Business Post*, 10 November 2002.

15   Steven King, 'Border Poll on Election Day Would Maximise UUP Vote', *Irish Times*, 19 September 2002.

16   Frank Millar, 'Wondering Which Way the Unionist Tide Will Turn', *Irish Times*, 27 July 2002.

17   Mitchel McLaughlin, 'Debate Must Accept United Ireland Question', *Irish Times*, 31 October 1997. See also 'McLaughlin Delivers United Ireland Message in Australia', *An Phoblacht–Republican News*, 7 March 2002; 'United Ireland Will Not Be a Cold House for Unionists: Adams in New York', *An Phoblacht–Republican News*, 7 February 2002.

18   Mitchel McLaughlin, 'Towards 2016 – A United Ireland', *An Phoblacht–Republican News*, 22 August 2002; Bimpe Fatogun, 'A United Ireland Could be a Reality', *Irish News*, 16 December 2002; Steven King, 'Don't Shout "Bingo" too Soon', *Belfast Telegraph*, 19 December 2002; Jack Holland, 'Census Results: A Blow to Republican Strategy?' *Irish Echo*, 19 December 2002; Anthony McIntyre, 'Victory 2016 Plus 40', *The Blanket*, 19 December 2002; Barry White, 'Counting the Days Ahead', *Belfast Telegraph*, 21 December 2002; Henry McDonald, 'Damned Statistics', *Observer*, 22 December 2002; Brian Feeney, 'Census Shows that Change will be Rapid', *Irish News*, 1 January 2003.

19   PRO, CJ 3/28, 'Referendum to Decide the Constitutional Position of Northern Ireland', 1 December 1969: the view is attributed to Callaghan by the official composing the memorandum. But see the view of Alvin Jackson, *Home Rule: An Irish History, 1800–2000* (London: 2003), pp. 318–19, to the effect that the steady increase in the nationalist vote could reconcile Sinn Féin to a quasi-autonomous Northern Ireland: if it does not, a 'future bloody endgame' might ensue.

20   In addition to the examples cited in the text above in Chapters III, VI and VII, see the verdict of Edward Heath, *The Course of My Life: An Autobiography* (London: 1998), p. 421: 'the bitter, tribal loathing between the hardline elements of the two communities, springing from an atavism which most of Europe discarded long ago'. See also Reginald Maudling, *Memoirs* (London: 1978), p. 180, for whom the

conflict was 'racial' rather than religious: 'It is very hard for an Englishman to understand the feelings of those who live in Northern Ireland. The history of their struggles is a long one, and they tend to cherish every moment of hatred in it. The deep divide between Catholic and Protestant, which, incidentally, is more racial than religious, had been handed down faithfully from generation to generation.'

21   The obvious exception to this expectation is Karl Marx, *The Communist Manifesto*, ed. Fredric L. Bender (New York: 1998), p. 56: 'Our epoch . . . possesses this distinctive feature: it has simplified class antagonism. Society as a whole is more and more splitting into two hostile camps.' However, his anticipation of the precise form of conflict that would afflict the age of 'equality' has not been exhaustively borne out by events.

22   David Hume, *A Treatise of Human Nature*, eds L. A. Selby-Bigge and P. H. Nidditch (Oxford: 1888, 1990), p. 377. On the dynamics of group jealousy and fear, see ibid., p. 379, where the account of Italian civil dissensions given in Francesco Guicciardini's *The History of Italy* is cited to exemplify the point.

B.

Index

Magilligan prison camp 114
Maguire, Frank 149
Maidstone 114
Major, John/Major government 290, 292, 317n10
Mallon, Seamus 408n61
Mandelson, Peter 305, 408n61
Mansergh, Martin: 'The Background to the Irish Peace Process' 313n1
Marighela, Carlos: *For the Liberation of Brazil* 378n56
Martin, Leo 87, 110
Marx, Karl: *The Communist Manifesto* 443n21
Marxism and Neo-Marxism 28, 32, 62, 356–7n90
Mason, Roy 231–2, 234, 235, 236, 237, 246–7
Mates, Major Michael 354n77
Maudling, Reginald 113, 159, 162, 201, 203, 316n6, 396n1, 407n57, 443n20
Mayhew, Sir Patrick 290
Maze Prison 147, 148, 149, 150–1, 152, 172
Meehan, Martin 355n81, 375n40
Melaugh, Eamonn 65–6
Mellows, Liam 322n12, 356n90, 371n19, 380n60
MI5 235
MI6 235
Mill, James 316n5
Mill, John Stuart 27, 389n11, 420n10
Considerations on Representative Government 316n5
England and Ireland 364n31
Millar, Frank 316n8, 388n4, 389n5, 437n43, 442n16
Millar, John 423n14
Milner, Alfred, Lord: *The Nation and the Empire* 423n13
Mitchell, Senator George 293, 296, 308

Mitchell, Rob 249
Molloy, Francie 370n12
Moloney, Ed: *A Secret History of the IRA* 339n42, 369n12, 372n24, 382n77, 385n84, 437n50
Molyneaux, James 222, 241, 243, 266, 289, 290, 291, 292, 438n53
Monaghan 266
bombing (1974) 248
Monson, Lord 202
Montesquieu, Charles de Secondat, Baron de 254, 423n14
Morley, John 427n40
Morrell, Leslie 213
Morrison, Danny 148, 153, 176, 370n12, 371n18, 382n75, 383n80, 386n95, 412n9
'Bodenstown Oration' (1977) 175, 376n48
Republican News articles (as 'Peter Arnlis') 166, 371n19
Murphy, Tom 372n24
Murray, Harry 216–17

Napier, Colonel 354n75
Napier, Oliver 212, 213
Napier, Sam 332n62
Napoleon III 27
Nasser, Gamal: *Egypt's Liberation...* 36, 325n25, 330n51
National Council for Civil Liberties, London 55
National Democratic Party 62
National H-Block/Armagh Committee 150–1, 152, 172
National Unity 62
Nationalist Party 60, 62–3, 66
NATO 401n15
Neave, Airey 237
'neo-colonialism' 31, 34–5
New Ireland Forum 207, 280, 283
New Statesman 236